A VIEW FROM THE BOTTOM

PERVERSE MODERNITIES
A Series Edited by Jack Halberstam and Lisa Lowe

NGUYEN TAN HOANG

A VIEW FROM

Asian American Masculinity and Sexual Representation

THE BOTTOM

Duke University Press   Durham and London   2014

© 2014 Duke University Press.
All rights reserved.
Designed by Heather Hensley
Typeset in Whitman by Tseng Information Systems, Inc.

Library of Congress Cataloging-in-Publication Data Nguyen,
Tan Hoang.
A view from the bottom : Asian American masculinity
and sexual representation / Nguyen Tan Hoang.
pages cm—(Perverse modernities)
Includes bibliographical references and index.
ISBN 978-0-8223-5672-1 (cloth : alk. paper)
ISBN 978-0-8223-5684-4 (pbk. : alk. paper)
1. Asian American gay men. 2. Masculinity—United States.
I. Title. II. Series: Perverse modernities.
HQ76.2.U5N49 2014
306.76089′95073—dc23
2014000759

Cover: Susan Choi, *Legs*, 2014, courtesy of the artist.

For Dredge

CONTENTS

PREFACE ix
ACKNOWLEDGMENTS xi

INTRODUCTION 1

CHAPTER ONE 29
The Rise, and Fall, of a Gay Asian American Porn Star

CHAPTER TWO 71
Reflections on an Asian Bottom

CHAPTER THREE 111
The Lover's "Gorgeous Ass"

CHAPTER FOUR 151
The Politics of Starch

CONCLUSION 193

NOTES 207
BIBLIOGRAPHY 253
VIDEOGRAPHY 271
INDEX 277

FIGURES P.1 AND P.2: *Forever Bottom!* (1999).

PREFACE

A close-up of an Asian man's face in pain-pleasure against a pink bedsheet. On the soundtrack, a male voice grunts and moans suggestively. Cut to two upturned legs swinging rhythmically against a plain white wall. A romantic Chinese ballad plays in the background. Close-ups of the same Asian man's face pushed against shower curtains, carpet, couch. Upturned legs poking out the window of a parked car, swaying in between redwood trees, rocking in front of crashing waves (figures P.1 and P.2). These shots are culled from a short, four-minute experimental video I made called *Forever Bottom!* (1999), a work that is the genesis for the book you are holding in your hands. Through simple camera techniques such as close-ups and low-angle shots, the video offers the point of the view of an Asian male "getting fucked" in a variety of settings: bedroom, balcony, kitchen, front lawn, parked car, park, beach. Though the title proclaims the temporal persistence and spatial ubiquity of an Asian man who "forever" revels in adopting the bottom role, the viewer never actually witnesses his anal penetration nor the top who is allegedly doing the penetrating. In fact, it is the viewer herself or himself who is positioned by the camera to take up the position of top, the invisible partner offscreen who is responsible for the reaction shots of the bottom imaged onscreen. *Forever Bottom!* pokes fun at the widespread assumption in gay Western male subculture that Asian men possess a propensity for the bottom position in gay anal sex. Such an attitude derives from the view of Asian men as feminized and less masculine than men of other races. Yet the video does more than merely highlight and dismantle this racialized, sexual stereotype. By refusing to offer a reverse angle, for example, advancing the counterclaim that Asian men are really butch tops, and by excessively performing Asian bottomhood, *Forever Bottom!* launches a critique of heteronormative narratives of Asian masculinity while simultaneously embracing Asian bottomhood in its capacity to produce sexual pleasure. *A View from the Bottom* aims to flesh out the racial-sexual-gender assumptions that the video humorously depicts. It is toward the delineation of this bodily knowledge, the erotics of bottomhood, that I now turn.

ACKNOWLEDGMENTS

I came to academia late, after dedicating my twenties to a video art practice. As a result, the learning curve was high. The entire process of writing a dissertation, then turning it into a book, was more challenging and drawn out than usual. Throughout this bittersweet adventure, I was blessed to have wonderful mentors, colleagues, friends, and family who regularly checked up on me with phone calls, e-mails, and Facebook postings. They frequently suggested that I leave the computer, go outside, and breathe the fresh air; offered to read drafts and revisions; invited me to give talks and screen videos; and encouraged me to stay on track, to keep writing, and to "send it off already." They calmly listened to me venting my frustrations at times and judiciously called my bluff on my procrastination tactics at others; in short, they kindly put up with me acting like the bossy bottom that I am. I am thrilled to finally get the chance to thank them for their efforts.

I count myself extremely lucky to have had a dissertation committee that is a model of intellectual generosity and compassionate mentorship. I have been a fan of Linda Williams since my undergraduate days, so it was a dream to have her as my dissertation director. Linda consistently held me to high standards and pushed me to perform at my best with her firm but affectionate guidance. My essay on Brandon Lee for her graduate seminar "Pornographies On/Scene" in spring 2001 jumpstarted this project. Elaine Kim's pioneering research in Asian American visual studies inspired my academic pursuit. I had known Elaine before I entered Berkeley's graduate program; before, during, and after my time at Cal, she never wavered in her support. Juana María Rodríguez showed tough love at the right moments, administering the gentle spankings I needed to get the manuscript out. I continue to learn from her sexy scholarship and to benefit from her whip smart advice. I will always be grateful to Chris Berry for flying all the way back from London for my PhD exams and for his unstinting belief in my scholarly and artistic work. I feel very fortunate to have come into contact with this brilliant scholar and gentleman.

My friends in graduate school made what might have been dreary seminars into opportunities for lively and fun dialogue. For steering late-night party conversations away from *Dialectic of Enlightenment* to *Deep Throat*, I thank Minette Hillyer, Rani Neutill, Jessica Davies, Jake Gerli, Amy Jamgochian, Sylvia Chong, Heather Butler, Amy Rust, Scott Ferguson, Curran Nault, Colleen Pearl, and Paul Rosenbaum These lovely souls demonstrated to me that there is indeed a glamorous life inside of academia.

Several other people must be singled out as being pivotal to the completion of the book. My dissertation writing buddy, Greg Youmans, diligently read draft after draft of chapters and provided meticulous feedback on how to transform half-baked ideas into fleshed-out arguments. During the arduous stage of manuscript revision, Arnika Fuhrmann gave incisive suggestions for streamlining and strengthening my central arguments. The volume has benefited greatly from Greg's and Arnika's essential contributions. I look forward to holding their brilliant books in my hands in the near future. Damon Young will find his stamp all over the following pages. His crucial interventions on the introduction forced me to surrender politically palatable but conceptually shaky claims; I couldn't have asked for a more intellectually kick-ass interlocutor. For their timely and astute responses to individual chapters, I'm indebted to Joe Ponce, Hiram Perez, Hentyle Yapp, Lucas Hilderbrand, Peter Limbrick, Rani Neutill, Eve Oishi, Petrus Liu, and Lisa Rofel. I'm especially grateful to Lisa and Juana Rodríguez for recommending my work to Ken Wissoker early on. I would like to extend my appreciation to Jack Halberstam, Martin Manalansan, and Thomas Waugh for their detailed, illuminating reports on the manuscript at critical stages.

Though it sometimes felt like I took a long sabbatical from it during the writing of this book, my art practice played a crucial role in my academic research. Indeed, every chapter here was manifested as a short experimental video somewhere along the line. My trajectory as an artist-scholar has been influenced and enabled by the following amazing figures: Richard Fung, Cecilia Dougherty, Jim Hubbard, Yong Soon Min, and Bruce Yonemoto. This project would not have been possible without Richard's foundational writings and videos. Cecilia turned me on to video making and impressed upon me the personal-political-ethical significance of depicting queer sex onscreen. Early on, Jim championed my video work and made an annual home for me at the MIX Festival. His steadfast commitment to queer experimental film and video and advocacy for younger artists constitutes a high standard that I still emulate. I was fortunate to have Yong Soon as my MFA thesis advisor at UC Irvine; since then, she has continued to inspire me with her intellectual curiosity and her drive to make art that interrogates geopolitical boundaries. The original conception of "bottomhood" came from a four-minute video I made for Bruce's experimental film workshop at UCLA; thus, I thank him for that little assignment on the close-up that resulted in *Forever Bottom!*

Closer to my present location, I want to acknowledge the support of my colleagues in the English Department at Bryn Mawr College. Their gracious collegiality was vital during the later stage of writing. For that, I am grateful to: Linda Susan Beard, Peter Briggs, Anne Dalke, Jennifer Harford Vargas, Jane Hedley, Gail Hemmeter, Raymond Ricketts, Katherine Rowe, Jamie Taylor, Bethany Schneider, Kate Thomas, and Michael Tratner. Across campus, Homay King, in her role as director of the Program in Film Studies, is a rare combination of savvy professionalism and personal integrity. Without fail, Bryn Thompson's gentle smile brightens up my days in English House.

My move from the Bay Area to the East Coast was made smooth and easy by new friends and colleagues in the City of Brotherly Love: Rosi Song, Homay King, Elena Gorfinkel, Lázaro Lima, Farid Azfar, Sharon Ullman, Saïd Gahia, Yvonne Lee, Nathanael Roesch, Bill Bellone, and Jerry Miller. I thank them for their remarkable modeling for how to balance work and leisure over the coffees, dinners, and cocktails we have shared together. Todd Shepard's constant friendship tenderly sustained me for the past six years and made them a lot of fun to boot.

It's only fitting in a book about gay Asian bottomhood that I should give props to my Gaysian Posse; these Gaysians have nourished and entertained me with their sweet presence over the years, as we gossiped over bowls of phở, soon doo boo, and tom yum kung. The OG and honorary members include: Cirilo Domine, Nodeth Vang, Erica Cho, Susan Choi, Việt Lê, Stephano Park, John Won, Julian Liu, Hentyle Yapp, Joe Ponce, Denise Tang, Eng-Beng Lim, Karen Tongson, John Tain, Mimi Nguyen, Feng-Mei Heberer, Lucetta Kam, Mike Atienza, Jih-Fei Cheng, Clifford Landon Pun, R. Benedito Ferrão, Patty Ahn, Ji Sung Kim, Margaret Rhee, Kukhee Choo, and Chris Vargas. Heartfelt thanks goes to Young Chung for his deep and abiding friendship since our trailer park days at UC Irvine. His work as an artist-curator-ambassador (including his eloquent camerawork in *Forever Bottom!*) never fails to surprise and excite me.

The writing of the book required me to lug heavy books and Xeroxed articles to many faraway cities. During those leaves of absence from Berkeley, I had a delirious time doing research and making the acquaintances of a few kindly Southern gentlemen at the Rancho Loco in Atlanta: Gerry Lowery, Charles Sinnett Register, and Tony Kight. In Berlin, I got to enjoy the fabulous company of Daniel Hendricksen, Anjali Michaelsen, Ming Wong, Dirk Schünemann, Marc Siegel, Susanne Sachsse, Nanna Heidenreich, Sascha Wölck, and Telémachos Alexiou. Anjali, Ming, and Telémachos deserve special shout-outs for welcoming me into their lovely Kreuzkölln flats for extended bouts of writing. In Bangkok, I found respite from the sticky, rainy summers over yummy meals shared with Phaisith Nick Khammanee, Arnika Fuhrmann, Brett Farmer, and Michael Shaowanasai.

Spread across the academic diaspora, the following folks motivated me to persevere in spite of the relentless beatings and poundings of academic life, with their dazzling wit and exacting humor: Glen Mimura, Amelie Hastie, Peter Limbrick, Mariam Lam, Celine Parreñas Shimizu, Gilberto Blasini, Lan Duong, Viet Thanh Nguyen, Nhi Lieu, Eve Oishi, Elizabeth Freeman, Ming-Yuen S. Ma, Elena Creef, Louisa Schein, Thomas Waugh, Lucas Hilderbrand, Joe Wlodarz, and Glen Helfand. I owe a special debt to Cindy Wu and Hiram Perez for keeping me grounded with their calming presence and clear vision. It's a tragedy we don't all live and work in one glorious bottom commune together!

I had the pleasure of presenting portions of this research at the Society for Cinema and Media Studies, the Association for Asian American Studies, and the American Studies Association annual conferences, as well as at the following colleges and universities: New York University, Pitzer College, Rutgers University, University of Bochum, UC Berkeley, UC Irvine, UC Riverside, UC Santa Barbara, University of Pittsburgh, University of Southern California, California College of the Arts, Swarthmore College, and Wellesley College. I'm gratified by the enthusiastic responses from those audiences and the generous hospitality of my hosts: Gayatri Gopinath and José Muñoz; Ming-Yuen S. Ma; Louisa Schein; Anjali Michaelsen and Astrid Deuber-Mankowsky; Petrus Liu; Simon Leung; Mariam Lam, Lan Duong, and Mike Atienza; Mireille Miller-Young; Colleen Jankovic, Mark Lynn Anderson, and A. Naomi Paik; Viet Thanh Nguyen; Việt Lê; Farid Azfar; and Elena Creef.

Earlier on in the project, I received a residency fellowship at the University of California Humanities Research Institute (UCHRI) in the research cluster, The Object of Media Studies. I extend my gratitude to its convener, Amelie Hastie, and the UCHRI's director, David Theo Goldberg, for taking a chance on a dissertating grad student and for the decadent quarter surfing the Net chatting up the GAMs of SoCal. I learned a lot about genuine intellectual dialogue and exchange in that seminar, especially with Amelie, Mary Desjardins, Lisa Parks, Kate Mondloch, and Laura Kang. I shall always cherish memories of wicked cocktails and hot tubbing behind the Orange Curtain in the fall of 2005.

A junior faculty leave from Bryn Mawr College during the 2011–12 academic year gave me the precious time to whip the manuscript into shape. A grant from BMC's Faculty Awards and Grants helped to offset the costs of final manuscript preparations. I am truly grateful for this generous support.

I have been thoroughly spoiled by my work with Ken Wissoker. Ken has been the consummate editor with his tremendous patience and keen perspective, especially during my moments of self-doubt. Jade Brooks, Heather Hensley, and Sara Leone facilitated the production process with utmost professionalism. A hug to the super-talented Susan Choi for the exquisite cover art.

I would be nowhere if it were not for my family. My parents, Nguyen Dinh Dai and Hoang Thi Nga, gave up everything and took their seven kids on a tiny fishing boat in the dark of night to seek a better life in America. My six sisters, Tien, Nu, Marie, Pauline, Linh, and Loan, have always complained about the special treatment their one and only brother received, but they persist in granting him the best kind of sisterly affection nevertheless. Along with my supportive brothers- and sisters-in-law, my ten nieces and nephews always remind me of the simple joy of life: spending time together with family.

Dredge Byung'chu Käng was there from the beginning. With good cheer, he has tolerated (and enabled) my impulsive eating habits, my phobia of the telephone, and the wacky ideas that eventually found their way into this final text. I continue to learn a lot from him and treasure his presence in my life in more ways than he'll ever know.

An earlier version of chapter 1 was published as "The Resurrection of Brandon Lee: The Making of a Gay Asian American Porn Star" in *Porn Studies*, edited by Linda Williams (Duke University Press, 2004). A much earlier version of chapter 4 appeared as "I Got This Way from Eating Rice: Gay Asian Documentary and the Reeducation of Desire" in *Resolutions 3: Video Praxis in Global Spaces*, edited by Erika Suderburg and Ming-Yuen S. Ma (Minneapolis: University of Minnesota Press, 2012).

INTRODUCTION

In July 2011, a blog called Douchebags of Grindr exploded onto the blogosphere. Claiming to satisfy "all your douchebag needs from the profiles of Grindr," the site gathers screen caps of Grindr profiles that readers and the blogger deem to be "douchebags" based on discrimination by body type, gender presentation, age, sexual self-identification, and other exclusionary caveats. For readers not familiar with it, Grindr is a smartphone app designed to help gay men facilitate sexual hookups. Grindr's innovation over web-based cruising sites lies in its GPS technology, which allows users to detect the distance of other users, down to the number of feet, from their own physical location.[1] In response to the hyperbolized demands and preferences posted on Grindr and other sex cruising websites, journalist Alex Rowlson opines, "You visit a hookup or dating website, cruise somebody's profile and are confronted with the list: no fats; no femmes; no Asians; no blacks; masc only; my age or younger; str8-acting, you be too; non-scene; and on and on." He cheekily continues, "What we find is a lot of hate when all we want is head."[2]

Among rejections based on numerous physical characteristics, the most common, and hysterical, rejection on Grindr is directed toward Asian men. Here are a few excerpts from profiles posted on Douchebags of Grindr: "Asians need not apply"; "I block more Asians than the Great Wall of China!!!"; "And Asians, prease reave me arone"; and "I'm scared about getting old and having to date a young Asian ladyboy." While these excerpts are culled from profiles of white users, these sorts of Asian exclusion are not restricted to them alone: "Into only GWM. Im not replying to asians" and "Let's chat, not into asians . . . into white guys." Posted by Asian users, these latter examples suggest that some Asian men themselves do not find other Asians to be desirable sexual partners. In a gay sexual marketplace that valorizes fantasies of "masc," "str8-acting," "DL," "bi," "married," "muscled," and "hung"[3]—that is, attributes of masculinity—Asian men appear to occupy the most unsexy, undesirable position of all, seen as soft, effeminate, and poorly endowed. I begin with these Grindr profiles because they crystallize the "problem" of Asian masculinity, queer and straight, in the American national imagination as well as in other parts of the West.

A View from the Bottom offers a new framework for oppositional politics through a reassessment of male effeminacy and its racialization. It challenges the strategy of remasculinization employed by Asian American and gay male critics as a defense against feminization and rewrites male effeminacy as socially and sexually enabling. I develop a concept of "bottomhood" that complicates the links between the bottom position and Oriental passivity. I deploy bottomhood as a tactic that undermines normative sexual, gender, and racial standards. The book conceives of bottomhood capaciously, as a sexual position, a social alliance, an affective bond, and an aesthetic form. Posed as a sexual practice and a worldview, this flexible formulation of bottomhood articulates a novel model for coalition politics by affirming an ethical mode of relationality. Instead of shoring up our sovereignty by conflating agency with mastery, adopting a view from the bottom reveals an inescapable exposure, vulnerability, and receptiveness in our reaching out to other people.

My book makes a crucial intervention into the fields of Asian American studies, queer studies, and film studies by turning to a queer Asian moving-image archive that has hitherto been deemed too peripheral to warrant serious academic inquiry. This bottom archive is composed of a transnational body of films and videos from 1967 to the present, drawn from a range of genres, including commercial American gay porn videos, a forgotten Hollywood movie, a French narrative film often dismissed as soft-core porn, and gay political documentaries drawn from the Asian diaspora (Canada, United States, and Australia). Across these texts, I demonstrate the ways that anal erotics and bottom positioning refract the meanings of race, gender, sexuality, and nationality in American culture, and in so doing, simultaneously enable and constrain Asian American men in visual representation. Adopting bottomhood not as a fixed role, an identity, or a physical act, but as a position—sexual, social, affective, political, aesthetic—facilitates a more expansive horizon for forging political alliances. Far from unequivocal condemnation or celebration, bottomhood is variously contested, repudiated, negotiated, and affirmed across these texts, in ways that force us to reconsider conventional understandings of desire, identity, pleasure, and politics. As such, bottomhood provides a framework for critique that can be mobilized for minoritarian political projects beyond the scope of Asian American and queer studies and politics.

Revisioning Asian American Masculinity

Sexuality constitutes an important and strategic arena in which to explore the intimate linkages between Asian American masculinity and discourses of power. In the past three decades, an impressive body of feminist and queer scholarship on Asian American sexuality has been steadily growing. However, little work has been done on sexuality in its vernacular meaning, that is, as sexual practice. In what follows, I bring together the two senses of sexuality—sex acts and sexual discourses—by reading a specific sexual positioning through the wider lenses of race, gender, sexuality, and visuality. A direct look at sex acts, rather than masking political operations, offers us a more nuanced understanding of the work of racial-gender formations. Discussion of explicit sexual representation remains euphemistic in everyday spaces and underresearched in academic domains. Yet pornography and other sexually explicit material are instrumental in shaping how we think about what is normal, natural, and possible in regard to sex, sexuality, and gender. Furthermore, ideas about sex, sexuality, and gender are always overlaid by commonsense understandings of race and ethnicity. *A View from the Bottom* contributes an analysis of the coconstitution of race and sexuality by exploring the multifaceted treatment of Asian American masculinity in critical scholarship and popular visual culture, with the goal of reconfiguring Asian American subjectivity and its relationship with bottomhood.

A failure to take Asian American masculinity and explicit sexual representation seriously can be attributed to the deep anxieties surrounding Asian

American masculinity, which has been historically marked by feminization and emasculation.[4] For example, Yen Le Espiritu has detailed the ways in which the racial construction of Asian American manhood has taken two divergent routes: on the one hand, the U.S. nativist movement at the turn of the twentieth century propagated the view of Asian men as lascivious sex fiends threatening white womanhood; on the other, a series of exclusion and antimiscegenation laws instituted forced "bachelor societies," which resulted in the view of Asian men as desexualized because they were prevented from forming heterosexual monogamous partnerships. As Espiritu elaborates, "Materially and culturally, Asian American men and women have been cast as *both* men *and* women and as *neither* men *nor* women. On the one hand, as part of the Yellow Peril that needs to be contained, Asian men and women have been represented as a *masculine* threat of military and sexual dominance and moral degeneracy. On the other hand, both sexes have been skewed toward the feminine side—a manifestation of the group's marginalization and its role as the passive 'model minority' in contemporary U.S. cultural lore" (2008, 113, emphasis in original).

Espiritu's keen observations build upon the Asian American cultural nationalist analysis of white racism. Frank Chin and his male coeditors' landmark literary anthology *Aiiieeee!* (1975) signaled a powerful challenge to the white male literary canon and created a new voice and visibility for Asian American writers. However, their antiracist and anti-imperialist project was accomplished via the installation of a very narrow conception of Asian American identity, one organized around a vision of the ideal, authentic Asian American subject characterized as male, heterosexual, American born, and English speaking. As Daniel Y. Kim points out, Chin and his colleagues compared the threatening traits attributed to other men of color ("the evil black stud, Indian rapist, Mexican macho"; Kim 2005, 137) with those docile traits ascribed to Asian men, who, as objects of "racist love," are seen as "'womanly, effeminate, devoid of all the traditionally masculine qualities of originality, daring, physical courage, [and] creativity'" (cited in Kim 2005, 68).

Feminist scholars such as Elaine Kim, Sau-ling Cynthia Wong, and King-Kok Cheung have argued that Chin and his cohorts' gesture of remasculinization simply reinforces white male patriarchal hegemony with their bid for an Asian American martial masculinity.[5] These feminist scholars point out that remasculinization is of limited efficacy because it recuperates Asian American masculinity by subscribing to a misogynist and homophobic agenda.

As Jachinson Chan contends, for some straight Asian American men, "the desire for inclusion within the dominant model of masculinity overrides the politics of alliance with other oppressed groups." Yet, Chan also notes, to reconstruct an "alternative" Asian American model of masculinity that is "nonpatriarchal, anti-sexist, and anti-racist," heterosexual Asian American men "risk the stigmatization of being effeminized and homosexualized" (2001, 11). But, instead of seeing the associations with women and queers as stigmatizing, I suggest it is more socially and politically advantageous to advocate such an alliance as an important strategy of dismantling racism alongside heteronormativity.

To cite a concrete example that has closer relevance to my focus on sexual representation, I refer to Asian American studies scholar Darrell Y. Hamamoto's porn video project, *Skin on Skin* (2004). Hamamoto enthusiastically promoted this work as the first porn video featuring a straight Asian American man fucking an Asian American woman. This attempt to "capture the pleasures of the flesh as enjoyed by Yellow people" (Hamamoto 2000, 81) is enacted here by inserting an Asian American man in the place traditionally occupied by a white man in heterosexual pornographic scenarios. However, in this substitution of one representative of male phallic potency (bad, objectifying white man) with another (good, sexy Asian man), it remains entirely unclear how this intraracial sex tape has transformed the "pleasures of the flesh" of the other constituents of "Yellow people," especially Asian American women, not to mention Asian American lesbians and gay men.

One witnesses this marginalization of queer sexualities in *Masters of the Pillow* (dir. James Hou, 2004), a documentary that chronicles the making of *Skin on Skin*. In a telling sequence, Rick Lee, owner of and sexual performer on the adult website Asian Man: The Sex Adventures of Asian Man, lectures on the participation of Asian Americans in the American pornography industry in Hamamoto's Asian American studies class at the University of California, Davis. To a crowded room of rapt Asian American students, Lee states that in the adult film industry, one encounters Asian women "getting screwed by everybody and their cousins. But an Asian guy, a straight Asian guy in the industry, [is] basically impossible to find." However, as he speaks, the camera cuts away to footage of Lee's own website featuring images of Lee fucking different white women in a variety of positions. This visual insert counters his oral testimony while attesting to Lee's pornographic performances as an exceptional intervention in the mainstream American adult film industry.[6] He goes on to say that if one does find an Asian man in porn, "he's basically gay, and he's a bottom." In response, the entire class bursts out in hysterical laughter. Lee's narration and the students' reaction effectively pose gay Asian American bottomhood as the butt of the joke, that is, as the typical, sorry state of affairs that requires scholarly and activist renovation.

In Hamamoto's and Lee's corrective efforts to promote straight Asian American men as potent pornographic studs, they leave dominant constructions of heteromasculinity intact by simply expounding a business-as-usual pornographic program, one that must dismiss gay Asian American male sexuality in order to shore up their status as proper desiring sexual subjects, as real men. Showing that straight Asian American men can and do fuck, too, merely points to the limits of an inclusionary politics based on the re-masculinization of heterosexual Asian American men, achieved at the expense of other Asian American subjects. These assimilationist moves call for a strong, forceful queer Asian American critique. In the words of David L. Eng and Alice Y. Hom, a queer Asian American critique "demands more than a deviant swerving from the narrow confines of normativity and normative heterosexuality; it demands subjecting the notion of Asian American identity itself to vigorous interrogation" (1998, 9). Heeding Eng and Hom's call, I advance bottomhood as a critical strategy that allows us to reflect on other meanings feminization and emasculation articulate besides being the effects of white racism on Asian American manhood. This consideration requires us to draw on the insights a long history of gay male critique can provide, a history that has sought to recuperate and redress the bottom position and its lowly and debased social ranking.

Gay Male Critique and the "Desiring Use of the Anus"

In the Western popular imagination, male homosexuality is often conflated with the perversion of sodomy; gay male sex is reduced to anal sex. The term "bottom," in gay male culture, designates the receptive partner in anal sex, the person lying on the bottom underneath the top, the insertive partner. The "lower" positioning of bottom is reinforced by the additional meanings of bottom to refer to the buttocks or anus. Assuming the bottom position, or, in sexual vernacular, "getting fucked," has acquired a host of negative associations, including being weak or humiliated. For a man to get anally penetrated by another man signals the ultimate act of emasculation. In a patriarchal society, to bottom is akin to being penetrated and dominated like a woman. It is to be lacking in power or to surrender one's power to the top. The top position is seen as being "active," "dominant," and "masculine," while the bottom role consigns one to the less privileged side of the binary: "passive," "submissive," and "feminine."[7] Top-bottom roles are not restricted to gay male sexual practice, but can also be found in s/m play (sadomasochism, both straight and gay) as well as lesbian sexual cultures.

Although dominant perceptions of top-bottom roles understand the top as dominant and active and the bottom as submissive and passive, the power dynamics between the two positions are much more multifaceted, as the appellation "butch bottom" attests. I will have more to say about these complications below. Here, I want to clarify that I am simply registering the dominant meanings of top-bottom, rather than endorsing these troubling dichotomies. The binary construction of top-bottom is creatively interrogated in gay male communities, in ways that question and reinscribe norms of sexual and gender expressions. In this section, my archive alternates between "high" gay male theory and "low" gay male cultural productions to activate a dialogue between the academic and the popular. Because it is within these two arenas that we find the most sustained and productive engagements with gay male anal eroticism, I characterize the approach I take here as "low theory," which Judith Halberstam defines as "a kind of theoretical model that flies below the radar, that is assembled from eccentric texts and examples and that refuses to confirm the hierarchies of knowing that maintain the *high* in high theory" (2011, 16, emphasis in original). Both gay male theory and cultural production are eccentric in their explorations of a topic considered impolite, illegitimate, or, in Interweb-speak, NSFW (not safe for work). Throughout this book, my readings of texts about bottomhood are consistently guided by a mode of reading that is informed by theories and practices deemed lowly, backward, and out of date.

Gay male critics such as Guy Hocquenghem, Leo Bersani, D. A. Miller, and Lee Edelman have challenged the assessments of bottomhood as feminizing and emasculating by revalorizing the derided anus. The traits of passivity, receptivity, and femininity ascribed to gay male anal eroticism, they maintain, can be harnessed for a radical undermining of aggressive, hard, impenetrable phallic masculinity. From Hocquenghem's ([1972] 1993) polemical *Homosexual Desire*, published at the height of the sexual revolution and gay liberation movements in France, to Bersani's landmark essay "Is the Rectum a Grave?" (1987) written as a response to U.S. right-wing scapegoating of gay men during the first years of the AIDS pandemic, these writers' work employed anal eroticism as a central part of their critique of civil society. Writing on the "desiring use of the anus," Hocquenghem argues that desublimation of anal sexuality wreaks havoc on a symbolic order based on Oedipal reproduction and phallic sociality. In a similar vein, Bersani (1995, 101) advocates gay male passive anal sexuality—which he couches in psychoanalytic terms as "self-shattering" *jouissance*—as a way of undoing phallocentrism and rejecting the assimilationist domestication of homosexuality.[8] He famously declared that, for heteronormative culture, passive gay anal sex engenders the "seductive and intolerable image of a grown man, legs high in the air, unable to refuse the suicidal ecstasy of being a woman" (Bersani, 1987, 212).[9] Since power and the constitution of the self are invariably linked, the value of ecstatic bottomhood lies in its embrace of a "radical disintegration and humiliation of the self" (217). Bersani offers tremendous insight about the attraction of bottomhood for gay men when he writes: "From within their nearly mad identification with it [heterosexual male identity], *they never cease to feel the appeal of its being violated*" (209, emphasis in original). In other words, gay men's passionate attachment to phallic masculinity is simultaneously coupled with the immense pleasure in violating its authority (i.e., through getting fucked up the ass by another man).

Evidence of the idolization of phallic masculinity, combined with its simultaneous defilement in receptive anal sex, can be found in gay male popular culture. Consider the following description from the classic American gay sex manual *The Joy of Gay Sex* under the entry "Bottom": "Some bottoms are particularly turned on by large cocks, actually, huge donkey dongs, not only large, but really thick. . . . This prize is the visual ambrosia of some bottoms. A cock's length is rarely a problem; its thickness may be. If an exceedingly thick cock fucks a bottom hard, the two sphincter muscles may get torn. Still, we know of men who have been damaged this way and, after recuperating, go back for more. We recognize the excitement of being plowed hard by a huge symbol of masculine authority" (Silverstein and Picano 2003, 23–24).[10] Along with the favoring of thickness over length, note the highlighting of the "visual ambrosia" of a cock's girth. The pleasure-pain of penetration is intensified by the visual prize of the top's "huge donkey dong." The insistence on the joy in being penetrated—not just being "plowed" but, more significantly, "damaged"—suggests the overwhelming appeal of submission and masochism in the bottom position. However, in contrast to contemporary queer theory's emphasis on the fluidity of gender performances and sexual desires, the positionings of top and bottom in contemporary American gay male cultures are more often constituted as social roles or identities. A perennial complaint in gay male communities about the disproportionate bottom to top ratio and the difficulty of finding "real tops" demonstrates the profound esteem of top masculinity in gay contexts. At the same time, the sentiment also reveals the immense attractiveness of bottoming, as an identification revealed to one's confidants rather than as an identity to proclaim or embrace publicly.

A key point in these gay male texts, of both the theoretical and self-help varieties, is the connections they establish between the physical experience of bottoming and the ideological perspective linked to that experience, or, to cite *The Joy of Gay Sex*, the continuities between "being plowed hard by a huge symbol of masculine authority" and "a state of mind, a feeling that one has about oneself in relationship to other men" (Silverstein and Picano 2003, 23). In popular gay male sexuality self-help literature, the physiological dimension of bottoming is often rendered as neutral and invoked to defend and justify the sexual practice (for example, by alluding to nerve endings, the prostate, and so on).[11] It is the ideational dimension of bottoming that generates the most intense cultural anxieties around gay male anal eroticism. At various times in the following pages, I use descriptions of the physical sensations of bottoming to affirm some of the ideological meanings assigned to anal eroticism, for example, feelings of exposure and defenselessness. At other times, I complicate cultural assumptions, for example, the idea that bottoming is necessarily passive and feminizing. Further, there are instances where the bodily and the psychic overlap in ways that cannot be thought apart from one another. Throughout, I take up the correlations, and discontinuities, between the sexual and the social in my conceptualization of bottomhood as a position that mediates between racial-sexual identities and acts.

The paradox concerning the popularity and disavowal of bottomhood necessitates a reconsideration of the treatment of femininity in gay male discourses. It is not unreasonable to assume that in gay/lesbian and queer studies one would find complex, and affirmative, analyses of diverse models of gender dissidence and their conjunctions with nonnormative sexualities. As sexual minorities stigmatized for being "failed" men, gay men would seem to be in the ideal position to question oppressive norms of gender and sexuality. However, in spite of assertions by some critics that the gay resignification of dominant masculinity operates to subvert and undermine its power, it should be noted that gay men's eroticization of dominant masculinity also constitutes a pseudoreligious devotion to such masculinity.[12] A cursory look at a key gay male popular culture form such as pornography, with its celebration of white, muscular, and hung male prototypes, lends strong support to Richard Dyer's observation that gay pornography, like its heterosexual counterpart, privileges the experience of the top.[13] Indeed, mainstream gay porn's visual logic consistently insists on larger-than-life penises, and its sexual numbers invariably conclude with performers—both tops and bottoms—jacking off to ejaculation. That is, pleasure, even for the bottom, is signified as the pleasure of the cock.[14]

At the same time, the genre accords an inordinate amount of attention to the bottom. The central sex act and narrative event that sets gay porn apart from straight porn is the penetration of one man's cock into another man's asshole. As Rich Cante and Angelo Restivo remind us, the "narrative wager" unique to gay porn concerns "a supplemental question about what will happen when there are two bodies with two penises. Who will, and/or who won't get penetrated?" (2004a, 162). Thus, I want to qualify Dyer's assertion about gay porn's romance with the top by suggesting that while porn conventions encourage viewer identification with the top (via the cum shot, for example), they simultaneously stage the fantasy scenario from the bottom's point of view. For instance, the sex acts in a typical scene progress from making out to fellatio to rimming to anal intercourse and ending with cum shots on the bottom's buttocks, back, chest, face, and/or mouth. Because the taboo, and erotic charge, of gay porn lies in a man getting fucked in the ass by another man, the narrative commonly directs its focus on the bottom performer. This privileging of the bottom's experience is reinforced by such visual-aural depictions as extremely low-angle close-ups of cock entering asshole; the sheer variety of fucking positions (missionary, doggie style, sitting on it, side to side, and so on) framed in numerous camera setups; moans, groans, dirty talk, and other verbal eruptions from the bottom; the duration of the ass fucking signaling the endurance of the bottom; and the look of satisfaction on the bottom's face after the top has shot his load (and the bottom following suit with his own cum shot). All of these elements tally up to a hot bottom performance.[15] Even when a scene includes many tops and one bottom, as in a gang bang, the fantasy is often organized around the viewer's identification with the bottom receiving the ass poundings. More accurately, these porn scenarios invite viewers to identify with the bottom as much as, if not more than, the top. What's more, the thrill is doubled when the bottom happens to be big, tall, muscular, and big dicked. Contemporary gay porn, like the mainstream American gay male community at large, remains enamored with its butch tops and butcher bottoms.[16] But the very constructions of top and bottom constitute a historically specific and shifting phenomenon. I now consider how these sexual positions were reconfigured from the early days of gay liberation in the 1970s to the AIDS epidemic in the 1980s to the present day.

The Polarization of Sexual Positions

The polarization of top and bottom sex roles and positions in contemporary gay pornography, it must be pointed out, is a relatively recent phenomenon. Although historians such as David Halperin have documented the inserter-insertee sexual roles and their correlations with superior-subordinate social status as far back as ancient Greece, the terminology of bottom and top in gay male sexual communities seems to have emerged in the post-Stonewall period. The first edition of *The Joy of Gay Sex*, published in 1977, lists various entries referring to positions for anal sex: "Bottoms Up," "Doggy Style," "Face to Face," and "Topping It Off"; however, there is no entry listed for bottom or top. It was not until the 1992 second edition, *The New Joy of Gay Sex*, that one finds entries for "Bottom" and "Top." These omissions suggest that, though undoubtedly practiced as sex acts, these positions did not constitute coherent sexual identities as they do in the present day. In an analysis of gay male personal ads from the 1960s to the 1990s, Daniel Harris notes that the terms "Greek active," "Greek passive," "French active," and "French passive"—or, in code of personal ads, "Gr/a," "Gr/p," "Fr/a," and "Fr/p"[17]—were used in the 1970s to describe gay male sexual preferences. According to Harris, these expressions "allowed gay men to liberate themselves from the stigma of effeminacy by redefining their passivity as a specific set of acts that occurred in a specific location—namely, during sex—rather than as a general style of flaming behavior that they were forced to adopt in public" (Harris 1997, 56). In other words, "Greek passive" signifies an act that a gay man enjoys engaging in in the bedroom, or the park, as the case may be; such a preference is not advertised through his effeminate bodily comportment. The emergence of "top" and "bottom" in the late 1980s, argues Harris, constitutes an even stronger delinking of sex acts from gender presentation (or more to the point, of getting fucked from effeminacy); that is, "bottom" as a position distances itself from the feminizing act of getting fucked. What the changes in gay personal ads and the different editions of *The Joy of Gay Sex* register, then, is the quite recent genealogy of "bottom." "Bottom" as a legible subject position seems to have emerged between the heady days of gay liberation and the height of the AIDS crisis. The absence of "bottom" and "top" in the 1970s can be attributed to the egalitarian tenets of gay liberation, one that deemed top and bottom as outdated heterosexist sex roles. To wit, in "Refugees from Amerika: A Gay Manifesto" (first published in 1970), Carl Wittman rejects topping and bottoming as a "mimicry of straights": "This is role playing at its worst; we must transcend these roles—we strive for democratic, mutual, reciprocal sex" ([1970] 1992, 306).[18]

The shift from role fluidity to a polarization of top and bottom positions can be traced in gay male popular culture from the 1970s to the 1990s. In his historical study of gay male pornography, Jeffrey Escoffier identifies a casual interchangeability of top and bottom roles in porn from the 1970s. According to Escoffier, rigid top-bottom positions emerged in the early 1990s due to the AIDS epidemic and the discovery of the greater risk of contracting HIV for the bottom partner. An idolization of the top role resulted in a "new kind of gay porn star" as embodied by Jeff Stryker, a straight-identified performer whose sexual repertoire includes fucking and getting sucked, with no reciprocation (Escoffier 2009, 215).[19] In a similar vein, it was not until the third edition of *The New Joy of Gay Sex*, published in 2003, that one finds an entry for "Versatility."[20] Rather than indicating a return to a prior polymorphous 1970s sexual free-for-all, the category of "versatility" demonstrates that top-bottom positionings have become institutionalized in gay male communities. That is, versatility allows for the switching and assumption of multiple positions, but not the transcendence of them.[21]

In the past twenty years, bottoming has also taken on a remasculinizing cast in both the American gay porn industry and in gay male theory. Returning to Bersani, we might say that the gay male bottom's "feminine" abdication of power provides a new kind of agency. Indeed, in separating sexual roles from gender performance, gay male critics have sought to retain male privilege while championing a subversive femininity: ecstatic bottomhood is maintained alongside a continuing investment in phallic masculinity. That is, the joyful abdication of power only makes sense in the context of those with something to give up. Indeed, the idea of agency, or the capacity to make choices and act in one's own interests, is already socially structured by existing relations of power. In her critique of Bersani's essay "Is the Rectum a Grave?" Mandy Merck observes that "in his comparisons of heterosexual women and homosexual men, Bersani seems at times to be describing two different 'femininities.' A cursory reading of his rendition of rectal sex reveals a heroic rhetoric of 'demolition,' 'danger,' and 'sacrifice' . . . that is nowhere attributed to vaginal penetration. Might it be Bersani's view that male 'femininity' is butcher than its female equivalent, precisely because the subject's masculinity is at stake?" (2000, 157). Similarly, as Tania Modleski reminds us, "It is clear that powerlessness and masochism have different ideological valences for women than for gay men" (1991, 149). These two feminist scholars' arguments expose the masculinist basis of Bersani's thesis, which rests on a surrendering of a male privilege that women do not possess.[22]

The masculinist bias found in gay male discussions of bottomhood such as Bersani's also is evident in some contemporary gay male sexual cultures. Take, for example, barebackers, those who specifically identify with a community of others in which condomless gay anal sex constitutes a transgressive act against mainstream norms (gay and straight) of sexual responsibility.[23] In bareback sexual discourses circulating online, the testimonies heralding the ecstasy of getting fucked without condoms reveal that these practices — far from attesting to an embrace of powerlessness, feminization, and self-shattering — function as hard proof of a masculinity powerful enough to endure endless ass poundings and the reception of "buckets of cum." Clearly, this "outlaw" brand of gay male bottomhood indicates not the disruption of masculine norms, but rather, an enthusiastic affirmation of those norms.

In his book *Unlimited Intimacy*, Tim Dean observes that "although not factored by class in any conventional sense, bareback subculture prizes an ethos of hypermasculinity and erotic transgressiveness that tends to be imagined in terms of working-class masculinity, with its military paraphernalia, skin head haircuts, tattoos, and muscular physiques designed to suggest a life of manual labor. What's necessary to perfect this image is often the kind of leisure and material resources enjoyed by more-affluent classes" (2009, 38–39). The "erotic transgressiveness" to which Dean refers concerns barebackers' decision to engage in unsafe sex, to share or risk contracting HIV. Dean's description of bareback subculture's gendered ethos reflects a sexual radicalism propped up on a hypermasculinity that is explicitly classed and racialized. Not surprisingly, the militaristic, muscled, tattooed, skinhead barebacker can easily be taken as a 2000s update of the 1970s gay macho clone. However, whereas the roles of bottom and top in the early decade of gay liberation were not explicitly connected to gender presentation, the assertions of sexual prowess in bareback discourses reek of a compensatory masculine appeal, especially for those occupying the bottom role. As Dean further explains, "Although the sexual bottom regularly is addressed by his tops in the most derogatory feminine terms (such as 'bitch,' 'pussy,' and 'cunt'), this misogynist rhetoric does not seem to impugn his masculinity.... No matter how one interprets such language, in bareback subculture being sexually penetrated is a matter of 'taking it like a man,' enduring without complaint any discomfort or temporary loss of status, in order to prove one's masculinity" (2009, 51). On the one hand, to assert that to be penetrated anally makes one "more of a man" goes against the homophobic perception that sees it as a demeaning, emasculating act. On the other, what is troubling with this move is the promotion of a very confining model of gay male subjecthood: the heroization of the gay male bottom position is achieved through the collusion with misogynist heteromasculinity (as in the barebacking vocabulary quoted by Dean) and the marginalization of male effeminacy and femininity.[24] Rather than equating bottoming with "taking it like a man," a more generative line of analysis would be to reexamine the stubborn attachments between bottomhood and feminine gender presentations. Such an effort would acknowledge, and affirm, various styles of embodying and doing bottomhood, allowing for the cultivation of social and political alliances between gay men and other subjects similarly situated at the bottom of social hierarchies.

It is my contention that the antiracist rhetoric of Asian American communities and the antihomophobic rhetoric in the mainstream gay and lesbian movement both employ the strategy of remasculinization in order to legitimize themselves and gain acceptance from the dominant culture. Significantly, their methods of achieving political voice and social visibility are maintained at the cost of marginalizing femininity and feminine embodiment. By contrast, I argue for a politics of bottomhood that opposes racism and heteronormativity without scapegoating femininity. On the one hand, the realignment of gay Asian American bottomhood with feminizing abjection would appear to reinscribe dominant constructions of race, gender, and sexuality. On the other, the refusal to redeem gay Asian American bottomhood through hyperbolic masculinity points to a more expansive political program, one that rejects token assimilation into existing social structures. I propose an alternative paradigm that recognizes femininity, vulnerability, and other negatively coded aspects of the bottom position.

Hurt So Good: The Pleasures of Bottomhood

In order to challenge "commonsense" notions of bottomhood as punishment and utterly lacking in pleasure, we must complicate the commonsense linkage of topness with absolute domination and bottomhood with total humiliation. A view from the bottom recognizes a potential for mutual pleasure and recognition between bottom and top,[25] as well as a rewriting of bottomhood as a mode of accessing sexual and social legibility. The appeal of the bottom position certainly involves a pleasurable surrender of power implicit in making oneself available to be surrounded and covered, mounted and penetrated, crushed and filled by a loaded symbol of male authority, the phallus. To open oneself up to the pleasure of anal penetration requires not only conscious control but also a letting go. In *Gay Men and Anal Eroticism: Tops, Bottoms, and Versatiles*, a book of personal testimonies about gay men's creative negotiations of the cultural taboos around anal sex, Steven G. Underwood describes the physical sensations of anal penetration: "The asshole is loaded with nerve endings and is extremely sensitive to erotic stimulation. The initial moment of penetration when the cock head breaks through the sphincter; the rubbing of the penis against the bottom's prostate during the actual fucking; the contraction of the rectum around the penis; these are the highlights of a memorable fuck session for both partners. The internal stimulation can be so intense that some bottoms . . . are able to cum without even touching their dicks" (2003, 8).

By calling attention to the actual physical experience of anal penetration as one loaded with sensitivity, stimulation, and pleasure, Underwood contests the moralistic, disembodied view of anal sex as dirty, perverted, and unnatural. The latter phobic perspective, if it admits pleasurable anal sex at all, would simply privilege the pleasure of the top and his penis; it cannot account for the pleasure of the bottom and his asshole (which is assigned a proper one-way, exit-only bodily function). Underwood's account of anal penetration, from the receiving end, effectively affirms the rich experience involving nerve endings and contractions, tension and release. Though his description of the embodied practice of bottoming constitutes an important corrective to familiar dismissals of bottoming as abject punishment, Underwood's interpretation is a common strategy used by bottom enthusiasts to explain bottoming: that is, it is justifiable because it is a physically enjoyable act.

However, this explanation of physiological satisfaction, while insightful, should also be read as a defensive tactic for coming to terms with the deep cultural anxieties associated with anal penetration. Even as both partners experience pleasures to various degrees, the social meanings assigned to each role differ significantly. While the pleasure of the top derives from the normative male prerogative of fucking, of performing as a masculine subject who penetrates another's hole to get himself off, the pleasure of the bottom signifies a fall from masculinity, a "feminine" pleasure in being fucked. By surrendering his asshole to be penetrated, the grown man accesses the forbidden pleasure of "being a woman" (or his fantasy of being one), and in the process forfeits his claims to masculine subjecthood. It is precisely this fall from masculinity attached to the pleasure of bottomhood that underwrites straight male anxieties about dropping the soap in the locker room shower. And yet what this splitting of top and bottom pleasures obscures is the proximity of a man's ass and his cock. For instance, Underwood's careful description of a "memorable fuck session for both partners" stresses the proximity of anus and penis. Due to this nearness, the internal stimulation of anus by cock has been described as being masturbated and massaged from the inside. The connectedness and blurring of anal and penile sensations obfuscate any strict division between top/bottom and cock/ass. For it is the case that penile orgasms also involve anal contractions, which are "most noticeable when the anus is contracting *against* something (finger, penis, etc.)" (Morin 1986, 99, emphasis in original); anal orgasms, as a result of prostate stimulation, can also produce ejaculations without penile contact. Further, some commentators multiply the meanings of anal orgasms by proposing that such orgasms involve both psychic and physiological release. What these orgasms have in common is not only the bottom's pleasure in being penetrated, but also a pleasure that is "relationally dependent" on the top's pleasure in fucking (Hoppe 2011, 203–204).

If we put the top back into the picture, it is more apparent that "passive" anal sex entails an ongoing negotiation of power between bottom and top, with neither position deemed a priori, outside of specific positions and scenarios, as exercising complete power and control. The following testimonies attest to the varying control a bottom takes and gives up:

> It's obviously passive because you're allowing someone to enter you, but then there's also controlling of the rhythm and controlling how deep it goes. In that sense, there's control in being receptive. (Underwood 2003, 51)

> He waits a moment or two . . . then moves his ass back onto my cock in one mouthful, dilating and clamping without a struggle. . . . He's undulating back and forth, sort of fucking himself with my body, so you could say he turns into an ass, an active one, turning me into a dildo. . . . His butt is a point of connection if not union—we *coexist* around the length of a few inches of skin. (Glück 2004, 5, emphasis in original)[26]

In these descriptions, the asshole is assigned an active function by physically regulating the rhythm and depth of penetration. So, while on a psychological level the bottom's role is to emotionally please and satisfy the top, the manner in which he goes about it reveals a certain degree of control, coming from a "top" headspace. In the second excerpt, the overwhelming stimulation of being penetrated reduces the receptive partner's entire body to his anal cavity. This anus voraciously swallows, dilates, and clamps, thus effectively turning the top's cock into a mere sex toy. These testimonies of bottoming consistently forge a link between the physical sensations of getting fucked with the broader psychological ramifications those sensations signify, specifically, the relative power and control of the bottom. Seen in this light, the claim that bottomhood is far from absolute passivity and powerlessness is not surprising, as the many adjectives denoting the different types of bottoms further prove: pushy, power, bossy, butch, hungry, verbal, aggressive, insatiable, and greedy.[27]

At the same time, gay male bottoms must also grapple with, if not overcome, the cultural taboos concerning bodily penetration and orifices connected to waste and pollution. Allowing another man access to one's anus constitutes the most intimate of sexual acts, rendering the bottom vulnerable physically and emotionally. Bottom enthusiasts in gay male and s/m communities designate this dynamic as receptivity, chosen in preference over the term passivity, due to the latter's connotations of "lack of involvement and loss of will" (Morin 1986, 134). Receptivity is an active engagement that accounts for the senses of vulnerability, intimacy, and shame that one necessarily risks in assuming the bottom position. Such a shift in terminology also forces a reconfiguration of physical, sexual, and social hierarchies, whereby bottomhood might be resignified from powerlessness to "active passivity," "strength in submission," and "passive agency."[28] Instead of regarding these different modes of openness as a loss of power, it is more profitable to regard "*the ability to relax, to receive, to voluntarily abandon control [as] a psychological and interpersonal asset, not a loss*" (Morin 1986, 133, emphasis in original). In describing top-bottom power dynamics in this way, I am not promoting a fuzzy, touchy-feely, sanitized view of gay sex. Rather, I want to foreground the interplay of power and to hold on to some sense of surrender and submission invariably tied to bottomhood.[29]

Clearly, the fact of boundary trespass involved in being penetrated is crucial in this discussion. As Susan Kippax and Gary Smith emphasize, "the corporeality of vaginal and anal intercourse renders the receptive person more vulnerable than the insertive partner: that having something inside your body or on top of your body can render your body more vulnerable" (2001, 428).[30] Indeed, I contend that this physical, and by extension psychic, vulnerability plays a pivotal role in our relationship with our own bodies and the bodies of others around us. Instead of an aggressive fortifying of our psychic and corporeal armor, a more socially and politically efficacious move would be to recognize and embrace this exposure and openness. Referring to the immense loss in the wake of AIDS, escalating global violence post-9/11, and everyday oppressions and injustices faced by women, people of color, and queers—and the lessons they provide about the limits of our sexual autonomy, Judith Butler writes, "we are constituted politically in part by virtue of the social vulnerability of our bodies; we are constituted as fields of desire and physical vulnerability, at once publicly assertive and vulnerable" (2004, 18). It bears noting that our patriarchal society continues to characterize these forms of psychic and physical susceptibility in a feminizing and racializing manner. The stakes of action are differently constituted for women, queers, and people of color. I thus now turn to the contribution a gay Asian American perspective makes.

A Race to the Bottom

Vulnerability and powerlessness hold a vastly different political import for gay Asian American men, subjects who are expected to be especially, if not exclusively, suited for the ecstatic passive anal sex championed by Bersani and other gay male critics. In "Looking for My Penis: The Eroticized Asian in Gay Video Porn," a landmark essay that brings a critical race analysis to bear on gay male theory, Richard Fung (1991) argues that due to the pervasive view of Asian men as deficient in masculinity, they are cast in gay video porn as passive bottoms who function as sexual objects for the enjoyment of dominant white tops. These racialized conventions in gay porn confirm Asian American critics' complaint that Asian men are emasculated in American culture. However, Fung carefully points out that there is nothing wrong with bottomhood or submission per se; the problem arises from the fact that Asian men are always consigned to this position in the videos. Extrapolating from Fung's insights, David Eng enlists the tools of psychoanalysis to argue that the conflation of Asian and anus in the popular imagination enacts a "reverse fetishism," signaling the white male subject's "refusal to see on the body of an Asian male the penis that *is* clearly there for him to see" (2001,

2, emphasis in original). This performance of "racial castration" underscores the ways in which the psychic traumas of sexual and racial difference powerfully constitute each other. Furthermore, Eng clarifies that queerness and deviant sexual formations already pervade conventional Asian American historiography, in such phenomena as bachelor societies, female prostitution, and paper sons; such a queer archive, then, might be mobilized to critique normative values such as heterosexual reproduction, the nuclear family unit, and traditional community ties.

These two critics' keen analyses alert us to the need for historicizing the claim of "humiliation of the self" put forth by Bersani. Humiliation and shame play a decisive role in the formation of Asian American male subjects. These constitutive effects of Asian American male subjectivity cannot simply be superseded by an embrace of suicidal anal sexuality as a way to negate phallic masculinity. For those already relegated to the lowest rung of the sexual and social ladder, an unqualified embrace of powerlessness only leads to an amplification of their subjugation and lowly position. What other routes are possible for thinking about gay Asian American bottomhood that would afford pleasure and agency (and, at times, a thrilling surrender of power and agency)? If we remain wholly within the terms of Fung's thesis, we would discover that to replace Asian-as-anus with Asian-as-penis is to reinscribe the penis and topness, that is, dominant masculinity, as the desirable end point. By contrast, my deployment of gay bottomhood exploits the deviancy attached to Asian American masculinity in order to affirm and celebrate an altogether different paradigm of gendered, racial, and sexual subjectivity, one that refuses to restore to feminized Asian American male subjects the refuge of heteronormativity. Identifying with bottomhood becomes a matter of disidentification with it, whereby the gay Asian American male subject "neither opts to assimilate within such a structure nor strictly opposes it; rather, disidentification is a strategy that works on and against dominant ideology" (Muñoz 1999, 11). We find a disidentificatory process at work in Joon Oluchi Lee's articulation of Asian American male castration as a state of joy. The "castrated [Asian American] boy" delights in being "mistaken for something" the world deems abject (2005, 54). Lee writes, "Embracing racial castration can be a potentially libratory willingness to embrace femininity as a race and, vice versa, race as femininity" (2005, 44). Affirming bottomhood, femininity, and race together rewrites abject masculinity without writing off femininity and the feminine, thus enabling a new mode of social recognition. Importantly, as Lee (2005, 46) further points out, while being aware of the "risk [of] psychic and bodily danger" in affiliating with femininity, a gay male performance of femininity must take care not to respond to that threat of danger with a recourse to masculinist self-preservation.

In addition to these developments in queer Asian American studies, this study has also profited from exciting queer of color critique scholarship that calls attention to the deep imbrications between race and bottomhood in other contexts, as can be seen in Kathryn Bond Stockton's (2006) exploration of the "switchpoint" between "black" and "queer" in *Beautiful Bottom, Beautiful Shame*, and Darieck Scott's (2010) examination of the generative force of black abjection in *Extravagant Abjection*. As Scott pointedly queries, "If we are racialized . . . through domination and abjection and humiliation, is there anything of value to be learned from the experience of being defeated, humiliated, abjected?" (2010, 6). Following these two writers' penetrating inquiries into the power-pleasure and attractions of black bottomhood, I attend to the specific experiences of gay Asian men, subjects who are obstinately positioned as social and sexual bottoms in the popular American imagination.[31] I am in full accord with Stockton's and Scott's exquisite analyses, especially their differing commentaries about the political utility of bottomhood.

Throughout this introduction, I have been hesitant about making definitive, totalizing claims about gay Asian American bottomhood as subversive, resistant, agential, and empowering. In this effort, I have benefited from Heather Love's caution about queer criticism's compulsion to rescue the "bad gay past" by "transforming the base materials of social abjection into the gold of political agency" (2007, 27, 18).[32] Following Love's observation that social abjection need not be proven to be politically advantageous in order to warrant critical attention, I maintain that we do not always have to attribute resistance and subversion to gay Asian American bottomhood in order to justify its existence and accord it serious analysis. In certain circumstances, bottoming entails the gleeful surrendering of power; its pleasures do not always depend on resistance and subversion. Even if we ascribe a transgressiveness to bottomhood, as many gay male critics rightly do, part of this transgressiveness involves the very relinquishment of power. Having said that, I do want to insist on the point that the racialization of the bottom position demands an acknowledgment of gay Asian American bottomhood's complicated relationship to questions of power and pleasure. To be sure, I agree with Scott when he glosses blackness-in-abjection by specifying: "The power or ability I examine . . . has to do with *the creation and use of pleasure*:

by this I mean the transformation of the elements of humiliation and pain . . . that, though abject, is politically salient, potentially politically effective or powerful" (2010, 163–164, emphasis in original). The transformation of "domination and abjection and humiliation" into pleasure by racialized subjects does reveal a degree of power. To reconfigure an imposition of the bottom role into a politics of gay Asian American bottomhood constitutes what Scott calls "a form of counterintuitive *power*" (2010, 9, emphasis in original). A consideration of this "counterintuitive *power*" forces a recognition that the assertion of agency in much of cultural theory often comes with a normativizing bent. For instance, Lauren Berlant has recommended that "we need to think about agency and personhood not only in normative terms but also as activity exercised within spaces of ordinariness that does not always or even usually follow the literalizing logic of visible effectuality" (2007, 758). The resistance against agency couched in nonnormative, noncoercive terms comes closer to a mode of agency that Anne Cheng describes as "a convoluted, ongoing, generative, and at times contradicting negotiation with pain" (2001, 15).

Bottomhood is neither crushingly powerless nor all-powerful. Ultimately, I am less concerned in locating instances of resistance than in analyzing the various meanings that accrue to bottomhood in specific texts and contexts.[33] To refuse to redeem bottomhood as resistance does not mean the denial of all political effects. By dedicating serious attention to the vicissitudes of bottomhood in the following pages, I demonstrate my firm belief in the important political stakes therein. Persistently branded as sexual and social bottoms, Asian American men are in an advantageous position from which to use the threatening force of bottom-as-abjection to confront the management of Asian American masculinity. Though the book focuses on gay Asian American men, its optic of bottomhood sheds light on Asian American masculinity in general, as queerness informs all formations of Asian American male subjectivity.

A View from the Bottom

In taking Asian American masculinity and sexual representation as its focus, *A View from the Bottom* concentrates on a queer Asian American sexual archive that has been marginal to both queer studies and Asian American studies. This oversight can be attributed to the fact that the films and videos I examine are dismissed as too stereotypical, damaging, and offensive for serious academic study.[34] Asian American scholarship on sexuality and gender has generally favored the written text (literature, historical documents) over domains such as the visual arts or cinema. Elaine Kim suggests that a major reason for the underdevelopment of visual criticism in Asian American studies is "because visual culture and visuality, such as through the media of photography and film, have traditionally been regarded with suspicion as colonial tools of silencing and deracination" (2003, 41). The need to rectify historical silences and rewrite inaccurate accounts can be found in two prominent genres of Asian American film, the social-political documentary and the historical trauma film. These genres typically employ "the politics of *ressentiment*" to seek redress for past injury (Okada 2005, 45).[35] Indeed, Asian American film history is frequently plotted from a sobering documentary tradition to its pinnacle achievement, the fictional narrative feature. Accordingly, this developmental narrative traces an itinerary from social exclusion to cultural acceptance. It is precisely this aspiration to normalization through the media that a bottom archive (in both form and content) disrupts.

Historically, visual culture criticism on Asian American gender and sexuality has been concerned with evaluating representations based on a set of narrow, realist criteria. In the past two decades, however, an exciting body of feminist and queer scholarship on Asian American film and media studies has pushed visual culture debates beyond the limiting boundaries of stereotype criticism. Scholars such as Darrell Hamamoto, Karen Shimakawa, Eve Oishi, Homay King, and Glen Mimura have pointed out that the call for "positive images" relies on a set of heteronormative criteria that further marginalize minoritarian subjects.[36] For instance, Tina Chen has compellingly argued that the common opposition between identity and stereotype, the "real" and the "fake," obfuscates the ways in which these two terms are "mutually constitutive, bound together by a shared desire for articulation and coherency in the project of producing a viable subjecthood" (2005, 60). Employing the evocative metaphor of "gaps," Peter Feng claims that Asian American independent film "fills the gap" while being fully aware of "its own inadequate referentiality" (2002a, 16). In her study of the cinematic "composition" of Asian American women, Laura Kang explores the ways in which "image, identity, and subjectivity do not and cannot line up with each other" (2002, 75). In the same vein, Celine Parreñas Shimizu posits that a more complex account of producing and consuming Asian female "hypersexuality" is needed in order to go beyond analyses that routinely evaluate hypersexual representations as transparently injurious, exploitative, and racist. Shimizu stresses that these analyses foreclose any possibility of agency, critique, and pleasure, thus arresting the "productive perversity" that potentially exceeds and undermines the "normative scripts for sexually and racially marginalized subjects" (2007, 21). Taken together, these critics fruitfully interrogate the framework of visibility politics organized about the nexus of positive-negative images by offering incisive analyses concerning oppositional modes of production and perverse viewerships. These sophisticated readings—informed by diverse schools of thought, including poststructuralism, semiotics, psychoanalysis, cultural studies, feminist theory, queer theory, sexuality studies, critical race theory, and diaspora studies— constitute an exciting new development in Asian American media studies with their vigilant attention to the politics of representation, one that never loses sight of the political stakes involved for minoritarian subjects who are seldom given the power to represent themselves.

One dynamic response espoused by Darrell Hamamoto, and one I enthusiastically endorse, is for Asian Americans to take up the camera to create a counterpornography or, to use Hamamoto's phrasing, a "Joy Fuck Club." As he observes, "Asian Americans have grappled with a psychosexual self-alienation that stems from a racialized sexuality shaped and sometimes deformed by social forces" (2000, 63). This statement usefully underscores the deleterious psychic effects of racial-sexual oppression and their transcription into moving-image media. While this point appears self-evident at first glance, a closer reading uncovers the problematic assumption that there exists an authentic, unalienated sexuality prior to racist regulation and discrimination. In short, it ignores the work of representation in shaping, forming, and deforming Asian American sexuality. In a more nuanced analysis, Celine Parreñas Shimizu responds to straight Asian American men's "straitjacket sexuality"—which she defines as the quandary of "asexuality/effeminacy/queerness"—with a radical call for an "ethical manhood" (2012, 15). Instead of protesting against the racial-sexual humiliations inflicted on Asian American subjects, the concept of ethical manhood, argues Shimizu, highlights how straight Asian American men assert power over others in some contexts even as they suffer from being stripped of power in others. A crucial component of ethical manhood involves the acknowledgment of vulnerability and the commitment to care for others. The emphasis on exposure and openness in this revisioning of heterosexual Asian American masculinity strongly resonates with my thinking around gay Asian American bottomhood. It is worth noting, however, that asexuality/effeminacy/queerness would only function as straitjackets for Asian American male subjects who remain enamored, even if residually, of the privileges of dominant masculinity. For those already excluded from the confines of heteronormativity, asexuality/effeminacy/queerness constitute, if not quite badges of pride, then insignias of social recognition and intelligible identities.

My study profits greatly from the groundbreaking work on Asian American sexuality and visual culture by scholars such as Hamamoto and Shimizu, alongside others noted above. Their incisive writings contest the phobic resistance by some Asian American culture critics to looking seriously at explicit sexual imagery. My concentration on visual culture constitutes a vital site for the investigation of Asian bottomhood due to these texts' expansive circulation and unpredictable modes of reception, especially when these texts depart from the familiar heterosexual scenario. For it is through the mass media such as film, television, video, and the Internet that one learns, recognizes, and resists one's racial, class, gender, and sexual positionings. By rendering on-scene what should remain obscene (off-scene), by screening and speaking "sex in public," the sexual representations I analyze in this book contribute to a queer Asian American world-making project that troubles and exceeds heteronormative intimate forms that are linked "to domestic space, to kinship, to the couple form, to property, or to the nation" (Berlant and Warner 1998, 322), referents that have been consistently privileged in conventional gay and lesbian and Asian American historiographies. Due to their queer sexual "content" and racial "inscrutability," these texts frequently fail to register as legitimate documents of culture. To be sure, an affirmative exploration of bottomhood disrupts the usual assumptions of what counts as political intervention. In a representational struggle centered around a politics of visibility (e.g., looking for and/or restoring the Asian penis), the redeployment of Asian American masculinity based on homosexualized, feminizing bottomhood would appear to compound the ample visible evidence of the hole (anus-as-cunt) in Asian American sexual representation. However, I maintain that deploying gay Asian bottomhood as a hermeneutic, a tactic of intervention, reconfigures gay Asian American bottomhood as a practice of joy.

My methodology of reading as a bottom—that is, reading like, alongside, nearby, and beside—combines what Eve Sedgwick calls a paranoid mode with a reparative mode of analysis. It unpacks the social, cultural, and political meanings of film and media texts and explores how the same texts affect viewers viscerally. Along with ideological exposure, my readings also reflect on the pleasures and surprises that touch and move the bodies of viewers. The unanticipated flashes of anger, attraction, arousal, disgust, and repulsion, these moments of being caught up and taken in by images, reveal the complicated ways in which viewers, naively and critically, sense and make sense of moving-image media. Attention to more embodied modes of experiencing the movies allows for a richer understanding of how their spectacles and sensuousness work and how they work on us. These embodied practices manifest themselves most sumptuously in "body genres" (e.g., melodrama, horror, pornography), experimental film, and digital media; but it is certainly the case that all types of moving-image media engage not just our sight and hearing but also the senses of touch and smell as well.[37] Throughout this introduction, I have remarked on the persistent tension between the social and political import of bottomhood (what it means) and the physiological experience of bottomhood (how it feels). The medium of film/video, with its passionate hailing of both our intellects and our loins, offers a fuller account of the subjectivities of those relegated to bottom positionings, on and off the screen. On the one hand, through its gendered and racialized formal codes and narrative conventions, dominant film and video portray Asian American men as feminized, emasculated, marginal subjects of representation. On the other hand, they also provide visual and aural access to how bottomhood can be experienced differently—socially, politically, and sensationally. That is to say, film and video mediate the pressures between bottomhood's ideological and carnal effects.

In the place of redress and reparation for representational harm, *A View from the Bottom* considers subjects that do not seek to overcome injury but those that have learned to live with past and present damage, in particular, everyday injuries marked by gender, race, and sexuality, that cannot find relief or make amends through legitimate social or political means. Inspired by a politics of the behind, the outmoded, the embarrassing, the chapters of the book do not follow a chronological timeline in which feminizing bottom positioning is surmounted by masculine topness. Instead, they proceed on a messier, nonlinear course, one that is deliberately itinerant and meandering, thus refusing any neat and tidy evolutionary development from oppression to liberation, from marginalization to assimilation. Each chapter explores the vicissitudes of bottomhood in their sexual, social, affective, and aesthetic dimensions, with emphasis on certain aspects depending on the text under discussion. Inevitably, there are overlaps, repetitions, and revisions of concepts, ideas, and arguments. A fledgling idea in one chapter gets a fuller examination in a later chapter; an argument about gay video porn recurs in a different guise in a discussion about a narrative feature film. Rather than an exhaustive survey of all the manifestations of Asian American bottomhood in the history of film and video, I zero in on a few key case studies drawn from different genres (U.S. gay video pornography, Hollywood narrative film, French art film, Asian diasporic experimental documentary, and gay sex websites). The range of texts suggests that Asian bottomhood permeates diverse portrayals of Asian manhood in different media genres and historical periods. One significant link across the chapters is the alignment of Asian bottomhood with the feminine, a link that contests the hypermasculinization of bottoming. Another is the manner in which bottomhood is variously acknowledged, challenged, rejected, and embraced. Emulating the complexities of top-bottom interplays of power and pleasure, I have resisted the imposition of a temporal order or narrative coherence onto these open-ended texts.

The first chapter, "The Rise, and Fall, of a Gay Asian American Porn Star," begins our investigation of Asian American masculinity and sexual representation through the dyad of top-bottom masculinities in the star text of porn star Brandon Lee. I posit that Lee's claim to fame as an Asian top performer in his early videos is secured through his "racial packaging" as an assimilated Asian American and the relegation of his FOB (fresh off the boat) Asian immigrant costars to the abject position of bottom. However, Lee's compelling performance in his recent videos as an aggressive bottom suggests that the borders between American/Asian, top/bottom, and dominance/submission cannot be steadfastly maintained. Unsettling these dichotomies, I argue for the position of the Asian immigrant as a desiring subject that buttresses and undermines the Orientalist fantasies animated in these porn videos.

Chapter 2, "Reflections on an Asian Bottom," expands the conceptualization of bottomhood by considering its manifestations as effeminacy, queer domesticity, social rank, and cinematic style. Focusing on the effeminate Filipino houseboy, Anacleto, in *Reflections in a Golden Eye* (dir. John Huston, 1967), the chapter analyzes the ways in which this marginal supporting character radically inverts the narrative's social hierarchies. Crucially, his bottom sensibility structures the very form of the film, inscribing a receptive filmic gaze, an "anal vision," that conscripts not only the other characters but also the spectator. In light of linear narratives of progress around LGBT media (e.g., global queering), I contend that Huston's Hollywood production actually grants Anacleto much more narrative influence than contemporary gay pornography affords its Asian bottom performers, a move that effectively severs any connection between a text's level of sexual explicitness and its political progressiveness.

Moving from a top porn star who (finally) bottoms to an "asexual" houseboy who wreaks social-sexual havoc in a military milieu with his effeminate acting out, chapter 3, "*The Lover*'s 'Gorgeous Ass,'" turns its attention to a romantic leading man whose physical weakness and emotional fragility seduce a young white girl. Looking at Jean-Jacques Annaud's *The Lover* (1992), I argue that even in a blatantly heterosexual love story, Asian male sexual prowess continues to be intimately linked with bottomhood. It finds expression here in the Chinese lover's shameful, "soft" masculinity and the literal exposure of his buttocks in the film's scandalous sex scenes. But rather than protesting the conflation of Asian and anus, I contend that the film's intense specularization of the lover's ass resignifies it, no longer as the sign of lack and absence, but instead as a pleasing site of sexual agency.

Chapter 4, "The Politics of Starch," continues the exploration of how Asian bottomhood functions as a catalyst for interracial desire examined in the previous three chapters. It returns to the central issues covered in the first chapter by looking at the ideological ramifications of top-bottom positionings in the context of gay male sexual representation. Whereas chapter 1 deals with the commercial gay porn industry, this last chapter focuses on work produced by gay Asian men as a critical response to those pornographic positionings of Asian men. It trains its analytic lens on a group of experimental documentaries made by gay Asian diasporic artists in the 1990s, including *Slanted Vision* (dir. Ming-Yuen S. Ma, 1995), *7 Steps to Sticky Heaven* (dir. Nguyen Tan Hoang, 1995), *China Dolls* (dir. Tony Ayres, 1997), and *The Queen's Cantonese* (dir. Wayne Yung, 1998). In an effort to retool Asian male sexuality, these works "reeducate" gay Asian subjects to jettison the passivity and objectification that are assumed to inhere in interracial (white-Asian) relationships in favor of the political empowerment found in egalitarian "sticky rice" (Asian-Asian) relationships. I then juxtapose another body of queer experimental and performative videos that rebuffs the documentaries' disciplinary impulse by exploring the unruly affects of bottomhood and the pleasures of subjection. That all of these projects frame their politics (and pleasure) in terms of a rejection or an embrace of bottomhood reveals the powerful hold that this particular racial-sexual positioning continues to exert over the erotic imaginaries of queer Asian subjects.

The conclusion turns to the Internet to survey the activities engaged in by gay Asian men (GAMs) on American gay sex hookup websites. In online environments deemed open and accessible, affording new sexual freedoms, GAMs come face to face with the same old offline bigotry and "sexual racism." I analyze the visual and textual tactics employed by GAMs to negotiate their exclusion from gay online spaces. The headless torso pictures and racialized screen names reveal the narrow conditions of visibility granted to gay Asian men. Within these limits, they nevertheless declare their sexual needs and wants, demanding full recognition as social subjects.

The unremitting focus on Asian men's bottoms in these diverse texts' portrayals of Asian male sexual competence articulates a particular relationship between race and visuality, and the problem that Asian bottomhood poses for dominant systems of visual representation. In her theorization of "the black femme function" in *The Witch's Flight*, Kara Keeling (2007) describes the black femme as a figure that cannot be accommodated or made to make sense within commonsense regimes of sexuality, sociality, and the cinematic. This failure of intelligibility is due to her status as "black," "woman," and "lesbian," a status that exceeds conventional organizations of subjecthood based on the requirements of compulsory heterosexuality. Keeling argues, "The black femme function points to a radical Elsewhere that is 'outside homogenous space and time' and that 'does not belong to the order of the visible'" (2007, 137). As my preceding comments in this introduction have made abundantly clear, gay Asian American bottomhood registers the incomprehensible, the obscene, or, to borrow Keeling's terminology, the "out-of-field" of both gay and Asian American discourses. Like the black femme, the Asian bottom embodies the social, sexual, political, and aesthetic point of view that no one wants to assume. In the following pages, I invite the reader to behold various embodiments of Asian male bottomhood in order to access another way of seeing, touching, feeling, and imagining the "radical Elsewhere" that bottomhood makes possible.[38]

CHAPTER ONE

The Rise, and Fall, of a
Gay Asian American Porn Star

In an article in the Asian American pop culture zine *Giant Robot*, journalist Claudine Ko (1999) recounts her search for Brandon Lee. She refers not to the son of Bruce Lee, who gained cult stardom after dying mysteriously and tragically at a young age while shooting *The Crow* (dir. Alex Proyas, 1994), but the other Brandon Lee, the gay porn star. Ko reports on rumors that Brandon Lee the porn star had been discovered while delivering Chinese food to a gay porn set. As the story goes, the director asked to see his egg roll and was so blown away by the sight that he immediately cast Lee in a porn video. Later in the article, Ko tracks down Chi Chi LaRue, one of the best-known directors in gay porn, who straightened out the story. LaRue claimed to have discovered Brandon Lee at a gay bathhouse in Los Angeles. Impressed by Lee's good looks and ten inches of manhood, she brought him to Catalina, the popular gay video company, which promptly signed him on, and the rest, as they say, is history.

I am not particularly interested in ascertaining which version of the story about Lee's discovery is true. Rather, what I find compelling is the way the two versions can be read as emblematic of how the image of Asian men in gay North American porn has shifted with the appearance of Brandon Lee.[1] Before Lee, Asian porn actors performed the roles of karate masters, Chinatown grocery boys, or their cousins, Chinese food delivery boys, which is to say, they constituted racialized sexual stereotypes. In contrast, Lee is frequently portrayed as West Hollywood boyfriend material, cast in mundane roles as well as pornotopic parts such as real estate agent, young man who inherits a gay brothel, army recruit, porn star, sex party host, biker dude, and most commonly West Hollywood twink.[2] In other words, Brandon Lee could well be just another random (American) gay guy one could easily find cruising in a West Hollywood bathhouse. He has left his parents' grocery store in Chinatown to live with his white boyfriend in the gay ghetto. This movement from one ghetto to another parallels Lee's transition from ethnic niche to mainstream gay video pornography.

By beginning my study of Asian American masculinity and sexual representation with an examination of gay male video pornography produced in the late twentieth and early twenty-first centuries, I address the common grievance about the representation of Asian American masculinity in American culture, registered in the complaint that mainstream media depict Asian men as effeminate and asexual. At first glance, it would appear that as a top porn star, Brandon Lee is a model of masculine sexual prowess and potency, the rhetorical and flesh-and-blood penis that Asian American cultural critics have been searching for. Put differently, his success would seem to satisfy the goals of Asian American media activism and scholarship. However, in what follows, I look at the ways in which the privileging of topness and remasculinization in the work of Brandon Lee serve to reinforce normative discourses of race, class, gender, nation, and sexuality. The chapter's investigation of contemporary gay male video porn shows how those modalities of difference get articulated through top-bottom sexual positionings. At the same time that I unpack Lee's claim to fame as an Asian top, I also point to the instabilities of his top status by highlighting significant moments in his videos when topness topples as well as instances when bottomhood exceeds its coding as Asian abjection. In addition, I suggest that Lee's emergence marks out a space for a queer, resistant Asian American porn spectatorship that enlarges previous models of porn viewing. Though not without its contradictions, Lee's exceptional porn persona proffers a new sexual visibility for gay Asian American men. His rise, and fall, unlocks heretofore unexplored possibilities for gay Asian men's social and sexual subjectivity, not least by animating new ways of thinking and doing bottomhood. To be sure, the instabilities of his topness illustrate how Lee maintains multiple boundaries (e.g., Asian/American, bottom/top) even as he embodies their blurring.

In his analysis of gay male porn videos employing Asian actors—the one arena where Asian men are depicted engaging in explicit homosexual sex—Richard Fung interrogates the "role the pleasure of porn plays in securing a consensus about race and desirability that ultimately works to our disadvantage [as Asian men]" (1991, 158). Fung describes the feminization of Asian men in gay porn within the context of racialized power relations. Examining the work of Vietnamese American porn actor Sum Yung Mahn, he demonstrates how pornographic depictions of Asian men focus on their submission to the pleasure of white men. In these tapes produced in the mid-1980s, Asian men almost always adopt the bottom role in relation to a white top. In *Asian Knights* (dir. Ed Sung, 1985), the only exception where an Asian top fucks a white bottom, the Asian character is portrayed as serving the white character domestically and sexually as a houseboy.[3]

The intended audience for these Asian-themed videos is primarily gay white men. A sex scene between two Asian men in *Asian Knights* is edited to conform to the point of view of a white man. What appears to be an Asian-Asian sexual scenario is undercut when the white man enters the scene and occupies the center of the sexual attention, much the way the man enters into a "lesbian" number in heterosexual porn. Most significantly, the white male fear of being fucked is displaced onto the bodies of Asian men. A scene in *Below the Belt* (dir. Philip St. John, 1985) has an Asian actor step temporarily into the role of a white character in order to articulate his anxiety about getting fucked. In this sequence, the Asian male body substitutes for the white male body to receive the punishment represented by anal sex.[4]

Despite the critical attention and popularity of Asian male actors in Asian cinemas and their successful crossover into Hollywood (e.g., actors such as Jackie Chan, Jet Li, and Chow Yun-fat in the late 1990s), as well as the more recent spotlight on Asian American actors Kal Penn, John Cho, Daniel Dae Kim, and Harry Shum Jr., the depiction of Asian men as sexually appealing scarcely figures in mainstream American popular culture. In the realm of explicit sexual representation, one finds that in marked contrast to the overwhelming presence of Asian and Asian American women in heterosexual pornography, there is a notable absence of Asian American men.[5] Thus, the

FIGURE 1.1: DVD cover. *The Best of Brandon Lee* (1999).

popularity of Brandon Lee as a gay Asian American porn star represents a startling and unique achievement that demands special attention.

Brandon Lee is the only male Asian American porn actor with the distinction of having a "best of" video compilation, *The Best of Brandon Lee* (dir. Chi Chi LaRue and Josh Eliot, 1999; figure 1.1). Starting in 1997, at the ripe age of eighteen, Lee began acting in gay videotapes geared toward an Asian niche market in Catalina's Far East Features series, in such popular titles as *Asian Persuasion* (dir. Josh Eliot, 1997), *Fortune Nookie* (dir. Chi Chi LaRue, 1998), and *Asian Persuasion 2* (dir. Brad Austin, 1998).[6] He then quickly crossed over into mainstream gay porn, appearing in *Dial "S" for Sex* (dir. Chi Chi LaRue, 1998), *Stag Party* (dir. Chi Chi LaRue, 1998), *Harley's Crew* (dir. Chi Chi LaRue, 1998), *Big Guns 2* (dir. Josh Eliot, 1999), *Throat Spankers* (dir. Josh Eliot, 1998), and *Peters* (dir. Dane Preston, 1999).[7] After a brief stint in the

U.S. Navy, he returned to making porn in 2004 as a Rascal Video Exclusive actor, appearing in a number of videos in 2004–2005.[8] The most significant of the videos produced after his comeback is *Wicked* (dir. Chi Chi LaRue, 2005), in which he bottoms for the first time. Concentrating on his work in the period before his comeback, I am interested in looking at the racial packaging of Brandon Lee in the Asian videos where he is depicted as American in relation to his Asian costars and how this process changed in the mainstream videos, where he is the only Asian (and frequently the only person of color), while his racial and ethnic difference is not remarked on. I argue that the making of this gay Asian American top porn star is accomplished through the coding of Brandon Lee as an assimilated (Asian) American. The case of Brandon Lee the porn star shows how American masculinity underlies topness, which then confers the status of gay porn star. His work serves as an exemplary "border study" of the conflicting categories of "American" and "Asian" as they are enacted and performed in top and bottom sexual roles in contemporary gay video porn.[9] An analysis of Brandon Lee's star text demonstrates how the two national categories have been constructed in mutual opposition and the manner in which their dichotomous differences manifest themselves through sexuality and gender. But before zooming in on Lee's racial packaging in the porn videos, we need to consider an earlier groundbreaking intervention in the visual representation of Asian masculinity in mainstream American popular culture.

From Kicking Ass to Fucking Ass

It is not insignificant that an Asian American adult performer takes as his *nom de porn* the name of Brandon Lee, son of martial arts superstar Bruce Lee. This choice of name clearly activates the one "positive" place Asian men occupy within the American popular imagination. The martial arts cinematic genre is set within a visual economy where Asian men are seen as physically powerful, energetic, and graceful. Yvonne Tasker (1997) has noted the importance of a remasculinization of Chinese national identity in the star text of Bruce Lee. The cultivation of the hard and muscular fighting body counteracts the view of Chinese men as soft and delicate, and thus foregrounds a Chinese national identity based on a macho muscularity. Tasker describes a scene in *Fist of Fury* (dir. Wei Lo, 1972),[10] in which a Chinese go-between, a traitorous character affiliated with the Japanese martial arts school, comes to the Chinese school to offer a challenge by taunting the students there as the "Sick Men of Asia." Responding to this insult, Lee's character goes to the Japanese school and defeats the students there to proclaim that he and his Chinese schoolmates are not sick men. Tasker writes, "This assertion of nationalism is very clearly inscribed through the revelation of Lee's body—as he ritualistically removes his jacket—so that discourses of masculinity and nationhood are complexly bound up together in his star image" (1997, 318). In other words, Lee's well-trained and disciplined hard body plays a crucial role in the assertion of national identity.

The most striking feature of the Bruce Lee star image in relation to our discussion of the eroticized representation of Asian men is his portrayal of an ascetic, sexually naive working-class hero. In most of Lee's films, his relationships with women are platonic and lacking in sexual tension.[11] In *The Way of the Dragon* (dir. Bruce Lee, 1972), the main female character is his cousin, who first doubts Lee's ability to help her fight against the Italian gangsters. Once she sees him in action, however, she develops a soft spot for him; but their relationship stays on a tender, familial level. The asexuality of the Lee character is especially pronounced in a sequence from *Enter the Dragon* (dir. Robert Clouse, 1973). In a brothel scene, Lee's cohorts, John Saxon and Jim Kelley, readily pick out several women from a lineup to join them for the night, while Lee requests only one woman to come to his room. The prostitute chosen by Lee turns out to be a fellow secret spy; needless to say, no romance ensues between them. Hsiung-Ping Chiao (1981) has observed that sex in the Bruce Lee oeuvre is seen as the "corrupting force" associated with decadence and linked with brothels, prostitutes, and slave trafficking. Lee's films subscribe to a puritan sexual morality, continuous with traditional Confucian values. Nevertheless, a contemporary viewer, who may already be cognizant of the work of recent Asian male action actors such as Jackie Chan, Chow Yun-fat, or Jet Li, can still be struck by the awesome erotic intensity of Lee's onscreen presence, which remains uneclipsed by other Asian actors working today. Chiao comments on the way in which the desexualization of Lee's fictional characters at the thematic level is undercut at the level of audience reception: "Puritan sexual morality have [sic] been paradoxically decoded by audiences as sexual stimulants.... It has been pointed out that his fights resemble sexual behavior. The open-legged posture before attacking, the slow-motion shots of his tense body, and the expression of excitement and elation intermingle to imply sexual provocation. The subtle tie between violence and sex thus transcends the overt layer of sex-inhibition and becomes emotional retribution for Lee's ill-fated destiny and plight" (1981, 40–41).[12] While Chiao calls attention to viewers' resistant reading of Lee's eroticism within his films, it should also be noted that Lee's fans, before and after his death, have been fully aware of his off-screen reputation as a ladies' man. They idolize his status as both a lover and a fighter (Nguyen 2007). According to Tasker, the martial arts genre, like the American Western and the action film, allows for the traditionally taboo looking of men at other men. However, Western critics' overemphasis on the aggression of Bruce Lee's films effectively downplays the sensuous and homoerotic force of his performances.[13] These critics' exclusive attention to the gory violence in his films disavows the homoeroticism of Lee's handsome face, onscreen charisma, and his half-naked body under duress.

Like the masculinist project of the martial arts film genre, the question of remasculinization in gay Asian American pornography occupies a central place in our discussion of Brandon Lee. Like the martial arts superstar, Brandon Lee plays a performer who acts on the bodies of other men, in the narratives and the reception of the videos. Thus, it is fruitful to examine the thematic correspondences and divergences between these two Asian American male stars. Bruce and Brandon Lee both work within film genres where spectacle and performance command more attention than narrative complexity.[14] The decisive moment of transformation underscores their emergence as physically powerful and sexually potent stars. Parallel to Bruce Lee's shift from nerdy country bumpkin to powerful kung fu master, the transformation of Brandon Lee from asexual Asian man to American porn star takes place when the motivating porn narrative gets established and the sexual episodes begin to unfold. While the kung fu movie builds up the viewer's anticipation of the moment when Bruce Lee finally decides to fight, gay pornography provides only minimal preparation leading to the performance of sex and thus offers the viewer little in the way of suspense. The selectively concentrated and distracted mode of porn viewing, the fast-forwarding and zooming in to where the real, exciting sexual performance occurs, calls to mind the kung fu viewer's anticipation of the instant when Bruce Lee, no longer able to contain his anger over the injustices surrounding him, exposes his muscular upper body and shows off his masterful martial arts skills. In the case of Brandon Lee, the metamorphosis from asexual Asian man to porn star is the thrilling moment when he finally exposes his hidden asset. In the words of the *Adam Gay Video Directory 2001*: "He can act, he's good sex, he's a top, and in case you hadn't noticed . . . that dick" (2000, 52).

The visual revelation of the martial arts star's compact, muscular torso and the porn star's erect, sizeable dick, as evidence of each man's "veiled" masculine prowess, is buttressed, and undermined, by aural effects. Accompanying Bruce Lee's exhibition of visually stunning movements is the involuntary eruption of convulsive grunts and wrathful yells, evoking intense rage. The overdubbing of Bruce Lee's films at these impassioned moments echoes the porn convention of postdubbing of dialogue and sex sounds: the generic dirty talk and repetitive moans in gay pornography. The porn soundtrack offers evidence of authentic sexual pleasure, provides proof of the final delivery of satisfaction, and adds realism by fleshing out the visual performance. But, as in the martial arts movie, the low-budget, out-of-sync, and poor verbal performance also suggests the sex sounds are excessive and faked. In the same way that Bruce Lee's animalistic shrieks are not commonly heard for their piercing sensuality, Brandon Lee's and his Asian costars' obligatory moans and groans are not perceived as adequately convincing sexual responses. (I will have more to say about the complicated relationship between this lack of a perfect match between the audio and visual tracks in the concluding section of this chapter.)

The most essential correlation between the genres of martial arts and gay video porn is their points of view in relation to the eroticized imaging of Asian male bodies. Whereas the sensuality of Bruce Lee is produced by the viewer's resistant reading, going against the grain of the narrative, the homoeroticism of Brandon Lee constitutes the key element of his status as a gay porn actor.[15] However, as stars commanding top billing (one an international martial arts superstar, the other a porn star in the smaller realm of gay male popular culture), both figures are set off narratively from the characters surrounding them. A "respectable working-class ghetto resident" (Kaminsky 1976, 63), Bruce Lee nevertheless transcends his downtrodden status through the performance of martial arts virtuosity. While Bruce Lee is presented as a man of the people who fights against imperialist forces, he stands out from the swarms of Asian male bodies that fight alongside him or more often, get beaten up by him. Similarly, Brandon Lee remains a recognizable, named actor, a fierce top among the anonymous hordes of interchangeable Asian bottoms. Though Brandon Lee is one among other men of the "Asian persuasion," he is marked off as different: he is an American real estate agent to the Japanese house buyer; he is the new owner of the boy brothel, where other Asians are sex workers; he is a porn star, a role model for another Asian character's porn ambition. These multiple differences are premised on an imbalance of power based on a higher economic, social, and cultural status. These power differentials relate to factors of nationality

(Americanness), race/ethnicity (unfixed, unstable), age (youth), size (dick, muscle), language (English speaking), and region (West Hollywood),[16] all of which contribute to his star status and top position. In what follows, I look more closely at these various components that go into the making of this gay Asian American porn star, with a sustained consideration of the spaces and mise-en-scènes in which these racialized pornographic fantasies unfold.[17]

The Making of a Gay Asian American Porn Star

Asian Persuasion opens with sunny skyline views of such landmarks as the Capitol Records building and the Fontenoy Apartments located in Hollywood, California. After the credits, the video cuts to two handsome young men asleep in a bed with white faux wrought iron headboards and plush off-white comforters. The porn decor evokes the bougie West Hollywood A-gay lifestyle of the late 1990s. Framed in identical poses on the bed—arms folded in front of their bare muscular chests—Brandon Lee and his boyfriend, Brad Davis Mikado, are awakened by a phone call. The caller is a client who wants to see a house in the Hollywood hills that Lee, the real estate agent, is trying to sell. Before Lee leaves, Mikado makes comments about the sexual nature of Lee's job, which requires meeting strange men at empty houses. Lee denies entertaining any sexual possibilities and suggests that Mikado, who is in the pool cleaning business, probably has more opportunities for sex with his clients, charges that Mikado also denies. Immediately, the viewer notices that the framing narrative of the video revolves around the two main characters' professions, and the familiar pornographic device of infusing characters' professions with homoerotic potentials. Lee is boyish, clean-cut, well built, middle class, and happily settled in a domestic coupledom. We are thus introduced to the world of a novel type of Asian porn character, an assimilated Asian American.

In the following scene, we see Lee, dressed in a pink Hawaiian shirt, finish showing the house to an older Japanese man.[18] The scene begins with Tenji Mito saying, "I like it. The neighborhood's great. And it's large." He looks down meaningfully at Lee's crotch. Lee responds, grabbing his crotch, "Yeah, it is large. And it gets bigger when somebody's lips are around it." Taking his cue effortlessly, the Japanese man proceeds to suck Lee and then gets fucked by him. Mito's comment about largeness refers first to the neighborhood and the house, then to Lee's cock, and we can infer from the context—a Japanese buying property in California—that the term also connotes the spaciousness of America in general. Throughout the scene, the sex is punctuated by Mito's heavily accented English emphasizing the big size and hardness of Lee's cock, crudely narrating how it acts on him: "Big cock. You've got big cock"; "I feel your hard cock"; and "Your dick make [sic] me come!" Conversely, Lee's verbal expression is limited to generic moans and stock phrases like, "Oh baby, feels so good" and "Yeah, baby, suck it." The position of top is aligned with Lee's coding as an American, associated with his Valley Guy English, his youth, butchness, muscularity, and big dick, set in opposition to the bottom's broken English (hence, marking him as non-American), older age, femmeness, skinny build, and smaller dick. Although the Japanese client may belong to a higher economic class — he is a potential buyer of the property — in the world of gay porn, other factors, such as physical endowment of muscle and genitalia, confer greater status than financial wealth. Nevertheless, a working-class status crucially informs the characterizations of Lee's other Asian costars. The other Asian actors in the video are the pool boys who work for Mikado's pool cleaning company, playing the roles of working-class immigrants.[19] None of them gets to fuck the two white special guest stars, well-known actors Mike Nichols and Sam Crockett. Significantly, unlike Lee and Mikado, whom we see moving between their swanky WeHo condo to their workplaces and back again (the last scene has them fucking in their state-of-the-art kitchen), the other Asian men are restricted to the spaces of their manual labor jobs, in the house of clients and around the backyard pool.

"Where Are You From?" The Spaces of Gay Asian Video Porn

Contrary to frequent dismissals by viewers and critics of gay male porn that too much storyline gets in the way of the real business at hand, namely, the sex, it must be pointed out that the particular settings in which the sex takes place and the narrative motivations for it to occur are of the utmost importance in these racially themed videos. Indeed, in light of the banal and formulaic repertoire of sex acts in the majority of mainstream gay porn productions, it is the specificities of the sexual fantasies and their mise-en-scènes that differentiate one production from another. What makes the sex hot is not merely the attractiveness of the actors' faces, the appropriate distribution of hair, the development of large pecs and tight abs, the shape and musculature of the ass, the length and girth of the cock, nor is it wholly the quality of their sexual performance and chemistry. Indeed what constitutes the hotness of a video can be attributed to how well it stages, repeats, and/or innovates on a preexisting collection of homoerotic fantasy scenarios that can potentially unfold at "all the key phantasmatic landmarks in the iconography of gay male porn itself: the locker room, the gym, the office, the park, the pizza delivery system, the plumber or UPS guy arriving at the door, the prison, and so on" (Cante and Restivo 2004a, 161). Although not especially imaginative or aspiring to originality, such staple "phantasmatic landmarks" allow viewers to pick and choose from the scripts structuring each scene with its attendant cast of characters (e.g., football players in the locker room, executive suits in the boardroom, gangsters in the prison) that would get them off the most effectively. Rich Cante and Angelo Restivo have persuasively argued for the importance of space and, more specifically, the world-making publicity of gay male pornography: "When the action is male-male sex, the spaces in which it transpires can never constitute neutral backdrops. This results from the fact that the acts themselves are nonnormative, whether one conceives the nonnormative as a violation of patriarchal law, or, more experientially, as the excess attached to feeling different and acting like an outsider. Therefore, visually recorded male-male sex acts are always situated in relation to a public via mechanisms distinct from male-female acts, even when their setting is a private space, such as a house or an apartment" (2004a, 142). They go on to claim that the intimate connection between gay male sex acts and public space "constitutes a key aesthetic dimension of the history of all-male moving image pornography" (Cante and Restivo 2004a, 142). While their comments offer insight about the queering of public space in gay porn, what is missing in the analysis is a consideration of how these spaces are racialized. All-male sex might "deneutralize" public and private spaces, but this deneutralizing occurs through various routes and intensities besides homoerotic ones, such as those framed by race/ethnicity, class, nationality, age, gender presentation, region, able-bodiedness, and so on. Cante and Restivo's "all-male" perspective assumes that all gay male viewers are evenly and seamlessly interpellated into these spaces of pornography, even at the phantasmic level. For, as we recall, in *Asian Persuasion*, it is the Americanized Asian characters (Lee and Mikado) who are allowed entry into various spaces of work and leisure, while the movements of the working-class Asian characters are severely circumscribed: they remain "housebound."

The portrayal of Lee's Asian costars as working-class foreigners/immigrants corralled within a constrained space with colonial overtones can also be found in *Fortune Nookie*, another video in Catalina's Far East Features series. In this video, Lee plays a young man who has inherited a fortune from a recently deceased uncle. The problem is that the white lawyer, Jacob Scott, refuses to tell him what the fortune is unless Lee pays him legal fees. Lee protests desperately, "But I have nothing! . . . Lawyers suck." To which Scott replies, "Yes, we do." Thus, Lee finds himself coerced into having sex with Scott in order to receive his fortune. Scott, dressed in a gray suit, orders Lee to take his clothes off and perform for Scott's pleasure.

The fortune turns out to be a brothel, where the sex workers are Asian men. They are managed and mistreated by a vicious white drag queen—in bad Japanese geisha drag—named Pixie (Vida de Ville). The Asian boy prostitutes are forced into working there for economic reasons. One of them, Niko Time, complains to Pixie that he wants to quit, but she reminds him that he has nowhere else to go. Another male prostitute, Tishiro Ho, tells his coworker, Erik Tenaka, that he is afraid that Pixie will fire him. Ho worries about his job security, especially since he has two kids to support. After taking over the whorehouse, Lee tries to make friends with Time, who also fears losing his job. Lee tells him, "I have a new job for you." Time replies, "OK, let's get it over with." But what Lee has in mind is giving Time the pleasure of firing the bitchy Pixie, who has been embezzling money from the business. They bond over the expulsion of the drag queen, and Lee gives Time Pixie's job. Time agrees to have sex with Lee and gets fucked by him.[20]

Sexual coercion and consent in *Fortune Nookie* are thematized around not only racial stratification but also class-inflected power relations. As in *Asian Persuasion*, an internal differentiation, and valuation, of the characters' sexual, gender, and economic capital becomes readily apparent in *Fortune Nookie*. Whereas Lee is coerced into having sex with the tie-wearing white lawyer (who tells him, "You have a lot of fees to work off, boy. . . . I'm pretty expensive"), after inheriting the brothel, Lee occupies the position of power over Time and the other Asian male prostitutes. Though he is poor at the beginning of the video, Lee's inheritance affords him a promotion in the economic and sexual hierarchy. However, the status of the immigrant sex workers under his charge remains relatively unchanged. The interaction between Lee and Time, though coded as more consensual in opposition to those between the two Asian men and their white sex partners earlier in the video (lawyer Jacob Scott and john Paul Morgan, respectively), continues to be structured by unequal power relations, with Lee's position as boss dominating over Time's status as employee. Sex in this video is tied to economic necessity, not utopian fantasy, sexual expression, or free choice. The use of Asian actors with heavy accents and FOB (fresh-off-the-boat) appearance and demeanor suggests an overlap of the actors' real-life situations with their characterizations in the porn narrative. Their actual low economic position and tenuous immigrant status resonate with their characters' marginalized positioning as sex workers threatened with unemployment. That is, their eroticization as sexual bottoms correlates with their bottom status in social and economic terms.[21] This dynamic corresponds with what Richard Fung has described as the lack of an empowering subject position for the gay Asian porn viewer due to the fact that these videos' ideal viewers are white gay men. While white subjects both within and outside the videos are accorded a multiplicity of social and sexual positions, Asian men's roles are extremely limited and fixed. In a more pronounced manner than the pool boys in *Asian Persuasion*, the male prostitutes in *Fortune Nookie* are firmly confined within the interior space of the boy brothel, unable to leave due to their dismal economic prospects outside of it. Time, as the only sex worker elevated to the position of manager, continues to be sequestered physically inside the walls of the brothel.

The spatial limitations imposed on Asian subjects in gay video pornography—as fantasy objects and as porn viewers—constitute a vital component of "how Asian porn obsessively catalogues the sexual uses of racial markings and racialized bodies" (Capino 2006, 208). The gym becomes the karate dojo; the pizza guy turns into a Chinese food delivery boy; the prison transforms into a boy brothel; Los Angeles's sunny Griffith Park morphs into "an out-of-the-way place located in a dingy back alley in San Francisco's famed Chinatown."[22] Paradoxically, as "Asian" categories—with dizzying racial and geographic connotations—become deployed to visualize Asian characters performing "gay male sex" for the camera, these videos effectively exclude these Asian characters from being seen as members of gay male communities. Recall that in *Fortune Nookie*, Tishiro Ho, one of the male sex workers, is depicted as "gay-for-pay," a father with two kids to support. The casting of Ho as heterosexual trade begs credibility due to his feminine gender presentation, soft nelly voice, and unconvincing enactment of a role usually deemed as a "straight-acting" or butch gender performance. With their FOB demeanors, it is inferred that these Asian immigrant characters (and actors?) live in poor ethnic ghettos far from the affluent gay neighborhoods of West Hollywood and the Castro. Their exclusion from gay membership parallels the depictions of Chicano/Latino men in contemporary gay U.S. porn. As Christopher Ortiz has argued, gay porn featuring Chicano/Latino men frequently sets their locations in Latino neighborhoods, "the barrio," or other class- and racially coded environments such as prisons and construction sites. A common fantasy figure that populates these sites is "the straight macho Chicano/Latino man who fucks 'me' (a white man)" without reciprocation; Ortiz (1994, 39) points out that such a stereotype prevents Chicano/Latino men from being seen as belonging to a gay community. Whereas Chicano/Latino characters are coded as macho, hypersexual, straight tops, and thus not qualifying as properly out and proud gay citizens, Asian characters are not conferred gay membership due to their effeminacy, desexualization, and exclusive bottom role (rather than the standard gay sexual versatility accorded to white men). Both groups of men of color are excluded from normative white gay American citizenship as a result of their racial-ethnic foreignness, working-class professions, and tenuous immigration status.

Looking at the spaces of Brandon Lee's Asian-themed videos and other Asian-niche productions, we get a fuller picture of how Asian sexuality is not only excluded from gay U.S. communities but also from the territorial space of America itself. Daniel Tsang, in a discussion of the mise-en-scène of gay Asian videos produced for the North American market, has noted the prevalence of the vague, timeless space of a remote land in the majority of these works. These fantasies of the sensuous East, of "lands far away from [Western] urban life" (Tsang 1999, 474–475), position the viewer as either an actual or a virtual sex tourist.[23] Other videos in Catalina's Far East Features Series corroborate this point, significant to note since they were released contemporaneously with Brandon Lee's Asian videos. Both *With Sex You Get Egg Roll* (dir. Peter Romero, 1999) and *Chew Manchu* (dir. Mark Jensen, 2000) exploit the associations of Asian sexuality with prostitution and sexual slavery, and thus, set their storylines in nebulous, mysterious, ahistorical interiors (although the exterior shots are all of Hollywood skylines): in *With Sex* the major narrative points occur in a dark, cavernous Chinese restaurant where the food delivery boys also double as call boys; similarly, the key scenes in *Chew Manchu* take place in the shadowy dungeon-like rooms of villain Chew Manchu (a low-rent gay porn version of Fu Manchu), called the House of Chew Manchu.

The logic of Asian porn actors stationed in Orientalist locales lends strong support to Jean Laplanche and Jean-Bertrand Pontalis's classic psychoanalytic insight that "fantasy . . . is not the object of desire, but its setting. In fantasy the subject does not pursue the object or its sign: he appears caught up himself in the sequence of images" (Laplanche and Pontalis 1986, 26)." To bring the quotation to bear on the Asian gay porn videos, we might say that their fantasies concern not only the bodies of Asian actors and the sex acts that they carry out, but, just as imperative, the mise-en-scènes in which they transpire. Though it is clear that, to some extent, narrative does take a secondary role in much of gay porn, it is also critical to examine the racially marked motivation of the staging of sexual fantasies in Brandon Lee's and other Asian-themed videos. The viewer of a video like *Asian Persuasion* is not just watching sex between men, but what the bodies and the sex with/between Asian men look like. The racial and ethnic coding of the actors occupies the central place of the sexual fantasy.[24] In watching the excerpt of a sex scene between Brandon Lee and Brad Davis Mikado in the *Best of Brandon Lee* compilation, a viewer might very well miss the point that Mikado, with his racially mixed appearance, is supposed to be read as Asian in this video. Seen outside the original context (*Asian Persuasion*), Mikado appears to be just another white porn actor.[25] The logic of these videotapes bespeaks the need to exoticize/eroticize racial difference by conjuring up a generic, slapdash Orientalia that, paradoxically, aims to reference vague notions of cultural authenticity. Consequently, we see credits in chopstick fonts, East Asian names, and characters having sex for money in settings like Los Angeles's Chinatown, Hong Kong, or Bangkok. Or, as Tsang notes, even when they are set in a no-place like anonymous hotel rooms in nameless countries, we are aware that this document of fantasy depends on the fact that the actors are from somewhere else, not here in the United States, but from an ahistorical, unspecified Orient. This point bears out Susan Koshy's claim about one of the primary features of American Orientalism, its deployment of "extraterritoriality." As she explains, "desire for the Orient/al is produced as a form of *extraterritorial desire*, a sign of the exotic that can be *acquired and consumed* . . . but is predicated on distance, on the foundational condition of belonging to another world, and hence must be *excluded from the space of the family and nation*" (Koshy 2004, 71, emphasis in original).

The emplacement of Asian men in another time and place, outside of Euro-American gay male spatial and temporal modernity, is confirmed on video box covers with their address to a specific type of consumer. The text for the video box packaging of *Fortune Nookie* is written on white elongated rectangles made to resemble paper strips from fortune cookies: "You will travel soon to the Far East for a pleasurable experience you won't forget," "Your love for men of Asian persuasion will increase and intensify," and so on. The second-person address replicates the phrasing of fortune cookies, but also positions the viewer as not of the Asian persuasion, a Western (and most likely) white viewer. The video promises to deliver the Far East to the viewer or to bring him there virtually, thus confirming Tsang's point that the ideal viewer of these tapes is the sex tourist. However, though it does not explicitly announce it, the setting of *Fortune Nookie* seems to be contemporary Los Angeles. We can deduce this from such clues as exterior shots of a Silverlake neighborhood, the use of a white drag queen to play the role of the bitchy madam Pixie, the Southern California architecture, "guppie" furnishings, and kitschy porno-set decoration of the rooms. Like *Fortune Nookie*, *Asian Persuasion* also mobilizes references to the Far East in its video box cover: "Do you need some persuading to experience a far east [sic] encounter? How about letting 8½ luscious inches make up your mind? How about smooth supple chested men giving you their eager, far east [sic] cocks standing firm in sweet scented nests of jet black hair. Super-hung Catalina discovery Brandon Lee has what it takes to persuade you. Just in case you need it!" The punning on the word "persuasion" activates two levels of meaning. The first refers to belonging to a religion or, in this case, a racial group, while the other meaning is a play on the verb "persuade," implying a sexual seduction.[26] While one can appreciate the cleverness of the double entendre and the gimmicky rhyming, this emphasis on the viewer's needing to be persuaded to try a "far east encounter," to find Asian men desirable, to buy the video, depends on the "common sense" of Asian men as undesirable and unsexy. The video box text must provide evidence—such as "8½ inches" of "far east cock standing firm," "smooth supple" chests, and "nests of jet black hair"—in order to persuade the potential (white) porn consumer to consider trying Asian cock. Again, like *Fortune Nookie*, *Asian Persuasion* is actually set in contemporary Los Angeles, as we can see from the exterior shots of the LA skyline in the credit sequence, in the house in the Hollywood hills that Lee shows the Japanese buyer, and the fancy Southern California home where Mikado and his pool boys go to work cleaning pools. What the discrepancy between video packaging and actual shooting locations suggests is that even when Asian men are removed from the ethnic ghetto of Chinatown and placed in the generic porno locales of West Hollywood, in conventional, pornographic historical time and space, they are still seen as carrying the timeless, mysterious, mystical Orient with them. Their inscrutable, exotic sexuality continues to hold hidden, unexploited "Far East" pleasures unknown to the white man.[27]

Shooting from Below

The novel intervention of Brandon Lee into this gay pornographic videoscape demonstrates that even as these titles include him in their publicity material referencing the discourse of Far Eastern sexual mysticism, in the videos themselves, he stands apart and in opposition to the other Asian characters. As enumerated above, his unique porn persona rests on his construction as an assimilated (Asian) American; more specifically, it is his prodigious genital endowment that constitutes the prized visual marker of difference from the foreign Oriental abjection embodied by other Asian actors. Various commentators have registered astonishment at the sight of such a dick on a small Asian man. Josh Eliot, the head director at Catalina who directed Lee in several videos, recalls being impressed by his cute face, but his great surprise came at the first sight of Lee's dick, which inspired Eliot to add another scene for Lee in *Asian Persuasion*. The porn magazine *XXX Showcase* puts it this way: "18-year-old Brandon has a hard-on almost as big as he is" (Lawrence 1998, 45). While this comparison stresses the large size of his cock, the comment implies that he has a small body that is out of proportion with his dick. In spite of the fact that so many commentators both inside and outside the videos keep remarking on the size of his penis—which "ranges" from 8½ to 10 inches, depending on which source one believes—it must be pointed out that in the world of gay pornography, the size of Lee's dick is not that extraordinary. The exaggeration and hype around Lee's sizeable equipment, I would contend, can be attributed to its attachment to the body of an Asian man. As suggested in the *XXX Showcase* citation, the big dick attached to the body of a five-foot-seven Asian man is considered out of proportion. This question of weight-height proportion does hold a positive valence in the gay male sexual marketplace, judging from the frequent invocation of this requirement in personal ads in gay newspapers and on gay websites.[28] Creative camera angles can easily correct any anomalous pairing of actors that might expose the secret of the vertically challenged yet well-endowed porn actor. A moment of mild shock registered for me when I was watching Lee in a four-way scene from *Dial "S" for Sex*. He is standing next to white performer Sam Crockett and merely reaches Crockett's shoulders. This medium long shot is held only for a minute or two before switching to a low angle underneath their cocks. From this worm's-eye view, Lee and Crockett, standing side by side, appear to be the same height; photographed this way, their similar stature—including the all-important cock size—thus implies their status as peers, as equal participants in the sexual scenario, as objects of desire standing upright while getting their cocks serviced by kneeling partners.[29]

The formal strategy of shooting from below visually showcases Lee's cock as it is licked and sucked by his costars (both white and Asian), and then as he fucks them with it. Lee's pleasure in getting sucked and in fucking constitutes the main sexual action and hotness of the videos, while his partners' pleasure derives from having Lee's cock penetrate their mouths and asses. In the scene between Lee and Tenji Mito in *Asian Persuasion* discussed above, a low-angle shot features Lee's cock in center frame as Mito, visible only by neck and chin, sucks it enthusiastically, his head bobbing from the top right edge to the center (figure 1.2). In the very same shot, in the upper left, we see Lee's face contorted, mouth agape emitting moans of pleasure, as he gazes at his cock going in and out of Mito's mouth. The shot economically and effectively aligns the viewer with Mito's pronounced enjoyment of Lee's cock as the "French active" partner in the scene. In the video's final scene, Lee and Mikado have sex after a long day at work. As porn conventions dictate, the scene ends with anal intercourse. The shots alternate between medium long shots of Lee fucking Mikado from behind (as the latter bends over a kitchen island countertop) and low-angle close-up shots of Lee's cock pounding Mikado's asshole (figure 1.3). Although the sequence concludes with high-angle shots showing the action from above, that is, Lee's top POV, the raucous verbal reaction of Mikado throughout the scene privileges his bottoming experience as recipient of Lee's vigorous pumping. Both of these scenes—the one between Lee and Mito that opens the video and the one with Lee and Mikado that ends it—submit to the rule of maximum visibility, displaying sexual acts from the best possible angles, especially those depicting intercourse (known as the "meat shot" in heterosexual porn with penis penetrating vagina). These exceedingly well-lit omniscient shots taken from the carpet looking up (documenting oral and anal sex), an "impossible" perspective that belongs to no one, actually serve to affirm the desiring perspective of the bottom, even at the risk of disrupting cinematic illusion.[30]

Indeed, in addition to attributing to Lee's big cock the powers to grant oral and anal pleasures to his partners, these videos also equip it with the capability of giving delight merely through the sense of sight. In *Fortune Nookie*, Lee's cock becomes a spectacle that arrests narrative flow. During various points during their foreplay kissing, Lee and Niko Time stop and look down at Lee's erect cock with their mouths wide open as if in awe (figure 1.4). After the two performers move from kissing to oral sex, Lee's cock re-

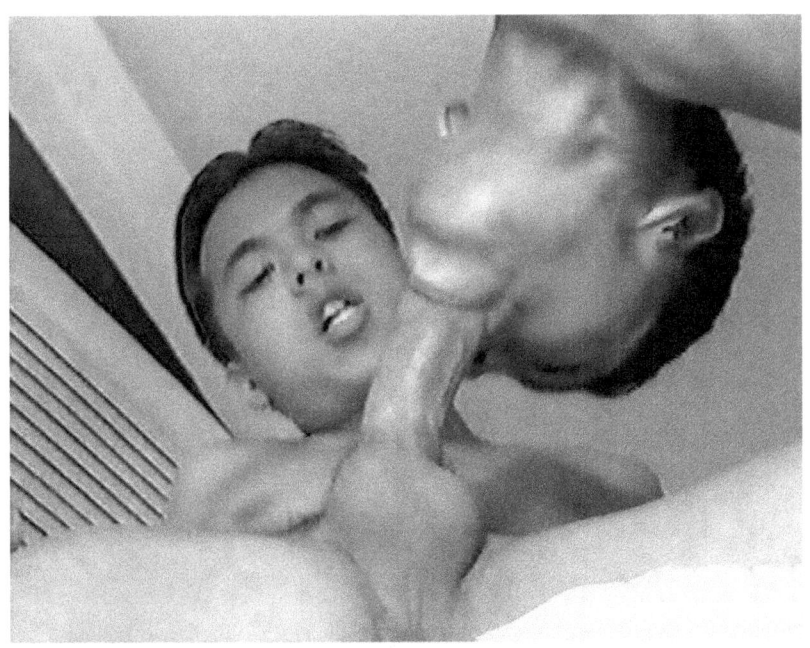
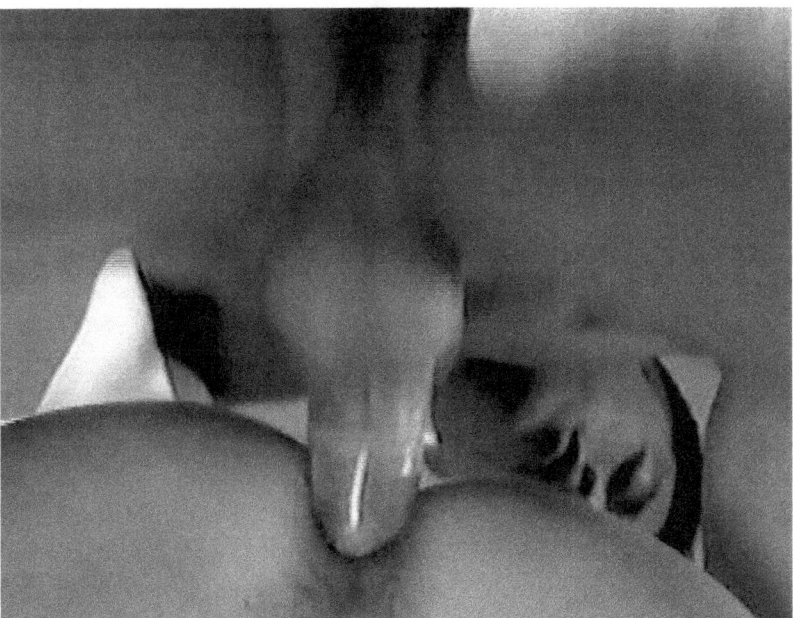

FIGURES 1.2 AND 1.3: Shooting from below. *Asian Persuasion* (1997).

FIGURE 1.4: Brandon Lee's cock. *Fortune Nookie* (1998).

mains the focal point as Time sucks on it while jacking off his own cock, which continues to be hidden away under his boxers. Such a visual fixation on Lee's endowment proves that such a "novel" sight in gay moving-image porn generates erotic thrill for Lee, Time, and us viewers. Here I want to sound a word of caution against the uncritical embrace of Brandon Lee, a big-dicked Asian American butch top, as what Asian American and other politically progressive gay porn fans have been waiting for. For although his work does invert the passive houseboy-bottom paradigm critics like Fung have protested against, this new and improved "positive image" of the Asian American top comes about at the expense of consigning other Asian men to the familiar position of unassimilable bottoms. Though the Asian penis has been found, there are only a few inches of it to go around, or it comes to resemble another white dick, tinted yellow. At the same time, it is vital that in acknowledging the shortcomings of Lee's top masculinity, we do not lose sight of the fact that the "image of servitude," or Asian bottomhood, is not only an injury and a liability, a position forced upon hapless, victimized Asian male subjects. We should also be open to viewing it as a position that can be enthusiastically assumed and pleasurably occupied. I examine these issues more thoroughly below in my discussion of Lee's "fall from the top."

Even though I have been discussing the Americanization of Brandon Lee in relation to his Asian costars, a similar process is at work in the mainstream gay videos in which he appears as well. *Big Guns 2* is a generic Catalina gay video that takes the military as a sexual background. Porn star Steve Rambo begins the tape by introducing the cast through a voice-over, read as if from a journal entry that he is writing. While conventional descriptions of white, macho, army-porno types comprise most of the voice-over characterizations, descriptions of the men of color exploit racial stereotypes. For instance, Rambo portrays the three black men as hypersexual studs; his voice-over makes references to a "six-foot-five monster of muscle and a tool between his legs that would make anyone's knees weak" and "a chest as hard as a rock and lips that could make a dead man come when he puts them into action." One Latino character is described as "streetwise from East LA," while another is said to possess a "burrito [that] was jam-packed with sour cream [and] was constantly being munched on." Whereas the black and Latino actors are ascribed racist characteristics, Lee's Asianness is not explicitly commented on: "And finally there's Brandon. You might call him our mascot. I guess when you're as youthful-looking and cute as he is and feature a giant, fucking dick to boot, everyone wants to be your friend." There are no crass references to his egg roll, teriyaki sauce, smooth, hairless skin, or his Oriental exoticism. The video begins with everyone being awakened in boot camp by Lee's moans while masturbating. Taking his role as mascot seriously, Lee here acts as the instigator of the orgy action that ensues. Not just an ordinary army recruit, he is painted as a special member of the unit, someone who everyone gets along with and gets off to.[31]

The distinctions between "American" and "Asian," big dick and small cock, top and bottom sex roles, Americanized and FOB, also extend to the mise-en-scènes of Lee's non-Asian-themed videos. The army barracks in *Big Guns 2* resemble your generic gay porn fantasy scenario, the only difference being the multicultural cast of characters detailed above. The living room in which the four-way orgy from *Dial "S" for Sex* takes place is the same setting, and in fact is the exact set for another of Lee's videos, *Stag Party*. It is a typical Southern California bungalow living room with French doors opening up onto a sunny backyard or balcony. This setting typifies most of the settings of Lee's other videos—the middle-class, gay, white milieu of West Hollywood. As I suggested at the beginning of the chapter, this constitutes a significant shift from the ethnic ghettos where previous Asian-themed porn videos were based.

In contrast to the persistent emplacement of Asian men in sexual encounters that can take place only in the Far East or the Chinatowns of the United States, Lee's crossover into the mainstream of gay porn videos concomitantly allows him to leave the ethnic ghetto once and for all and set up residence in the contemporary urban gay male ghetto of West Hollywood. In these videos, Lee is portrayed simply as a West Hollywood twink whose Asianness is seldom noted. In *Dial "S" for Sex*, he comes home to find his white boyfriend, Drew Andrews, jerking off while talking on the phone with an anonymous caller. Lee and Andrews proceed to have sex together, and later are joined by two white friends who drop by unexpectedly for a four-way orgy. At the end of the scene, we find out that Lee came home on a lunch break and must go back to work. Before doing so, he reminds his boyfriend, "Don't forget that Mitch is coming by to pick up those papers. Don't forget to call him, OK? Gotta go. Bye." Neither the preceding sex scene nor anything that comes after narratively motivates this line. Its only purpose, it seems to me, is to establish Lee as a regular guy living in generic pornotopia, in a tame coupledom occasionally spiced up by kinky sex. In addition, the throwaway line establishes Lee's class credentials as a white-collar executive type who inhabits a vanilla world far away from that of Asian porn characters with their dirty manual labor and/or commercial sex work.

The video that locates Lee most firmly in the West Hollywood gay scene is *Peters*, which is a porn remake of the Winona Ryder vehicle *Heathers* (dir. Michael Lehmann, 1989). Lee plays the Winona/Veronica character, here called Daniel Sawyer. This typical American name erases any connection to any "Far East" identity. After throwing up on one of the circuit-partying Peters at an exclusive sex club, Daniel/Lee is rebuked by one Peter Chandler (Patrick Allen), who threatens to reject Daniel/Lee from their West Hollywood in-group by telling him, "Might as well move to the Valley, Daniel."[32] Another reference to the West Hollywood gay scene is invoked when Daniel/Lee and his cohort Jack Long (Gage Michaels in the Christian Slater role) make a rendezvous with the two bullies Buzz and Rahm at the Hollywood Spa, the largest gay bathhouse in Los Angeles. Taken together, these narrative elements demonstrate how Brandon Lee's appearance in mainstream gay porn recodes him into just another gay pornotopic character, carousing within the hegemonic space of gay, white, male, affluent West Hollywood.

The color-blind casting of Lee in the starring role of Daniel Sawyer in *Peters* signals the most extreme instance of his legitimation as an American.[33]

"No, Where Are You *Really* From?"

In a milieu dominated by an ideal of white, American, masculine physical perfection, what is it about Lee that has enabled him to enter into the segregated world of mainstream gay pornography? I propose that Lee's crossover is made possible by a certain degree of racial instability accruing to his star image. This ability to penetrate into the mainstream is part and parcel of an undecidable (inscrutable, unfixed) Asian ethnicity.

In addition to their name, the other "coincidence" linking Brandon Lee, cult star of *The Crow*, and Brandon Lee, porn star of *Fortune Nookie*, is their racial ambiguity. The son of Bruce Lee was hapa (half-Asian, half-white), a fact that is seldom mentioned as a result of Hollywood's typecasting of Brandon Lee as a martial arts actor. Consequently, most commentators are invested in establishing a patriarchal lineage by emphasizing the connections between father and son (the Little Dragon and Son of the Dragon). The racial/ethnic ambiguity of Lee the porn star proves trickier. In his first foray into gay porn, he appeared in a video titled *Glory Holes of L.A.* (dir. Bianco Piagi, 1997) under the name of Sean Martinez. It was not until his second video, *Asian Persuasion*, that he took on the name Brandon Lee. In the context of mainstream gay video pornography, where young, white, well-built actors are the unquestionable norm, any departure from this type represents a special niche, a zone in which differences such as race become heavily commodified.

The "trouble with Asians" is the difficulty of telling them apart. But in the world of gay video porn, it is not necessary to discriminate the "minute" differences among Asians. Rather, it suffices to connote cultural authenticity by conjuring an all-encompassing Orientalia. Thus, most Asian actors have East Asian or, more specifically, Japanese-sounding names, such as Tenji Mito, Hiro Sukowa, Erik Tenaka, and Niko Time. Other actors take on Japanese first names and Chinese last names, like Tishiro Ho. Others Orientalize their names for an Asian video, as in the case of Brad Davis Mikado and Jean Russo Chen. The former usually goes by Brad Davis in his other videos. The addition of "Mikado" implies a hidden Japaneseness in his person. Josh Eliot, director of *Asian Persuasion 1* and *2*, suggests the practical necessity of using "not quite Asian" actors like Davis in the Asian-themed videos in order to safeguard against the risk of Asian actors changing their minds and reneging on their commitment to appear in a video on the day of the shoot.[34] This bit of extratextual information notwithstanding, the mixed-race reference in these actors' names also exploits the exoticism traditionally associated with interraciality in the United States. This transgression draws upon the historical prohibition against miscegenation. For instance, Gina Marchetti has called attention to Hollywood cinema's depiction of Eurasians as evil, deceitful, and dangerous. In the context of gay porn, the bi-/multiculturalism of mixed-race actors also provides a form of "the-best-of-both-worlds" exoticism, invoking difference but also similarity—threat and spice, as well as comfort and familiarity.

Far from being merely camp and kitsch (like the short, butch names used by white actors), naming in the Asian-niche videos plays a large role in the racial packaging of the tapes, since the producers are selling eroticized-exoticized racial and ethnic difference. Quentin Lee, who played Peekay Chan in *Shanghai Meat Company* (dir. Tony Chan, 1991), claims that the white producers of the video gave themselves Asian names in the credits in order to sell it as being an authentic "by-Asian-for-Asian" videotape. Along these same lines, we can appreciate Brandon Lee's assumption of a recognizable Asian American name from a cult martial arts celebrity. This choice of name exploits the cultural association of Asian men in the popular imagination with the kung fu action genre. Inadvertently, he may have inherited the racial ambiguity of the real Brandon Lee as well.

Brandon Lee's real name is Jon Enriquez. He was born in Mobile, Alabama, on March 18, 1979. His ethnic background is Filipino, with a mix of Chinese, English, and Spanish. I propose that Enriquez's previous appearance in gay porn as Sean Martinez reveals an attempt to present himself as Latino, hence drawing on the closer association of Latinos/Chicanos with hypersexual appeal.[35] It's significant that Enriquez's choice of porn name is aligned with East Asian and Asian American connotations after he decided to appear in Asian-themed videos. In the United States, there is an automatic association of Asia with East Asia. The Far East/East Asia axis grounds the Orientalist fantasies of gay pornography. To support this observation, I mention here several other titles in Catalina's Far East Features series: *Pacific Rim* (dir. Mitchell Dunne, 1997), *With Sex You Get Egg Roll*, *Chew Manchu*, and *Crème of Sum Yung Gai* (director uncredited, 2004). In the discourse of Oriental sexuality—based on an *ars erotica* (erotic art), with its links to Eastern knowledge and experience of pleasure—the sexuality of Filipinos does not figure strongly. Regarded as dirty and impure, too mongrelized and Westernized due to four hundred years of colonial contact with Spanish and American cultures, Filipinos are excluded from this exotic framework.

In an article about the taxi dance halls in Filipino immigrant communities of the 1920s and 1930s, Rhacel Salazar Parreñas (1998) refers to the threat posed by the interracial mingling between the "little brown monkeys" (the male Filipino laborers) and "white trash" (women who worked at these dance halls) to the hegemonic American discourse around racial purity represented by the eugenics movement. Jinqi Ling has noted that the classification of Filipinos as U.S. nationals and as Malays (rather than Mongolians) in the same period allowed Filipino men relative freedom of movement and interaction with white women. Ling writes, "The invention of Filipino males' threatening sexuality is thus bound up with white men's concern about securing their social power, a concern brought to the point of crisis by Filipino workers' participation in the labor movement" (1997, 319). My brief mentions of Filipino male labor history in the United States aim to emphasize the historical coding of Filipino men as sexual threats to white American manhood. Along with the "corruption" of the Philippines by Western colonial forces, the image of Filipino men as "irresistible studs" prevented the incorporation of Filipinos in the exoticized, feminized, and domesticated discourse of Orientalist, racial fantasies. It is this particular historically inflected, racialized sexual dynamic that enables, even in the late 1990s and into the 2000s, the transformation of Jon Enriquez/Sean Martinez—identities that are couched in the threatening, opaque, and vexed framework of Filipino American sexuality—to the more culturally intelligible (and easier-to-consume) Brandon Lee.

I contend that the conventionally handsome face of Brandon Lee functions as a product of a mongrelized Filipino American interracial mixing after many generations.[36] The colonial and imperialist legacies of the Philippines have produced what some of my Filipino friends jokingly refer to as a "mutt," a mixture comprising indigenous Filipino, Malay, Chinese, Spanish, and American biological and cultural, somatic and psychic ingredients. One can see this mutt mixture reflected on the face of Brandon Lee as a set of hybridized, Westernized facial features: most meaningfully, the double eyelid, the tall nose bridge, and the brown skin. It is also this "unplaceable" face that permits a crossing of ethnicities. Because "all Orientals look the same," the face of Lee animates a variety of racial connotations, going from Jon Enriquez to Sean Martinez to Brandon Lee. Enriquez, Martinez, and

Lee's ability to pass resides precisely in exploiting this hidden disguise of the exotic, inscrutable Asian mask in order to put forth a legible, average American face. As an Asian American fan of Lee observes, "Compared to the other Asian guys he's with in the videos, he's definitely a better watch. The other guys usually aren't cute. . . . They make funny noises when Brandon Lee fucks them and have that annoying Asian edge to them—kind of like my brethren that I shy away from at gay Asian clubs."[37] In contrast to the "closed," single-lidded eyes and foreign, FOB demeanor of his Asian costars with their often unintelligible verbal recitals, Lee's open American face is "a better watch," and the English-speaking, American viewer can hear his Valley Guy accent without great effort. Furthermore, doesn't the register of surprise and pleasure of seeing an "American" dick attached, out of proportion, to the face and body of an Asian American man indicate another *passport*? Isn't this big (enough) dick the appeal and the prerequisite, the pass for admittance into the world of white gay mainstream pornotopia? Is this the dick that is finally big enough to rival, and fuck, white men?

The Fall of Brandon Lee

Up to this point, I have focused on the early phase of Brandon Lee's career, from the beginning in 1997 to his departure from the industry in 1999. This brief period was pivotal to the construction of his image as a gay (Asian) American porn star, largely due to his crossover from an Asian niche market to a more mainstream one. In 2004, after serving in the U.S. Navy, Lee returned to gay porn as an exclusive actor for Rascal Video. No longer the clean-cut Asian American twink from his early years, Lee reemerged in the industry with an edgier look: thick muscular build, body decorated with copious tattoos, cocky demeanor, and an aggressive performance style. The most significant change in Lee's porn persona was his decision to bottom for the first time in *Wicked* (figure 1.5). It appears as if his butch makeover were created to offset the turn to bottoming. Before discussing *Wicked*, let me backtrack and propose that his previous videos amply prepared the viewer for Lee's momentous "fall from the top."

From the beginning of his career, Lee's topness has always been a shaky affair. Adding a new dimension to the argument I made above about Lee's persona as an American top, here I highlight moments in his videos when bottomhood makes itself felt. For instance, I referred above to the scene in *Fortune Nookie* with Jacob Scott as the lawyer who coerces Lee into having sex with him in exchange for Scott's lawyer fees. Even though Lee tops Scott

FIGURE 1.5:
DVD cover.
Wicked (2005).

in this scene, Scott, the consummate "bossy bottom," holds the upper hand throughout the sequence as he repeatedly calls Lee "boy" and orders him to "fuck me like a man." Before they even get to the fucking, Scott demonstrates his power when he directs Lee to strip naked and pose in a variety of positions—standing, bending over, sticking up his ass—while Scott remains clothed, watching, and rubbing his cock through the trousers of his business suit. Lee's function in this scene (incidentally, what many viewers consider the hottest scene in *Fortune Nookie*) as a passive top who is bossed around and objectified by the bottom is reinforced when at the end of the sequence, he kneels on the floor while Scott jacks off and comes on Lee's face and chest.

Another moment when Lee's topness is called into question can be found in *Asian Persuasion 2*. The scene in question shows Tommy Lin, an aspiring porn actor, seated in the waiting room of Catalina Video watching Brandon Lee, the porn star, perform a solo jerk on a TV monitor. Lee directly addresses Lin (and by implication, the porn viewer), throughout his masturbatory routine. This video within a video mirrors the porn viewing situation, and thus can be said to teach the viewer "how to watch Brandon Lee," characterized here as an autoerotic top, a top that must constantly acknowledge his susceptibility to bottomhood. Throughout the sequence, there is a constant switching between his position as top—the subject acting upon the viewer—and as bottom—as the object of someone else's desire. While on his stomach humping a pillow, Lee looks at the camera: "I want my ass eaten out really good. . . . Nice tongue in my hole." He fingers and spreads his hairless asshole. But then he shifts from this bottom position (getting eaten out) to top: "Bend your knees so I can fuck you. . . . I need a tight ass for my cock." However, what we immediately see is his spread butt cheeks. At the end of the scene, he flips over on his back, shoots on his own face, and ends by wiping his cheeks and eating his own cum, while looking directly at the camera. To be sure, in the context of the post-AIDS solo jerk, the eating of cum constitutes a resignification of risk and sexual taboo associated with the exchange of bodily fluids.[38] The ingestion of his own cum crystallizes the constant switching between top and bottom that Lee directly solicits, visually and verbally, from the viewer throughout this solo-jerk scene; put differently, he performs this switching in addition to soliciting it. Lee's self-facial dramatizes the enormous pressure brought to bear on the racially inflected fantasy of an Asian top porn star performing for another Asian man who desires him and desires to be like him. Moreover, the coming and shooting on his own face can be seen as a complex negotiation of the ways in which an Asian American top porn star must also address the desires of non-Asian spectators, particularly in the context of North American gay porn, spectators who are not used to seeing an Asian American actor in the role of a top. These moments of Lee's autoerotic topness, then, exemplify what José B. Capino has argued is the determining component that makes Asian porn Asian, namely, sexual availability. Capino writes, "The pleasure of Asian porn's plenitude is intensified by the compulsory sexual availability of virtually all the Asian figures within the diegesis of video pornography" (2006, 212–213). However, against Capino's observation that this Asian sexual availability is made possible by the ways "the racialization and sexualization of Asianness are hyperbolized equally and together" (209), Lee represents a special case because, as I argued at length above, his hyperbolic sexualization as a top porn actor is accomplished through a process of deracialization or, more precisely, a racial disavowal, albeit a process that remains uneven and unsustainable. The self-sufficient sexual repertoire he performs for the viewer (rimming and fucking his own ass, eating his own cum) demonstrates his racially unremarked sexual availability for the viewer, acting in turn as an invitation for the viewer to perform these same acts on him.

The destabilization of Lee's top status traced in these examples finds its full realization in *Wicked*. Looking closely at the narrative motivation for Lee's bottoming in this video can tell us how Lee's relatively secure status as an American top porn star mediates and accommodates this radical shift in his porn persona. In *Wicked*, Lee plays himself, the porn star Brandon Lee, but one whose celebrity has inflated his head to diva proportions. The first scene in the video pairs Brent Everett and Jan Fischer in a mechanic's garage. As the scene ends, Lee enters the porn set and throws a hissy fit, claiming that that was supposed to be his scene. The director (Doug Jeffries) replies that since Lee doesn't bottom, he had to cast another actor who was willing to bottom for Everett, who only tops. The following scene shows another pair of white actors, Tag Adams and Tommy Ritter, on a country barn set. Lee barges in, interrupting the two actors' conversation, saying, "Do you know who I am? Everybody kisses my ass around here. Let's start with you!" In response, Adams eagerly dives in to rim Lee's asshole. The end of the scene finds Adams and Ritter jacking off and ejaculating all over Lee's face. As the director yells "Cut!" a furious Lee shouts, "This will be the last time I get cum on my face!" Back in his dressing room, Lee is visited by the Ghost of Porn Past (Kurt Young), who advises Lee to change his prima donna ways because they are negatively affecting the people around him. Lee replies that everyone loves him, but the Ghost tells him differently. They look into a magic mirror and observe a scene between two of Lee's former costars, both of whom left the porn industry due to their bad experiences working with Lee. Next, Lee is visited by the Ghost of Porn Present (Chi Chi LaRue), who espouses the positive power of cooperation and teamwork, of what can happen when "everybody work[s] together to get the job done." Through the same magic mirror, she allows Lee to witness a very hot three-way sex scene between Johnny Hazzard, Joey Milano, and Luca DiCorso. Lee is impressed: "I wish I had been in that scene!" Back to reality, the assistant director comes to tell Lee that the actor who was supposed to bottom in the final scene canceled, thus putting the whole production in jeopardy. Having learned his lessons from the two Ghosts' visitations, Lee heroically volunteers to fill in for the missing actor. In the final scene, Lee bottoms for Shane Rollins. After taking turns sucking one another, Lee declares, "I want you inside me." Rollins takes his time preparing Lee's ass, by rimming it, spitting his saliva into Lee's asshole, fingering it, and finally penetrating Lee. As a dramatic turning point in Lee's career and the climactic scene of *Wicked*, Lee takes Rollins's cock enthusiastically, performing his role as an aggressive and extremely verbal bottom, much more so than in his performance as a top in the video's barn scene. To signal the momentous occasion, Lee is shown coming not once, but twice. The first time has Lee jerking himself off and shooting while Rollins fucks him. After jacking Rollins off, Lee jerks himself and comes again. Lee looks up and smiles at the two Ghosts above, who smile and wave approvingly down at him.

Writing about gay-for-pay actors in gay pornography, Jeffrey Escoffier observes, "Virtually every actor who makes a name for himself as a top is challenged to bottom at some point in his career" (2003, 544). Famous examples include such figures as gay-for-pay, or sexually ambiguous, performers Jeff Stryker, Ryan Idol, and Rod Barry. Escoffier notes that in order to sustain fan interest and maintain their marketability, porn actors must periodically modify their persona by enlarging their sexual repertoire. While the question of gay-for-pay is a moot point in the case of gay-identified Lee, it is notable that he decided to bottom right after his return to porn from a five-year sabbatical, suggesting that this vital addition to his sexual repertoire was as carefully orchestrated as his new edgy, buffed, tattooed image. But, unlike a white gay-for-pay actor like Rod Barry, whose decision to bottom was based solely on financial compensation (Escoffier 2003, 544), Lee's repackaging from a total top to a versatile performer cannot be adequately understood without taking his Asianness into account. Indeed, the press around Lee's decision to bottom invariably references his status as an Asian porn star known for being an exclusive top. For example, the credit sequence at the beginning of *Wicked* is composed of close-ups of box covers of Lee's early Asian-niche videos, such as *Asian Persuasion 1* and *2*, and *Fortune Nookie*; the sequence establishes Lee as a porn star and links his past work as a top with this new phase as a versatile performer.

Wicked narrates Lee's bottoming as a morality tale à la Dickens's *A Christmas Carol*. The moral dilemma for Brandon Lee is whether to persist in his porn star arrogance and egotism or to do good by sacrificing his status as a top for the betterment of the group (i.e., the success of the video production). Although *Wicked* is the porn vehicle that showcases Lee's bottoming,

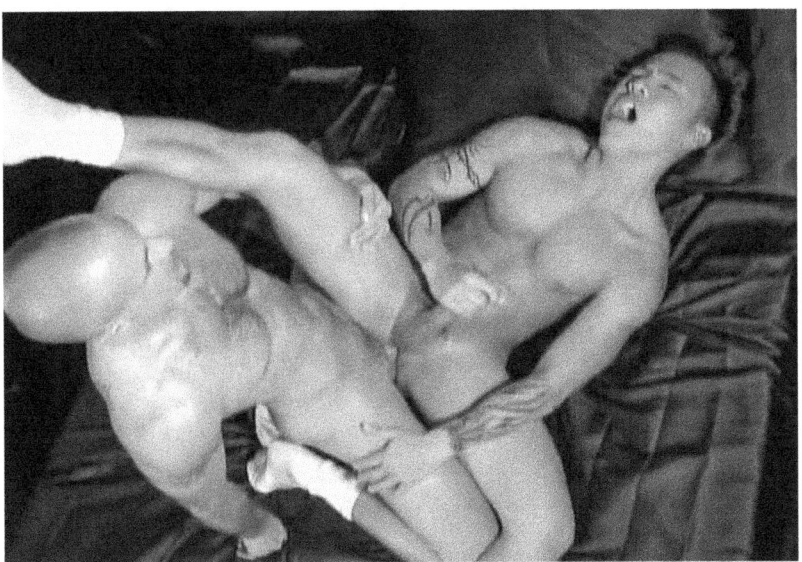

FIGURE 1.6: Brandon Lee bottoms. *Wicked* (2005).

the narrative, curiously, is not organized around the desire to get fucked or the pleasure of bottomhood. Rather, it functions here as a way of disciplining Lee's porn stardom gone awry, as a means of reining in its excesses. Lee's porn diva shenanigans are explicitly linked to his role as a top: from the first scene when he storms the set fuming because he has been replaced by another top (Everett) to the later scene when his topness is compromised after two costars give him facials. Though not exactly a sign of punishment and submission, Lee's bottoming in *Wicked* nevertheless implies that Asianness and topness are ultimately incommensurable. Relatedly, it also indicates that his unremarked and unremarkable racial position—as an assimilated (Asian) American—cannot be steadfastly maintained and stabilized. Instead of signifying strength, discretion, and confidence, Lee's brand of topness—as manifested in the narrative of *Wicked*—is marked by bitchiness, hysteria, and insecurity. Put differently, his porn stardom is coded as feminizing: Lee's top is less Jeff Stryker and more Lucy Liu. In *Wicked*, Lee's redemption, the only way he can repair his bad porn image, lies in giving up his status as a top, hitherto the defining trait of his fame.

Yet to read Lee's bottoming as a containment of Asian American masculinity is not the whole story. Lee's turn as an aggressive bottom challenges a purely ideological reading. His insistent, verbal entreaties to Rollins—"fuck me, fuck me, oh yeah"—and his raucous moans of "uh uh uh uh fuck uh," even if partly exaggerated and overly theatrical, encourage us to think beyond the framework of bottomhood cum Asian abjection (figure 1.6). The fact that Lee is able to maintain an erection while being fucked and to come twice in one sex scene suggests involuntary bodily responses that exceed the narrative framing of Lee's bottoming as a lesson about cooperation, teamwork, and humility.[39] The pleasure manifested by Lee's bottoming, whether seen as involuntary, excessive, or perhaps even faked, triggers an alternative reading. Asked in an interview about his experience bottoming for the first time onscreen, Lee replies that unlike in real life, you can always say "Cut!" when bottoming in front of the camera. He goes on to say, in real life, "I just take it," whereas on a video shoot, "I had time to get used to my partner" (Corday 2005, 20). For Lee, bottoming for a porn production is "easier" because he has more control over the process. While the logistics of pornographic performance do not override the narrative framing of Lee's bottoming in *Wicked*, they do call attention to the performance of bottomhood, and by extension, the performance of topness as well. In distinguishing his experience of bottoming on and off camera, Lee suggests that his sexual practice in real life does not necessarily correspond with, and might be counter to, the top activities he performs in videos. This potential discrepancy opens up a space for Lee's agency as a porn performer who makes a choice to add bottoming to his sexual repertoire as a strategy of extending his marketability in the industry. Further, Lee's bottoming can be read as less a fall from the top and more a way of tapping into the full range of sex acts that gay male video porn ratifies.[40] As a versatile actor who performs fiercely as a top sometimes and aggressively as a bottom at other times, Lee exploits and to a certain extent challenges the racial codes that underpin top and bottom positionings in contemporary gay video porn.

In addition to performance, another way to read Lee's bottomhood as something beside the regulation of Asian American masculinity is by considering the changed mediascape that has recently discovered a new Asian desirability in the realms of culture, including film, television, music, the Internet, and popular culture. Since his emergence in the late 1990s, Lee has made a big impression in a global gay Asian mediascape for being the first Asian top porn star in North American gay pornography. His fame is disseminated not only through his actual videos but also through the circulation of his star text across various media platforms. The first hit that comes up on a Google search for "gay Brandon Lee" takes one to a Wikipedia entry on Lee.[41] The gay press readily recognizes him as a "living legend" of gay pornography. *Unzipped*, one of the most popular American gay magazines chronicling the contemporary gay porn industry, credits Lee with "busting stereotypes [about] Asian men" and names him "porn's reigning Asian superstud" (Corday 2005, 18–20). As part of its "Asian Invasion Issue!," New York City's gay glossy weekly *Next* puts a buffed and naked Lee on its cover, posed in a three-quarter view that accentuates his smooth, firm, meaty pecs and smoother, firmer, and meatier buttocks. The writer of the cover story compares Lee's accomplishments as a gay Asian American porn star and his "aggressive total-top-ness" with what B. D. Wong did for Asian American actors with his Tony Award–winning performance in *M. Butterfly* (Angelo 2005, 12). In the same vein, the Paris-based gay magazine *Baby Boy* includes Lee in its top ten list of gay Asian icons. As the only porn actor, he rounds out the list at number ten in an international roster that includes Bruce Lee (no. 1), Takeshi Kaneshiro (no. 4), and Wang Lee Hom (no. 9). In light of these examples, I want to reassess my claims throughout the chapter that the ideal viewer of Lee's work is (always) a gay white man.[42] Doing so offers us a broader understanding of the ideological work behind Lee's revised persona as a versatile Asian American porn star.

An Accented Pornography

I began this chapter by arguing that the construction of Brandon Lee as a desirable (Asian) American top porn star is established in opposition to his less-than-appealing Asian costars with their working-class status, Chinatown address, bad accents, bad hair, flat faces, small dicks, and propensity for bottomhood. It should be amply clear by now that in linking sexual dominance and desirability with porn stardom, topness, and hegemonic white American masculinity, one risks perpetuating the association of bottomhood with Asian submission, abjection, and anonymity. In addition, this essentialist and binary coding of white American/top and foreign Asian/bottom serves to foreclose any consideration of the pleasures and agency of the bottom, whether white, black, Latino, or Asian. A rethinking of the dynamics of top and bottom must acknowledge that for some gay Asian male subjects, adopting the bottom position can be an enjoyable and affirming sex act. To invoke the title of the well-known sex-positive feminist, lesbian magazine, they are perfectly happy "on their backs." A more nuanced critique of normative racial-sexual discourses might proceed with a different aim, that is, not by flipping on top, but by interrogating the values underpinning these social-sexual positionings. It would also attempt to submit these anonymous

FOB bottom porn characters to a wholly different set of social, sexual, and aesthetic viewpoints.

Brandon Lee's conversion from a clean-cut West Hollywood twink top to an older buffed-out, heavily inked versatile performer was accompanied by a persona makeover into an egotistical diva. After the decisive *Wicked*, the porn diva persona became even more dramatically altered. In *Lights & Darks: An Interracial Spin* (dir. Doug Jeffries, 2005) and *Affirmative Blacktion: An Interracial Takeover* (dir. Doug Jeffries, 2010), Lee's star text takes on an explicitly racializing cast when he adopts "yellowface" in both videos. In the former, he is a suit-wearing proprietor of a modern-day laundromat who speaks broken English and exhibits an offensive racist suspicion of his black customers; in the latter, Lee plays a greedy, imperious heterosexual Chinese bar owner, complete with a white girlfriend and a coterie of butch, muscular white and black minions-employees who cower and jump at his every command. It would appear that as part of the project of diversifying his sexual repertoire by adding bottoming to the list, Lee's porn persona has begun, for the very first time in his career, to exploit the potentials of "Asian roles" that his deracinated American image had previously left untapped. I analyze this latest development in Lee's image in the broader framework of the deployment of sound and the voice as they pertain to Asian characters in gay video porn. The stereotypical roles of his Asian costars and Lee's own turns in various Asian stereotypes in his more recent videos create the opportunity to argue for an accented pornography, a mode of porn performance and reception that, while drawing on toxic racialized sexual roles, also allows for the envisioning and inhabiting of a different subject position vis-à-vis these Orientalist gay fantasy scenarios.

By moving the analysis away from diagnosing the ways that these FOB characters have been made abject due to their relegation to bottom status, I propose to examine the characteristic that most brands them as irredeemably foreign: their voice, or, more specifically, their bad, accented English.[43] It is through their accented English that Asian porn performers communicate another sexual subjectivity, one that is not less than, or lacking, in relation to the idealized white gay performers, but one that evades intelligibility within conventional pornographic image- and soundscapes. My use of "accented pornography" borrows from Hamid Naficy's powerful theorization of accented cinema. In Naficy's formulation, accented cinema refers to an artisanal and collective method of filmmaking that challenges the dominant mode of cinematic production, a task accomplished "from the filmmakers' and audiences' deterritorialized locations." Acknowledging that "all accents are not of equal value socially and politically," he employs the discussion of nonnormative vocal performances to signify various forms of linguistic, social, and political marginalization (Naficy 2001, 22). In the context of gay porn, accents constitute a shorthand for depicting a character's sexual appeal, most significantly, his masculinity quotient: a deep voice in a non-region-discernible accent that evokes butch, red-blooded, all-American manhood.[44] By contrast, the strong accent of some Asian actors—as aural evidence of their racial/ethnic, class, national, and gender alterity—indexes their exclusion from U.S. gay community membership. Consequently, I want to draw on Naficy's argument for accented cinema's deterritorialization to describe certain viewers' willingness to grant the Asian FOB actors a new hearing. In contrast to some critics, I do not perceive in the FOB porn subjects' accents a failure to speak and perform as idealized white porn stars; nor do I detect in their slow, belabored voices an intentional resistance and undermining of the mainstream gay porn soundscape, in the vein ascribed by Naficy to an accented, intercultural cinema. Instead, I seek to make room for listening to and witnessing these subjects' authenticity-in-abjection differently, as toxic in normative terms, to be sure, but more importantly as legitimate in their own right, without justification, translation, or special accommodations. My use of "accent" refers not only to the actors' English, but also to their voices' scripted, soft, hesitant, effeminate quality—the grain of their voices that doesn't carry the authoritative butch masculine tones adopted by white American (top) actors.

Numerous critics have identified the vital role that sound plays in moving-image pornography. In her landmark study of heterosexual pornographies, *Hard Core*, Linda Williams argues that the female voice (along with the female face) is used to stand for and signify female pleasure due to the fact that its true source evades visual representation. Other critics writing on gay male moving-image porn have made similar observations about the phantasmic function of the voice. For instance, Cante and Restivo (2004a, 158) point out that sound in gay male porn, such as the unsynced "improvised-in-postproduction mishmash of moans, breathings, gasps, cries," effectively constructs a utopian, phantasmic pornographic space. In the same vein, Cindy Patton argues that unsynced sex sounds in pornographic loops suggest that "sexual subjectivity is something like 'tapes' that we run" (1999, 475). She continues:

> Where older porn ran its endless grunting and groaning loops, 1980s porn intersperses sex noises with phrases like "suck my big dick." ... The mismatch between the visuals and the word "big" reminds us that even without exotic scenes or spectacular sex acts, today's porn is truly fantasy. Such phrases operate not as referential signs, but as verbal fetishes which compress and miniaturize a narrative of desire. When the actor asks to have his dick sucked and it happens, we are as (or more) excited to hear him ask as we are scopophilicly satisfied to see him get it. (476)

The mismatch between image and sound constitutes a crucial aspect of an accented pornography. The dissonance produced by the foreign Asian accent being asked to recite a conventional American porn script generates the sexual charge in an Asian-themed video, or, to borrow Patton's wording, the Asian actors' poor pronunciations become "verbal fetishes." We can appreciate the ways the phantasmic spatial dynamic gets played out in Brandon Lee's Asian porn videos: the heavily accented English and the slow, awkward, and sometimes unintelligible delivery of lines by his Asian costars work to accentuate their limited facility with the English language. This lack of a perfect translation between the porn script and its verbal recitation paradoxically fits into the theme of the porn narrative, which is premised on the exotic foreignness of the Asian actors. In other words, their poor English authenticates and enhances the Orientalist fantasies the videos aim to achieve. Building on Cante and Restivo's thesis concerning the link between sound and the utopian, phantasmic space of gay porn, I amend and specify how pornographic voices and vocalizations manufacture racialized sexual fantasies in these videos, especially since Asians are often deemed to be non-English speaking, incapable of speaking it correctly, or, left to their own devices, speaking in a gibberish ching-chong nonlanguage. The clash between "Asian sounds" and porn fantasy is most piercing when FOB characters are inserted into scenarios not marked as "Asian," but those of the generic, white "phantasmic landmarks" variety, as is the case when a Chinese food delivery scenario is replaced by a pool boy scenario.

I contend that it is where the lack of fit between FOB bodies and the generic pornographic soundtrack occurs—the instance when the voice drowns out the image—that possibilities for a different sexual subjectivity begin to emerge. Breaking and entering into dominant fantasies not written by or for him, the FOB immigrant subject effectively reterritorializes, or "tape[s] over," conventional scenarios with his own, overlapping soundtracks of desire. In a scene from *Asian Persuasion 2*, Tommy Lin, an aspiring porn actor, has a meeting with porn producer Rusty (Rob Lee) at the offices of Catalina Video about his audition tape. It transpires that the interview requires Tommy to demonstrate his sexual skills with Rusty right there and then. Though it animates the predictable proverbial casting couch scenario, multiple elements in the scene don't quite add up to a seamless production: unimaginative writing, bright nonnaturalistic lighting, and distracting synthesizer music. Most conspicuous is the wooden, amateurish acting, especially in the stilted, belabored delivery of lines of dialogue: Tommy with his soft, feminine voice, which is quite at odds with the young hunky ingenue type he's meant to project; and Rusty and his heavy Asian accent, idiosyncratic enunciations of syllables, and staccato pauses, as if he were reciting spoken-word poetry: "I guess you know now / why we called you in / We want you to be in / our new / Asian / VIDEO!" and "THEN! / I suggest you get over here / and show me just how bad / you really want that part!" To be sure, this awkward delivery of lines may be appreciated for its camp effect, an effect that is heightened by the actors sounding like they are giving it their best shot. At the same time, I suggest that some viewers might find the dialogue sequence sexy precisely because it is performed so poorly and with the utmost sincerity.

Following Patton's insight that the unmooring of the voice from the image track activates a different level of sexual fantasy, I suggest that these unsuccessful attempts to sound like an (Asian) American porn star point to a wholly different porno economy, what I have been calling an accented pornography. The inability to "speak sex" in standard English shows that these FOB characters don't own the space in which they are inserted;[45] yet their mispronunciations encourage us to prick up our ears and listen for other sounds. Though the scene between Tommy and Rusty (young aspiring porn actor and older porn producer) echoes that of Brandon Lee and Tenji Mito (young real estate agent and older prospective house buyer), the dynamics between the former couple differ in many ways, but most crucially, in that both of them are strongly coded as Asian immigrants in a way that Lee never was. Hence the power differentials between Tommy and Rusty are relatively smaller, but by the same token, more complicated. For instance, though Rusty initiates and orchestrates the sexual activities, he does most of the work as the sucker and fuckee; that is, his is the consummate bottom position. And yet the slow, relaxed manner in which he licks and sucks Tommy's cock and eats out Tommy's asshole, along with the joy he exhibits in getting fucked, complicate any clear characterization of Rusty as a passive, powerless bottom. Indeed, the video privileges his bottom positioning to such an extent that Rusty is not accorded a money shot—the obligatory jacking of one's cock to ejaculation at the end of a scene—nor does the viewer catch any glimpse of his cock at any point. The ethics of reciprocity of "I do you, you do me" is entirely absent; instead, the video wholly endorses Tommy's top pleasure, or more precisely, Rusty's bottom pleasure in administering to Tommy's desires. Most tellingly, the only moment in the scene when Rusty's performance comes across as involuntary (which is not to say that it is authentic) is when his mouth erupts into moans and Mandarin mumbles when he is being fucked by Tommy. In other words, his bottom pleasure is specified as being so intense that it makes him revert back to his "foreign tongue." It is through porn sound that his anal pleasure is heard, registered, and validated.[46]

At this point, it bears asking, what viewer would find the scene to be hot and sexy? Whose fantasy is this? A conventional ideological reading would answer that it's hot for the white viewers who get off on depictions of the Orientalist foreignness of Asian men, as revealed in this instance by their accented voices. I contend that such a reading is impoverished because it cannot countenance fantasy scenarios not propped upon a porn literacy of the white, U.S., English-only variety, one that can only read racial difference through an exoticizing lens and hear in accented voices an inability to speak proper English. What if we consider the scene from the perspective of viewers who look and talk like Rusty and Tommy, not in their roles as naive, duped FOBS coerced into sex work, but as sexual subjects who know quite well the name of the gay porn game (figure 1.7)?

Instead of the usual focus on the Asian male as the object of somebody else's fantasy, of the body that is acted on by another, I propose that we examine identification and desire beyond hetero- and homonormative configurations of the U.S. nation-state; such a consideration would entail a challenge to place the gay Asian male immigrant-subject at the center of the pornographic fantasy scenario. I take my cue here from David Eng's influential call for "queer diaspora" as a new methodology for political and scholarly intervention: "If earlier Asian American cultural nationalist projects were built on the political strategy of claiming home and nation-state through the domestic and the heterosexual, a new political project of thinking about this concept in Asian American studies today would seem to center around queerness and diaspora—its rethinking of home and nation-state across

FIGURE 1.7: FOBs kissing. *Fortune Nookie* (1998).

multiple identity formations and numerous locations 'out here' and 'over there'" (2001, 219). Following Eng's lead, I urge a shift away from the identification of Asian American as the only desirable sign of enfranchisement and belonging, such as that embodied by Brandon Lee in the earlier stage of his porn career. To wit, Lee's porn persona has diversified over the years, from American top twink to yellowface bottom chink, indicating patently that porn stardom according to a static home-nation-state and homonormative standard cannot be maintained. As Lisa Lowe reminds us, "the Asian immigrant—at odds with the cultural, racial, and linguistic forms of the nation—emerges in a site that defers and displaces the temporality of assimilation" (1996, 6). It is in the spirit of attending to an alternative national temporality that I coin the phrase "accented pornography" to account for the fantasies of the gay Asian male immigrant-subject.[47]

I have suggested that the "bad accent" of the Asian actors, such as Rusty and Tommy Lin, can intimate an FOB sexual subjectivity that, while fulfilling Orientalist fantasies, might also evade them. In a similar vein, the functions of Brandon Lee's "chinky accents" in his recent videos can be read as signifying on Asianness itself as performative. Lee's adoption of Orientalist roles in *Lights & Darks: An Interracial Spin* and *Affirmative Blacktion: An Interracial*

Takeover exemplifies a knowing, tongue-in-cheek riff on Asian characters in gay porn. In these two videos, Lee plays characters that are explicitly coded as negative stereotypes of Asian men, connoting villainous Fu Manchu traits with a prominent dosage of dragon lady stylings thrown in for good measure. Similar to the way that his transition to bottomhood was anchored by a firm reputation as a top porn actor, what sets off Lee's enactment of the stereotype of the evil Asian businessman from his Asian costars' Orientalist parts of pool boys and male prostitutes is the viewer's awareness of Lee as an Asian American from his previous roles. Because we already know Lee doesn't actually speak with a chinky accent, a sense of self-awareness and theatricality infuses his performance and our reception of it. Yiman Wang's concept of "yellow yellowface" is clarifying here. For Wang, yellow yellowface accounts for the self-conscious strategy an Asian American actor employs in performing a toxic Asian stereotype in order to remark and ironize on it. The casting of Brandon Lee certainly accomplishes such a task.[48]

The sexiness and humor of both of Lee's recent Asian videos reside in Lee's discernible delight in playing such over-the-top roles. An early sequence in *Lights & Darks* illustrates the improper pleasure of Lee's acting quite distinctly. An interracial couple, Blu Kennedy and Rick Razor (white and blatino,[49] respectively), drop off their laundry at Lee's laundromat and demand aggressively that it be done by 6 p.m. Lee, dressed professionally in wire-rim glasses, black dress shirt, pink tie, and black slacks, responds obsequiously, mumbling in an accented, broken English that he always does his best to deliver their laundry on time. After the couple leaves, a white customer, Luca DiCorso, asks for his assistance. Lee responds in a curt manner that the next free machines belong to him (Lee); however, in contrast to his deferential attitude toward Kennedy and Razor, his treatment of DiCorso is brusque and bitchy. Most remarkable is that he switches from broken English to a normal voice when addressing DiCorso. Dismissing DiCorso, he claps his hands at two black customers lounging on a counter and barks, "Off! Now!" Later, as he hurries from the laundromat to make his delivery, he tells DiCorso, "Listen, if you watch the place, I'll give you fifty bucks. I don't trust those two," as he points to the two black men.

Lee's portrayal in *Lights & Darks* updates the manual labor worker as a respectable, sharply dressed professional. His chinky accent references the stereotype of the subservient Chinese laundryman aiming to serve his customers; at the same time, an underlying eroticism pervades his playacting of racialized submissiveness. The abrupt switch to standard English, along with the subsequent domineering attitude toward DiCorso and the two black men, cue the viewer to the fact that his subservient behavior earlier was merely an act. While his groveling manner toward Kennedy and Razor doesn't get fully explained until the end of the video (as part of an elaborate s/m dungeon role-playing scene), the sudden transformation from obsequious Oriental servant to bitchy Asian queen illustrates Lee's camping along to the role written for him, his winking collaboration with it. In the same vein, the atrocious racism directed against the black characters is meant to denote a politically incorrect, unrepentant Asian villain whose moral compass is so beyond the pale as to beg credibility, thus conjuring up "a sort of Oriental drag" (Capino 2006, 215).[50]

As the various iterations of an accented pornography discussed thus far have elucidated, to make the Asian American immigrant the central desiring subject of the pornographic fantasy scenario does not mean creating and prescribing more politically palatable positions for him as either a butch top, a controlling bottom, or a bland, versatile, polymorphous sexual performer. Rather, it seeks to mobilize, in a self-reflexive manner, a multiplicity of sexual scenarios (including those that cannot be recuperated for a politically progressive program, such as in *Lights & Darks*), all the while retaining and exploiting the sexual turn-on of power differentials. The precise form and content these pornographic scenarios might take should remain open ended and undefined; what is more essential is the creation of a fresh angle, a view from below that offers new ways of imagining how armpits and tongues, fingers and mouths, teeth and nipples, cocks and assholes, bodies and subjects, might caress, rub, lick, bite, swallow, push, penetrate, move, and talk to one another.

IN LIGHT OF MY foregoing discussion of Brandon Lee's vicissitudes as a conscientious American top citizen and a campy Asian bottom villain, and the multiple accents that his Asian costars articulate to interrupt the discourse of Asian abject bottomhood, let us disarticulate the conflation of bottomhood with social disempowerment. Let me amend my earlier proposition to put the immigrant-subject at the center of the pornographic scenario and specify this desiring immigrant-subject as the embarrassing, abject, repudiated FOB subject. He is both the effeminate Asian immigrant bottom performer in Brandon Lee's videos and the viewer who gets off on watching those same videos. Instead of regarding the FOB's bottom positioning as something imposed on him by the white gay porn industry, what if we consider that the desiring FOB immigrant-subject takes pleasure in his bottomhood, a position that affords him a degree of sexual agency?[51] I suggested that Lee's early Asian-niche videos already contain this bottom-line analysis. His solo jerk as an autoerotic top porn star in *Asian Persuasion 2* teaches Tommy Lin (and by extension, his gay Asian porn audience) the pleasures of top and bottom (e.g., eating ass, getting eaten; fucker, fuckee). Similarly, the sexual excitement in the scene of Lee, the brothel owner, topping Time, the sex worker, in *Fortune Nookie* is generated by the novelty of "sticky rice" eroticism, along with the problematic, and sexually exciting, power differentials that accrue between boss and worker, assimilated American and foreign Asian, big-dicked top and small-dicked bottom.

From the point of view of the FOB spectator-performer, the instabilities of Lee's topness are not only the results of the dominant culture's management of Asian masculinity; rather, they constitute a way of signaling and affirming the call of bottomhood. Lee's bottoming can also be seen as a refusal to uphold the bond between topness and masculine self-sufficiency. As a result of his confirmed status as an Asian American porn star (and all the requisite traits such a status entails), Lee's transition to bottomhood speaks differently to his gay Asian viewers. Unlike other manifestations of Asian bottomhood in gay porn, it does not read as coerced, abject, feminizing, demeaning, or as a default of Asianness, but as a complex negotiation of racial, gender, national, and economic meanings attached to this most loaded of sexual positions, in gay porn in particular and dominant culture in general. Brandon Lee's aggressive, enthusiastic, and strategic fall from the top shows that one can indeed remain an Asian American porn star that tops and bottoms. The trajectory of his porn stardom demonstrates that even in a media genre inordinately obsessed with the cock, the penetrable ass ultimately beckons. In chapter 2, we witness the seduction of bottomhood enacted in the most revered of patriarchal establishments, the American military, and exhibited in America's most cherished institution, the Hollywood silver screen.

CHAPTER TWO

Reflections on an Asian Bottom

On the first page of her novel *Reflections in a Golden Eye* (1941), Carson McCullers writes: "There is a fort in the South where a few years ago a murder was committed. The participants of this tragedy were: two officers, a soldier, two women, a Filipino, and a horse." In 1967, Hollywood turned McCullers's novel into a big-budget production directed by John Huston and starring Oscar-winners Marlon Brando and Elizabeth Taylor. The film royally flopped at the box office in spite of its stellar credentials and its treatment of such juicy themes as "nudity, mutilation, fetishism, homosexuality, masochism, sadism, and murder."[1] In this chapter, I do not expound on the aesthetic and industrial reasons why the film failed financially, nor do I speculate on the behind-the-scenes shenanigans of its high-profile stars. Instead I focus on a minor character in this drama, one situated toward the end of McCullers's list: a Filipino. In the character Anacleto (played by Zorro David), we witness one of the most flaming Asian homosexuals who has ever graced the Hollywood screen. It is a good twenty-six minutes into the film when we first encounter Anacleto at the bedside of Alison Langdon, trying to feed his ailing white mistress a spoonful of medicine. The camera adopts a close-up on Anacleto scrunching up his face as Alison swallows her medicine. The close-up on his face doesn't reveal to us Alison's reaction offscreen, but rather renders visible Anacleto's empathy with Alison's discomfort. On the one hand, the Filipino houseboy's overidentification with his white mistress demonstrates his obsequiousness, that is, the skill of a servant in attending to the needs of his mistress; on the other, such servile doting also communicates a queer Filipino American male's confirmatory identification with white femininity.

In chapter 1, we observed how gay Asian bottomhood has been consistently joined to Asian male feminization, foreignness, and abjection. To be sure, gay Asian bottomhood does find affirmative expression in Brandon Lee's recent reemergence as a versatile performer; yet his adoption of the bottom role is qualified—indeed, made possible—by his well-established status as a singular Asian American gay male top porn star. This chapter makes explicit the critical force of bottomhood only hinted at in chapter 1. My argument for critical bottomhood is based on a figure one might describe as a polar opposite to an Asian American male porn star: an asexual, effeminate Asian houseboy. Whereas Lee's topness paradoxically strengthens the linkage between Asian and anus that underlines commonsense understandings of racialized sexuality, Anacleto's bottom positioning revalorizes the association between Asian and anus. By examining the negative characterization of the Filipino houseboy within the narrative context and formal strategies of the film, I demonstrate how Anacleto's effeminacy should be read differently. In Huston's film, effeminacy and femininity can be read as desirable and enabling qualities.

Reflections in a Golden Eye takes place at a military base in the American South during the post–World War II period.[2] Marlon Brando plays Major Weldon Penderton, a repressed homosexual who harbors a secret obsession with one young, hunky Private Williams (Robert Forster) after catching sight of him riding a horse naked in the woods. This is the same Private Williams who likes to sneak into Penderton's house at night to watch Penderton's wife, Leonora, sleep while he sniffs her perfume and fondles her lingerie. For her part, the overripe Southern belle Leonora (Elizabeth Taylor) devotes most of her time and energy to her horse, Firebird, and an open affair with her husband's best friend, Lieutenant Colonel Morris Langdon (Brian Keith), who happens to live next door. Langdon's wife, Alison (Julie Harris), is a woman on the verge of insanity, whose only meaningful human connection is with her Filipino houseboy. Anacleto entertains himself and Alison by playing Rachmaninoff records, painting Surrealist watercolors, and hatching various schemes to run away together. The assorted sexual and other intrigues on the army base serve as desperate attempts by the cast of characters to deal with the deadening uniformity of military life. Conforming to its Southern gothic generic convention, the boredom and repetition of army life are broken only by tragedy. As the quote that opens, and closes, the film proclaims: "There is a fort in the South where a few years ago a murder was committed." The murder that I am interested in investigating is not the one referred to in this quotation, but the one enacted on the Filipino houseboy. Anacleto's disappearance from the film is not considered weighty enough to deserve a spectacular shootout, and yet, his swishy, effeminate movements continue to haunt the film's final frames.

While the portrayal of Anacleto as an effeminate, subservient houseboy would be categorically dismissed as dehumanizing in the Asian American critical context, what seems more perplexing is how Anacleto's effeminacy is vehemently rejected in gay quarters as well. For example, Vito Russo maintains in *The Celluloid Closet* that Anacleto resembles "a screaming queen out of a Warner Brothers cartoon" ([1981] 1995, 166). Similarly, a contemporary viewer remarks on the Internet Movie Database website that David's "reviling, degrading" portrayal of Anacleto sends the gay movement back some thirty years.[3] Indeed, what these gay critics are protesting against is the film's employment of gender inversion in its depiction of Anacleto's queerness. While the sexological discourse of sexual inversion was strongly discredited by post-Stonewall queers as heterosexist and homophobic, the deployment of inversion, sexual and otherwise, in *Reflections*, I would argue, operates as a trenchant critique of the white military universe of the film. In what follows, I adopt Anacleto's view from below to look at the ways in which this brown sexual invert radically upends the heteronormative constructions of gender, race, sexuality, and nation within *Reflections*'s white American military world. Most significantly, he accomplishes this not through the familiar route of remasculinization but by embracing femininity and racial castration. Reassessing the Filipino houseboy's bottom agency forces us to interrogate the limits of contemporary minoritarian politics and scholarship in their inability to accommodate subjects who deviate from conventional social and political agendas, in particular, those who forge alliances that privilege marginalized feminine values in the place of legitimated masculine ideals. My reparative reading of a film that predates the historical emergence of lesbian and gay and Asian American political movements enables us to explore unforeseen openings for resistance in historical contexts deemed culturally backward and politically behind.

Examining the problems of temporality and body politics, reading as a bottom, the chapter traces the numerous manifestations of Anacleto's bottomhood across the body of *Reflections*: the performance of effeminacy, the queer domestic bond between him and his white mistress, the anal erotics permeating the mise-en-scène, and the inscription of a receptive filmic gaze. Released two years before the official beginning of the modern lesbian and gay liberation movement (i.e., Stonewall), *Reflections* never once mentions the word "homosexuality," nor does it depict explicitly a homosexual act.[4] Though the film images a range of sexual perversions, the "spectacle of gay sex" cannot be visibly and coherently rendered (for example, the romantic homosexual dyad prevalent in post-Stonewall gay cinema); rather, it is reflected and felt through the means of legible invisibility, the nothing-to-see of homosexual desire that is (Asian) bottomhood itself. Consequently, my analysis of Anacleto's bottomhood encompasses not only narrative content but also the ways in which bottomhood crucially informs the formal style of the film. It should be noted that while the following chapters treat the question of Asian male bottomhood in an explicitly sexual manner, this chapter explores the ways in which bottomhood is expressed more figuratively and seeks to expand the conceptualization of bottomhood beyond its restricted, vernacular sense of a sexual position in gay male sex or in S/M play. Yet, as I will show, the threatening yet thrilling force of exposure, vulnerability, and receptivity underpinning the physical act of passive anal sex pervades this affective account of bottomhood.

Flaming Little Brown Brother

The predominant manner in which homosexuality is signified in *Reflections* is through effeminacy, or, in Russo's words, the "assumption of the female role" ([1981] 1995, 166). In its depictions of both Anacleto and Major Penderton, the film's exploitation of the inversion model of homosexuality relies on the view of the "passive homosexual": a man who "wants to be female, and his desire, like that conventionally expected in a woman, is for a man. He may be said to have a woman's soul in a man's body" (Sinfield 2004, 18). In other words, homosexuality in such a system is manifested visibly as gender dissidence; it must be marked on the body for others to witness.[5] It is precisely the obviousness of effeminacy, its unmistakable legibility, that challenges the common claim that homosexuality, unlike skin color for instance, is not immediately visible but something that has to be purposely revealed.[6] The lesbian and gay movement's premiere strategy, from its early days to the present, has been to encourage queers to make themselves visible, on an individual and a group level. Yet the rallying call for lesbians and gays to come out of the closet was framed from the point of view of the straight-appearing and straight-acting gay man or woman who, theoretically, could choose to pass. The screaming queen, like his female counterpart the butch lesbian, was always already too visible.[7] In a fascinating essay, Daniel Harris describes effeminacy as a socially denigrated repertoire of speech and movement that inspires contempt and disgust from both conservative and progressive observers. He argues that effeminacy constitutes a body language spoken "in the very register of the voice, in the gait, the demeanor, the sense of humor, and even the prose style" (Harris 1991, 72). Effeminacy is an elusive manner or, better, a set of too-recognizable mannerisms that gloriously brands its performer: "legs that involuntarily seek each other out and braid under the table or hands that oscillate like pendulums at the wrists" (77). These marvelous descriptions capture well the ways that the Filipino houseboy inhabits his body and moves through his environment. Unlike the stiff postures and measured movements of the two officers, Langdon and Penderton, Anacleto's bodily comportment is exhibitionistic, exaggerated, extroverted, his silhouettes outlined by soft round contours rather than hard sharp edges: from his pageboy haircut to his graceful amble, the theatrical sway of his arms to his animated facial expressions, from his loose-fitting shirts to his well-timed entrances and sudden exits, from his thick Filipino-accented, flowery English to his awkwardly translated French phrases (figure 2.1). As an impertinent talking back to the constraining masculinist ideology of the body, Anacleto's effeminacy is delightfully broadcast, proclaimed, worn.[8]

Not surprisingly, reviews of *Reflections* in the popular press unfailingly affix Anacleto's strangeness with his feminine qualities. He is described as not measuring up to his assigned sex ("half-male"), as tipping toward the female side, thus indicating a demotion of masculine gender status ("effeminate" and "sissy"), or ascribed traits belonging to both sexes ("epicene"). These value-laden descriptions bear out Alan Sinfield's assertion of effeminacy as being grounded in misogyny, due to the fact that the stigma attached to effeminacy arises from the devaluation of anything connected to the feminine in our culture.[9] In effect, this formulation aligns male effeminacy with

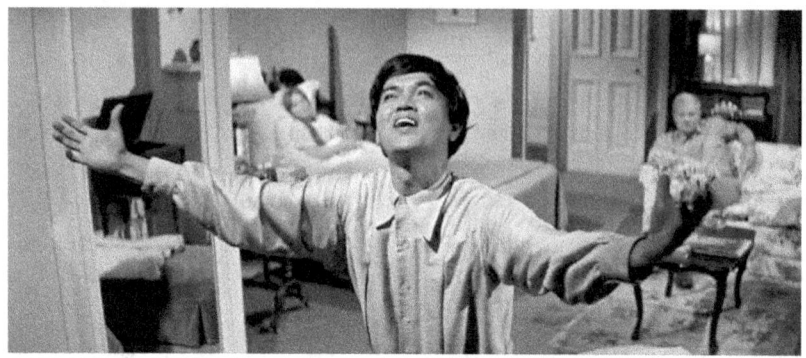

FIGURE 2.1: Anacleto's dance. *Reflections in a Golden Eye* (1967).

being female and thus inferior and works to regulate and maintain proper gender and sexual boundaries (Sinfield 1994, 26). However, *Reflections* accords a moral authority to those marginalized due to an embodiment of the feminine. Consequently, the film assigns Anacleto's effeminacy an important function in undercutting the hierarchy of military rank, gender, race, nationality, and species established in the film. Moreover, Anacleto is not only marked by his peculiar gender. In addition to the popular reviews' attribution of an in-betweenism to Anacleto's gender presentation, the term "child-man" in another review ascribes his difference to an in-between physical and mental development.[10] As a Filipino child-man, Anacleto is a ward of the Langdon household, akin to how the Philippines functions as a ward of the United States. Indeed, American colonial discourse deployed "the home and the family structure . . . as a way to narrativize the colonization of the Philippines" (See 2009, 117). Anacleto's arrival on American soil constitutes a consequence of U.S. colonial and imperialistic actions in the Philippines. His low rank of brown houseboy—refracted and reinforced through his effeminate nature—makes him doubly suited for bottom status.[11] Anacleto's racialized gendering, his effeminacy, cannot be broken down into discrete components of essentialist identities or denaturalized acts. His effeminacy, mimicked inexactly and excessively, is composed by acts which in turn produce identity and identity made legible through acts. Far from being invisible, or something that can be voluntarily and discreetly disclosed, Anacleto's gender and sexual deviance, like his status as a racial alien, is both clearly written on and read off his body.

In addition to resisting the masculine regulation of the body, Anacleto supplants the military's mental discipline with his own feminine-coded aesthetic and moral system. By embracing high culture—classical music, ballet, painting, and French—Anacleto appropriates the cultural accomplishments of the West for himself and powerfully asserts his sensual world of the arts not as an alternative, but as superior to, the harsh military universe of bodily deprivations and psychological conditioning. The houseboy and his white mistress cope with the humdrum sterility of army life by having recourse to the life of the imagination; the world opened up by art appreciation allows them to surmount the limits of their physical world, prompting them to become conscious of, and to question, its social restrictions. The association between femininity, homosexuality, and the arts has persistently functioned to relegate women and gay men to the realm of the feminine, devalued and dismissed as frivolous and inconsequential and set in opposition to the serious, productive, manly world of business and industry (Sinfield 1994, 190). Interestingly, gay men have claimed the sphere of aesthetics as a way of affirming and legitimizing homosexuality in the face of homophobic oppression.[12]

While the male invert's strategy of using the creative arts as a sign of homosexual superiority would seem to account for Anacleto's high-culture aspirations, it should be noted that the Filipino houseboy's artistic cultivation is just that—aspiring. His French is poor and poorly improvised, his knowledge of ballet and classical music gathered secondhand through Alison, his experience of fine cuisine, not surprisingly, extremely limited. In the novel, the narrator describes Alison's appraisal of Anacleto's artistic skills thus: "at bottom he was imitative—almost, as Morris said, a little monkey" (McCullers [1941] 1966, 74).[13] But instead of judging Anacleto's inadequate high-culture connoisseurship to be a detrimental flaw signaling some sort of innate racial inferiority (the mindless imitation of a "little brown monkey"), a reparative reading would consider his imperfect mimicry as an ambivalent postcolonial critique of Western high culture itself. Indeed, a cogent example of Anacleto's strategic deployment of postcolonial mimicry can be found not only in his dedication to the arts, but in his improper use of Western languages, the tongues of colonial and imperial forces. For example, a joke told by a group of soldiers at a party ridicules the Filipino houseboy's snobbish pretensions when they refer to Anacleto's description of himself as a *garçon de maison*; not content to stand passively by as the butt of the joke, Anacleto surreptitiously dumps a pitcher of water on the group of soldiers. Although the joke trivializes the Filipino's pretension, Anacleto's renaming can be read as an attempt to elevate his social status, aiming to promote his standing by translating it into a "sophisticated" foreign tongue. Another example of how Anacleto seeks to remake his world through language can be seen in his everyday use of English. For instance, the Filipino houseboy often mispronounces words on purpose—at one point substituting "certainly" with "suddenly"—as a way of garnering attention from Alison and getting her to correct him. At the same time, he announces to her and his other interlocutors that he is not speaking in his native tongue. In this way, Anacleto proudly marks his difference from those around him, intimating that his allegiances (linguistic, cultural, affective) potentially lie elsewhere. Anacleto's appropriative enunciations render these dominant languages exotic and alien, transforming them into his very own queeny argot. To be sure, in the eyes of the white officers like Langdon and Penderton, the very fact that the Filipino houseboy dedicates his time to painting watercolors, listening to classical records, and speaking in French, regardless of how talented or well versed he might be in these endeavors, attests to the Filipino's wholly foreign, femininized difference.

No Fats, No Femmes, No Asians

In assigning a critical function to Anacleto's homosexuality as expressed through his effeminacy and sexual inversion, I am collapsing a number of categories that some gay male theorists have sought to keep distinct from each other and from what they have called modern homosexuality. In his well-known essay, "How to Do the History of Male Homosexuality," David Halperin distinguishes premodern models of homosexuality—namely, effeminacy, active sodomy, male love/friendship, and passivity/inversion—that he claims foreground "gender over sexuality" from a modern homosexual model that "privileges sexuality over gender" (2000, 92). In his narrative, the prehomosexual models, which were often shot through with social hierarchies, have been superseded by a modern formation, whereby "homosexual relations cease to be compulsorily structured by a polarization of identities and roles (active/passive, insertive/receptive, masculine/feminine, or man/boy). Exclusive, lifelong, companionate, romantic, and mutual homosexual love becomes possible for both partners" (112). Although he admits that gender deviance continues to be associated with homosexuality today, Halperin's description of a modern male homosexuality based on "sameness and mutuality" and normative masculinity may be read as a compelling symptom of an anxious defense against the enduring stigma of effeminacy. According to Halperin's scheme, the Filipino houseboy would not qualify as a "modern homosexual" at all, invested as Anacleto is with the defining traits of a premodern homosexual subject: traits such as effeminacy, inversion, and passivity. In response to such periodization and cultural categorization, Carla Freccero argues that Halperin's analysis demonstrates how "temporality is spatialized into cultural difference" (2005, 39) and has the unfortunate effect of "homogeniz[ing] modern sexual subjectivity by universalizing a U.S. (or Euro-American) model of gay identity across national, cultural, and spatial boundaries" (40).[14] For it is certainly the case that in many non-Western cultures within and without the borders of Western nation-states, same-sex eroticisms continue to be strongly marked by gender difference and sexual roles. For example, in *Global Divas*, Martin Manalansan persuasively argues that the Filipino *bakla* (the indigenous appellation often translated as homosexual), although characterized by effeminacy and cross-dressing, should not be deemed an anachronistic precursor to the modern "gay," but "rather, in diasporic spaces, *bakla* is recuperated and becomes an alternative form of modernity" (2003, 21). Furthermore, Manalansan points out that in diasporic contexts, *bakla* and "gay" might be more usefully understood "not in terms of self-contained modes of identity but as permeable boundaries of two coexisting yet oftentimes incommensurable cultural ideologies of gender and sexuality" (21).

While a contemporary gay viewer—say, one who subscribes to the post-Stonewall homo-ideal of a straight-acting Euro-American gay man—might balk at the stereotypical portrayal of Anacleto as a screaming queen, another possible reading would be to see Anacleto's racially marked Filipino flaming as a gleeful rejection of gender policing found in military milieus (and contemporary gay male culture). Framed by an alternative cultural lens articulated through Manalansan's diasporic *bakla*, one might add that Anacleto's effeminacy is an expression of his "female heart" housed in a male body, a gender expression that complements his object of desire, the straight macho man (Manalansan 2003, 25). Even if we remain within the sexological model of sexual inversion employed within *Reflections*, one resting upon a coercive heterosexist framework that naturalizes the sexual union of male-female, man-woman, we still must admit that it does make room for dissident gender presentations that exceed coherent and respectable gender norms.[15] As noted, a major problem arising from Halperin's (2000, 112) history of homosexuality is that it relegates all queer subjects who fail to privilege "sexuality over gender" (for that matter, those who fail to privilege sexuality over any other marker of social difference), those who persist in "lopsided . . . erotic pleasure or desire," to a space-time outside of and prior to modernity. My insistence on strategically reattaching gender deviance (i.e., effeminacy) with homosexuality in my formulation of bottomhood is meant as an affront to the oppressive and tyrannical deployment of "sameness and mutuality" that allegedly constitutes legitimate, modern homosexual relations. Indeed, the shift from gender-deviant to gender-normative homosexuality might be better characterized as a shift (a promotion?) from gay effeminacy to gay hypermasculinity. Nevertheless, effeminacy continues to attach stubbornly to gay men in spite of several decades of gay liberation. Part and parcel of that attachment is the fact that the screaming queen—pre- and post-Stonewall—remains the most abject and least desirable figure in gay male communities in the West.[16] Instead of distancing oneself from the taint of effeminacy by postulating a manly gay style, a more productive strategy for undermining a heteronormative social order would be to make space for a plurality of gender expressions, including effeminacy. Such a move affirms at least one vital component of "stigmatized gay traditions" (Sinfield 1994, 197), rather than casting it out as an unfortunate anachronism.

Another tradition in which male effeminacy occupies a constitutive position is Asian American history. Scholars of Asian American studies have noted the key roles of sexuality and gender in the racialization of Asian Americans. Citing such phenomena as immigrant bachelor communities and the relegation of Chinese men to feminized professions, Lisa Lowe has argued that Asian American men's racialized "gendering" constitutes "the material trace of the history" of their "'feminized' position in relation to white male citizens" (1996, 11–12). In other words, Asian American masculinity continues to be indelibly marked by a long history of feminization, as a consequence of racist immigration policies, labor discrimination, and anti-miscegenation laws. Yen Le Espiritu lends support to Lowe's analysis of the gendered racialization of Asian American men in her discussion of the labor of Filipino enlistees in the U.S. Navy in the period following World War I. Prevented from joining the upper ranks, Filipino enlistees were assigned the posts of stewards and mess boys, forced to perform domestic duties for higher-ranking officers: cooking, cleaning, laundry service, and other forms of menial housework, including "walking the officers' dogs and acting as personal servants for the officers' wives" (Espiritu 2003, 29). Espiritu notes that the "relegation of Filipino men to 'feminized' work illustrates the interconnections of race and gender in that the racialization directed at them takes the form of sexism. That is, the indignities braved by these men are similar to those endured by women who traditionally performed both paid and unpaid domestic work" (131). Clearly, the assignment of bottomhood to Asian American male subjects constitutes a lasting trace of Asian American racialized gendering. In the same way that a reclaiming of effeminacy can be said to constitute an affirmation of a stigmatized gay tradition, an acknowledgment of Asian bottomhood — as the node where gender, race, sexuality, and sexual practice crisscross — can be read as an affirmation of an essential, yet often disowned, feature in the history of Asian American racial formation.

In his groundbreaking study on "racial castration," a project that reverberates strongly with my project on Asian bottomhood, David Eng employs psychoanalytic discourse to address the interplay of psychic and social forces in the construction of Asian American masculinity. Building on Freud's theory of fetishism and the negotiation of sexual difference, Eng argues that the management of Asian American masculinity operates from a disavowal of sexual and racial difference. Eng utilizes a queer analysis to warn against the inadvertent reinforcement of heteronormativity: "Asian American activists and critics must refrain from seeking antifeminist solutions to predicaments of Asian American masculinity" (2001, 16). Though persuasive in its delineation of the ways in which racial and sexual differences mutually constitute one another, Eng's cogent analysis has little to say about the possibility of resignifying racial castration, of redeploying it productively. Couched within the psychoanalytic paradigms of the dream work, the mirror stage, the primal scene, fetishism, and hysteria, Eng reads the social experience of the Asian American "emasculated sissy" through these structures of psychic trauma and lack. In exposing how Asian American male subject formation is determined by the successes and failures of "(de)idealized sexual and racial identifications" (29), he is unable to account for subject positions that refuse, contest, and exceed this psychoanalytic framework.

From a more historical perspective, Susan Koshy argues that effeminacy is "a reductive formulation for capturing the gender and sexual variations that have refracted the racial meanings of various Asian American masculinities over time" (2004, 14). Rejecting Asian male feminization as a mode of analysis, she focuses instead on Asian American male sexual potency in relation to the racialization of Asian Indians and Filipinos. For example, Koshy points out that because Filipino men were able to attract the sexual attention of white women, the regulation and containment of Filipino masculinity ascribe to Filipino men a deviant (hetero)sexuality marked by a threatening sexual savagery and degeneracy. In the writings of Carlos Bulosan, she locates a complex negotiation of Filipino American sexualization, in particular, in Bulosan's rewriting of white-Filipino miscegenation, one that bears remarkable resemblance to Alison and Anacleto's relationship: "Bulosan's writings highlight the contradictions in American democracy by representing its oppression and injustices as masculine and its enlightenment and uplift as feminine. Within this framework, the Filipino American subject's platonic desire for white women comes to figure the migrant's love for the highest ideals of America. The Filipino American's desire for America is thus naturalized through the symbolic structure of the heterosexual romance even as the sexual purity of this love challenges popular attributions of deviant heterosexuality to Filipino Americans" (Koshy 2004, 23–24). Interestingly, even as Koshy attends to the complicated response by Bulosan to the management of Filipino American masculinity, her reading makes evident that Filipino American virile sexuality continues to be haunted by the specter of Asian male effeminacy: that is, sexual potency must be refunctioned into sexual purity as "a means of challenging colonial inscriptions of Filipino sexual degeneracy" (116). My main point here is that while Koshy's emphasis on Asian American male sexual potency and its role in Asian American "sexual naturalization" addresses a blind spot in Asian American scholarship, her dismissal of effeminacy problematically assumes that effeminacy as a mode of analysis offers us only one (limited) way of seeing how Asian American masculinities have been understood, that is, as a transparently negative construction. Thus, Asian male effeminacy is seen as self-evident and needs no further interpretation.[17]

What these commentaries illustrate is the lack of imagination inherent in Asian American readings of effeminacy: they fail to perceive the potential that effeminacy might be socially and sexually enabling for some Asian American male subjects who profess no loyalty to heteronormativity. As noted, the rhetorical search for the Asian penis depends on the view that sexuality, masculinity, and subjecthood can be located only in that organ. But what if we look elsewhere, at other bodily zones, alert to other sensations, attuned to other meanings? If we move outside the constraining purview of heteronormativity, we would be able to entertain the notion that effeminacy and sexual desirability are not automatically antithetical, that male feminization does not necessarily entail desexualization.

The Queer Domestic

One of the most interesting things about Anacleto's effeminacy is the ways in which it works to form a coalition between him and his mistress, Alison Langdon. Their relationship can be seen as a creative alliance between male homosexuality and femininity. Anacleto's political alignment with femininity is mediated through a queer domestic relationality that rewrites minoritarian politics' residual investment in the couple form and its capacity for reproduction.[18] Anacleto represents a strange, foreign presence in the Langdon household due to his dual status as a "racial alien" and a "sexual deviant" (Koshy 2004, 2). Hence, the Filipino houseboy must be domesticated and "house-trained." To be sure, the reason why the Filipino servant is admitted into the Langdon household and permitted in close proximity to his white mistress is certainly due to the sexist racialization of Asian men that Espiritu salutarily outlines; that is, he is deemed harmless due to his effeminacy, infantilization, and desexualization.[19] Jennifer Ting has noted that in late nineteenth-century California "bachelor Chinamen" were deemed safe, comforting friends to white families. Ting points out that the historical endorsement of these intimate interracial relationships relies on the view of Chinese men as celibate, "[lacking] sexual interest in white women and, conversely, the unlikelihood that they will arouse the sexual interest of white women" (1995, 274). However, it is clear that a disturbing strangeness and erotic threat attach to the Asian houseboy's relationship with his white mistress as well. In contrast to Ting's description of the houseboy's domestic feminization, Robert G. Lee sees the Asian domestic servant as a "figure of forbidden desire" that transgresses the codification of normative gender roles and sexual conduct. Lee argues that the houseboy was essential to the proper functioning of the bourgeois household while simultaneously embodying the danger of "racial pollution" (1999, 9). His presence in the white household disrupted the traditional structure of the white patriarchal family in terms of labor and sexuality through the displacement of female labor and by animating the potential for cross-racial and interclass intimate relationships (88). The twofold characterization of the houseboy as comforting servant and sexual menace recalls the unique place of the Philippines in U.S. colonial discourse, a role that differs markedly from the unequivocal exclusion of other Asian ethnic groups from the U.S. nation-state. As Sarita See perceptively observes, "A racial formation that emerges out of the colonial construction 'foreign in a domestic sense,' Filipino America is a simultaneously inassimilable *and* assimilable entity in the 'house' of the American empire" (2009, 116, emphasis in original). As a subject situated in- and outside, within and without the American "home," Anacleto occupies a liminal position that at once confirms and confounds conventional relationality.

While the multiple pairings in the narrative—Major Penderton and Leonora, Penderton and Private Williams, Private Williams and Leonora, Leonora and Colonel Langdon, Leonora and her horse Firebird—undoubtedly reek of one sexual perversity or another, the coupling that wreaks the most havoc for the white masculinist universe of the film has to be Alison and Anacleto's relationship. Interestingly, their bond, though unusual for an association between mistress and servant, cannot be slotted into ready-made categories of sexual perversion, such as homosexuality, voyeurism, adultery, sadomasochism, impotence, and bestiality, which arguably account for the other characters' relations. A mother-child dynamic can be said to animate their relationship, a dynamic borne out by Lee's proposition that in mid-nineteenth-century America, the Chinese houseboy's alien presence in the white household was accommodated to the role of "surrogate child," a role that conformed to the family's structure of gender and desire. This surrogate child status is reinforced by the colonial construction of the Philippines as an infant in need of civilizing uplift and care. (In McCullers's novel, we find out that the Langdons first employed Anacleto as their houseboy when Morris was stationed in the Philippines; it was part of their "rescuing mission" to bring him back with them to the United States.)[20] Yet, as Robert K. Martin points out, Alison Langdon's self-mutilation—cutting off her nipples with garden shears after the death of her baby, Catherine—constitutes a violent renunciation of her maternal function and "symbolically indicates her exclusion from the world of women" (1992, 100). Both Alison and Anacleto might be said to come together and connect in their repudiation of their assigned social roles. This negation exemplifies, not their wholesale rejection of femininity, but the pair's queer feminine embodiment, one that "radically reconstruct[s] not only femininity but, in effect, the entire field of gender signification" (Farmer 2000, 131). Just as Alison's infirm mistress barely constitutes proper heterosexual Southern white femininity, Anacleto's effete brown houseboy also fails to measure up to gender-sexual-national norms.

Alison's preference for the company of the Filipino houseboy over her husband exemplifies her unequivocal rejection of the role of army wife. For his part, Langdon responds to Alison and Anacleto's relationship as an annoyance and irritation; his facial expression registers exasperation and disgust when confronted with the two. For example, in the scene of Anacleto at Alison's bedside, Anacleto cajoles his mistress to spend money on a new suit.[21] While Alison hesitates, Langdon, eavesdropping in the background, chimes in impatiently, "Oh, go on and buy the dress, for God's sake!" Clearly, Langdon is unable to hear their conversation as playful, affectionate banter, only seeing it as a silly, trifling argument that should be resolved through financial means. Neither Alison nor Anacleto acknowledges his verbal interruption, let alone his presence in the room. A more explicit example of the rewriting of mistress-servant relations occurs late in the film when Alison, Anacleto, and Langdon first arrive at the sanitarium. As Alison draws a cigarette to her lips, both Anacleto and Langdon reach out to light it for her. Anacleto beats the colonel in lighting Alison's cigarette. The Filipino houseboy, dressed in suit and bow tie, flashes the colonel a look of smug satisfaction. Anacleto's gallant, masculine gesture shows him to be an attentive and more adequate partner to Alison than Langdon himself.

The "strange private bond" between Anacleto and Alison exemplifies what historian Nayan Shah has named "queer domesticity."[22] Shah's affirmative conceptualization of queer domesticity contests the normalizing rhetoric of Asian American historiographies that tend to privilege middle-class heterosexual domestic arrangements at the expense of other models of domestic relationships deemed perverse and lacking. Shah elaborates, "The space and social relations of queer domesticity countered or transgressed . . . normative expectations. It included emotional relations between men and women that upset normative heterosexual marriage, as well as homosocial and homoerotic relations. . . . Exploring deviant sexualities and queer domesticities allows us to conceive of alternatives that do not funnel all valued erotic and sensual relations into heterosexual marriage and reproduction" (2001, 78–79). As a "desexed" neurotic female and an "artistic half-male," Alison and Anacleto critically reconfigure the vexed relationship between an army wife and her Filipino houseboy.[23] Their deep intimacy arising out of a queer domestic bond destabilizes the conventional borders of private/public, female/male, masculine/feminine, mistress/servant, mother/child, and lover/best friend. As Shah's capacious formulation of queer domesticity suggests, Alison and Anacleto's unconventional relation forces us to reconceptualize what sorts of relationships are legible, legitimated, and deemed valuable. It calls attention to multiple forms of relationality that lie beyond state-championed heterosexual marriage and state-sanctioned lesbian and gay domestic partnerships. Their deep attachment is reminiscent of the intense friendships between women and gay men that Jennifer Doyle has characterized as "couplings . . . in which mutual recognition converts not into a [marriage] proposal, but into a lifeline" (2007, 328).

As one critic writes, the Filipino houseboy is "Alison's alter-ego; he imitates her in all things, improves upon her fantasies, and understands her every thought" (McPherson 1996, 144).[24] To be sure, Anacleto's involuntary and theatrical effeminacy, while ostensibly "authentic" and "natural" (due to his racial otherness), is indelibly informed and nurtured by the example of Alison's troubled white American femininity. Consider the following scenario in which Morris Langdon recalls the difficult childbirth that Alison had to endure, an event he could not bear to watch. As Langdon recounts to Leonora, "The Filipino was there, sweat pouring down his face. The doctor told her she wasn't bearing down hard enough, so he'd bear down right along with her, bending his knees, screaming when she'd scream." As narrated by Langdon, Anacleto's behavior reveals a brand of naive selflessness that can be attributed to his primitive disposition, what Koshy has labeled "hypercorporeality," by which she means "the reduction of Filipino subjectivity to primordial sensations, appetites, and propensities" (2004, 14). And yet the intensity of his mimicry suggests a remainder, a surplus that exceeds a straight ideological critique. It is significant that the Filipino houseboy's identification with his mistress's pain—not just any pain but, most specifically, the female pain of giving birth—is physically taken on and performed by him as an attempt to assuage her agony. In this sense, it is possible to read Anacleto's hypercorporeality positively, as a manner of communicating his sympathy with his mistress, his affirmative response to her bodily call.[25] Alison's hysterical body and Anacleto's careful ministrations to it represent a manner of caring for the self that contrasts sharply with the militaristic goal of subjugating the body, of privileging the mind over the body. The fact that this story of Anacleto's sympathetic labor is recounted by Langdon while mourning the death of his wife shows us that he considers Anacleto's act to be an admirable feat that Langdon could not perform; in other words, the Filipino houseboy's feminine mimicry signifies the support of a husband that Langdon could not provide his own wife.

Cinematically, we witness their queer bond imaged through the use of two-shots and close-ups, formal techniques commonly reserved for romantic leads. In their scenes together, the camera visually privileges their interaction and marginalizes other characters, most notably Alison's husband

FIGURE 2.2: Anacleto and Alison. *Reflections in a Golden Eye* (1967).

Langdon. One particular scene of intimacy between Alison and Anacleto bears comment. They are dropping clams into a fishbowl and marveling at the spectacle; the camera magnifies the two in extreme close-ups, revealing their delight and contentment in being in each other's company (figure 2.2). To Alison's query, "Anacleto, are you happy?," Anacleto replies, without missing a beat, "Well, certainly, when you are well." Since the film has told us nothing about his backstory, Alison's question about Anacleto's happiness allows a unique glimpse into his state of mind. Instead of adhering to an individualistic perspective, his response reveals that he deems happiness to be relational, reliant on the well-being of another. It brings to mind something a lover might say to a beloved, or what a mother might say to her sick child. However, as a query posed by a mistress to her servant, Alison's question is far from innocent, infused as it is with a gross imbalance of power. Though she herself is unaware of it, her question involves a degree of coercion for Anacleto to produce an answer that she would want to hear. He qualifies his initial affirmative response by deferring his happiness to the uncertain future ("when you are well"). But this future does not include a change in status, say, from dependent houseboy to independent man, but in Alison's transformation from an ailing mistress to a healthy one, a future in which the houseboy succeeds in his task to make her well.

The spirit of selflessness and generosity in Anacleto's comments about his happiness is vividly undercut in the following scene. Alison and Anacleto's reverie is interrupted by Leonora, who has come to ask Alison if she could have Anacleto's help at her upcoming party. Without consulting Anacleto, and in spite of her own distressed reaction to Leonora's party announcement, Alison tells Leonora that he would be glad to help out. In response,

Anacleto angrily leaves the room. Following right after Anacleto's colorful delineation of how his own happiness is intimately linked to his mistress's physical and emotional well-being, Alison's casual loan of Anacleto's labor to Leonora exposes the immense social gap between Alison and Anacleto. By lending out Anacleto, Alison asserts her power as mistress, thus reinforcing their proper roles within the household. Though Alison clearly detests the social rituals within the army base, she nevertheless participates in them and benefits from the base's social hierarchies. As a woman with no military rank to speak of, she at least holds power over the Filipino houseboy, a power she casually wields. She fails to recognize that his willingness, even pleasure, in serving is reserved for her; it is not a natural propensity for servitude that might be casually transferred to another white mistress such as Leonora. Alison's lapse of consideration gives us pause in making any totalizing claim about the ways in which their intimacy might rewrite dominant configurations of race and class, that it might completely override the power and privilege arising out of those inequalities. This incident illustrates how Anacleto's agency in the film, even as it is enabled by his close relationship with Alison, is partial and constrained. Anacleto's choice to identify with Alison's infirm femininity and the expression of his effeminacy come closer to what Eve Sedgwick describes as "the middle ranges of agency that offer space for effectual creativity and change" (2003, 12). Displacing what she finds to be the limiting binarisms of repression and liberation, hegemony and subversion, Sedgwick postulates a more capacious definition of agency as a template for "thinking otherwise" about social and political transformation without succumbing to an inane consumerist analogy—that is, having "one's choices narrow to accepting or refusing (buying, not buying)" (13). Following Sedgwick, we might speculate on the "choices" made by Anacleto that led him to the Southern U.S. army base. For instance, in addition to economic reasons, they might also be guided by other motives: "personal longings, dreams, and fantasies about different worlds and different possibilities" besides heteronormative ones (Espiritu 2003, 36).

The patent disparity in power between mistress and servant, alongside their unconventional attachment to one another, prompts one critic to characterize Anacleto as "both slave and equal" to Alison (Feld 1996, 28). Keeping that paradoxical formulation in mind, I suggest that the difficulty of reconciling the imbalance of power between mistress and servant is augmented by the fact that it is the woman here who holds the upper hand in the relationship. Although such a move renders Anacleto an abject masculine subject to a certain extent, his negotiation of power operates as a complicated critique of domination in that his alliance with Alison enables him to craft a model of relationality and belonging that readily accommodates those on the bottom rung of the white patriarchal structure, subjects considered always already marginalized and oppressed, robbed of all agency. The intimacy between the two suggests that social, affective, and political alliances can be generated not only from sameness and mutuality but, even more striking, on power differentials. Interestingly, the public legitimacy of the white female mistress–male Filipino servant relation allows Alison and Anacleto to enact their queer domestic intimacy. Far from preventing the two from forming a deep social bond, the radical differences between Alison and Anacleto— female/male, mistress/servant, white/brown, American/Filipino — operate as the catalysts for their lasting union. It is precisely the inequities arising out of differences of gender, class, race, and nation that become eroticized in their unique and abiding connection. As slave and equal to Alison, Anacleto occupies a bottom position in relation to Alison (at least in this one instance), and yet such a positioning lends their relationship a certain frisson.[26] At the same time, however, Anacleto's emotional outburst in response to Alison's lapse of judgment reveals the underbelly of affective care work, what Martin Manalansan has theorized as "the performance of disaffection." Manalansan defines disaffection as the "emotional distance, alienation, antipathy, and isolation . . . and [the sense of] disloyalty to regimes of power and authority" experienced by those tasked with providing expert care that ostensibly arises out of natural maternal feelings, those charged with attending to the needs of others without calling attention to their own needs (Manalansan 2010, 217). Anacleto's hissy fit, then, constitutes a disaffected response to Alison's betrayal, but, more importantly, it also intimates a secret, unnarrated backstory that threatens to unravel the bond between houseboy and mistress. Seen in this light, Anacleto's performance of doting servility marks a necessary, and precarious, survival strategy, a move that communicates his being "unmoved" by the deadening, never-ending demands of domestic labor. His disaffection reveals that "agency can be an activity of maintenance, not making; fantasy, not grandiosity; sentience, without full intentionality; inconsistency, without shattering; embodying, alongside embodiment" (Berlant 2007, 759). For the flaming brown houseboy, bottomhood is not a melo-traumatic event, but a practice, and an embodying, of everyday life.

Although it trades in the processes of inversion, Huston's film refuses the ready-made inversion of heterosexual to homosexual; it refuses the substitution of the conjugal dwelling with some idealized notion of outlaw queer existence.[27] Instead, the film offers a more expansive redrawing of sociality, what I have termed queer domestic relationality, a queerness more troubling because it is already located within the home. As noted above, this queer domestic realm is not some bland feel-good space stripped of power relations. Like the white women in Bulosan's writings analyzed by Koshy, Alison embodies the highest ideals of America in Anacleto's eyes, but with a crucial difference: these ideals depart radically from the heteronormative social order represented by the masculinist military world. They include a tribute to the imagination as well as an immersion in a life of the senses. Their interracial intimacy does not serve to shore up Anacleto's wounded masculinity, but rather, reflects and affirms his sissy subjectivity. Instead of vying for a place at the table, Anacleto and Alison's reconfiguration of national belonging is based on queer, feminine values, where sissy houseboys, mutilated mistresses, and dead infants are granted membership. Unfortunately, the transformative politics inherent in their new queer vision of America remains unrealized.

Their utopian rewriting of relationality cannot be sustained within the military milieu of *Reflections*. Alison and Anacleto's attempt to escape the conjugal home with the colonel tragically lands them in the big house—not a literal prison, but a mental institution. Once ejected from the legitimated space of conventional sociality, where they exist and pass as mistress and servant, Alison and Anacleto's deterritorialized outing effectively spells their respective tragic ends. Alison suffers a fatal heart attack soon after arriving at the sanitarium. The Filipino houseboy doesn't fare much better. After Alison's death, Anacleto packs up her things and expediently exits the film, never to be seen and heard from again.[28] Yet this rare bird is profoundly missed. Colonel Langdon proclaims repeatedly to Leonora and Penderton, "I wish Anacleto would come back," thus signaling the Filipino houseboy's crucial role in safeguarding narrative coherence.[29] Anacleto's sudden, unexplained disappearance mirrors what Kara Keeling has called "the out-of-field" that often marks marginal, queer of color characters in dominant cinema. The out-of-field "points to a radical elsewhere that is 'outside homogenous space and time' and that 'does not belong to the order of the visible'" (Keeling 2007, 137). Anacleto and Alison's simultaneous excisions from the film reinforce their codependent existence; in the world of *Reflections*, one simply cannot go on without the other.

From Hairdresser to Houseboy

Numerous critics have characterized the Asian houseboy—also spotted in the guises of laundryman, domestic, cook, and manservant—as deferential, loyal, and asexual, but also invisible, duplicitous, and threatening. He is commonly regarded as one of the most persistent and maligned stereotypes of Asian men in the American cinematic imagination. As a figure of desire and danger, the houseboy resonates strongly with the operations of the "supporting character" theorized by Patricia White in her study of lesbian representability in classical Hollywood film. White points out that supporting characters provide indispensable "support" to Hollywood cinema's ideological structure of "heterosexual romance and white American hegemony" (1999, 142). However, supporting characters, often coded as queer through their gender liminality ("effeminate men and masculine women" [141]), also play a critical part in unmasking the narrative's maintenance of gender and sexual normativity. In addition, because Hollywood cinema frequently consigns people of color to supporting roles, White cautions that it is also crucial to examine "how racial stereotypes are gendered and sexualized" (151). To simply detect racism in representations of people of color as asexual or hypersexual risks verifying heteronormativity without an examination of how such sexual codings might be available for resistant queer readings. According to White, the supporting character constitutes "a site for a range of unpredictable effects" (148), such as defamiliarizing narrative structures, activating viewers' responses to specific character types, and through the over-the-top quality of an actor's performance.

Other critics have emphasized a supporting actor's performance style as conducive to expressing a character's true-to-life qualities. Writing against the common assessment of character actors as exaggerated caricatures, Rudolf Arnheim tells us that while "the character actor shows man as he is[,] the heroic character shows man as he would like to be" ([1931] 2004, 205). For David Thomson, the supporting player often serves as "a fond witness, a model for us . . . by virtue of their color, eccentricity, vivacity *and* fidelity" ([1989] 2004, 207, emphasis in original). In contrast to White's observation that a supporting character's excessive performance calls attention to his or her narrative function, Arnheim and Thomson focus on how supporting characters' idiosyncrasies, their "individual aura of the genuine" (Arnheim [1931] 2004, 205), actually draw them closer to spectators; that is, minor characters' flaws and ticks make them resemble us. On the one hand, if we follow White's formulation of the double function of the supporting character, we would see that the flaming Filipino houseboy is deployed as a "normalization of hierarchy" (1999, 150)—recall that he is situated between "two women" and "a horse"—and yet, at the same time, he effectively exceeds narrative assimilation and containment, a move made even more spectacular by Zorro David's flamboyant performance. On the other hand, if we take into account Arnheim's and Thomson's arguments about the closer match between character actors and viewers, we would have to admit that a screaming queen like Anacleto, with his willful indifference to normative military masculinity, serves as "a [better] model for us" in the audience, especially those who, like Anacleto and Alison, find themselves in the good company of "people behind footlights, midgets, great artists, and such-like fabulous folks" (McCullers [1941] 1966, 33).[30]

In spite of a fair number of positive reviews of David's performance in the popular press, publicity around the film and subsequent interviews given by Huston about *Reflections* focused overwhelmingly on the high-profile stars involved. For his part, Huston was especially effusive in his descriptions of Brando's and Taylor's acting chops. What little information there is about David paints a picture of the actor as simply playing himself.[31] He was reported to have been discovered at Saks Fifth Avenue in New York City, where he worked as a hairdresser. Additional anecdotal evidence in the behind-the-scenes book exposé *Troubles in a Golden Eye* further conflates character and actor. Like Anacleto, David emigrated alone without friends or family to the United States from the Philippines. He did not have much education and acquired his hairstylist training at a young age. David took great pride in his profession, viewing it as more than a job: "Once I cut someone's hair, that head belongs to me, because the lady has become my walking advertisement" (Russo and Merlin 2005, 84). In a letter to McCullers, David expressed gratitude and optimism that the role of Anacleto would afford him entrance into a new professional and artistic arena, that of "Acting!" He related his strong identification with the Filipino houseboy by announcing, "I am Anacleto" (107). Throughout *Troubles*, David's performance is problematically reduced to merely showing up and being "a Filipino fag" (84), whereas the performances of Brando and Taylor are attributed to their formidable craft. The conflation of character and actor poses a challenging double bind for thinking about David's performance. On the one hand, the blurring of role and performer, a process in which David himself felt obliged to participate, has the problematic consequence of robbing David of any agency and self-consciousness, a self-reflexivity critics such as Vito Russo readily credit to white male actors playing sissy roles. Such a view colludes with racist formulations of people of color as childlike, mindless mimics, lacking the requisite creativity, intelligence, and dramatic skills befitting sophisticated artists. On the other hand, the similarities between Anacleto and David enable us to reassess the success of David's performance. For instance, the fit between role and actor calls to mind the cherished fundamentals of American Method acting, "living the part" and "playing oneself," as well as the Soviet Montage filmmakers' formulation of *typage*, the physical and social resemblance of (nonprofessional) actors and the characters that they play. Seen from this angle, another reading of David's overidentification with Anacleto is possible: as a newcomer to the world of Hollywood moviemaking, he might have wished to convince McCullers and the public that he was authentic and right for the part. His resemblance to Anacleto would compensate for the lack of acting experience. Indeed, the producers did hire him due to his biographical likeness to Anacleto. Referring to his casting practices, director Huston states, "I prefer using an actor who is not only very talented but also has a personality like that of the character he plays" (Phillips 2001, 141). While Huston's comment begs the question as to its relevance for his main actors (Brando as closeted homosexual army major and Taylor as his sex-crazed adulterous wife), it certainly overdetermines his casting of David for the role of Anacleto. Production assistant Bill Harrison recalls that one of his more difficult assignments on the film was to fill the request by the producers: "find us a Filipino fag" (Russo and Merlin 2005, 84). Whereas the film's leads were carefully chosen from a pool of well-known actors, the role of the Filipino houseboy was deemed negligible enough to be recruited not by auditioning professional actors but by locating someone who embodied that abject racial-sexual identity.[32] In other words, the framing of the casting of Anacleto as the search for "a Filipino fag" suggests that, unlike the roles of closeted army major or sex-crazed army wife deemed worthy to attract Oscar-caliber actors, the role of Filipino houseboy would not be desirable, respectable, or even possible (?) for any serious actor to play.

Anecdotes in *Troubles* demonstrate that David caught on quickly that Huston expected him to play his part très gay. As the director was too reticent to ask him outright to act effeminately, David first butched it up for a scene in front of a crowd of observers. However, after realizing that Huston wanted him to "be gay," David played his part as a flaming queen, to Huston's relief and satisfaction.[33] As performed by David, Anacleto willfully defies the rigid military stance of the other white male characters by flaunting his feminine mannerisms and taking pleasure in their annoyance at his exhibitionism. Consider the scene in Alison's bedroom where Anacleto suddenly breaks out in an improvised ballet. Emerging from the closet holding one of Alison's nightgowns and humming a classical tune, he lifts his arms toward the ceiling and exclaims, "Look! Just this moment made me compose a ballet." He turns around suddenly, opens his arms wide, looks off into space, and sets up the scene: "Black velvet curtains. And a glow like winter twilight. Very slowly with the whole cast." A high-angle camera frames his outstretched arms as Anacleto bends his knees, bows forward, and dramatically rises up and turns, arms reaching up toward the ceiling once more. "Then a spotlight follows solo like a flame." His arms curve and sweep about dramatically; his body twirls dizzyingly around the room. "Very dashing. And with the waltz . . . Mr. Sergei Rachmaninoff plays." His dance is performed for Alison ensconced in her bed as well as for the camera. Indeed, he looks directly at the camera at several points during the dance: this unusual acknowledgment of the film viewer works to include the viewer as part of Alison and Anacleto's community of two, as a witness who would appreciate Anacleto's improvised dance. (By contrast, Langdon, seated on a couch in the background making faces throughout Anacleto's performance, is wholly ignored by Anacleto and Alison.) His movements and narration effectively transform the cramped, dreary bedroom into a fabulous stage. At the end of the dance, Alison claps enthusiastically. "Bravo, bravo, Anacleto!" Anacleto blows kisses to her and tiptoes gingerly backward "offstage," out the bedroom door. Consumed by his performative trance, he inadvertently falls down the flight of stairs, an accident that we become aware of only through offscreen sound. Langdon walks out of the room to investigate as Alison asks, "Is he all right?" The camera cuts to a high-angle shot of Anacleto splayed on the floor at the bottom of the stairs. Anacleto reassures her, "I'm fine, Madame Alison." At the top of the stairs, the colonel mouths the words, "I wished you had broken your neck." Anacleto quickly picks himself up, and with a flamboyant flip of the head, marches off, refusing to give Langdon the satisfaction of his insulting taunt. This imperious, queeny gesture, in keeping with the dance that preceded it, exemplifies Anacleto's blatant disregard for the military code stipulating a soldier's proper bodily comportment, a body that must be stiff, rigid, and kept in check.

 David's performance in this sequence is indicative of his over-the-top acting throughout the film. Negative reviews of his performance blame it on his "overdoing things greatly" (Baker 1967, B23), in other words, acting too much the screaming queen. As film scholars have noted, good acting in Hollywood film entails a naturalistic, invisible style. In place of grand gestures common to the stage, the film actor must restrict himself to small, subtle "mute expression" (Balazs quoted in Wojcik 2004, 3). According to Kracaucer, "The film actor must act as if he did not act at all but were a real-life person caught in the act by the camera. He must seem to *be* his character. He is in a sense a photographer's model" ([1960] 2004, 20). The imperative of playing oneself in order to produce a believable, compelling performance finds its ultimate manifestation in Method acting. The Method encourages the actor to draw on his psychological interiority as reservoir for an authentic performance. As Virginia Wright Wexman explains, "The specific techniques used in Method performance—improvisation, relaxation, the cultivation of psychologically meaningful pauses, and the use of emotionally charged objects—are designed to reveal psychic conflict" (1993, 162). The actor most closely associated with Method acting in *Reflections* is Brando, and one can clearly identify components of his performance in the techniques outlined by Wexman, most notably his Southern-accented, mumbled delivery of lines; his employment of homo-coded symbolic objects (postcard of Greek male statue, Baby Ruth wrapper, cold cream); and his alternation between emotional repression and violent outburst.[34] True to the requirements of Method acting, Brando's success in disappearing into his role is accomplished by rendering his character's psychological state as so many conflicts: between discipline and chaos, surface and depth, blindness and sight, uniform and flesh, and desire and violence. In direct opposition to Brando's Method style that oozes profound psychic conflict and pain, David's externalized performance is stripped of psychological depth. He enunciates his lines, exaggerates his facial expressions, hyperbolizes his bodily movements; he overacts, overreacts, camps it up. Whereas Brando represents his military closet queen as a complex psychological personage, David presents his outrageous screaming queen as an amateur photographer's model, or better, a melodramatic diva always ready for her close-up. Therein lies the difference of meanings in "playing oneself" (and their attendant valuation) in Brando's and David's respective performances. To produce a convincing performance of the tortured, closeted Penderton, Brando's Method techniques amount to "a series of quasi-theatrical exercises . . . designed to 'unblock' the actor and put him . . . in touch with [buried] sensations and emotions" (Naremore 1988, 197). In Julie Harris's admiring description of Brando's acting, it was "almost as if he was exploring his own sexuality. . . . [His performance was] so pure that there was no explaining where it came from" (Russo and Merlin 2005, 111). Paradoxically, the emphasis on Brando's uncanny talent in assessing his inner truth to play Penderton works to create a safe distance between Brando and the role. By contrast, David's playing himself in playing Anacleto collapses any distinction between actor and role, reinforcing his lack of talent, while at the same time lending an authenticity to the character.

A careful examination of the seeming opposition between being and acting enables us to read the resemblance of David and Anacleto—both characterized as Filipino screaming queens—in a different, more productive manner. Indeed, we get the sense that David/Anacleto is constantly aware of his effect on others, whether one of amusement (Alison), disgust (Langdon), or satisfaction (Huston). Put differently, David/Anacleto is not merely caught in the act by the camera. The camera—or its stand-in, the interested look of other characters—inspires him to be, and allows him to act, his flamboyant Filipino fag self. Instead of seeing the role of effeminate Filipino houseboy as an abject, irredeemable figure created by a racist movie industry, what if we take the continuities between actor and role seriously and entertain the possibility that David played the part of Anacleto honestly, with full conviction, drawing on his own experience as a "Filipino fag"? As an alternative to diagnosing Huston's exploitation of David's racial-sexual authenticity as a naive and racist casting practice, we might consider the deployment of authenticity as an enabling move for David, that he in fact enjoyed playing the part, performed the role as he saw fit, and found satisfaction in presenting visibility to "Filipino fags" in a Hollywood movie. This reading of Asian bottomhood makes room for subjects such as David who might embody toxic stereotypes; it seeks to recognize and affirm these subjects without the need to apologize, justify, or deconstruct those stereotypes.

My point in belaboring David's casting and acting is to activate a reassessment of his portrayal of a negative Asian male stereotype. In effect, the bad reviews of David constitute the critics' (including mainstream straight reviewers and gay critics) polite rejection of the abject role of Anacleto, a Filipino houseboy who is happy playing house, that is, a role that is unimaginable, uninhabitable by anyone. What would constitute a good performance of a Filipino fag, then? One whose Filipinoness and faggotry are less over-the-top and more discreet, coded, legible only on the level of connotation? To be sure, such a requirement would amount to the complete erasure of all Filipino screaming queens, on- and offscreen. A truly queer reading would be attentive to these representational dilemmas, but must also recognize and acknowledge David's sincere, dignified contribution, that he in fact plays his part extremely well. In an adoring tribute to B-movie actress Maria Montez, Jack Smith famously compares "good" Hollywood acting to the efficient functioning of a car engine: "GOOD PERFS. that give you no magic" ([1962] 1997, 25). By contrast, he maintains that the magic and integrity of Montez's performances exceeded the common rules of acting. The conviction in her own beauty, her flaming image, transcended the cheap plaster sets and idiotic scripts. In a similar way, David's playing himself with absolute conviction ratifies his performance's truthfulness. But, like Montez playing the larger-than-life movie star in film after film, David's playing himself in *Reflections* exceeds the film's purview: it cannot contain his wonderful, overdone and hence unbelievable performance.

A Bottom with a View

Unlike the assortment of sexual perversions frankly depicted in the film, Anacleto's bottomhood is never allowed to manifest itself as a viable sexual practice. In this sense, the Filipino houseboy's obedience and devotion to his white mistress would appear to corroborate the charge of asexuality commonly attributed to Asian American men in mainstream cinema. And yet, in critiquing the desexualization of Asian men, we must not reconsolidate the category of sexuality or the process of sexualization based on a heterosexual logic founded on masculine supremacy. Anacleto's asexual bottom, precisely by evacuating the top, succeeds, then, in exploiting bottomhood's potentiality for radical difference, since he ultimately refuses to act as support for top masculinity. I argue that Anacleto as asexual, nelly houseboy poses much more of a threat in *Reflections* than Anacleto as a well-rounded, straight-acting, out character who openly engages in homosex onscreen. This is because the menace he represents is intimately linked to a bottom worldview that structures both the film's narrative content and cinematic form. In the following, I trace the ways in which the irrepressible Filipino queen colors the portrayal of the other homosexual personage in the story, Major Penderton. Even more striking, however, is how the film consistently endorses not just Anacleto's but, more radically, the view from below that is taken up by different characters.

The flaming gay and Filipino visibility presented by Anacleto is responsible for keeping Major Penderton a "constipated closet case," according to Russo's ([1981] 1995, 166) tidy description. In other words, the queeny Anacleto is the type of indiscreet queer that the butch Penderton fears he might become. Though they occupy opposite ends of the social chain of command and each vehemently detests the other, a steadfast connection binds the two together: Anacleto can be said to serve as a negative model for Penderton, but a model nonetheless. For both, bottomhood is figured as a literal and metaphorical fall: Anacleto's fall down the stairs after a campy ballet improvisation effectively puts him in his place; Penderton's fall off Firebird (discussed below) exposes his desire to demote himself to the same level as Private Williams. The Asian bottomhood that Anacleto gleefully performs to provoke the major and his best pal Langdon is evident not only in his effete superiority and flamboyant exhibitionism, but also through the ways in which his bottomhood gets transmitted to the other participants in *Reflections*: from the head honcho, Major Penderton himself, to Private Williams, to Leonora, right on down to the horse at the bottom of the pecking order. I am referring to the plentiful exposure of bottoms, which are spread throughout the film. More specifically, these exposed buttocks, observed by (and on) Penderton, have the predictable effect of triggering his military compulsion for discipline and punishment. At the sight of Leonora's flaunting of her voluptuous naked backside walking up the stairs, Penderton, from the landing below, threatens to kill her. Spying Private Williams riding gracefully on his horse bareback and bare-assed in the woods (figure 2.3), Penderton "purse[s his mouth] in anal outrage" and volunteers to "attend to" the young enlisted man.[35] While Leonora's voluptuous bottom taunts Penderton for being a prissy tight-ass, serving as ample evidence of his lack of manly desire, Private Williams's taut bottom inspires the major to loosen up his ass. That is, the private's bare bottom arouses in the major desire for another man, conveyed here not through penetrating another's ass but by becoming the horse's ass himself. Observing Penderton's clenched bottom stiffly atop a horse (figure 2.4), a soldier at the stable cracks, "If the major could see himself from behind, he would never get on a horse."[36]

But get on a horse he does, partly to be a good sport by joining Leonora and Langdon in their equestrian pastime, and, perhaps more strikingly, because he wants to fall off. In one amazing sequence, Penderton takes out his wife's horse, Firebird, for a ride in the woods by himself, knowing full well that the horse is out of his league. Not surprisingly, Penderton immediately loses control of Firebird as it gallops erratically through thick bushes and brambles. The tracking camera lurches and staggers wildly alongside them, cutting quickly from long to medium to close-up shots, from below on the

FIGURE 2.3: Private Williams riding bareback. *Reflections in a Golden Eye* (1967).

FIGURE 2.4: Major Penderton looking on. *Reflections in a Golden Eye* (1967).

ground showing the horse's flanks and Penderton's panic-stricken face to the trees and sky hurtling dizzyingly by in blurry flashes. As if to signal its own loss of control, the camera falls behind as it tries frantically to keep horse and rider within the frame. The sense of chaos is compounded by the music on the soundtrack with its persistent, pounding horns and cacophonous crescendos. The ride ends with Penderton sliding under the horse, dragged along and finally released on the ground. After savagely beating Firebird and collapsing on the floor of the forest weeping hysterically, Penderton lies still and exhausted. From nowhere, a buck-naked Private Williams appears, steps gingerly over Penderton's supine body, and slowly leads Firebird away by the reins while Penderton remains awestruck and speechless on the ground.

Though one can certainly read Penderton's riding accident as a self-administered masculine trial, a more compelling interpretation would be to consider the ride as the desire to surrender control, to give in to the stallion's greater strength and potency, to activate his own descent. Clearly, his falling for Private Williams stimulates Penderton's desire for this rapturous fall. This causal link is made explicit when Penderton, struggling to hold on to the wildly galloping horse, catches sight of Williams sunning himself naked on a rock.[37] By failing at this equestrian test of strength, endurance, and control, and what's more, to have his failure witnessed by an enlisted man, Penderton plunges downward into the terrain of bottomhood. Penderton's desired fall gets manifested in a wish to renounce "honor and rank" by rechristening himself "Private Weldon Penderton" (McCullers [1941] 1966, 96).[38] On the one hand, this effort to remove the obstacle of rank that separates Penderton from Private Williams appeals to the construction of homosexual relations as based on sameness and mutuality advocated by post-Stonewall activists and scholars. On the other, the fact that Penderton wants to demote himself in order to "get his guy" bespeaks the erotic excitement inherent in surrendering power; the sexual thrill comes from bottoming for a man of lower rank.

In a text consumed with rank and hierarchy, *Reflections* charges its lowest-ranked human character, the Filipino houseboy, with the film's moral authority. In addition to the literal representation of asses, Anacleto's bottomhood is also registered on a formal level, in the ways the film sanctions various views from below, as can be seen in Penderton's irresistible, eroticized fall. From the beginning of the film, multiple low angles are offered as challenges to those at the top. In an early scene, Penderton belittles Private Williams for his incompetence as a soldier. Leonora, swinging to and fro on a hammock, looks up at her husband, who stands upright. She counters Penderton's judgment by stating that Williams is great with her horse, Firebird. Penderton dismissively retorts, "Firebird is a horse." To which Leonora fiercely responds, "Firebird is a stallion!" Thus, Penderton's authority and manliness are explicitly questioned by Leonora, who implies that her horse and the private possess more masculine potency than her husband. A scene in the Pendertons' parlor reveals the adulterous relationship between Leonora and Morris Langdon through the agency of another low perspective. The Pendertons and the Langdons are relaxing in the Pendertons' drawing room after dinner. Langdon and Leonora play blackjack, Penderton makes drinks, and Alison knits on the couch. An extreme low angle shows Leonora rubbing her foot against Langdon's under the table; tightly framed in the shot's upper half is Alison's head as she catches a glimpse of their playing footsie underneath the table (figure 2.5). This low-angle shot economically reveals the hypocrisy underlying polite after-dinner conversations and its role in maintain-

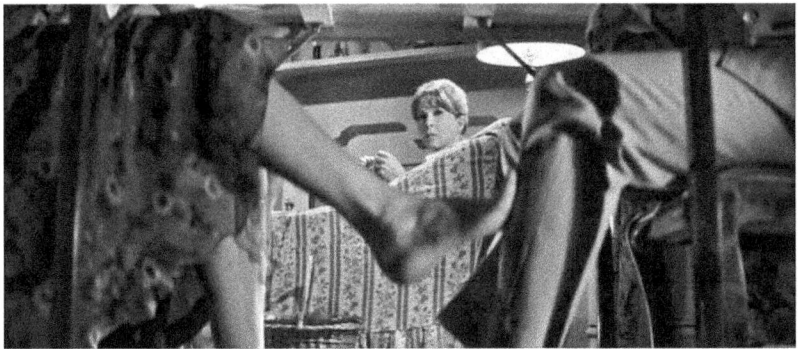

FIGURE 2.5: Alison's view from below. *Reflections in a Golden Eye* (1967).

ing civilized interactions within the army base. It also succinctly spells out at an early stage of the narrative the dynamics among the central protagonists. Like Leonora's earlier challenge from below, posing her horse Firebird as superior to her husband the major, here the subversion of social conventions also comes from below. Significantly, this insight from the bottom is attributed to Alison, odd girl out, the crazy, unstable nonplayer in this scenario. The most sustained view from the bottom comes from Private Williams, the voyeur who lurks outside the Pendertons' house at night, watching. A number of interior scenes are ascribed to Williams's point of view: Leonora walking up the stairs naked, the after-dinner card game at the Pendertons,' and Major Penderton's contemplation of his Greek statue postcard, as well as Anacleto's improvised ballet in the Langdons' house next door. Although all of these critical scenes are attributed to Williams—that is, the camera frequently cuts back to his face half-cloaked in shadow at the opening and end of these scenes—what is curious is that his point of view appears physically impossible. In addition to the limited field of vision offered by the curtained windows, a few of the scenes that he ostensibly sees actually take place upstairs on the second level (Leonora's naked backside, Anacleto's dance). At times, the camera shows his face watching intently, and the reverse shot is only of the house with the upstairs windows lit up (figures 2.6 and 2.7). In effect, what this demonstration of faulty camera angles and erroneous point-of-view shots reveals is the degree to which the view from below is insisted upon in *Reflections*, even at the risk of disrupting the operations of invisible editing and the maintenance of realist diegetic space.[39]

FIGURE 2.6: Private Williams's view from below. *Reflections in a Golden Eye* (1967).

FIGURE 2.7: The Pendertons' house. *Reflections in a Golden Eye* (1967).

Anal Vision

Another reading of Williams's impossible perspective is as Huston's visual translation of the film's title, *Reflections in a Golden Eye*. To a greater extent than Taylor, the female lead, Forster monopolizes the position of to-be-looked-at-ness in the film. He appears nude multiple times in *Reflections*: riding a horse bareback and bare-assed, sunbathing nude on a rock, and walking in the woods naked to retrieve the wounded Firebird. Even as he plays a Peeping Tom lurking in the dark, the camera returns again and again to show his face watching. Huston's camera objectifies the looker as much as the objects of his look. Williams's eye and the reflections of what it sees are rendered in giant close-ups. We first catch sight of the extreme close-up of his eye as he watches Leonora walking up the stairs naked. As Stephen Cooper notes, the magnification of this male eye calls attention to the mechanics of cinematic looking: "The gigantic close-up of his gaze, which has earlier confronted our own eye, has alerted us to the self-consciousness built into the film and in turn imposed upon us. We are not looking, in other words, at the naked Elizabeth Taylor . . . ; we are looking at an enormous film image of an eye staring back into ours, so that our own eyes must be reflecting the nude reflection in its corner—and so on, ad infinitum" (1993, 106). Attributed to a character who speaks only a handful of lines throughout the film, who exposes his body for our homoerotic vision, and who does nothing but watch impassively, Williams's gaze can be said to function less like an aggressive, penetrating male gaze (in the mode of say, Hitchcock's *Vertigo* [1958] or Michael Powell's *Peeping Tom* [1960]) and more like a gaze that simply receives, mirrors, reflects. He often acts as the film viewer's stand-in, the one watching unobserved in the shadow, just barely visible by the dappled light emitted from the windows. Even when he does trespass the boundary between outside and inside by sneaking into the house and into Leonora's room, all he does there is sniff her perfumes, fondle her negligee, and gaze at Leonora in her drunken slumber. As Parker Tyler points out, the soldier's only activity is to "patiently watch her for hours while she sleeps"; far from any perverse "hands-on" contact, "he just wants to *look* his fill" (1973, 260, emphasis in original). With this description, Tyler frames perception as an activity that seeks satisfaction, like a mouth that copiously consumes or a butt that wants to get stuffed.

The direct reference to the golden eye of the film's title comes from Anacleto. During one of his painting sessions with Alison, Anacleto holds up a watercolor of a peacock and remarks on the peacock's giant golden eye with its "reflections of something tiny and . . ." When he is unable to find the right word, Alison finishes the sentence for him: ". . . grotesque." The camera then cuts to an image of Williams's eye quietly observing Leonora while she sleeps, thus effectively connecting the peacock's eye referred to by Anacleto with Williams's vision. The portrayal of the golden eye as belonging to a peacock aligns the organ with a male animal known for its beauty and exhibitionism. As such, it is an eye that sees but also advertises itself to be looked at. Besides Williams, the other figures in the film who might be described as peacocks—males engaged in theatricalized self-displays—would have to be Anacleto and Penderton. Like Williams, both Anacleto and Penderton often adopt a receptive gaze. As a servant, Anacleto watches and registers what he sees without being empowered to intervene in that vision; yet his unacknowledged servant gaze arms him with crucial knowledge. For example, during a big party scene in full view of all the guests, Leonora repeatedly

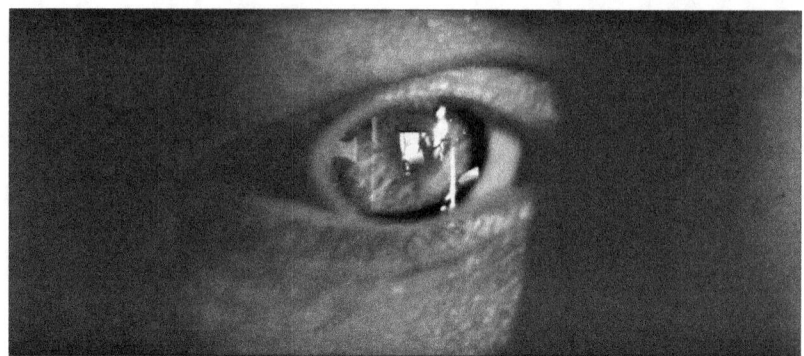

FIGURE 2.8: Reflections in a glassy eye. *Reflections in a Golden Eye* (1967).

strikes Penderton across the face with a riding crop in retaliation for his physical abuse of Firebird. Later, Anacleto tells Alison that while everyone thought that Leonora was drunk when she struck her husband, as the bartender during the party, he was the only one aware that she was completely sober during the incident. In a very different manner, Penderton's persistent, searching look at Williams in the course of the film oscillates between mastery and surrender. While his first accidental glimpse of the private riding naked in the woods arouses Penderton's indignation at the soldier's impropriety, as the film progresses, Penderton becomes obsessed with Williams, as is evident by his seeking out the private sunning in his birthday suit in the woods or stalking the private strolling around the army base.[40] Unlike Williams's impassive looking at the goings-on inside the Penderton and Langdon households, a golden eye that reflects "things . . . grotesque" without reaction, and thus without judgment, Penderton's obsessive, searching look for and at Williams aims to uncover a truth, an acknowledgment, some sort of recognition or reflection back from the object of its gaze. Ironically, in its obsessive quest to exert mastery, Penderton's tunnel vision or, better, his anal vision, renders itself desperate, hysterical, and vulnerable to being blindsided in the film's tragic, violent end. Sarah Gleeson-White (2003, 56) points out that in McCullers's novel, "eyes do not see, they merely reflect": Firebird's eyes reflect Penderton's image; Penderton's eyes are described as "glassy"; and Williams's unseeing eyes mutely survey Leonora (figure 2.8).

The powerlessness of these male gazes (Williams's, Anacleto's, and Penderton's) calls to mind Steven Shaviro's account of film spectatorship as a fascinated and passive activity. As a corrective to psychoanalytic film theory's romance with the aggressive, sadistic, mastering male gaze, Shaviro (1993,

33) shifts the focus to the visual pleasure to be had in giving oneself over to the "voyeuristic fascination" and "agitation of the senses" of the cinematic experience. Following Shaviro, we can say that the golden eye in Huston's film is "continually distracted, and passively absorbed" (48) by what it reflects. Confronted by grotesque reflections (the numerous sexual shenanigans of the film, to be sure, but also the film's obsession with exposed bottoms and multiple views from below), the viewer is rendered speechless, or has her speech deauthorized. The exhibitionism of these male gazes also conjures up Christian Metz's description of an introjective vision: things that I see "come to be deposited within me"; that is, the objects of my vision "have been 'projected,' on to my retina" (Metz quoted in Clover 1992, 207–208). Carol Clover (204–205) has dubbed this obverse of the voyeuristic, assaultive gaze the "reactive gaze" or "punctured" vision, as a more expansive model for film spectatorship. The golden eye of *Reflections*, then, takes not the visible male phallic organ, but that other invisible unisex one, the anus, as a model: an anal vision that reflects, receives, stretches, envelops, grips, releases; it observes, records, bears witness. As Arnheim explicates, "If you take the camera . . . as a receptive organ and if you use the camera as something which takes, which is being impregnated by the world almost passively without doing anything about it, because your [sic] taking whatever comes, you have a very passive quality in this use of the receptor instrument, don't you see?" (quoted in Katz 1996).[41] The critic's provocative figuration of the camera as a receptive organ that simply "tak[es] whatever comes" not only puts the finger on the anal erotics spread throughout *Reflections* but also captures Huston's desire to induce such a mode of receptive viewing in his viewers.

One of the things that *Reflections* is known for is the color experiment by Huston to give the film an absolutely novel look. As the director explains, "Vivid Technicolor would, I felt, get between the audience and the story—a story of minds, thoughts, emotions. So I was looking for a particular kind of color. . . . Weeks and months of experimentation were involved, starting well before the commencement of the picture and continuing after the final shots. What we achieved was a golden effect—a diffuse amber color—that was quite beautiful and matched the mood of the picture" (Huston 1980, 32). On the one hand, we might interpret Huston's color experiment as a concerted effort to package *Reflections* as a serious film dealing with important adult themes. (Its tagline, after all, was "Leave the children at home.") Along with its impressive literary pedigree, the film's treatment of controversial subject matter having to do with "sexual perversions" allows it to compete with European art films popular (and profitable) at the time for their sophisticated and daring handling of sex and sexuality.⁴² In the same vein, the color experiment can also be read as a strategy by Huston to temper the film's sexploitative subject matter; that is, the arty formal experiment seeks to elevate the narrative's trashy elements to the level of Film Art. However, in spite of these potential good intentions, the color experiment failed miserably with audiences when the film was released. Most viewers interpreted the amber hue as faded film stock or an inferior version of black and white; the desaturated version of the film was quickly replaced by Technicolor prints.⁴³ I suggest that Huston's desire to make the film golden constitutes an attempt to make the film reflect a bottom perspective in the viewer's eye. As Huston's quote above testifies, his motivation for the color experiment was to evoke the psychology and mood of the narrative, to present "a story of minds, thoughts, emotions." To recall Cooper's description of the close-up of Private Williams's golden eye reflecting Elizabeth Taylor's naked backside: "we are looking at an enormous film image of an eye staring back into ours, so that our own eyes must be reflecting the nude reflection in its corner—and so on, ad infinitum." By reflecting Williams's fascinated, enraptured seeing on the screen, his receptive anal vision is mirrored and replicated in our own eyes. The resistance on the part of critics and viewers to adopting this alternative vision, coated in a "golden wash" (*New York Times*), a "brownish monotone" (*Motion Picture Herald*), and "touches of lavender" (*Box Office*), bespeaks their refusal or inability to see differently, to simply receive, rather than to master, the reflections in their fascinating field of vision.⁴⁴

"Scraping about the Round Hole"

Depicted as the consummate top throughout the film (albeit a poor, anxious, insecure one), one charged with the tasks of training soldiers on such matters as military maneuvers and leadership, toward the end of the film Penderton delivers a brief speech that flies in the face of what we have been given to understand is his defining worldview. The following is a conversation between Langdon and Penderton on the subject of Anacleto:

> LANGDON: It's a pretty awful thing to see a grown man dancing around on his toes to some kind of silly music, and painting all kinds of funny-looking pictures and watercolors. Oh, we would have run him ragged in the army all right. And he sure would have been miserable. But anything would have been better than . . . all that other mess.

PENDERTON [responding to Langdon's complaint about Anacleto]: Any fulfillment obtained at the expense of normality is wrong and should not be allowed to bring happiness. In short, it's better because it's morally honorable for the square peg to keep scraping about the round hole rather than to discover and use the unorthodox one that would fit it.

LANGDON: Don't you agree with me?

PENDERTON: No. No, I don't.

According to both of these officers' evaluations, Anacleto's dishonor is a result of his failure to abide by the rules of normative masculinity. Although Penderton's analogy designating the Filipino houseboy as a "square peg" who refuses to "scrap[e] about the round hole" makes adequate sense in expressing Anacleto's nonconformity, the choice of the term "square peg" to describe Anacleto seems grossly awkward and imprecise. Though the analogy appears appropriate in relation to the question of conformity (shapes fitting into preconstituted molds), what could the crude imagery of square pegs scraping about round holes also signify if not penile-vaginal sexual intercourse: a "morally honorable" mode of sociality that Anacleto refuses to partake in? In this economy of sexual difference, with its options of square pegs and round holes, Anacleto would clearly be aligned on the side of round holes, not the vagina, but rather, the other "unorthodox one," the asshole. Doesn't Anacleto's masculine dishonor lie precisely in obtaining fulfillment and happiness as an unorthodox hole discovering another unorthodox hole to reflect and fulfill it, that is, his abiding bond with Alison? Although Penderton's comments are purportedly about Anacleto, it is evident that the square peg under question is none other than Penderton himself. It is about Penderton's own search for other unorthodox holes to fit his square peg that he rhapsodizes in the speech. What this link establishes is that, contra Russo's assertion that Anacleto's screaming queen works to keep Penderton a constipated closet case, Anacleto's frivolous fairy has a more productive influence on the major. The Filipino houseboy's bottomhood forces Penderton's closet door, which is to say, his anal vision, to open more than a narrow crack.

The "threat and promise of homosexuality," mirrored in *Reflections in a Golden Eye* as bottomhood and represented most powerfully by the minor character Anacleto, finally come to a tragic end in Major Penderton's house. On the fateful night, Penderton sees Private Williams entering his back door and thinks that the soldier has finally come to see him. When the soldier goes into Leonora's room instead of Penderton's, the major violently penetrates the private the only way a top military man can respectfully admit to, by riddling him with bullets. Yet the specter of Asian bottomhood reasserts itself over the entire proceedings. Anacleto, long gone from the film, has the last word. After Penderton's gun goes off, Leonora wakes up and screams hysterically, as the camera swings wildly from Penderton with stunned expression to Leonora screaming to the dead private on the floor back to Leonora screaming back to Penderton stunned, and so on. This concluding shot has been faulted by critics as erratic and amateurish. I would argue, however, that it expresses most ecstatically the bottom sensibility championed by the Filipino houseboy throughout the film: it constitutes the most sustained swish pan in the history of Hollywood cinema.

AT THE BEGINNING of this chapter, I suggested that a major reason for the critical rejection of *Reflections* by gay critics such as Vito Russo lies in the film's outmoded depiction of homosexuality, in particular, the film's dependence on discourses of sexual inversion. Clearly, such a critical diagnosis derives from a specific assumption of political progress, as a development from offensive screaming queens to heroic, manly gays in the military. This framework of visibility politics cannot countenance bottomhood as a viable position of critique. Reviewers and critics also postulated other reasons for the film's failure, including its preoccupation with sordid sexual intrigues, bad acting, and Huston's color experiment. As I argued above, all these elements crucially underpin the work of critical bottomhood in *Reflections*.

Indeed, the film's scathing critique of white American masculine hegemony—as represented by Brando's Major Weldon Penderton—is couched in terms of a fall from the top, or more precisely, a surrendering of control and mastery. In spite of the matter-of-fact assertion of homicidal violence that bookends the film ("There is a fort in the South . . ."), there is a marked absence of explicit military conflict in the film. As Stephen Cooper points out, there is also a lack of any reference to the Vietnam War in major reviews of the film, a glaring omission for a film that arrived in theaters at the height of public protest against the military conflict in Vietnam. Situating the film in relation to Huston's war documentaries produced in the 1940s and 1950s, Cooper observes a shift in Huston's portrayal of the American soldier in *Reflections*: "Gone is the declarative emphasis on the soldier's defining quality, his selflessness; gone too the profound respect for devotion to duty" (1993, 98).[45] Cooper's historical contextualization thus links the film's less-than-glowing characterizations of its military personnel to a political critique of American society at the end of the 1960s. Significantly, the deflation of the upstanding patriotic soldier that Cooper outlines is drawn in *Reflections* in terms of sexual deviance (Penderton's homosexuality, Williams's voyeurism, and Langdon's adultery). I have been arguing that a pivotal catalyst for Penderton's rejection of his military duty is none other than a subject most unsuited and unqualified for military discipline: the flaming Filipino houseboy. It is Penderton's decision to follow another trajectory, the course of bottom-hood modeled by Anacleto, that causes the downfall of the film, its rejection by viewers and critics during its initial release and subsequent critical neglect.

In recent years, *Reflections* has been slowly rediscovered and incorporated into a gay film canon, appearing on the retrospective programs of queer film festivals and repertory theaters. In the former context, the film is featured for its nostalgic, perverse pre-Stonewall sexual excesses as well as the performances of its stars Brando and Taylor, now read as self-parodying and camp. Its recent recovery as a gay film also reads the film through the lens of contemporary gay politics, that is, as a pre-Stonewall treatment of "gays in the military" (Benshoff 2007). For example, writing on a cycle of "Hollywood homo-military films," Harry Benshoff maintains that these films, whether tragic or comic, "actually indict the *repression* of homosexual desire and not homosexuality per se" (72, emphasis in original).[46] While valid and perceptive, such a reading focuses attention on the butch Major Penderton and his hunky object of desire, Private Williams, as the central homo couple of the film. If we go along with this privileged pairing, the tragedy of the narrative, as played out in the film's dramatic conclusion, lies in Penderton's killing of the object of his lust, the person responsible for activating his homosexual desire. Unlike the repressed military homo in *The Sergeant* who shoots himself, Penderton remains physically, if not psychically, intact. Nevertheless, there is no happy ending in Huston's film: Penderton does not get his guy after all. I contend that the emphasis on repressed homosexual desire enacts its own repression: namely, of other kinds of queer desires, identifications, and relationality that exceed the homo-masculine couple form. As noted, the eruption of the swish pan at the film's dramatic conclusion offers another kind of payoff, a campy camera movement that revels in and pokes fun at the film's serious, tragic ending. As Douglas Crimp points out, the "fixation on the guy getting the guy" invariably reinforces "the drive to normalcy—the drive toward happy endings, [and] the reverence for the dyadic couple" (2004, 5–6)—and hence, cannot recognize pleasures that exist outside the conventional economy of desire. The insistence on the happy (or for that matter, tragic) homo ending prevents us from, in Crimp's words, "revel[ling] instead in Liz's slatternliness, Brando's self-parody, [and] Zorro David's faggotry" (6), and, I would add, the queer pleasures of ecstatic bottomhood that Liz's slatternliness, Brando's self-parody, and David's faggotry embody so well. Adopting the film's lowly perspectives allows us to discover the perverse enjoyment in this mainstream Hollywood narrative.[47] In chapter 3, I employ this bottom point of view on a film explicitly lauded, and reviled, for its sensational showcase of Asian bottomhood. In shifting our gaze from the bit part of Filipino houseboy to the romantic lead of Chinese lover, we witness once more the complex manner in which Asian masculinity finds sexual expression and critical leverage in a politics of the behind.

CHAPTER THREE

The Lover's "Gorgeous Ass"

The headline of an article on the film *The Lover* (1992) in the October 1992 issue of *Glamour* magazine teases, "Did they or didn't they?" This titillating query speculates whether the two leads, Jane March and Tony Leung Ka Fai, actually did have sex in the movie. Since the lovemaking appears "so sensuous, so erotic," the writer wonders, "How did they make it look so real?" In his response, director Jean-Jacques Annaud proposes that in order to make a film erotic, one mustn't show too much: "You don't want to kill the dream. If you see too much, you feel unwelcomed. It is very difficult to film in such a way that you say, 'See, there is nothing to hide. Look how beautiful,' without giving the impression that you are a Peeping Tom" (Krupp 1992, 195). Interestingly, a number of critics dismissively compare the film's sex scenes to pornography. More specifically, they link *The Lover* to the soft-core sex travelogue classic *Emmanuelle* (dir. Just Jaeckin, 1974) by dubbing the film *Emmanuelle in Saigon* (Billson 1992, 20–21). It seems especially salient that a film portraying an explicitly sexual relationship between an Asian man and a white woman should bear the charge of pornography. Of the many major articles and reviews in the mainstream Anglo-American press I perused, only one asks (in parentheses) whether this was the first time that "an Asian [appears] in a full nude scene in a major film" (Lurie 1992, 154). The writer neglects to specify that in this case it is an Asian male in a full nude scene, and that "a major film" here refers to a film from Europe or Hollywood.[1] Bracketing *The Lover*'s artistic pretensions and did-they-or-didn't-they publicity stunt, I contend that, by failing to acknowledge the novelty of Tony Leung's "overexposed" flesh in this high-profile international production, commentators on the film ignore the crucial difference such an eroticized representation of the Asian male body makes in mainstream Western cinema, which had never before eroticized this racially abject body on its larger-than-life screens. Instead of attending to the complex power dynamics in a love story marked by racial, sexual, class, and age differences, these critics disavow the threat of a naked Asian man fucking a white girl in the colonies by relegating the film to the soft-core generic trash bin.[2]

This chapter asserts that even in a blatantly heterosexual love story, Asian male sexual potency continues to be informed by bottomhood, which is manifested here in the Chinese lover's wounded masculinity and the inordinate amount of interest directed at his naked buttocks in the film's notorious sex scenes. Like Brandon Lee's inevitable transformation from an Asian top to a versatile performer who bottoms, we find a similar pressure brought to bear on the Chinese lover's performance of sex onscreen: his top missionary position can only be made legible by his "gorgeous ass." Parallel to Alison and Anacleto's queer domestic bond forged out of a bottom coalition, the young French girl and the Chinese lover's interracial affair is based on the creation of an alliance across feminizing shame. Hence, my discussion of *The Lover* brings together the previous chapters' delineations of bottomhood as sexual positioning as well as affective receptivity. What makes this particular text different from the previous two is the fact that whereas bottomhood seems a natural fit for a gay porn actor and an effeminate houseboy, we find that bottomhood can attach to heterosexual Asian masculinity as well; that is, bottomhood functions to effectively queer, and thus to undermine, *The Lover*'s claim to normative masculine sexual potency and prowess.

It should be noted from the outset that I situate my reading of this international production (French-British-Vietnamese) within an Asian American critical framework. I focus on the American context of reception of *The Lover* to examine a local manifestation of a transnational circulation of

Asian masculinity, especially a model of masculinity that exceeds the familiar nexus of martial arts hero and urban gangster. Bear in mind that the trans-Asian projection of Leung's image in *The Lover*, from Hong Kong to Ho Chi Minh City to Paris to San Francisco, occurs several years before the different waves of Asian cinemas made a splash on American movie screens.[3] As such, the sight of Leung's "gorgeous ass" in 1992 reveals the dismal marginalization of Asian men in Western cinema while at the same time providing a rare glimpse of a different model of masculinity. Even though its narrative concerns an interracial love affair in 1930s Indochina, the reception of the film in the United States was invariably informed by the history of Asian American sexual-racial-gender formation. Like the other texts in this book, the film has not received much serious critical examination, partly due to its representation of explicit sex, and most likely due to its affirmative treatment of Asian bottomhood.[4]

My analysis of Asian masculinity in *The Lover* seeks to revalorize depictions of Asian American masculinity dismissed and overlooked for their feminizing and emasculating operations. The specularity of bottomhood in *The Lover* surpasses the narrow scope of visibility/invisibility and negative/positive registered in certain strains of lesbian and gay and Asian American cultural criticism. Because "sexuality is regulated through the policing and the shaming of gender" (Butler 1993, 238), we cannot afford to respond to the shame of Asian American male feminization by erecting the pride of Asian American remasculinization in its place. By contrast, this chapter argues for the Chinese lover's feminization, his shameful bottomhood, as a more expansive model of Asian American masculine embodiment, one that serves as a searing critique of a dominant masculinity marked by the desire for a confrontational and aggressive penetration of the other. This resignified Asian bottomhood engages openness, vulnerability, and receptivity to others: other looks, bodies, agencies.

One striking modality of bottomhood animated by the sight of the Asian man's smooth posterior is the activation of touch. The shift from opticality to tactility is consonant with a transfer of value from a phallic economy of visible evidence to an anal economy of felt receptivity. In the same vein, the mutuality of touch compels the shift of attention from the absent potency of the Asian penis to the vulnerability of the Asian ass. Indeed, the movements of the hand play a vital role in the intimate encounter of the young female protagonist and the Chinese lover through and across racial and sexual shame. These hesitant hands reaching out and blushed faces turning away intimate the ways negative affects—such as shame, loss, grief, and anger—underline our social alliances and political identifications. A more careful reconsideration of negative affect encourages us to adopt a more capacious view of what might constitute social agency for racialized subjects. I postulate bottomhood as a positioning that affords a difficult but fruitful path to social recognition, and not simply as an abject identity that one has to renounce and get over. Hence, in the place of moralistic outrage and blanket dismissal, I look closely at the film's sex scenes to trace the lovers' itinerary from shame to shamelessness. It is precisely in the scandalous soft-core sex sequences that we witness the Chinese lover's powerful eroticism, one that is shot through with inhibition and self-doubt but also scandalous specularity. An unrelenting focus on his beautiful buttocks allows us to see the limits of a critique—performed by Asian American, feminist, and postcolonial scholars—that continually evaluates the Chinese man's bottomhood as emasculating, objectifying, and colonizing. Before turning to the productive operations of shame and how they play out in The Lover's presentation of tactile vision, let us examine the ways in which Duras's text rewrites the conventional romance narrative with its foregrounding of racial and sexual antagonisms, a gesture that imbues her award-winning international best seller with important political ramifications. As part of my strategy to repoliticize the film, I read Duras's book alongside Annaud's adaptation, as most critics and commentators tend to do, even when they end up condemning the film or both film and novel. I will have more to say about the differences between Duras's novel and Annaud's film below; here I would like to note that I aim to tease out the book's extended exploration of the two protagonists' "shame consciousness and shame creativity" (Sedgwick 2003, 63) in order to show how they are translated visually in the film.

"Love, Nothing Else": Racializing the Romance

Based on Marguerite Duras's 1984 novel L'Amant, The Lover narrates a torrid sexual affair between a young white girl and an older, wealthy Chinese man in colonial Saigon in 1929.[5] Their fateful first meeting takes place during a ferry crossing on the Mekong River. Stuck on a crowded bus with the natives, she readily accepts a ride from him in his fancy limousine back to her boarding school. A few days later, he returns to pick her up and brings her to his bachelor apartment in Cholon, the Chinese quarter in Saigon, where they have passionate sex. From the beginning of the affair, both are fully aware of the racial and sexual taboos underpinning their relationship. She states,

"I don't like Chinese very much," while he admits that it would be impossible for them to get married since she has had sex with him. The central conflict in the story hinges on the girl's motivation in her dangerous liaison with the Chinese lover. The viewer remains uncertain as to whether she is only interested in him for the money he gives her to help her impoverished family or whether she is in fact in love with him despite her disavowals of love. For his part, the Chinese lover must contend with his father's wish that he marry a Chinese girl from a rich family; if he does not, his father will cut him off financially. In the end, he goes through with the arranged marriage, while she is sent back to France as part of her punishment for engaging in the scandalous affair.[6]

Many writers have leveled criticism at the work of Duras (beginning with her screenplay, *Hiroshima Mon Amour* [dir. Alain Resnais, 1959]) by accusing her of domesticating historical complexities to heterosexual romance. Pointing to the ahistoricism in Duras's semiautobiographical text, Sylvie Blum-Reid (2003, 28) argues that Duras portrays herself as a courageous figure defying racial and cultural taboos while completely ignoring the historical context of decolonization under way in Indochina. Similarly, Panivong Norindr maintains that the violent and bloody history of French colonization of Indochina is rewritten as "a stormy love affair" (1996, 132).[7] He cites feminist film theorist Mary Ann Doane's observation regarding the depoliticizing process at work in transforming social history into individual drama: "rather than activating history as mise-en-scène, a space, the . . . love story inscribes it as individual subjectivity closed in on itself. History is an accumulation of memories of the loved one" (Norindr 1996, 135). However, it is possible to unpack the ideological operations of the text in the things left out and unsaid. For example, Susan Koshy has uncovered the ideological work performed by interracial romance narratives, in spite of their manifest refusal to deal with social issues. Although her topic concerns Asian American miscegenous love stories, Koshy's argument offers much insight for our discussion:

> Fundamentally, these narratives marshaled an emotional logic to test the political logic of social boundaries. But while tragic stories about the impossibility of love between the races often enlarged the sympathies of readers, they also engendered a pragmatic apprehension in an audience that acknowledged the necessity of racial divisions. . . . Narratives of interracial desire came to be so influential because of *their ability to ad-*

dress social questions precisely by seeming not to. They transformed political questions of difference that were the basis of social hierarchy by rendering them in the simulacrum of a "universal" language of the human heart. (2004, 20–21, emphasis added)

While in accord with other scholars' critique of Duras's reduction of social and political antagonisms to the "language of the human heart," Koshy's analysis brings to the fore the social, historical, and political implications that interracial romances attempt to elide. Building on Koshy's astute reading, I suggest that arguments about Duras's avoidance of the Indochinese historical context, while correct to a certain extent, should be qualified if we examine the ways she reworks the conventional love story by engaging the knotty power relations of a taboo interracial relationship in the colonial period. For example, we can point to the ways that *The Lover*'s interracial coupling, while heterosexual, can hardly be described as heteronormative, let alone amenable for recruitment into the hegemonic narrative of French colonial order. At least one critic has identified in the film "a thinly veiled allegory of French colonial ideology's account of the French experience in Indochina—its imagined Franco-Asian coupling (marriage), the native population's rejection of the French suitor, the departure of the French, the abiding longing of the people of Southeast Asia for the departed French, and the French lover's nostalgia for its lost object of desire" (Winston 2001, 72). Although this allegorical reading confirms observations about Duras's reduction of French colonialism to heterosexual romance, this reading problematically reduces the significance of the lover's Chineseness into the all-encompassing sign of "Southeast Asia." For as I argue below, his Chinese identity troubles the ready-made binarisms of colonizer and colonized and European and native. In a dynamic that recalls the queer bond between Alison and Anacleto in chapter 2, it is precisely the Chinese lover's and the young French girl's failures to live up to their assigned social roles that bring the two together. As one reader comments, "the incongruity of the girl outside of her 'place' seems to lie at the core of the Chinese man's desire for her, of his desire to be other, seen already in his cultural affectations" (Yeager 2001, 228). Note this critic's crucial point that the Chinese man's desire for the girl is part and parcel of his desire to be other than himself. In the same vein, it is his racial otherness and class difference that attract the girl in her desire to escape from the material and moral restrictions imposed by her family and the white colonial community. Each character is attracted to the other's failure, and refusal, to take up their proper place in the racial, class, gender, and sexual hierarchy.

If we look at the romance genre itself, we can see the ways Duras reworks its codes and conventions to account for the improper ways both partners adopt their roles in the script. Taking inspiration from the violation of border divisions between high and low genres, serious art film and soft-core porn mobilized in the media buzz around Annaud's film, I turn to Tania Modleski's groundbreaking feminist study of the Harlequin romance.[8] Consider her description of the Harlequin formula: "A young, inexperienced, poor to moderately well-to-do woman encounters and becomes involved with a handsome, strong, experienced, wealthy man, older than herself by ten to fifteen years. The heroine is confused by the hero's behavior since, though he is obviously interested in her, he is mocking, cynical, contemptuous, often hostile, and even somewhat brutal. By the end, however, all misunderstandings are cleared away, and the hero reveals his love for the heroine, who reciprocates" (1982, 36). Modleski's outline of the narrative conventions of romance novels sheds light on the ways Duras's text conforms to but also departs significantly from the Harlequin formula. We have the poor, inexperienced young girl and a handsome, experienced, wealthy older man. In the place of the Harlequin romance's narrative goal of convincing the hero to accept the "preeminence of love and the attractions of domesticity" (Modleski 1982, 17), *The Lover* reverses and complicates this trope by giving us a shy, awkward, and sickly Chinese playboy who falls head-over-heels in love with our white heroine. The impossibility of a romantic happy ending is signaled from the start by his Chineseness, her whiteness, his seduction, and her loss of virginity. Disrupting the romance's convention of the older man exploiting and corrupting the young girl and teaching her to submit to his sexual dominance (in the tradition of *Emmanuelle*), the young girl in this case comes to profit financially and experientially from their affair. It is she who is "mocking, cynical, contemptuous, [and] often hostile" to his pronouncements of love, who appears to be in it only for lust and money. By contrast, his Chineseness, older age, and wealth render him "afraid," consigning the performance of his male potency and sexual agency within private interior spaces. Instead of the clichéd colonial fantasy of the white male colonizer and his female native lovers—insert here Lieutenant Pinkerton and his Butterfly, or Gauguin and his Tahitian women—the Chinese lover and the French girl's transgression of racial-sexual boundaries comes about through a concomitant failed performance of gender roles, thus effectively infusing the text with political undertones.⁹ Nevertheless, the simple reversal of gender roles doesn't quite capture the complicated nuances of their relationship; the power dynamics are not so clear-cut as to who always has the upper hand.

Another element that complicates traditional racialized sexual dichotomies can be seen in the physical mobility of the two characters in colonial Indochina, especially that of the young girl. In her study of the integral role played by gender in the European colonial project, Ann Laura Stoler posits that imperial authority and colonial power relied on the policing of European women's sexuality, which was closely linked to the maintenance of white sexual morality and racial purity. More specifically, European male colonial regulation of white female sexuality entailed the protection of European women against the sexual threat of native men. As Stoler explains, "A defense of community, morality, and white male power was achieved by increasing control over and consensus among Europeans, by reaffirming the vulnerability of white women and the sexual threat posed by native men, and by creating new sanctions to limit the liberties of both" (2002, 60). In light of these social constraints on French women in colonial communities, the relative freedom of movement enjoyed by the young French girl is remarkable. Her mobility can be attributed to her lower-class status, her youth, and, paradoxically, her whiteness and French citizenship.¹⁰ Indeed, Norindr has named the girl's ability to move through the spaces of the city her "errance," in order to reference both "the meaning of swerving both from the path and from truth—as deviation or perversion—and wandering from one place to another, an accidental journey more than a process of forced displacement" (1997, 109). He goes on to say that her errance contests the colonial order's rules and regulations and their aims to produce "'fixed' positions of intelligibility" (111). Her physical and moral wandering astray from the trajectory of normative white femininity provides the young girl with a critical perspective into the hypocrisies undergirding the colonial status quo. It is not surprising, then, that some commentators have noted the subversion of colonial sexual mores by Duras's young female protagonist in choosing to engage in a sexual affair with a Chinese man.

At the same time, such a subversion has been fiercely interrogated. A number of scholars have asserted that the young girl's accession of desiring female sexual subjectivity is accomplished by relegating the Chinese man to the position of feminized sexual object. They maintain that the female protagonist exerts power over the Chinese lover by adopting an objectifying male gaze, in effect, "feminizing him as other men's gazes have feminized her" (Staley and Edson 2001, 293). Another critic argues that the young girl shores up her sexual and racial dominance by evoking the prevailing image of Asian men in the white colonial imagination, one that regards Asian men as "weak, submissive, subordinate, and at times, asexual" (Ruddy 2006, 91). In addition to these feminist objections, the book (along with the film adaptation) also came under attack from Asian American critics who fault Leung's Chinese lover for not adequately measuring up to how romantic leading men ought to be. In her introduction to the landmark Asian American literary anthology *Charlie Chan Is Dead*, Jessica Hagedorn characterizes "The Lover . . . [as] the pathetic Chinese millionaire boy-toy completely dominated by his impoverished, adolescent, blondie waif dominatrix in both Marguerite Duras' popular novel and the recent film version." She finds such depictions of Asian masculinity continuous with how Asians have been "portrayed as loyal servants and children, . . . humorless, non-assertive, impotent—yet we are eroticized as exotic playthings in both Western film and literature" (1993, xxii).[11] Slotting Duras's and Annaud's texts into existing analyses of Asian American male feminization, Hagedorn's interpretation readily brands Asian male feminization as a racial injury and a sexual liability. To be sure, it is clear that the female narrator animates stereotypical traits of Asian men in her characterization of the Chinese lover. What I find more disconcerting, however, is the ways in which, in detailing the Chinese man's feminization, these critics' arguments remain caught within the binary logic of racial hegemony and gender normativity. That is, desiring sexual subjectivity can only be described as masculine, white, and colonizing; inversely, to occupy the position of desired sexual object can only be seen as feminine, Oriental, and colonized. In explaining the female protagonist's acquisition of sexual autonomy as mined through her racial privilege, these critics dispossess the Chinese lover of any agency—whether in his older age, his money, his wealth of experience, or his surrender of dominant masculinity. As such, their readings cannot imagine the possibility that the Chinese lover's "weak, submissive, subordinate" qualities might be received and felt differently, that they might be appreciated and desired.

By racializing the romance, Duras troubles the paradigm governing colonial interracial sex: the active white male subject acts upon the passive native female object. By extension, her portrayal of the young French girl and the Chinese lover upends the traditional binarisms of subject and object, looker and looked upon, activity and passivity, and lover and beloved. The Chinese man's wealth, weakness, and vulnerability, alongside the girl's poverty, sexual precocity, and opportunism, reveal their deviations, or "errances," from normative colonial, racial, gender, class, and sexual mores. Significantly, both characters' brazen display of their social vulnerability encourages us to think about desire and pleasure "in the very specularization of the self" (Cheng 2001, 53), the complicitous pleasure taken in the process of subjection.[12] In both the novel and the film, the specularization of the Chinese lover's body is marked by lack: the lack of force, strength, muscle, hair, and virility. And yet it is evident that such "shameful" feminine qualities—moans, cries, soft skin, and erect nipples, not to mention emotional vulnerability and sexual hesitations, all qualities I would characterize as manifestations of a bottom sensibility—are here accorded positive valences, inspiring sexual passion in the young girl.[13]

A Touch of Shame

Reading Duras's novel, one readily recognizes the key affect animating the lovers' sense of themselves and their sexual congress across racial and class lines, namely, the affect of shame. Early in the novel, Duras writes: "We were white children, we were ashamed, we sold our furniture, but we weren't hungry, we had a houseboy and we ate" (1985, 6–7). After the first time they have sex, the girl narrator tells the Chinese man about her family's poverty: "Shameless, that's what we were. That's how I came to be here with you" (45). Clearly, the shame of being a destitute white girl in the colony constitutes the driving force in her relationship with the Chinese lover. An explication of recent developments in feminist and queer studies on shame theory will prove tremendously useful in unpacking this driving force in *The Lover*.

In a series of essays on shame and queer performativity, Eve Sedgwick describes shame as "deconstituting and foundational" of identity. Drawing on the work of psychologist Sylvan Tompkins, Sedgwick identifies the childhood scene in which the pleasurable looking relations between child and adult suffer a break: "the moment when the adult face fails or refuses to play its part in the continuation of mutual gaze . . . [resulting in the child's] social isolation and signaling the need for relief from that condition" (2003, 36). Here shame functions as a critical moment in which identity is formed and put into crisis. Moreover, Sedgwick notes that the protoform of shame—"eyes down, head averted"—highlights the "painful individuation" as well as the "uncontrollable relationality" activated by shame. She argues that the strangest feature of shame, and the most salient in "offer[ing] the most conceptual leverage for political projects, is the way bad treatment of someone else, bad treatment by someone else, someone else's embarrassment, stigma, debility, bad smell, or strange behavior, seemingly having nothing to do with me, can so readily flood me" (2003, 37). Sedgwick questions the conventional social-political response that would call for getting rid of shame and replacing it with pride, anger, dignity, or truth telling (for example, in political and therapeutic discourses tied to the civil rights movement, gay and lesbian liberation, feminist consciousness-raising, incest survivor therapy, and so on); instead, she proposes harnessing shame's capacity for production, at once personal, social, and political, and advocates for shame's potentiality for critical and affective transformation and resignification.

Other critics have extended Sedgwick's important insights on queerness and shame and brought them to bear on other registers of social difference. Judith Halberstam posits shame as "a gendered form of sexual abjection" and goes on to say that shame "belongs to the feminine, and when men find themselves 'flooded' with shame, chances are they are being feminized in some way and against their will" (2005b, 226). The gay reclamation of masculinity—celebrated by some gay male theorists as a critical undoing of dominant masculinity—she suggests, demonstrates a troubling recuperation of masculine privilege in order to compensate for gay white men's shameful feminization in childhood: their former abject status as sissy boys. In opposition to the gay white male deployment of gay pride as the antidote to homophobia, Halberstam contends that people of color and women have responded to shame formations by employing various political strategies, including feminism and queer of color critique.[14] The text that abuts most closely to my interest in exploring racial-sexual shame and bottomhood is Kathryn Bond Stockton's (2006) *Beautiful Bottom, Beautiful Shame*. Investigating the switch point between "black" and "queer," Stockton examines their crossings with affects such as shame, debasement, abjection, and humiliation, and their attachments to "bottom pleasures" (7–8). Stockton reminds us that "there is no purely black form of debasement—nor a queer one. Only blended forms of shame" (23).[15] This last point is critical when we consider the coconstitution of various forms of social factors underlining the characters' shame in *The Lover*, specifically the roles of race and femininity. In addition, I augment shame theory's interest on the face by drawing attention to the body in my analysis of how the two protagonists inhabit their shame through bodily gestures and movements: hands reaching out, backs arching up, buttocks thrusting away.

Both Duras's text and Annaud's film allow us to see the overdetermined blending of racial and sexual shame in the lovers' interracial affair. A sequence of their first meeting from the film shows the ways their attraction to one another is activated by their status as outsiders. Film techniques emphasize how they stand out, and apart, among the hordes of natives that populate the mise-en-scène. On the bus to the ferry, a medium shot shows the back of the girl's head as she sits among the native riders; seen in the background of the frame, she almost fades into the crowd as the female voice-over narrates, "So that day I'm going back to Saigon. I'm wearing my cabaret shoes and my man's hat. No woman, no young girl wears a man's fedora in that colony in those days. No native woman, either." With the remark about the uniqueness of her donning of the fedora, the camera zooms in on the girl's head, drawing her out from the rest of the bus riders, as the voice-over continues, "That hat, I never leave it. I have that, this hat. That all by itself makes me whole." In the next scene, the camera tilts up the girl's body in medium close-up, spotlighting her black high-heeled shoes bejeweled with rhinestones, her oversized sacklike dress, her little girl's braids, and again the man's hat. The camera cuts to a reverse long shot of the girl standing by the ferry railing; relegated to the far background, she's rendered miniscule, yet standing out among the faceless natives wearing conical peasant hats. A big black limousine enters from the right of the frame, dwarfing the girl's small figure in background left (figure 3.1). In a 180-degree reverse shot, a low angle shows the Chinese man's limo in the background, squeezed between her legs in the foreground (figure 3.2). With their contrasting scale and framing, this series of shots highlights the French girl's and the Chinese man's difference (signified by her fedora and his limousine, respectively) from their environment. They also introduce the interplay of power and desire between the two: her youth, whiteness, and sexual precociousness are juxtaposed against his wealth. The provocative framing of his big black limo intruding into the frame to render her French *coloniale* status insignificant is countered by the shot of her legs looming around and above his car, turning his conspicuous wealth into a mere sexual plaything.

These visual metaphors exemplify both characters' relationships to their outsider status, which, though steeped in shame, are rerouted into shameless exhibitionism. The shame of poverty underscores the young girl's attraction to the wealthy Chinese man; it is also the component that sustains their relationship. The girl's distinctive costume of man's hat, lamé shoes, and low-cut dress constitutes a deliberate mixing of gender codes, with its ambiguous association of trash and glamour, setting her apart from natives and whites.[16]

FIGURE 3.1: The French girl. *The Lover* (1992).

FIGURE 3.2: A limousine between her legs. *The Lover* (1992).

It is noteworthy that the "ambiguous signifiers" of the female protagonist's costume are derived from her shame-inducing poverty: the "marked-down markdowns" shoes, the sacklike dress made from her mother's old dresses, and the hat that is "link[ed] with poverty" (Duras 1985, 24). In making her abject poverty into an eroticized public spectacle, the young girl renders her social marginalization hypervisible, amplifying the threat she poses to the colonial social order. As Stoler reminds us, poor, single white women, along with white prostitutes, were marginalized in European colonial communities because they existed outside the spatial and moral boundaries of respectable European bourgeois family formations, which were deemed the "cultural bases for imperial patriotism and racial survival" (2002, 61).

The female protagonist's re-presentation of "white-trash" femininity elucidates the ways in which class-inflected shame gets transfigured through adolescent female subjectivity, the cross-cutting of class and female shame. Lending support to Halberstam's description of shame as "a gendered form of sexual abjection," Liz Constable maps out shame's distinctive contours that shape female sexual subjectivity. Constable draws on Simone de Beauvoir's rearticulation of Sartre and explains that while "Sartre defined the invasively paralyzing impact of another's contemptuous, or shaming, gaze . . . [Beauvoir observed that] being shamed for women has more to do with the *absence of response* from others than with Sartre's descriptions of penetrating shaming gazes" (Constable 2004, 677, emphasis in original). In light of de Beauvoir's delineation of how shame differentially affects women, Constable suggests that for young women in the West, shame arises "through an absence of response to their feelings as emerging sexual subjects" (677). Constable's insight helps us delineate another crucial element governing Duras's female protagonist's precocious exhibitionism, one complexly determined by the ways in which French colonial privilege and racial pride are undercut by humiliating poverty and female sexual shame. A response to these processes of humiliation and shame can be seen in the young girl's distinctive costume, which she uses "to flaunt the body without shame" (Norindr 1996, 121). To flaunt the body without shame presupposes that one is full of shame to begin with; this point verifies Sedgwick's observation that "shame and exhibitionism" come from the "same glove" (2003, 38). Such a display attempts to compensate for the experience of being unrecognized, unseen, unattended to. The spectacular flaunting of the adolescent female body throws off the cloak of shame at the same time that the gesture accesses pleasure in the girl's self-objectification.

Shame inundates the Chinese lover's self-display as well. Fastidiously dressed in his expensive white suit, exceedingly well-groomed with his perfectly-styled hair, and chauffeured around in his big black limousine, the Chinese man plays the part of a rich Parisian playboy, but, significantly, without a playboy's self-confidence. We first see him during the ferry crossing as he gets out of the car and approaches the white girl standing against the ferry railing. The camera adopts a low medium shot and shows him dominating the foreground in midframe, while she appears below him in the background. Asking if she'd like a cigarette, he holds out his fancy cigarette case;

FIGURE 3.3: Crossing the Mekong. *The Lover* (1992).

a close-up registers his trembling hand. A quick close-up shows her glancing at the case and then at his face as she declines the offer. Cut to a close-up of his face, looking nervous, awkward, and crestfallen. A medium two-shot frames them standing by the railing again, but now in a reverse shot, with her in the foreground center frame and him in the background (figure 3.3). Trying a different tack, he articulates his surprise at seeing a young white girl on a native bus and comments on the originality of her donning a man's hat. He states: "And you're pretty. You can do anything you like." Finally, she asks who he is. Delighted that she finally exhibits an interest in him, his face lights up; he tells her that he lives in the big blue house with the terraces in Vinh Long. She: "It's a Chinese house." He: "I am . . . Chinese." The camera cuts back to her, looking at him, and then looking away.

Throughout this pickup scene, there is none of the sustained shot–reverse shots and eyeline matches typical of classical Hollywood film during a dialogue sequence. Instead, we have furtive glances and averted eyes. The only exception occurs when he looks directly at her and enunciates his identity as Chinese. Besides his car and fancy clothes, this pronouncement clinches the fact of his wealth, a fact reinforced by Jeanne Moreau's voice-over explaining the status of the rich Chinese "financial minority that owns all the popular housing in the colony."[17] Despite his self-exhibitionism and conspicuous consumption, cracks in the cool veneer immediately become visible in this early attempt at seduction. Reviewers of the film readily equate the trembling hand with the Chinese man's failure to adequately perform the role of smooth, suave masculine lover. Though rich and male, his Chineseness prevents him from full accession of racial privilege, from entering the sexual playground of Parisian playboys on equal footing. It is as if his Chinese family's enormous affluence embarrassed and unmanned him. In the same way that he positively acknowledges her poverty-induced femininity (e.g., her donning of a man's hat), she recognizes his shame-prone demeanor in the self-display and giveaway of the trembling hand and the shame-pride in the assertion "I am . . . Chinese."[18]

The above scenario of the couple's meeting on the ferry demonstrates the "painful individuation" of the pair's awareness of their shameful differences, that is, her poverty performed as a shameless masquerade, a "body without shame," next to his racial difference undermining his picture-perfect masculine performance, the shame "he has to get the better of." Hence, while their self-displays draw on the repertoire of conventional gender norms (her white-trash feminine glamour and his suave masculine Chinese playboy getup), both characters inevitably expose the seams of their mimicry, and their failure to effectively pass.

The interrogation of conventional dichotomies of masculine/feminine, subject/object, shame/shamelessness can be extended to the binary of colonizer/colonized in the depiction of the lover as Chinese. During the French colonial era, the Chinese functioned as an "indispensable intermediary" between the French and the Indochinese population due to the Chinese's comprehensive knowledge of the natives and their customs. The economically successful Chinese were deemed hardworking and reliable by the French in comparison to the Vietnamese, whom they branded as lazy and childlike. Yet, despite their long-term presence, the Chinese's position remained very tenuous in Indochina. Chinese economic dominance in the region frequently resulted in anti-Chinese attitudes, which at times manifested in Vietnamese nationalist calls for boycotts of Chinese businesses.[19] Though a similar resentment of the Chinese can be found in other Southeast Asian countries, anti-Chinese sentiments were compounded by an extensive history of Chinese domination in Vietnam. Their financial dominance was qualified by their status as "merchants without empire," demonstrated by the fact that their economic strength did not translate to social and political power (Rigg 2003, 100, 112). It is this simultaneous "exclusion and embeddedness" of the Chinese in Indochina that distinguishes the standing of the Chinese lover as neither colonizer nor colonized.[20] It remains the case, however, that because he is Asian, he is metonymically infected by the specific gendering of indigenous men. As Frank Proschan has noted, "French colonial observers constructed the Vietnamese male as androgynous, effeminate, hermaphroditic, impotent, and inverted" (2002, 436). The liminal status of the Chinese in colonial Indochina and the conflation of Chinese and Vietnamese masculinities as lacking vis-à-vis white French masculine norms work to reinforce the marginalization of the Chinese lover in his encounter with the female narrator.

Thus far, I have been discussing Duras's novel and the film adaptation almost interchangeably. I suggested above that critics and reviewers commonly interpret the film in light of the book, that is, intertextually. Commentators frequently cite the other two texts that constitute Duras's Indochinese trilogy, *Un barrage contre le Pacifique* (*The Sea Wall*, 1950) and *L'Amant de la Chine du Nord* (*The North China Lover*, 1991), which cover the writer's childhood in colonial-era Vietnam.[21] Sharon Willis (1987) has commented that with their recurring "fragments, scenes, details, and figures," Duras's texts encourage not final closure, but constant rereadings. Nevertheless, it is useful to tease out the differences between *L'Amant* and *The Lover*. As already mentioned, numerous critics have charged Duras with disregarding the social and political context in which her tale unfolds. Although these assessments are valid, it is important to note that the depoliticization of Duras's work is located not only in the texts themselves. Indeed, Jane Bradley Winston has called attention to the commodification of the author-function "Duras" and its deployment to consolidate consumer desire, both domestically and in the international market, for a nostalgia-tinged "Indochina" and "the exotic-erotic consumers had come to expect and desire of the French culture niche" (Winston 2001, 71). In addition, Winston suggests that the depoliticization of Duras's work is also the consequence of actions by the male-dominated French literary establishment to contain the feminist critique in her work by relegating it to the feminine sentimental genre.[22]

In a more vehement manner than the dismissal of Duras's novel *L'Amant*, many commentators condemn Annaud's film adaptation for its nostalgic depiction of French colonialism, or what Norindr names a "phantasmatic Indochina," a meticulous re-creation of contemporary Vietnam into a colonial fantasy stripped of any traces of French colonial and imperialist violence and exploitation.[23] Filming his thirty-million-dollar production on location in Vietnam, Annaud and his crew set out to renovate buildings, pave roads, plant trees, and repaint entire neighborhoods to transform dilapidated Ho Chi Minh City into colonial-era Saigon. They went as far as shipping a 1929

Morris Léon Bollée limousine from Seattle to Vietnam, as well as an old ocean liner from Cyprus. Though these painstaking efforts by Annaud and his crew strongly confirm critics' assessments of the film as being stripped of social, political, and political context, it is certainly possible to read into the film's omissions and failures a way to repoliticize it. For example, many critics' disdain for the film can be linked to its depiction of explicit sex; instead of phobic rejection, however, I believe it is profitable to take this salacious appeal seriously and to subject the sex scenes to careful analysis. To reiterate yet again the novel's or the film's lack of historical grounding is to continue to perpetuate the same familiar analysis, to restrict rather than open up the text to alternative readings in new times and contexts. In other words, it is not enough to diagnose and dismiss the film for being an exotic travelogue cum soft-core sexual spectacle. In addition to submitting Annaud's fetishized colonial fantasy to interrogation, we might also propose that the extravagantly re-created mise-en-scène can be read as a mode of shameful/shameless exhibitionism (not unlike the two protagonists' shameful/shameless social and sexual exhibitionism), as a symptomatic recuperation of the shame of white male colonial subjectivity confronted with the threat of its expired hegemony. This is not an endorsement of Annaud's ahistorical, prettified reproduction of Indochina or his reduction of Duras's imaginative fiction to the naked requirements of the real, one that can only be captured on location. Rather, this reading considers other routes of reading the interracial love story that forms the heart of the novel and film. Although I readily admit the limits of claiming the interracial relationship as posing a serious threat to colonial authority, I do want to tease out the mutual recognition enabled by the couple's meeting across difference in order to form a bottom alliance. This recognition is performed through unabashed specularity, but even more strikingly, through the animation of touch.

The Hand: Organ of Love and Labor

In the car ride back to Saigon, the Chinese man continues his seduction of the girl, again effected with his trembling hand. After an awkward silence incurred during a crossing of a rickety bridge, the Chinese man tentatively reaches across the seat to touch the young girl's hand. A medium shot of the backseat shows them seated apart with ample space between them (figure 3.4). With surreptitious glances at her bare, white, skinny hand resting on the brown seat, he looks out the window as he slowly inches first his pinky, and then his well-manicured brown hand (only slightly larger than her own)

FIGURE 3.4: In the limousine. *The Lover* (1992).

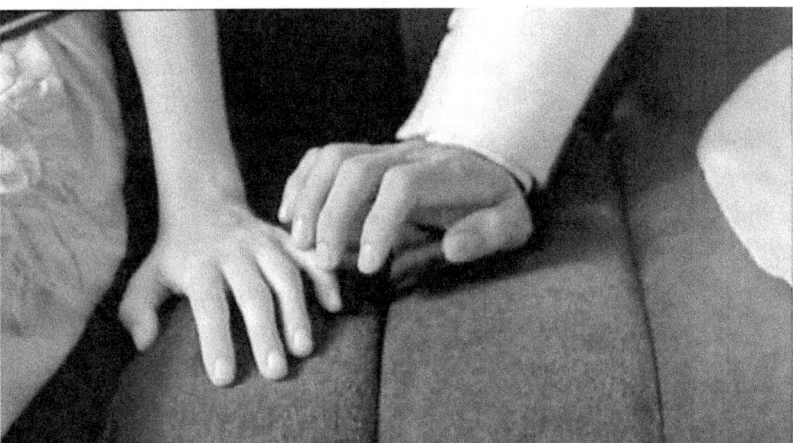

FIGURE 3.5: Digital caress. *The Lover* (1992).

over hers (figure 3.5). The periodic honking and insistent engine noise of the car are drowned by nondiegetic flute music as the camera cuts from close-ups of his impassive face to close-ups of the lingering digital caresses and maneuvers to a measured zoom of her flushing face, eyes half-lowered, mouth partly open, looking away out the window. As his hand clasps and interlaces with hers, the girl's facial expression is orgasmic as she tightens her fingers around his, while he parts his own lips and looks straight ahead. The camera then cuts to an exterior long shot of the car speeding across the frame amid a grove of rubber trees, a visual ellipsis for the manual intertwining taking place within the speeding limo.[24]

The digital cruising in the backseat of the car, though conventionally signifying an innocent heterosexual eroticism, suggests queer uses of the hand. Mandy Merck has observed that in lesbian cultural production, from Radclyffe Hall's novel *The Well of Loneliness* (1928) to the Hollywood neonoir film *Bound* (dir. Andy and Larry Wachowski, 1996), the hand functions as an "instrument of sexual contact and as a marker of gender transitivity" (Merck 2000, 127). Not merely a fetish substitute for the penis, the hand in the lesbian texts she considers represents a threat to a phallocentric field of vision in its participation in another sexual economy, one enabling a reciprocal exchange of sexual pleasure between women. Merck cites Engels, who noted that in addition to being "an organ of labour, [the hand] *is also the product of labour*" (quoted in Merck 2000, 144, emphasis in original). She reminds us that "historically, the touching of hands has been a powerful performative, binding the parties to vows, contracts, and wagers" (145). As the organ of love, labor, and binding contracts, the hand and its multiple functions are set in motion in this reaching out, across, and into the interstitial space of the brown car seat in between the two protagonists. While the lowering of eyes, heads turning away, and faces flushed bespeak their painful individuation, this erotic handshake binds the two in their mutual shame. Significantly, it is this recognition of shame as a difficult but vital mode of relationality that allows for a movement across their respective differences.

By the time the limo arrives at the girl's school, the Chinese man's hand is shown resting on the girl's upper thigh. She turns from the window and finally looks at him, stating breathlessly, and meaningfully, "That's it. It's here." The Chinese man then draws his hand back and folds it with his other hand, resting both on his delicately crossed knees. A few scenes later, the girl is shown in bed at the boarding school under the gauze of the mosquito net; the camera cuts from close-ups of her face to her hand as it lingers over and presses the fabric of the nightgown at her crotch, touching and pleasuring herself. Later on, after their first intercourse, the Chinese lover asks if she would like him if he were poor. Replying that she likes him as he is, that is, with his money, she becomes aroused once more and guides his hand with both of hers down to her crotch, thus instigating their next bout of fucking. As the lovers writhe on the bed, Jeanne Moreau narrates on the soundtrack, "I think . . . he's used to it. This is what he does in life. He makes love, nothing else. Obviously I'm very lucky. It's as if it were his profession." Even his status as a jobless playboy who doesn't have to lift a finger to maintain his extravagant lifestyle, this unproductiveness is resignified and reconfigured by his hand, as an organ of love and labor, pivotal to his true profession of love. The young girl's attribution to her Chinese lover the profession of "love, nothing else" sounds as if he himself were the prostitute, in surrendering his body to her in exchange for love.[25] The catalyst for sexual activity in these scenes is the agency of the hand—feeling, exploring, guiding, discovering, recognizing. The modality of touch repairs the break in relationality that shame activates. Conventionally signaling purposelessness and hence susceptibility to vice, his idle hands in this case become gratifying and profitable for the both of them.

Witness the tension and negotiation in the play of power between the two lovers in the first, and most spectacular, sex scene. Adopting the part usually ascribed to the female partner in the conventional romance, the Chinese lover fears that physical intimacy will lead to emotional attachment. When they first arrive at his bachelor flat in Cholon, looking down, he confesses, "I'm afraid. . . . I'm afraid of loving you." In response, the girl requests that he follow the script: "I'd rather you didn't love me. I want you to do as you usually do with other women." Although taken aback by her directness, he undresses her and carries her to the bed, while he himself remains fully clothed in his immaculate white suit. The camera dollies in closer for a better look at her completely nude body as he leans over it. However, unable to continue playing the part of the masculine seducer, he sits up and looks away from her. The voice-over explains: "Once on the bed, he's overcome by fear. He says she lied to him, that she's too young, that he can't do such a thing." Another reversal occurs in this scene in which the man's greater sexual experience incapacitates him. Instead of being passionately ravished by the male lover of paperback romance, here the virginal young girl takes the lead. The dangerous itinerary of taboo interracial sex is identified and traced by her curious, searching female hand on his soft masculine body. With her eyes closed, she unbuttons his shirt, kisses his chest, removes the sleeves one by one, while we see him throw his head back in profile, eyes closed. As Moreau intones on the soundtrack ("The skin!"), a close-up frames his supine hairless torso as her hand travels from his smooth chest with its dark erect nipples down to his crotch (figure 3.6). Sitting up on the bed, she reaches down and unbuttons his white slacks and puts her hand under the fabric, as he dramatically inhales, causing his lean stomach to shrink and his skinny ribs to protrude. The female voice of experience narrates the scene: "The skin is of a sumptuous softness; the body is hairless without any virility at all other than that of the sex. She doesn't look him in

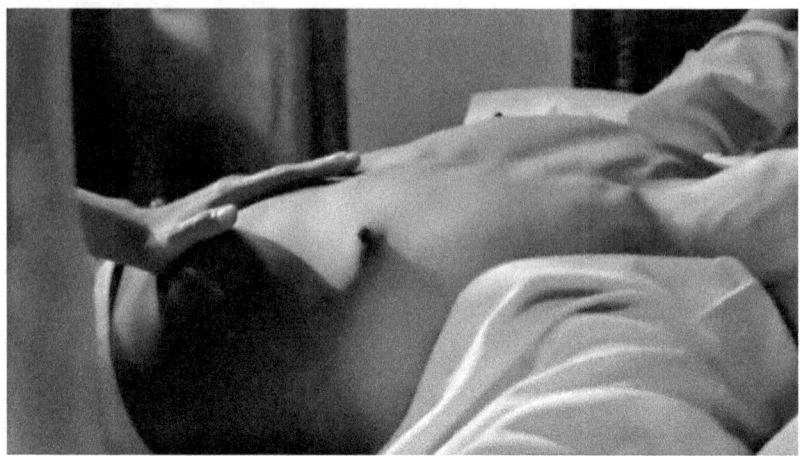

FIGURE 3.6: Her hand on his torso. *The Lover* (1992).

the face. She touches him. She touches the softness of the sex, of the skin. She caresses the golden hue. The unknown novelty." The camera cuts back to a close-up on his face, eyes closed, head thrown back on the pillow. Next, he sits up to kiss her shoulder and mouth. The camera then cuts to a medium shot to show him fully nude for the first time, seen from behind, his body on top of hers, in between her legs thrusting slowly and rhythmically.

With her eyes closed as she undresses and caresses his body, the sense of touch is privileged over the sense of sight, with its common associations with objectification and aggressivity; her hand on his soft, sumptuous body awakens and activates desire in both of them.[26] The maneuvers of the hand— her hand disrobing him and sliding underneath his pants to touch the "only" virile part of his body—function as a binding instrument. His hand reaching across in the limousine earlier is here answered by hers reaching under to meet his sex, also blindly, with face turned away. The movements of hands (reaching out, across, down) and their withdrawal (back, away, into), from trembling and shy to bold and gripping, demonstrate their centrality in these critical scenes of the lovers' meeting across shame and into desire, in which traditional dichotomies of passive and active, pleasured and pleasuring, self and other are temporarily destabilized. As Sedgwick reminds us in *Touching Feeling*, "the sense of touch makes nonsense out of any dualistic understanding of agency and passivity; to touch is always already to reach out, to fondle, to heft, to tap, or to enfold, and always also to understand other people or natural forces as having effectually done so before oneself" (2003, 14).²⁷ The link between touch, shame, and eroticism also calls to mind Leo Bersani's formulation of the hand as the instrument that foregrounds "the limits of power." Although his comments concern the little boy's early lesson in the pleasure associated with a divestiture of power, Bersani's argument offers us a powerful impetus to rethink questions of passivity and agency: "in masturbation the hand produces an excitement indissociable from a certain form of surrender, from, ultimately, a loss of control" (1995, 101).²⁸ In submitting to the other's caress, grip, hold, the two lovers bare themselves; they relinquish self-control by putting themselves in each other's hands.

To be sure, it is vital that the two protagonists' rapprochement across and through "shame consciousness" is here executed through the shedding of clothes. This risky act constitutes the lovers' passage from shame to shamelessness, from self-protection to self-exposure. Richard Dyer observes that nakedness invariably entails vulnerability, in terms of exposure to "the elements" as well as social vulnerability. He elucidates, "Clothes are bearers of prestige, notable of wealth, status, and class; to be without them is to lose privilege. Nakedness also reveals the inadequacies of most bodies by comparison with social ideals of both the female and male body" (Dyer 1997, 299). It is the revelation of the two lovers' naked flesh that enables their overcoming of social shame. While the young girl's white, nubile body remains unremarked upon in both the book and the film, as embodied by Jane March it is clearly a conventionally beautiful body that unmistakably conforms to the social ideal. However, as we witnessed above, it is the Chinese man's body—fleshed out by the slim, toned physique of Leung—that fails to live up to the social ideal of the (white) male built body. It is the female protagonist's desire and lust for his vulnerable, socially inadequate, "feminine" body that reconfigures his racialized, feminizing shame into, not pride, but pleasure, the pleasure of submission.

An examination of vulnerability and shame as mediated through the modalities of specularity and touch in Alain Resnais's classic art film, *Hiroshima Mon Amour* (1959), will provide us further insight into complex interplay of power and desire in *The Lover*. Based on a screenplay by Duras, *Hiroshima* constitutes an important intertext for Annaud's film with its treatment of similar themes such as interracial desire, French female sexuality, and Asian masculinity. To be sure, *Hiroshima* demonstrates a much more nuanced exploration of these issues with its nonlinear, avant-garde formal structure and a narrative that draws on multiple historical, social, and political contexts. It is clear, however, that the dynamics of power and the appeal of its surrender are just as complexly rendered in *The Lover*. Interestingly, the hand plays a critical role in *Hiroshima*'s scenes of the lovers' coming together and drawing apart. As in *The Lover*, hands erotically bind characters and effect a breach in that productive binding, thus showing that the sense of touch can be comforting as well as terrorizing.

Emmanuelle Riva plays a French actress (referred to as She) who comes to Hiroshima to act in a film about peace. While there, she has an affair with Eiji Okada (He) that sparks memories of another affair with another forbidden, foreign other in a different time and place: her first love, a young German soldier, during World War II in occupied France. During a thirty-six-hour period, She and He engage in an extended dialogue about their respective pasts and presents, hers in Nevers and his in Hiroshima, as they move in, through, across the hotel rooms, ruins, squares, streets, restaurants, cafés, and monuments of Hiroshima as well as the interior and exterior spaces of Nevers, France (portrayed via disruptive flashback sequences). Ultimately, the film deploys the overdetermined site of Hiroshima to meditate on the potentialities and limits of desire, memory, knowledge, and representation *tout court*.

The film's justly famous opening sequence foregrounds the ways collective memory and individual history, group violence and personal shame intermingle, vis-à-vis the modalities of specularity and touch. *Hiroshima* begins with a series of medium close-ups of fragmented, writhing limbs covered in thick coatings of glittering ashes that gradually dissolve to images of limbs soaked with glistening sweat. The viewing experience is disconcerting and destabilizing as one is not quite sure what one is looking at and how these limbs are connected to one another: a bicep, an upper arm, a shoulder, an elbow, a back, a thigh, a hand, fingers. It is not until the end of the sequence that one makes out a darker arm wrapped around a lighter-skinned back and sees that it's two people embracing—whether in love (sweat) or in death (ashes) remains unclear. As this ambiguous image dissolves into one depicting a broad back with two hands clutching the top of it, we hear on the soundtrack an incantatory voice-over:

>HE: You saw nothing in Hiroshima. Nothing.
>SHE: I saw everything. Everything. I saw the hospital—I'm sure of it. The hospital in Hiroshima exists. How could I not have seen it?

HE: You didn't see the hospital in Hiroshima. You saw nothing in Hiroshima.

From the outset, the viewer's attempt to comprehend and grasp the visual and verbal information proffered by the film is frustrated. Our doubt and misapprehension do not give way to knowledge and certainty, even as the ambiguous interior shots of the two partners' lovemaking suddenly switch to newsreel documentary footage of Hiroshima. A verbal rhythmic pattern emerges counterposing the woman's verbal assertions and the man's negations of her claim to sight, experience, knowledge, and understanding, which is echoed by the visual alternation between the lovers' passionate sexual embrace and the Hiroshima victims' intense physical suffering. Due to such visual alternation, the spectacle of the lovers' exposed, intertwining limbs eroticizes the violent imagery of the ruins of Hiroshima.

Specularity in *Hiroshima* simultaneously reassures and menaces. The wholeness of the lovers' body parts—their sexual merging, their love story— is threatened by the sights of Hiroshima, in particular, the bodily disfigurations of its residents: his smooth, strong, expansive back finds a visual echo in a man's back that is horribly burned and scarred; her fingers passionately gripping his back are juxtaposed against images of forceps wiping a small child's hand riddled with sores and a young girl's hand with twisted and deformed fingers; and her persistent claims of seeing and knowing are repeatedly scored over images of subjects deprived of sight (blind children and women with blank expressions). To be sure, pleasure also saturates our viewing of the exposure of the lovers' flesh and that of the Hiroshima victims' due to the masterful avant-garde aesthetics of the film, renowned and canonized in world cinema for its innovation in cinematography, editing, and narrative structure, even as it thematizes the difficulty and impossibility in accessing pleasure in seeing and knowing. Her fetishization of his Japanese male body ("You have such beautiful skin") activates desire but also conjures up pain and loss: the atomic destruction of Hiroshima and, as we find out later, the death of her German lover.[29]

Indeed, the hand and its sense of touch occupy center stage in these scenes. From the start, we are forced to perceive haptically, since we cannot make out what the limbs are doing, how they connect and relate, to whom they belong. In the museum sequence, an omniscient bird's-eye view of a diorama model of Hiroshima transforms into close-ups of scorched metals, melted bottle caps, pieces of human flesh preserved in jars, and mounds of human hair, views that animate a tactile vision. It is as if these textures of skin, flesh, and body parts constituted evidence of the woman's knowledge, anchoring our perception of the sequence, while at the same time revealing a certain opacity. These images' textures and layers of meanings are too dense and too close to make out and fully comprehend. Her persistent claims ("I saw"; "I know"; "I am endowed with memory") finally admit defeat ("I forgot") and give way to submission and surrender: "You're destroying me. You're good for me. . . . Please devour me. Deform me to the point of ugliness." Even as she tries to shore up her authority to speak by establishing the commonalities between them ("Like you, I know what it is to forget. . . . Like you, I too have struggled with all my might"), her shameful past affair with the German lover haunts and overwhelms her present liaison with the Japanese. For his part, the national shame of being on the losing side, the shame of being decimated by the atomic bomb, paradoxically provides him with the authority to challenge her claim to occupy the privileged center. As in *The Lover*, the two characters in *Hiroshima* creatively transfigure their past histories of shame into sexual heat in their present love affair.

A powerful image punctuates her assertions and her subsequent capitulation: the newsreel footage returns again and again to shots of her disembodied hands clutching his broad, smooth back.[30] His strong back becomes a smooth, blank screen onto which she projects her story of love and shame. Her hands gripping his bare back in sex bespeak control, need, and desire, as well as loss, desperation, and submission. But even in her surrender, the story of *Hiroshima* remains hers to narrate. Her hands actively dictate the rhythm of the sequence, whereas his passive, sleeping hand (in a later shot) conjures up the dead hand of the German lover. This graphic match becomes embodied by the film's end when the Japanese man responds to the woman in the German lover's voice. Yet, by then, we still know very little about the Japanese and his backstory. Ultimately, she retains narrative authority while ostensibly giving it up. Her repetitive assertions of having seen everything in Hiroshima can be read as an attempt to disavow the shame of not knowing, that is, the shame that constitutes her subjectivity. Although a similarly authoritative female voice is also found in *The Lover* (registered by Jeanne Moreau's evocative voice-over narration), a more dynamic negotiation of power occurs in *The Lover* than in *Hiroshima*, especially during the former's sex scenes. The potent receptivity of the Chinese lover's back, and ass, takes pride of place in these negotiations.

FIGURE 3.7: The lover's gorgeous ass. *The Lover* (1992).

Mounting Tony Leung's "Gorgeous Ass"

At the beginning of the chapter, I noted that the intense anxiety activated by the sight of an Asian man fucking an adolescent girl is managed by reviewers in their dismissals of the film as soft-core porn; in effect, their dismissals function as an act of shaming the actors for daring to perform such sex acts onscreen.[31] A similar process of shaming, this time directed solely at the Asian male lead, can be witnessed in the excessive concentration on Leung's Oriental rear end, a preoccupation articulated by the camera's unrelenting focus on his naked bottom. Conforming to mainstream cinema's sexual double standard, *The Lover* displays quite a bit of female flesh (March's nude body is displayed in all its back-and-frontal glory) during the love scenes, which take up more than twenty minutes of the one-hour-and-fifty-two-minute film. Yet the film never once gives us a glimpse of Leung's soft, golden novelty, his sex. Instead, it offers the viewer the usual signifiers of parted lips, glistening beads of sweat, and abstract close-ups of conjoined body parts, as well as, very unusually, Leung's naked ass, which "play[s] a major role" in the film (Bernard 1992, 29). Interestingly, even as the Chinese lover gets on top, the viewer can only make out his bottom (figure 3.7).[32]

The Lover's sensual showcase of Leung's bare buttocks revises conventional representational codes of sexual verisimilitude. According to Mandy Merck, pornographic realism depends not on narrative credibility or psychological subtlety; rather, the question turns on the actuality of the sex act itself. She notes that porn realism is based on "nudity, genital conjunction and, conventionally in men's porn, the 'come shot'" (Merck 2000, 141). Similarly, in her influential study of hard-core pornography, Linda Williams traces the development of the "quest for greater knowledge of the truth of pleasure" from the stag film's "genital show" (the exhibition of hidden body parts), to the "genital event" of the "meat shot" (genital penetration) embedded in some sort of narrative, and finally the convention of the "money shot" (the male's visible coming) in order to provide proof of sexual pleasure (1989, 181).[33] Adapting these two critics' insights, one might say that in addition to the two leads' nudity and the proximity of their bodies, sexual realism in *The Lover* is also firmly located in Leung's "gorgeous ass . . . pumping away between Marsh's [sic] coltish legs" (Brown 1992, 84).[34] As *Time* magazine movie critic Richard Corliss states, "Her back arches as prettily as the chords in the lush background music. His buttocks tense as his passion surges" (1992, 70).[35] Corliss simultaneously accounts for the condensation and displacement of Williams's genital show and genital event, wherein the tensing of the fully visible backside is directly linked with a surging of passion, or more precisely, the surging (forward) of the obstructed, invisible full frontal. The reader might protest that there is no notable difference in the exhibition of Leung's rear end in the love scenes here from those of love scenes in other mainstream films where (non-Asian) men's buttocks are shown to signify the honesty of the sex act, due to the fact that frontal male nudity still operates as a social and industrial taboo. I would rejoin by stressing that Leung's buttocks take on an entirely different function here. Unlike the exhibition of white actors' asses, Leung's is expected to do double duty due to the fact that the Asian penis is almost never found in Western cinema, whether in the licit genres of Hollywood film or the illicit genre of pornography.[36]

From the first sex scene at the Chinese lover's bachelor apartment, the organ of love and labor is transfigured from the trembling hand to the tense buttocks. Above we witnessed the multiple itineraries taken by the hand to connect the lovers across their mutual shame. It is clear that Asian male sexual prowess is managed by the camera's (and viewers') overwhelming interest in his naked buttocks. Here, we encounter the crucial element linking the extended hand and the exposed bottom: the sense of touch and the ways it "makes nonsense out of any dualistic understanding of agency and passivity" (to recall Sedgwick's compelling formulation). The groping hand's sensitivity to surfaces and textures redirects our interest from the blocked penis to the sensational display of the smooth buttocks. The Chinese lover's bottomhood functions not only as an instance of shaming, but also constitutes a shameful position available for readjustment and revisioning. Whereas the sight of naked male asses (whether actual or imagined) provokes in some heterosexual men intense anxiety of (homosexual) emasculation, rape, or, simply, gay male sex,[37] for other viewers the sight of male asses produces a different set of possibilities. More so than any part of the male body, the male ass derives its erotic charge from the combination of power and vulnerability: the buttocks' strong, taut musculature is qualified by the asshole's potential for penetrability.

My claim finds support in Molly Haskell's feminist analysis of the Chinese man's nakedness. She interprets the depiction of his bare buttocks as Annaud's attempt to portray the woman's viewpoint in her lust for and appreciation of a male body. The director, she suggests, makes the Chinese man's "skin palpable to us, the back above all as somehow innocent, vulnerable, unaware" (Haskell 1992, 33). Echoing the depiction of the Japanese man's broad, smooth back in *Hiroshima Mon Amour*, Haskell's reference to the palpability of skin in *The Lover* conjures not only the soft, sumptuous texture of Asian male skin (as expressed in the stereotype of smooth Asian skin and Duras's feminist reworking of it). More radically, Haskell intimates that the film encourages us to put ourselves in the Chinese lover's skin in this scene of sexual congress, to recognize his innocence and vulnerability, to be sure, but, more importantly, to sense our own body opening up to receive another's desiring touch. This marking out of a space for the viewer's cohabitation with a character saturated with shame is very different from some critics' readings of the Chinese man's sexual penetration of the young girl as a recuperation of his masculinity, as an evacuation of shame.[38] Haskell adds, "The lover allows himself to be *caught from behind*" (1992, 33, emphasis added). This last sentence indicates an invitation to desire the Chinese male body, a body that offers itself up to be caught from behind, that is, to be seen, held, penetrated. In effect, the constitutive frisson of *The Lover's* sex scenes rests firmly in the Asian man's backside. At the same time that the Chinese man and the young French girl give, and receive, sexual pleasure via the strategic conjunction of their genitals, the viewer obtains pleasure from watching his behind thrusting rhythmically between her legs. Getting on top, he simultaneously offers up his bottom for the viewer's visual-tactile consideration. In mounting the Chinese lover's ass, the sequence collapses the hierarchy between phallic penetration and anal receptivity. Leung's ass covers and blocks March's genital area while at the same time exposing itself to our tactile vision, surrendering to our desire and pleasure in seeing and feeling what an Asian man in the throes of sex looks like.

The cinematic pleasure in being sexually solicited by Tony Leung's ass, as I am tracing it here, finds support in the work of scholars such as Vivian Sobchack and Laura Marks, who employ a phenomenological perspective to explore "embodiment relations" in moving-image media. For example, Marks advances a theory of haptic visuality as a bodily relationship between the viewer and the image, whereby "the eyes themselves function like organs of touch" (2002, 2). In contrast to optical visuality, a mode that entails distance between beholder and object and encourages identification and projection, haptic visuality operates more on proximity and invites an embodied perception.[39] Marks's intervention into Lacanian-based film spectatorship studies challenges routine observations about visual pleasure, masculine and feminine positionings, agency and passivity, desire and identification. A serious consideration of tactile visuality forces us to move beyond conventional theorizations about cinematic identification and visual objectification to a more capacious model of cinematic engagement that embraces "a series of *mediated* exchanges between our bodies, the film's body, and the bodies on the screen" (Williams 2006, 328). Incorporating all of these bodily negotiations into our reading of Asian masculinity in *The Lover* allows us to imagine other possibilities besides a hard, exit-only brand of masculine body, one that rigorously disavows its anal permeability. Perceiving haptically, working to reconstitute the image, one senses and makes sense that Leung's trembling ass opens up other ways for thinking about not just Asian masculinity but masculinities at large.

Shifting our attention for a moment from the Asian American context that has delimited my discussion of the film, let us consider the casting of Leung as the Chinese lover. Annaud's choice for his male lead certainly draws on the transnational popularity of Hong Kong cinema in the late 1980s and 1990s, as can be seen in the international popular and critical recognition of such directors as Stanley Kwan, Wong Kar-wai, Ann Hui, Tsui Hark, John Woo, and others. In light of our present focus on gender and sexuality in *The Lover*, we might point to the explorations of gender-bending in such movies as *Peking Opera Blues* (dir. Tsui Hark, 1986), *Swordsman II* (dir. Ching Siu-Tung, 1992), *The Lovers* (dir. Tsui Hark, 1994), and *He's a Woman, She's a Man* (dir. Peter Chan, 1994), and the treatment of homosexuality in such films as *Oh! My Three Guys* (dir. Derek Chiu, 1994) and *Boy's?* (dir. Hau Wing-choi, 1996). Writing about the queering of masculinity in these Hong Kong films,

Travis Kong (2005, 67) notes the increasing visibility of "gender-blending," "homosocial overcoat," and overt representations of gay male homosexuality. The destabilization of conventional masculinity in Hong Kong cinema during the same period as *The Lover*'s production and reception offers another valuable perspective to bring to our analysis of Leung's performance. Indeed, before his appearance in *The Lover*, Leung's credits include roles in such action films as *Prison on Fire* (dir. Ringo Lam, 1987) and *A Better Tomorrow 3* (dir. Tsui Hark, 1989). In these two violent movies set in male-dominated environments (prisons, wars, arms dealing), Leung costarred with Chow Yun-fat in storylines that privilege intense homosocial male bonding between the two male leads. Kong suggests that the loosening of conventional formations of Chinese masculinity can be understood through "two intertwining ideals—the *wen* ideal ('cultured behavior, refinement, mastery of scholarly work') and the *wu* ideal ('martial prowess, strength, mastery of physical arts')" (2005, 67). Whereas the *wu* ideal accounts for the homosocial bonding found in Hong Kong male buddy action films, the *wen* ideal might explain the softer, desexualized brand of masculinity commonly attributed to Chinese men, especially when examined according to a Western standard. Interestingly, neither model can adequately explain the Chinese lover's bottomhood; he would appear to fail to measure up to both *wen* and *wu* ideals. In a fascinating essay examining these ideals, Julian Stringer analyzes the transformation of the representation of masculinity in the male buddy action films of John Woo through the lens of 1997, the year of the handover of the territory from the United Kingdom to China. Focusing on *A Better Tomorrow* (1986) and *The Killer* (1989), Stringer argues that the two films combine the male action genre and the female melodrama genre, or in his words, "doing" and "suffering" genres, whereby one finds macho male protagonists who perform hostile and violent acts while at the same time undergoing extreme emotional agony. Stringer attributes the mixing of sadistic and masochistic modes to Hong Kong's looming political uncertainty, which "produced narratives of loss, alienation and doubt, imprinting upon many movies the traits of an anxiety" (1997, 25). I do not mean to imply a one-to-one correspondence between Stringer's thesis and Annaud's casting of Leung; rather, I contend that the decisive change in the representation of Hong Kong masculinity must be kept in mind as part of the visual constellation of how Asian masculinity is produced and understood in a globalizing mediascape.

Hong Kong cinematic portrayals of alternative masculinities in the 1980s and 1990s offer us one historically and culturally specific reference for the analysis of Tony Leung's bare buttocks in *The Lover*. American genre cinema of the 1970s provides another crucial comparative perspective. Cinematic representation of black male sexual potency, to invoke another prominent model of racialized masculinity, has also focused on men's uncovered behinds. In addition to the famous pumping ass of Melvin Van Peebles in his blaxploitation classic *Sweet Sweetback Baadasssss Song* (dir. Melvin Van Peebles, 1971), we can also point to boxer Ken Norton's powerful buttocks generously displayed in the blaxploitation-inspired plantation drama *Mandingo* (dir. Richard Fleischer, 1975). These spectacular black male asses function as visible signs of black male sexual prowess in a cycle of films that deploy such sexual power as a key element in the struggle against white racism. On the one hand, the exposure of muscular, imposing black male buttocks confirms Darieck Scott's observation that the category of "black male" evokes a "position at once hypermasculine and feminine, exemplifying an erection/castration paradox" (2010, 19); furthermore, "racialization is accomplished through subjugation by containing or marginalizing threats of *penetration* to black male figures" (19, emphasis in original). In other words, this exhibition of black male asses does reveal a certain feminine vulnerability. On the other hand, a strong case can be made that the overwhelming spotlight on the black man's backside in these films works to displace the threat (and hold out the promise) of the imaginary big black phallus lurking on the front side.[40] For example, in an analysis of the interracial sex scene between the slave Mede (Norton) and his mistress Blanche (Susan George) in *Mandingo*, Linda Williams (2004) points out that the camera directs a persistent gaze on Norton's muscular rear end; his body is visually privileged over hers.[41] If we compare this scene to the first sex scene between Leung and March in *The Lover*, we find a striking difference in the appearance and function of the exposed male buttocks. Whereas camera placement and mise-en-scène in *Mandingo* exaggerate the black man's disproportionate mass towering over the white woman's diminutive frame, in *The Lover* cinematic techniques show the two protagonists' bodies corresponding more closely in size and proportion to one another.[42] Instead of the tall black slave visually dominating his white mistress in *Mandingo*, in *The Lover* it is the virginal young girl who looms over the older, more experienced Chinese man's supine torso, she who reaches down to touch the "softness of the sex." The different roles taken up by the black male slave and the Chinese lover in their respective interracial sex scenes demonstrate how racialized masculinities play out differently: the black man readily adopts the role of the dominant masculine lover; the Asian man performs in a shy and hesitant fashion. It is not until the female partner sexually initiates and gets on top that he actively responds. As noted, the viewer is continually reminded of his precarious sexual agency via the camera's concentration on his moving buttocks. Confronted with the sight of his buttocks looming above and between her spread legs, the viewer beholds the Chinese lover's sexual prowess for the first time. Leung's ass is "gorgeous" due to its leanness, litheness, and graceful quality. Low-key lighting and a three-quarter perspective dramatically articulate the sinuous lines and supple curves from back to ass to thigh to calf and up the other side. The slow, intense, rhythmic thrusts of Leung's clenched ass cheeks further accentuate their striking tautness. However, instead of offering ocular proof of phallic endowment (albeit displaced a few inches from front to back) as in the case of bare black male asses, the insistent focus on the Chinese lover's uncovered behind—both by the camera and by critics and viewers—would seem to back up the dominant view of the Asian male's small, negligible, or otherwise nonexistent penis.

Let us tease out the differing racial resonances between penis and buttocks in order to interrogate a critical framework that can only glean from the site of an Asian ass a sign of Asian male lack, evidence of a small, negligible, missing Asian penis. In his work on the sexual representation of the male body in Hollywood cinema and the wider realm of visual culture, Peter Lehman observes that patriarchal society maintains itself in the ways it "dominates, restricts, prohibits, and controls the representation of the male body, particularly its sexual representation" (1993, 9)—that is, by specifically veiling the penis. He goes on to say, "The awe surrounding the penis in a patriarchal culture depends on either keeping it hidden from sight . . . or carefully regulating its representation" (28). A cursory look at the enduring taboo against male nudity in mainstream Hollywood cinema strongly confirms Lehman's insight about the policing of penises in visual culture. The restrictive, and sexually prudish, Motion Picture Association of American (MPAA) ratings system commonly assigns any film containing a glimpse of a flaccid penis an R rating (all viewers under age seventeen must be accompanied by an adult). A sight of an erect penis would automatically guarantee an NC-17 (viewers must be age eighteen and over), a rating that severely limits the film's commercial theatrical release.[43] In comparison to the much more flexible standards for female nudity, Hollywood's strict regulation of the visual spectacle of the penis constitutes compelling evidence of a sexist, patriarchal, and heteronormative regime of sexual representation. Not surprisingly, this regime caters to the heteromasculinist desires and visual pleasures of those accorded political, economic, and social power, a power that is "hidden from sight" but regarded as unquestioned common sense. Indeed, this phallic visual economy masquerading as invisibility and absence structures the manner in which the Chinese lover's wounded masculinity and erotic expertise are comprehended in *The Lover*: his "gorgeous ass" signifies his "racial castration" *and* his sexual potency. Such a manifestation shows that, as a result of the cultural interdiction against full frontal male nudity, the male ass has come to stand in for male sexual prowess in the movies. But as my discussion of black and Asian asses above intimates, exposed male buttocks on movie screens contain different racial valences.[44]

Lehman aims to articulate and thus to demystify the link between phallus as powerful patriarchal symbol and penis as pathetic literal organ. He advocates for making the vulnerable, "real" small penis visible in order to displace the fantastic, incredible large penises on display in genres such as pornography. As we have seen, North American pornography—the one arena where penises are accorded visibility—equips white men with large cocks and black men with larger-than-life ones. To follow the logic of Lehman's exposure-and-demystification argument, to uncover and verify the "fact" of the small (Asian) penis would constitute an effective gesture of dismantling (white) patriarchy. Yet in privileging small over large and advocating for transparency over opacity, Lehman's project is ultimately interested in assimilating into another normative standard of valuation, rather than postulating a new, transformative politics of representation. In other words, it remains caught within a heteronormative framework that sees and assigns sexual subjectivity and gender identity according to the presence or absence of a penis. A phallocentrism persists that can establish sexual subjectivity only in and from the penis. Thus, although I appreciate Lehman's endeavor to shed light on the invisible workings of patriarchy by severing the link between size and power, I find his reliance on the revelation of the taboo penis, "that much-shamed organ" (Bersani 1995, 101), as the tool for undoing patriarchal authority a limited, short-sighted strategy. As gay male critics such as Bersani, Guy Hocquenghem, Lee Edelman, and D. A. Miller have demonstrated, the eroticization of the male anus represents much more of a threat to the social order than exposing the "phallacy" of the big powerful cock.[45] Furthermore, lesbian theorist Sally Munt reminds us that the anus, as "the marker of sexual *indifference*," has the potential to undermine the "edifice of gender differentiation intrinsic to heterosexuality" (1997, 209, emphasis in original).⁴⁶ To problematize Lehman's optimistic investment in making the racially unmarked penis visible, I examine a pivotal scene in *The Lover* in which the reassertion of Asian masculine authority is accomplished through an aggressive displacement of feminizing shame. On the one hand, this move corroborates Lehman's observation that phallic power depends on masking the male body; on the other, it simultaneously necessitates the veiling of the Asian ass so prominently displayed in the film's prior sex scenes. By blocking Leung's gorgeous ass, the scene reinstates the Chinese lover, if only temporarily, into the domain of normative masculinity, where men wield their ability to penetrate, to fuck, as a demonstration of their sexual and social prerogative. At the same time, such an act denies the power and pleasure of the fuckable ass, its receptivity to penetration that allows for an alternative, and more fulfilling, route to social agency.

The rape scene warrants particular consideration because it does not appear in either of Duras's texts (*The Lover* and *The North China Lover*) but constitutes an intervention on the part of Annaud and his co-screenwriter Gérard Brach. The scene takes place directly after the restaurant and dance hall sequence in which the Chinese lover is humiliated by the girl, her mother, and two brothers, who, while gorging on the expensive food and drink paid for by the lover, refuse to speak to him, and thus to recognize and acknowledge him as an equal. As the female narrator explains, "In my family's presence, he ceases to be my lover. . . . He becomes a reason to be ashamed of, that has to be hidden." At the dance hall, the older brother derisively snickers at the Chinese man for dancing with his sister. In response to the brother's challenge that it would take "at least two of you" to fight with him, the Chinese man retorts, "It would take four of me, you mean. You have no idea how weak I am."⁴⁷ The public declaration of his extreme weakness demonstrates a refusal to engage within the terms of the older brother's aggressive, hysterical masculinity and appears consistent with the elegant and fragile comportment of the Chinese man. In the following scene at his bachelor apartment, this embrace of castration is fiercely repudiated as the lover exacts revenge for his public humiliation. Striking the girl across the face and knocking her down on the bed, he proceeds to pull off her panties and, while still wearing his impeccable dark suit, brutally rapes her. The addition of the rape scene fundamentally breaks with the depiction of the Chinese man's wounded masculinity up to this point in the film. The insertion of a scene of sexual violation rewrites the lover from a figure who is treasured precisely for his softness and femininity into a weak, inadequate char-

FIGURE 3.8: Head averted. *The Lover* (1992).

acter who is intent on redeeming his failed manhood by resorting to physical force and sexual violence.

In the restaurant scene, the Chinese lover's presence in front of her family threatens to expose the girl's dirty secret, highlighting her shameful desire. Disowning her own shame founded in this very familial scene ("Our common history of ruin and shame, of love and hate is in my flesh"), she effaces it by projecting it onto the lover: "because he's Chinese, because he's not white . . . he becomes a reason to be ashamed of." His sexual assault acts as retaliation for her refusal to uphold their bottom alliance. Earlier in the film, the clasping of hands in the limousine represents a binding in which the mutual recognition of the other's vulnerability to being shamed is redirected and transformed into attraction, lust, and desire for the other. In the restaurant and dance hall sequence's violent aftermath, his hand striking across her face effects a breach in their contract. This brutal gesture demonstrates the terrorizing force of touch, thus pointing to the limits of claims for its desired sensuality. Some touches are unwanted; others cannot be felt or responded to. As Iain Morland argues, "Touch and tactility are not the same; the former is an action, whereas the latter is a sense. Hence a body can touch without tactility, for instance, if one's hands are numb from exposure to cold weather" (2009, 296). This scene of sexual violation is depicted generically, in a very matter-of-fact manner, as if it were a business transaction. His assaultive, instrumentalizing touch is silently tolerated by her passive, supine body. The Chinese lover's pinning of shame onto the French girl is reinforced cinematically. Throughout the rape, the camera adopts an unflinching high-angle medium close-up on the girl's face. Obliterated by his shadow, she closes her eyes, looks to the side off into space, twirls her hair, her face flushed (figure 3.8). His aggressive thrusting is relegated off-scene, ob-scene. While the close up on her mute face encourages the viewer's identification with the young girl's traumatized state, the use of the close-up renders the rape scene generic and conventional in its clear articulation of male violence and female victimhood, that is, a gender binarism that has been contested throughout the film.[48] Unlike the previous sex scenes with their scandalous showcase of the two actors' nude bodies, the fact that both remain fully clothed (except for her panties and his unbuttoned fly) further underscores the violence and shamefulness of this sex act. It is precisely through careful camera framing and discreet costuming that a relationship of male power and female powerlessness is established. The veiling of the male body in the scene transforms the small, negligible Asian penis into a dangerous, threatening phallus capable of inflicting sexual violence. By the same token, the covering of the vulnerable, permeable Asian ass prevents us from seeing Asian masculinity embodied alternatively, toward a wholly different, deviant end.

Licking the Lack

A disarmingly simple narrative involving money, sex, love, and colonialism constitutes Duras's novel and Annaud's film adaptation. As the young girl puts it at one point in the film, "They say I'm a slut who goes to the shady part of town to have her body fondled by a Chinaman." Toward the conclusion of the movie, when the two lovers attempt to come to terms with the inevitable ending of their affair, the Chinese man holds her face in his hands and asks her to recite the script to their relationship, its raison d'être: "I want you to say it to me once. You came here so that I'd give you money." In their citations, these two synopses of the interracial affair concede the "'necessarily "aberrant" relation' between a performative utterance and its meaning" (Crimp 2002a, 64). Stated differently, these two attempts to reduce their relationship to one of prostitution, lust, or love, reveal the excess, the infelicity of these utterances themselves. These multiple enunciations, or quotations, bear out critics' observations that throughout her career, Duras repeatedly revisits this primal story of forbidden love, reworking it in different genres. One key function of the intertextuality of these cover stories is that a knowing self-reflexivity becomes attached to the shocking elements of the narrative. It is precisely the transparency and lack of depth in the film's quotations, citations, and iterations of the same old story that denaturalizes its own performance and reveals its own sensational staging. To wit, when she makes a declaration such as "I don't like Chinese very much" or when he follows suit with, "If I wanted to marry you, well, it would not be allowed. We can't tolerate the idea of that," they do so over a lavish dinner in a fancy restaurant. These gleeful pronouncements reveal a certain enjoyment in their defiance of social rules and regulations. But even as they acknowledge these public restrictions, they do so by relishing their freedom in pushing against these social regulations. These performative reiterations of immoral transgressions of racial and sexual boundaries must be kept in mind as part of the critical effects of Duras's text. Although some critics read the young girl's disavowals of love for the Chinese lover as unerring proof of the girl's racist affirmation, her ultimate allegiance to the colonial order, by contrast, I would argue that the young girl's schematic recounting of the affair—"a slut who goes to the shady part of town to have her body fondled by a Chinaman"—trades precisely on the violation of multiple taboos (racial, sexual, class, and age) that gives the affair its erotic intensity. Hence, one might say that the young girl's obviously sexist and racist rendering of the affair between a little white slut and a filthy Chinaman operates as an ironic and mocking explanation for their mutual lust and love over the years, an enduring attraction fueled by fear and desire, shame and shamelessness.

Writing on the carnal knowledge gleaned from interracial relationships cultivated in European colonial and imperial contexts, Stoler posits that "sex was not a leveling mechanism but a site in which social asymmetries were instantiated and expressed" (2002, 57). Similarly, Williams argues that "all depictions of interracial lust develop out of the relations of inequality that have prevailed between the races" (2004, 302). Yet Williams importantly acknowledges that interracial sexual couplings do allow for "transgressive erotic recognitions across racial difference" (292). In this chapter, I have attempted to account for both lines of analysis by examining the scenes of sexual congress between the two lovers, effected through and across the mutual recognition of racial and sexual shame. This recognition develops out of their being marginalized and privileged, but each in their own way due to their specific social positioning. In particular, I have foregrounded the deviant masculinity of the Chinese lover which, though steeped in shameful bottomhood, nevertheless functions as a vital catalyst for the lovers' emotional bind and sexual passion.

The voluptuous, tactile moving image of Leung's exposed backside inspires a new itinerary for the study of Asian American sexual representation, what Elizabeth Freeman in a different context has labeled a "'bottom' historiography" that confers value on the "transmission of receptivity" (2005, 64). Instead of looking for, and locating, Asian masculinity in the penis, one would do better to grope around, and behind, for that gorgeous Asian ass. Gazing at Leung's bare buttocks, one critic observes, "You get to see an awful lot of them . . . for what must be 100 of the movie's 103 minutes. The other three are for the credits and a couple of establishing shots" (Bernard 1992, 29). Inspired by this critic's hyperbolic anal vision, I urge us to quit bemoaning Asian men's absence "down there," to lick the lack and consume what is already there, overwhelmingly present in all of its contradictory effects and thrilling potentialities. My affirmative reading of bottomhood transforms the trembling hand into a winking ass, one that advertises itself as a fulfilling and pleasurable site of social and sexual alliance: for the lovers in the film certainly, but also those of us on the other side of the screen, looking on.

CHAPTER FOUR

The Politics of Starch

In the previous chapters, I paid close attention to how bottomhood productively informs the portrayal of Asian masculinity in a variety of cinematic texts, most clearly in contemporary video pornography but also, more surprisingly, in mainstream films not specifically about queer Asian masculinity. For example, in chapter 2, the main narrative of *Reflections in a Golden Eye* is concerned with the social disconnection among the central protagonists and how these relational failures find expression through numerous sexual perversities. Though his is a minor part, the Filipino houseboy wields much narrative influence in inspiring the downfall of the film's highest-ranked character, Major Penderton. Furthermore, while Anacleto can certainly be read as another example of Asian male racial castration, such a diagnosis ignores the ways in which his bottomhood fruitfully troubles heteronormative frameworks of sexual legibility and social bonds. In chapter 3, the dominant themes of *The Lover*'s tragic love story include memory, loss, taboo interracial desire, and female sexual subjectivity. Yet I showed that the Chinese man's shameful bottomhood plays a decisive role in activating the girl's sexual awakening and sustaining the lovers' affair. Indeed, it is the exposure of his gorgeous ass that enables the Chinese lover, the young girl, and the film viewer to transform individualizing shame into sexual arousal and emotional receptivity. These forays into Hollywood cinema and European art film suggest that the rubric of bottomhood is not wholly constraining of Asian masculinity but also remarkably generative of other, more productive, ways of conceiving the interconnections among race, gender, and sexuality.

This final chapter returns us to the question of interracial relationships and hard-core sexual representation laid out in chapter 1. There, I argued that in the commercial gay pornography of Brandon Lee, top and bottom sexual positions mediate the borders between masculinity and femininity, activity and passivity, American citizenship and Asian foreignness. Lee's original claim to fame as an Asian top contests the stereotype of the Asian bottom; yet his more recent turn as a bottom allows us to read bottomhood as a position that can be desirable and chosen. A double movement of disavowing bottomhood and mining its potential for pleasure can also be found in the gay Asian documentaries and queer experimental videos that are the focus of this chapter. These works illustrate a critical engagement with bottomhood as a sexual and social positioning in gay Asian male cultural politics in general and contemporary gay male video pornography in particular. As a direct talking back to the casting of Asian men as racialized sexual objects for white gay male consumption, the gay Asian documentaries seek to articulate gay Asian male sexual subjecthood through a sexual-political program of "sticky rice" desire. These documentaries adopt a rather negative, and at times ambivalent, view of bottomhood, associated with exploitation, inequality, false consciousness, and racial-sexual objectification. Challenging this ideological assessment, the chapter also considers queer experimental Asian videos that present more playful, ironic, and multilayered explorations of bottomhood.

The Reversible Gaze

In Ming-Yuen S. Ma's experimental documentary *Slanted Vision* (1995), film scholar Laura Marks describes her pleasure in watching hard-core gay male pornography in a sequence titled, "Confession of a Porn Viewer, Part 2." She proposes her "fag hag gaze" as part of her theory of an s/M model of looking, one that aims to break out of the impasse in feminist debates about the male gaze. In the place of the phallic gaze's fixed opposition between the male sub-

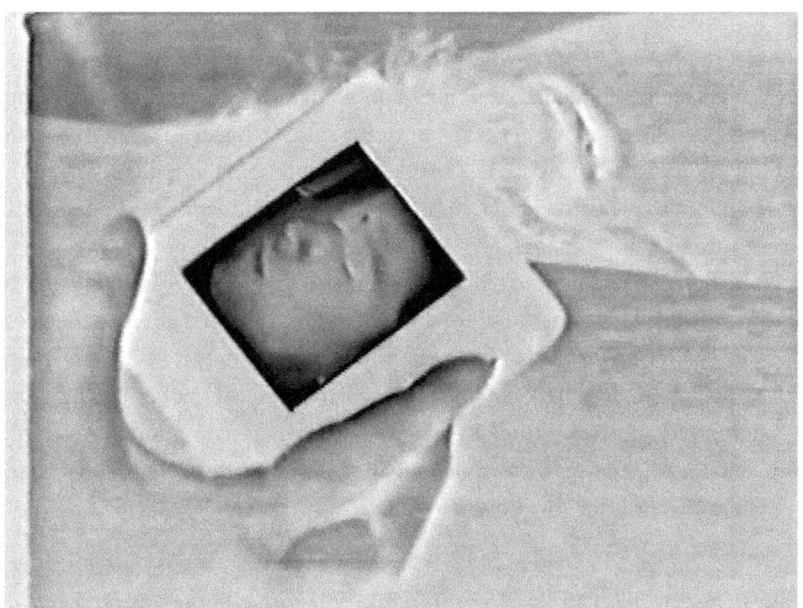

FIGURE 4.1: Scanning camera. *Slanted Vision* (1995).

ject of the look and the female object to be looked at, an s/m model of erotic looking offers a "fluidity of movement" (Marks 2002, 77) between subject and object, domination and submission, a process of looking in which power is negotiated and exchanged, producing pleasure and play. In this sequence, a female hand holds a small video monitor showing a generic porn clip of an Asian man getting fucked by a white man; the hand-sized video monitor tracks the length of the prone body of an Asian man shown in blue negative tone (figure 4.1). As the sequence juxtaposes two views of eroticized Asian male bodies, characterized by Marks as "haptic and optical" looking (86), we hear Marks's narration:

> When I look at images of gay men that are made for gay men, I can look all I want. I can devour the image. My eyes can move over this man's ass, his thighs, his cock, his nipples, like my eyes are hands or a tongue. I can do whatever I want to this image with my eyes, and I can fantasize being in that position to dominate that would be hard, just about impossible to do, if the image were directed to me as a woman.
>
> Looking at gay porn, I borrow a gay man's look at another man. If a man has a desiring gaze at another man, I could sort of drop in on it. I can take it for a ride. It feels especially liberating for me in gay porn because

it's two men, so they're at least potentially equals. There's this feeling of playfulness I so long for between two people who can take turns looking and being looked at, touching and being touched, fucking and being fucked, being the top, being the bottom. There's this feeling that they can always switch. And also, the image of a man being vanquished, a man giving in to pleasure, and to being done to, is exciting for me because it's so rare in hetero images.

I hate these theories that say we must disarm the objectifying, phallic, powerful gaze upon other people's bodies. I think that these theories give too much power to this kind of look. . . . I don't want everybody to be disarmed, equal, touchy-feely, always treating each other like full, autonomous subjects. I think this is a tedious democracy of looking. I think it's a bore. Sexuality is not about equality; it's about an exchange of power. What I want is for that power to flow around more.

Marks delineates how, as a straight woman, watching two gay men fucking allows her to "look all [she] want[s]" and to adopt a dominant position by "borrow[ing] a gay man's look at other men." I appreciate her frank rejection of a "disarmed, equal, touchy-feely, . . . tedious democracy of looking" and her astute point that the erotic charge of looking derives precisely from assertion of and submission to power.[1] I must register, however, my reservation with the ways in which Marks glosses over the specific relations of power in gay male porn that remain resistant to the kind of mobility and play that she privileges. As gay Asian North American cultural critics and artists have noted, the playfulness and negotiation between "looking and being looked at, . . . fucking and being fucked, being the top, being the bottom" continue to be inaccessible for gay Asian men, who are relegated to only one side of the equation, that of bottomhood, when they figure in the equation at all. Marks claims that an S/M model of looking draws on the undermining of power in its fluidity and reversibility of dominant and submissive roles. Yet I would suggest that such an experiment with dominance and submission within a "*safe, delimited . . . fantasy space* of the cinema" (Marks 2002, 78, emphasis added) risks corralling and neutering the sexual frisson that looking and objectification entail. The model of fluidity and reversibility that Marks positively invokes—one she posits is not available in heterosexual relationships—derives from a specific construction of homosexuality based on gender egalitarianism. For Marks, such a play with dominance and submission is possible because both partners are men. However, this privileging of gender symmetry subsumes other kinds of differences, such as age, class, race, and ethnicity, that strongly short-circuit the mobile exchange of power in these sexual scenes.[2]

In spite of its problems, her argument resonates with me because it refutes the claims of a group of documentaries produced by gay Asian men in the United States, Canada, and Australia in the mid- to late 1990s. These experimental documentaries include the aforementioned *Slanted Vision* by Ming-Yuen S. Ma (1995, United States), my own *7 Steps to Sticky Heaven* (1995, United States), Tony Ayres's *China Dolls* (1997, Australia), and Wayne Yung's *The Queen's Cantonese* (1998, Canada).[3] These videos construct an erotics of looking that exploits the sexual charge of interracial sexual representation only to cast it out—that is, to replace this politically troubling representation with a more equal, touchy-feely, and politically palatable representation. They sought to contest the feminization and desexualization of Asian men in gay visual culture in general—and in gay video porn specifically—by presenting self-consciously performative, sexually explicit material, which acts in part as an urgent counterpornography. A central component of the reeducation of desire for these films' intended gay Asian male audience is the goal of replacing the so-called wrong, misguided desire for white men with a supposedly more empowering desire for other Asian men—that is, the conversion of "potato queens" into "sticky rice." To paraphrase Marlon Riggs's famous dictum concerning gay black male identity, the politics of gay Asian sticky rice desire can be summed up thus: "Asian men loving Asian men is the revolutionary act." The political project of the documentaries operates from the assumption that gay Asian men living in the West do not consider other Asian men as desirable sexual partners. The "natural" coupling comprises a younger Asian and an older white man.[4] In gay Asian vernacular, the term "sticky rice" is derived from the definition of Asian men as rice. For instance, a rice queen is a white man who likes Asians. Asian men hooking up with Asian men are described as rice that sticks to other rice. Depending on the context, sticky rice can easily be resignified from a term of empowerment into a term of insult. Related to discussions of sticky rice and the novelty of the phenomenon (novel enough to have a label attached to it[5]) is the common reason stated by some gay Asian men for why they do not find other Asians attractive: it would be too incestuous, akin to having sex with a "sister." In effect, these characterizations suggest that sex between two Asian men (read two effeminate gay men, two bottoms) does not quite count as properly homosexual.

In response to a gay sexual marketplace that puts a premium on the white masculine ideal and consigns Asian men, and those who love them, to the category of exotic sexual fetishists, intra-Asian desire is advanced as a political stance against white racism and as a collective affirmation of gay Asian identity. The shift from potato queens to sticky rice signals a concomitant shift in masculine agency: from passive sexual object (Asian boy toy) to active sexual subject (politicized agent). I contend, however, that this politically correct lesson fails to account for desires and identifications that cannot be so easily disciplined, especially those desires that embrace bottomhood and femininity. In other words, such a reeducation of desire ends up arresting the play of desire and marginalizing a gay Asian male subject's desire for submission and domination — in effect, a move that curtails a gay Asian subject's choice and sexual possibilities.[6]

By describing these videos' ideological project in this way, my defense of the gay Asian male desire for bottomhood and femininity ironically circles back to Marks's championing of an s/m erotics of looking. Instead of viewing these competing claims as irreconcilable (my critique of both Marks and the gay Asian documentaries' prescriptive reeducation of desire), a more illuminating perspective would be to consider Marks's position as demarcating the prevailing social and political context into which the gay Asian documentaries provide a fundamental critique. More specifically, the documentaries contest Marks's subsuming of race under sexuality and gender. As Richard Fung notes, while "'the spectator's positions in relation to the [gay male pornographic] representations are open and in flux,' this observation applies only when all the participants are white. Race introduces another dimension that may serve to close down some of this mobility" (1991, 154). The fact that the gay Asian videos also end up closing down some of this mobility in their highlighting of same-race desire does not undermine their important and necessary intervention into the discourse of gay Asian sexual representation at the specific historical juncture of mid-1990s sexual-racial politics. My interrogation of Marks's s/m model of looking and the gay Asian documentaries' sticky rice lesson seeks to challenge both projects' relegation of bottomhood to a low status. Instead of advocating for an equal-time, reversible s/m scopic and sexual play or to legislate meaningful sex acts with partners of the right race, a more radical lesson would be to endorse a politics that enables a multiplicity of desires and identifications, including those that insist on fixity rather than mobility. For certain subjects, dwelling in the abject space of bottomhood and femininity can be a powerful mode of accessing social and sexual recognition.

Documenting Sticky Rice

In his landmark study of gay and lesbian cinema, *Now You See It*, Richard Dyer (1990) identifies three central goals of gay and lesbian affirmative documentary (his corpus is all pre-1980). To combat negative portrayals of queers in dominant culture, gay affirmative documentary advocates positive representation, which entails "thereness, insisting on the fact of our existence; goodness, asserting our worth and that of our life-styles; and realness, showing what we were in fact like" (Dyer 1990, 274). Significantly, Dyer points out that a conflict exists between the first two goals, thereness and goodness, and the third, realness. In other words, gay documentaries from the early years of gay liberation frequently sideline "conflict, contradiction and difficulty" (246) within gay communities in order to project a unified public face. One dominant stylistic strategy in the films described by Dyer is the dominance of the voice. The voice functions as the "source of knowledge and vehicle of truth" (243) and is privileged over the image: for example, the favored talking head common to documentaries. Multiple voices are gathered together to articulate a coherent social group, which, while diverse, is tied together by gay identity. Gay affirmative documentary follows a narrative structure whose aim is the realization of one's homosexuality, that is, the decisive moment of coming out. Gayness is purported to be invisible, unlike the immediate legibility of sex or skin color.[7] Thus, the act of proclaiming one's homosexuality in the face of pathologization and stigmatization constitutes a political gesture. The underlying assumption behind the exclusive focus on coming out is the idea of homosexual identity as inherent, fixed, hidden, but always ripe for revelation.

In his article "Walking on Tippy Toes: Lesbian and Gay Liberation Documentary of the Post-Stonewall Period 1969–1984," Thomas Waugh (2000) extends Dyer's discussion by focusing on the performance strategies adopted by gay documentaries that depart from standard, straight documentary practices. Waugh observes that to adequately address community concerns about the ethics of authentic and fair representation of lesbian and gay subjects, gay documentaries employ such performance-based approaches as dramatization; role-playing and reconstruction; rehearsed statements and monologues; and the use of music, dance, gesture, and bodily movement. These performative strategies allow subjects of the film to actively contribute to the process; they also creatively compensate for the drawbacks of traditional documentary form (Waugh 2000, 250). Waugh calls attention to a subgenre of performance documentaries, autobiographical sex performance films such as Curt McDowell's *Loads* (1980), Barbara Hammer's *Women I Love* (1976) and *Multiple Orgasms* (1976), and Rosa von Praunheim's *Army of Lovers* (1978). Watching the explicit sexual performances in these films, "the spectator was engaged, linguistically, politically, and affectively, but also physiologically. Minority politics is not only asserted but 'performed' as sexual exchange" (Waugh 2000, 266–267). Performance documentaries thus effectively combine "cumming out" with "coming out."

It is within this rich gay documentary tradition that includes Dyer's affirmative documentary lineage and Waugh's performance-based documentaries that I would like to situate the gay Asian videotapes in the discussion below. These works also owe their aesthetic and political debts to the films and videos produced by queer of color filmmakers coming out of the United States, Canada, and the United Kingdom in the 1980s, such as Marlon Riggs, Isaac Julien, Pratibha Parmar, Cheryl Dunye, and, most important, Richard Fung—filmmakers of color who investigated the interpenetration between homosexuality, race, and sexual representation in their independent and alternative film and videomaking. These pioneering works—which are mostly experimental documentaries—also pose a critical challenge to the hip "homo pomo" narrative films of the early 1990s hyped as the New Queer Cinema, which did not explicitly concern themselves with questions of racial politics. Produced in the same period (late 1980s–1990s), the works of Riggs, Parmar, and others were "ostensibly and explicitly *about* queer black, Latino, or Asian identity . . . [and represented] a certain committed identity politics necessitated by the state of queer cinema and activism, the politics of communities of color, and the alternative invisibility or demonization of queers and people of color within conservative political climates" (Oishi 2000, 226).[8] The groundbreaking work of these queer of color filmmakers motivates this chapter's analysis of the sticky rice documentaries. I seek to challenge the conventional archive of LGBT cinema filled with bland narratives about affluent white gay men looking for love in Chelsea/West Hollywood/the Castro. Instead, I focus attention on experimental queer work by artists of color that mounts powerful critiques against the homonormative productions that constitute the queer cinema canon.

As these different, overlapping filmic genealogies make clear, the work of queer of color filmmakers constitutes a dramatic intervention in independent gay and lesbian film and videomaking with its attention to racial matters, expanding the concerns of ethnic-based film and video productions with its analysis of sexuality. In their formulation of the emerging field of queer Asian American studies in their anthology Q & A, David Eng and Alice Hom take Asian American studies to task for not directing adequate attention to sexuality and gender in its critical analysis; by the same token, they fault lesbian and gay studies for prioritizing sexuality over and above race and class. They argue that "one does not become queer merely though sex or sexuality" and that "one may also become queer in opposition to other queers" (Eng and Hom 1998, 12). In that volume, Jasbir K. Puar's compelling, measured analysis of "queer diaspora" offers an incisive critique of the trendy celebration of "transnational sexualities." She cautions against the careless importation of visibility politics, couched in terms of "coming out or being out," across cultural and national borders: "This privileging of being out sets forth sexual identity as separable from other identities, or at least as primary and uninflected by other subject positionings. This narrative posits a domestic perspective as a diasporic perspective that becomes a globalizing tendency" (Puar 1998, 415). Here, Puar cautions against the imposition of a Western LGBT political agenda onto other parts of the world, an imposition that homogenizes and flattens out cultural differences.

It is precisely these vexed intersections of domestic and transnational, queer and diaspora that the gay Asian documentaries thematize. As Hiram Perez provocatively asserts, "Being gay always involves, to some extent, being someplace else" (2005, 177). He further points out that the dominant trope of Western-style gay politics, coming out of the closet, implies real or imagined travel and freedom of movement that remain unavailable to the majority of queers. I argue that these gay Asian videos imaginatively produce this "someplace else" in queer Asian diasporic space. It should be noted that the "sticky rice field" cannot be located either in the United States/Canada/Australia or in Asia, but it might be identified as an in-between, hybrid space formally constructed in the videos themselves as well as in the videos' subsequent circulation in gay and lesbian as well as Asian (American/Canadian) film festivals, gay Asian community spaces (support groups, community organizations, social events, HIV/AIDS education), and university classrooms and libraries.[9]

Speaking, Translating, Spatializing Sex

In constructing this other impossible space, a queer diasporic space that allows for the enactment of sticky rice desire, these gay Asian videotapes critically rework the project of gay affirmative documentaries in two essential ways: the first is the deconstruction of the centrality of the voice; the second is the deployment of sexual performance. For example, in contrast to the groundbreaking 1977 documentary *Word Is Out*'s near-exclusive reliance on talking-head testimonials from its gay and lesbian subjects, the gay Asian documentaries consistently question the privileging of the voice as a source of knowledge, truth, and authenticity. A key issue here is the fact that for the majority of these interview subjects, English constitutes a second language. Again and again, these videotapes cogently thematize the difficulty of speaking about sex and sexuality on camera in a foreign tongue. The issue of the verbal articulation of sex echoes my discussion of accented pornography in chapter 1. However, whereas accented pornography constitutes more of a mode of reading or, more precisely, listening otherwise, accented voices are encoded in the production of the documentary videos themselves. For example, *Slanted Vision* deploys multiple conceptual and aesthetic strategies to emphasize processes of translation and mistranslation by offering awkward literal translations of terms for private body parts such as broccoli, jade flute, and chicken's ass and sex acts such as shooting aeroplanes, playing the flute, flying a kite, sitting on a candle, and squeezing black beans. My video *7 Steps to Sticky Heaven* foregrounds the politics of the interview through the use of unsynced audio, voice-over dubbing, ambient sound, redundant subtitles and onscreen texts, and extended video strobing and freeze-frame.

Wayne Yung's video, *The Queen's Cantonese*, most compellingly examines the role of language and the dominance of the speaking voice with its investigation of gay Asian North American identity and sexual politics in the framework of a conversational language course. In place of heteronormative roles and rituals presented in conventional language tapes, the exercises and dramatizations in Yung's language lessons include such gay-sensitive and GAM-specific scenarios as cruising Chinese men in the park, bargaining at the bathhouse, and politely asking your white trick to leave after sex.[10] At the beginning of "Lesson I," the "Occupations" dramatization introduces us to the three protagonists who will accompany us on our Cantonese language excursions. The first is a bleached-blond young Asian man who announces in Cantonese, "I am a potato queen, which is someone who likes to do it with white men" (figure 4.2). The second, a dark-haired white French Canadian, states, "I am a rice queen, which is someone who likes to do it with Asian men" (figure 4.3). The third, another young Asian man, tells us, "I mostly do it with white guys, so that makes me a potato queen, but now I like Asians too, so maybe I'm sticky rice" (figure 4.4). In the parallel universe of *The Queen's Cantonese*, to learn Cantonese is to become socialized as a proper gay Cantonese subject, which in this case is split into three available subject positions: potato queen, rice queen, or sticky rice. Learning the Cantonese language entails "understanding the Cantonese mind" and taking up one of these subject positions. Yet, as the lessons in the rest of the video indicate, a central part of this endeavor is to learn to appreciate and adopt the position of sticky rice, which represents the ideal speaker constructed and addressed by the language lessons. In its construction of a sticky rice field, the video trains its student to become a queen fluent in proper gay Oriental argot and versed in sticky rice politics.

In their essay "The Cultural-Aesthetic Specificities of All-Male Moving-Image Pornography," Rich Cante and Angelo Restivo (2004a) posit that public space has been central to the construction of contemporary gay sexuality (at least in the United States); they maintain that gay porn constitutes a privileged site for the articulation of this queer "world-making publicness." They specify, "In its continual reinscription of all the spaces surrounding us, all-male pornography at some point also *becomes* the field for the (utopian) reinvention of the world eternally promised by identity politics" (Cante and Restivo 2004a, 143, emphasis in original). It is necessary to qualify this insightful observation about gay porn's "(utopian) reinvention of the world" by pointing out that such an "all-male pornography" operates through a series of exclusions—most significantly for our discussion, gay Asian subjects. With this in mind, one can see that the sticky rice field in *The Queen's Cantonese* is clearly not a racially unmarked gay pornotopia, but where the gay and the ethnic magically come together to produce a distinct queer diasporic space, unlocatable in everyday homo- and heteronormative time-space. In this pornographic field, the utopian reinvention of the world not only shows us "the *homoerotic* leaking into everyday reality—offices, gyms, rodeos, wherever" (Burger 1995, 41, emphasis in original), but provides evidence of the homoerotic leaking into everyday Cantonese reality: gay rice bar, queer cogender bathhouse, dim sum safe-sex restaurant, outdoor sex market, and cruisy bamboo park. Being out in this sticky rice field shows us that sexual identity is inseparable from other identities, and that this sticky rice narra-

FIGURE 4.2: Potato queen. *The Queen's Cantonese* (1998).

FIGURE 4.3: Rice queen. *The Queen's Cantonese* (1998).

FIGURE 4.4: Sticky rice. *The Queen's Cantonese* (1998).

tive must, tactically and campily, transform a gay domestic perspective into a queer diasporic perspective in order to register gay Asian male presence. It is significant that this sticky rice space is set in neither China nor Canada, but in a "Pearl of the Orient" in Vancouver, also known as Hongcouver.[11]

One useful way of thinking about this queer diasporic space is to emphasize the field's sticky nature, as the glue between the domestic and the diasporic; another is as "the clash of homoscape with ethnoscape," which is how Waugh accounts for the "identity disjuncture of queer and Asian" in the video work of Richard Fung.[12] Reworking Arjun Appadurai's influential theorization of the different "scapes" mediating the flows between the local and global, Waugh writes, "Shifting the notion's application from the ethnic diasporas to that of the queer diasporas or the queer global village, the homoscape is the transnational scene of sexual spaces, commodities, communications and identity performance. . . . It is inhabited by the coded rituals of looking and cruising, the negotiations of consent, and ultimately of course, the protocols of sexual exchange" (2002, 68). In this explication, it appears as if the homoscape were accorded mobility in the "transnational scene," but a mobility accomplished by leaving the ethnic diaspora behind, stuck at home (?) in the space of the heteronormative host nation.[13] In opposition to such a supplanting of the homely ethnic by the sexy homo, *The Queen's Cantonese* generates sexual humor and erotic tension by exploiting (rather than seeking to resolve) the clash between ethno- and homoscapes even as it provides lessons in the protocols of sexual exchange in the brave new queer diaspora.

The Reeducation of Desire

While we can see a pedagogical function most clearly in Yung's video, a pedagogical impulse pervades the other videos as well. All four videos contain material of differing levels of sexual explicitness, from lyrical soft-core to raunchy hard-core, imagery that could be said to function as a counter-pornography, combating the ways that Asian men have been stereotyped in the mainstream media as powerful but desexualized martial arts masters and typecast in gay pornography as passive, submissive bottoms. The production of an alternative field of sexual representation is consonant with these works' collective project of mapping a queer Asian diasporic space. Gay male critics have pointed out that pornography occupies a central place in gay male culture, for it is the one arena where gay men see our sexuality imaged and affirmed. In a homophobic and sex-negative culture, gay porn serves as an essential how-to manual for gay men. For years before Stonewall and many years afterward, "it was pretty much only in gay pornography that we could regularly see representations of gay men at all" (Cante and Restivo 2004a, 147). In addition, Richard Dyer has famously observed that although pornography gives us important experiential knowledge of our bodies, porn as it exists teaches us the "wrong" kind of knowledge. Gay pornography, like its straight counterpart, privileges the experience of the fucker and his relentless drive toward visible coming. Dyer writes, "At the level of public representation gay men may be thought of as deviant and disruptive of masculine norms because we assert the pleasures of being fucked and the eroticism of the anus, in our pornography this takes a back seat" ([1985] 1992, 128).[14] As numerous critics of color have asserted, the education provided by gay male porn (at least in North America) possesses a racializing cast. North American gay porn persistently relegates Asian men to the backseat, where they automatically lift their legs in the air and are taken for a ride by white tops.[15]

In contrast to the revisionist project of *The Queen's Cantonese*, for gay Asian men coming out in the West, coming into our gayness often means being socialized as a proper white gay subject. As Tony Ayres writes, "When I first became conscious of being gay, there was not a particular kind of male body I was attracted to. To be honest, anything with a dick would have done. However, as I became a participant in the gay world, I found myself increasingly influenced by the imagery which determined what was desirable. An 'Ideal Body' . . . became increasingly attractive: muscled, tanned, and buffed" (1999, 91). He adds, "The sexually marginalized Asian man who has grown up in the West or is western in his thinking is often invisible in his own fantasies. Our sexual daydreams are populated by handsome Caucasian men with lean, hard Caucasian bodies" (91). While gay pornography affirms gay Asian men's homosexual desire, it simultaneously curbs their participation in the sexual scenario. As Ayres's testimony illuminates, mainstream white gay sexual representation plays a pivotal role in how gay Asian men see themselves as sexual subjects, and by extension, influences how they regard one another. One can see how such a dynamic plays itself out in the "rice bar," as shown in the following analysis by Eric Wat in his oral history of the emergence of a gay Asian community in Los Angeles:

> The experiences of the narrators in rice bars prove that it was not only the alienating environment of being a minority in a mainstream gay establishment that kept most gay Asians apart. Instead, I argue that the white/mas-

culine and Asian/feminine binary reinforces the dependency of gay Asian men on their white counterparts. Not only were gay Asian men led to believe that other gay Asian men were not desirable, but feeling unworthy themselves, they could only find validation from white gay men, and not each other. Even when one gay Asian man met another, there were already sets of expectations that informed how they were going to relate to each other. As long as those expectations were left unchallenged, no matter what kind of space gay Asians occupied, or how many of them occupied it, those expectations would inevitably be inscribed in the spaces around them. (2002, 84)

In my own personal experience of spending many weekends in a well-known rice bar in San Francisco in the mid-1990s, I can attest to the power imbalance that underlies the interactions between white and Asian patrons. The racialized gendering articulated by Wat manifested itself thus: the white men were positioned as the active choosers, while the Asian men were the ones waiting around to be picked. However, the rice bar also enabled Asian men to meet one another in a context less inflected by the racism of mainstream gay bars, where they could gather in a gay Asian-friendly space to socialize as friends as well as to pick up potential tricks.[16]

Returning for now to the gay "racial hierarchy of desire" traced by Wat above, we find this dynamic unfolding in a sexually explicit sequence from *7 Steps to Sticky Heaven*. In "Step 3: XXX," characterized as a "commercial interruption" to the video's presentation of "sticky rice boys," a gay Asian informant testifies in voice-over that "everyone falls for . . . images of white men with tight bodies, six packs, and bulging biceps" and that the speaker himself wants to have "some white gay man . . . take me [and] dominate me." Another man confesses that he likes to have rough sex with Caucasian men but attributes more meaning to the sex he has with Asian men. On the image track, we see the "dominant trip" and "rough sex" enacted by the Asian video maker himself; he gets his nipples twisted, his ass spanked and fucked by his white ex-boyfriend. It is important to note that the voice-over descriptions (and disavowal) of the dominant trip and rough sex are culled from interviews conducted with subjects who appear in other parts of the video. Instead of using a clip-on microphone as is customary for on-camera interviews, the use of the built-in camera microphone for these interviews results in ambient noise interfering with the interviewees' testimonies. Consequently, the public nature of the interview is reflected in the audio quality, evident by the intrusion of laughter, street sounds, and other conversations taking place nearby. The scoring of public interviews over images of private sex acts undermines the traditional separation of sex talk from sexual action. More to the point, such a juxtaposition of public declarations of sticky rice desire and private potato queen practice brings to the fore the inherent contradictions in the project of reeducating desire. Following the insights offered by Dyer and Fung, I contend that this sexually explicit sequence stands in for the bad knowledge that porn offers—the fantasies of domination and submission responsible for what Fung identifies as the conflation of Asian and anus. And yet the inclusion of such a sequence in a video that is supposed to extol the joys of Asian men getting together betrays the irresistible attraction to this allegedly bad knowledge based on racial objectification and abjection.

At the end of his essay "Coming to Terms," Dyer cites a scene from a gay porn film in which one performer "gently licks the semen off [another performer's] penis . . . [thus] express[ing] a tender emotional feeling" ([1985] 1992, 130). This scene of tenderness represents for Dyer an example of a reconstructed gay male pornography that can reeducate desire. Interestingly, toward the conclusion of "Looking for My Penis," Fung gestures toward moments in which an Asian porn actor's performance style exceeds the codes of white gay male porn that would ordinarily domesticate his racial difference. Fung elaborates:

> There are several moments in *International Skin* [N'wayvo Richhe, 1985], for example, in which the focus shifts from the genitals to hands caressing a body; these moments feel to me more "genuine." I do not mean this in the sense of an essential Asian sexuality, but rather a moment is captured in which the actor stops pretending. He does not stop acting, but he stops pretending to be a white porn star. I find myself focusing on moments like these, in which the racist ideology of the text seems to be temporarily suspended or rather eclipsed by the erotic power of the moment. (1991, 158–159)

Both Dyer and Fung refer to individual performances that destabilize the rigid conventions of porn, resulting in rare moments of romance and "erotic power." In pointing to these singular moments of "good knowledge" (as Dyer states wistfully, "If porn taught us *this* more often" [130]), both critics engage in what Leo Bersani has described as the "*redemptive reinvention of sex*"

(1988, 215, emphasis in original).[17] The goal of redemptive reinvention mirrors the rehabilitative tenor of the gay Asian documentaries as well.

If these gay Asian videos are invested in a pedagogical project, a task of reeducation, what is the lesson being taught? A lesson in sticky rice eroticism. The rehearsal of various subject positions in these tapes—namely potato queens, rice queens, and sticky rice—sets up a crucial appendix to the coming-out narrative found in conventional gay-affirmative documentaries. In addition to realizing one's gay feelings and making them audible and public, these works complement the coming-out narrative with the coming into consciousness as sticky rice. In fact, these works bypass the coming-out-as-gay narrative altogether; their narratives center instead on gay Asian men who come to realize their desire for other gay Asian men. Interview subjects begin by confessing their desire for white men in embarrassed tones and nervous giggles and end with giddy, celebratory proclamations about discovering the novel and familiar sexiness of Asian men. We see such an itinerary in the language lessons in *The Queen's Cantonese*, which dramatize the disintegration of a relationship between a young Chinese man and his white lover due to his budding romantic feelings for another Chinese man. My own video instructs the intended gay Asian viewer how to reach sticky heaven in seven easy steps. Interestingly, the video not only defines but also justifies sticky rice desire. My voice-off questions include, "What's sticky rice all about?" and "What kind of rice do you like?" as well as "Why did you turn sticky?" and "How is sex different with Asian men?" The seven steps progress from white "ex-boyfriend" to "ricedicks" to "ricing on the cake." On the one hand, if we recall the testimony of one sticky rice subject who claims that he engages in "no-strings" rough sex with white men but invests more emotional connection in the sex he has with Asian men, it appears that *7 Steps* conforms to Dyer's and Fung's critical desires for a reeducated gay pornography. On the other hand, for all of its sexual explicitness, the affective tone of the video corresponds more to an antiporn feminist definition of erotica, which views sexuality as "a way of bonding, of giving and receiving pleasure, bridging differentness, discovering sameness, and communicating emotion" (Steinem quoted in Champagne 1995, 43). Consider the testimony of another sticky rice subject detailing his first sexual encounter with another Asian man in the same video: "Well, it was strange, because I felt like I was touching my own body, touching something that was really familiar, like touching my own brother.... You know, we had the same frame of body, so everything seems in place in proportion to mine." In spite of the interviewee's discovery of connection with another Asian man through their sameness, in the video this talking-head testimony is presented like a voice-over, in that the audio is purposely not synced up with the movement of the speaker's lips. That is, the separation of image and audio tracks serves to undercut the speaker's confession of ultimate bonding with another and getting in touch with himself. In detaching the accented-English voice from the racially marked body, I foreground the mediation of the video apparatus in the authentic proclamation of sticky rice mutual recognition, thus registering the different processes of translation involved in creating a queer Asian diasporic space for the enactment of sticky rice desire: from one language to another and from a material body to an electronic one. By enabling the articulation of sticky rice desire and denaturalizing such an enunciation, I point to the alternative itinerary taken by a gay diasporic Asian subject coming into sexual and political consciousness as sticky rice.[18]

Up to this point, my discussions of *The Queen's Cantonese* and *7 Steps to Sticky Heaven* have highlighted the ways in which the construction of a sticky rice field, as an in-between queer Asian diasporic space, rests on the maintenance of a sexy, productive tension between the homoscape and the ethnoscape. I now turn to an example that encourages us to interrogate the assumption that queer diasporic discourse is necessarily always oppositional. Queer theorists of color such as Puar, Manalansan, David Eng, and Gayatri Gopinath have cautioned against the uncritical celebration of queer diasporas by suggesting that both queer and diaspora possess the potential to be harnessed for the heteronormative project of the nation-state. For instance, Gopinath advocates for a deployment of queerness as "a way to challenge nationalist ideologies by restoring the impure, inauthentic, nonreproductive potential of the notion of diaspora" (2005, 11). Gopinath advises us to remain alert to "the implications of privileging sexuality as a primary 'identity' throughout the diaspora"; she asks, "What possible alternative narratives of sexuality may we be shutting down in such a move?" (1996, 123). This question is critical when we look at the manner in which *China Dolls* imagines the sticky rice field in which Asian-Asian desire unfolds. Exploiting food analogies, the sequence titles in *China Dolls* track a trajectory similar to *7 Steps* with its shifts from "Forbidden Fruit" to "Potato Queen" to "Sticky Rice" to "Fruit Salad." In the "Sticky Rice" segment, Ayres describes a formative sexual encounter with another Chinese man when he traveled to China for the first time on a work assignment. While the image track shows Ayres

FIGURE 4.5: Asian men kissing. *China Dolls* (1997).

snapping pictures and the images of his trip projected onscreen, we hear his narration: "I was looking for my roots, a sense of my Chineseness. Unfortunately though, most people on the mainland mistook me for a Japanese tourist." From the snapshots of outdoor market scenes, the video cuts to two shirtless, muscular Asian men embracing and kissing one another in a studio setting (figure 4.5). Ayres's narration continues: "But one significant thing happened. I met a man called Robert, and we spent the night together. I had never slept with a Chinese man before. But it was as familiar as touching myself. Chinese skin: hard and smooth and polished. Perhaps for the first time, I felt desire which had nothing to do with race. He didn't want me because I was Chinese; I didn't not want him because he was Chinese. We were simply attracted to each other. It was the most liberating experience of my life."

If we recall the demonstration of a racial hierarchy of desire in *7 Steps*, a sex scene between the video maker and his white ex-boyfriend constitutes one of the required steps a gay Asian must accomplish to reach the goal of loving another Asian man. As I briefly suggested, the sexual excitement generated by that sequence — constructed by the jarring spanking and moaning on the audio track along with filmic techniques such as a handheld camera and a shot–reverse shot structure switching from the perspectives of the

THE POLITICS OF STARCH 169

Asian bottom as well as the white top—is presented only to be dismissed as an incidental commercial interruption. That sequence, while trading in and exploiting the thrilling interplay of power, desire, and difference, resolutely situates Asian men on the side of the dominated, the passive partner who submits himself in rough sex. In contrast, the erotic charge of sticky rice coupling in *China Dolls* results not from difference and power imbalance but from familiarity and symmetry. As Ayres narrates his desire for another Chinese man, a desire that "had nothing to do with race," we see two young handsome Asian men kissing and caressing each other's "hard and smooth and polished" skin. Moody lighting, dramatic close-ups, a chroma-keyed background of fuzzy yellow swirls, and slow-motion frame rate work together to blur distinctive physical differences between the two Asian men. In watching what Ayres posits as "the most liberating experience of [his] life" reenacted onscreen, we are shown both partners partaking in an erotically tasteful and identity-affirming sexual interlude. It is noteworthy that this mirroring of desire is only possible through Ayres's returning to his roots. Such a nostalgic gesture depends on the logic of finding oneself by going back to "the old country"—that is, the past. Ayres's sticky rice epiphany subscribes to what David Eng calls the "nostalgic demands of diaspora," conforming to "the normative impulse to recuperate lost origins, to recapture the mother or motherland, and to valorize dominant notions of social belonging and racial exclusion that the nation-state would seek to naturalize and legitimate through the inherited logics of kinship, blood, and identity" (Eng 2010, 13–14). Instead of a sticky rice field that exists in an undefinable "someplace else," resting between and resisting the critical tension created by the pull of homoscape and ethnoscape, for Ayres, the "demand for evidence [of sticky rice desire] . . . result[s] in a recourse to roots, culture, origin, and ultimately the nation(s)" (Puar 1998, 419)—that is, China, without the scare quotes. Exploiting his position as a queer cosmopolitan elite with the mobility to boldly cross borders of nations and temporalities, Ayres's sticky rice lesson learned is accomplished at the expense of erasing other narratives of same-sex eroticism. Like the affirmative documentaries Dyer discusses, conflict and contradiction are smoothed over in the liberation afforded by Asian-Asian eroticism. National, class, and linguistic differences become subsumed under the banner of race and ethnicity. The similarity of the Asian male bodies in Ayres's sticky rice dramatization bespeaks their physical symmetry, but it cannot account for other illegible asymmetries and the social, cultural, and political meanings attached to them. Never mind the fact that the Chinese locals mistook him for a Japanese tourist; in the end what mattered was, as Ayres eloquently pronounces about his first Chinese lover, that "he didn't want me because I *was* Chinese; I didn't *not* want him because he was Chinese. We were simply attracted to each other" (emphasis added). Although such a claim might simply be read as a description of a desire unadulterated by race (and racism)—an attraction exceeding history, space, and time—the use of a double negative suggests another potential claim: "I wanted him *because* he was Chinese."

Lest the viewer miss the point that this fateful sticky rice rendezvous functions as the magical salve for racial exoticization and sexual objectification, the end of the sequence has the "China doll" (represented throughout the video as an Asian man in elaborate Chinese opera drag) dramatically remove his feminine headdress. While the video maker's sexual contact with a different-yet-familiar Other releases him from the rice queen's colonial mind-set that would see him only as an exotic sexual plaything, such a release is achieved by leaving Robert, the real China doll, behind, after having realized his role as a conduit (and ground) for Ayres's sexual and political liberation via Robert's hypervisible cultural authenticity and unproblematic homosexual origin.

In discussing its troublesome politics, I don't mean to minimize *China Dolls*'s remarkable feat of intervening in mainstream sexual representation. Its imaging of two half-naked, hunky Asian men in homosexual embrace, a rarely seen—and "hard to imagine"[19]—sighting in the cinema (whether in mainstream, independent, or experimental genres), points to the valuable and difficult political project that these Asian documentaries undertake in siting a sticky rice field across the queer Asian diasporas. Of the four videos discussed here, *Slanted Vision* concerns itself most clearly with the subject of gay Asian men and pornographic representation (in this sense, it builds upon the analysis begun by Fung in *Chinese Characters*); hence, it deals directly with the question of how to reenvision such representation. One reading of the title suggests the slanted, distorted manner in which gay Asian men's "sexuality [has been] blue-screened onto pre-existing scenes, where the standards of beauty and desirability have been defined by others, and where our gestures have been already scripted" (Ma 2002, 60). In addition, the term "slanted vision" also evidences the manner in which gay Asian male subjects look at and consume these images—that is, askance, critically, from an improper angle. Early on in this visually and theoretically dense video, Ma confesses his inability to enjoy porn videos featuring Asian men because these videos often cast Asians in offensive, stereotypical roles, such as waiters, houseboys, masseurs, and exchange students. Consequently, Ma's video progresses from a dry, intellectual analysis of the pornographic representation of Asian men in such badly dubbed titles as *Shanghai Meat Company* (dir. Tony Chan, 1991), "Eggroll for Two" (an episode from *Asian Force* [dir. Tony Chan, 1991]), and *Pacific Fever* (dir. Frank Ross, 1991), to a sequence later in the tape titled "Non-Gratuitous Sex Scene," in which Ma engages in sex with another Asian man. This sequence cogently demonstrates the function of sexual performance in the gay Asian works I have been discussing.

Unlike the "gratuitous" sex scenes in the generic gay porn videos featuring Asian actors quoted previously in the documentary, this particular sex scene announces itself, because "non-gratuitous," as a corrective to what had been shown before. Instead of the progress from jacking to sucking to fucking in the porn videos, the sex acts in Ma's reconstructed sex scene emphasize a nonlinear repetition of caresses, kissing, licking, jacking, and sucking; significantly, fucking is not included in the repertoire of sex acts. Self-reflexively pointing to the conditions of its making, the scene cuts between two views of the sexual action. One is composed of medium shots in blue grainy Super-8 film stock from the perspective of an outside cameraperson (Quentin Lee); the other view, shot with a video camera, resulting in red-hot hues and set in slow motion, is from the perspectives of the participants in the scene (Ma and Napoleon Lustre), as they hand the camera back and forth (figure 4.6). The sequence is backed by the hypnotic West Javanese popular song "Tongeret," by Idjah Hadidjah, along with a whispery recitation of a litany-like poem by Lustre.[20] Toward the conclusion of the sequence, the aural lyricism is interrupted by an interview voice-over in which the HIV-positive narrator relates an incident in which he had to stop his sexual partner from swallowing his cum. What is interesting for our discussion at hand is the manner in which the scene of sticky rice sexual coupling is culturally, politically, and aesthetically situated—that is, the scene's multilayered self-reflexivity calls attention to this sticky rice space neither as a field of dreams waiting to be found nor as a fantasy of origins to be discovered, but as one that is self-consciously constructed in a specific time and place. As a queer Asian diasporic invention, this sticky rice field is made up of heterogeneous, impure, inauthentic, and competing elements: shaky cameras, underexposed Super-8 film footage, electric video colors that bleed, an exotic- and traditional-sounding (because untranslated) Indonesian song, a poem being recited in accented English so hushed that the viewer can barely make it

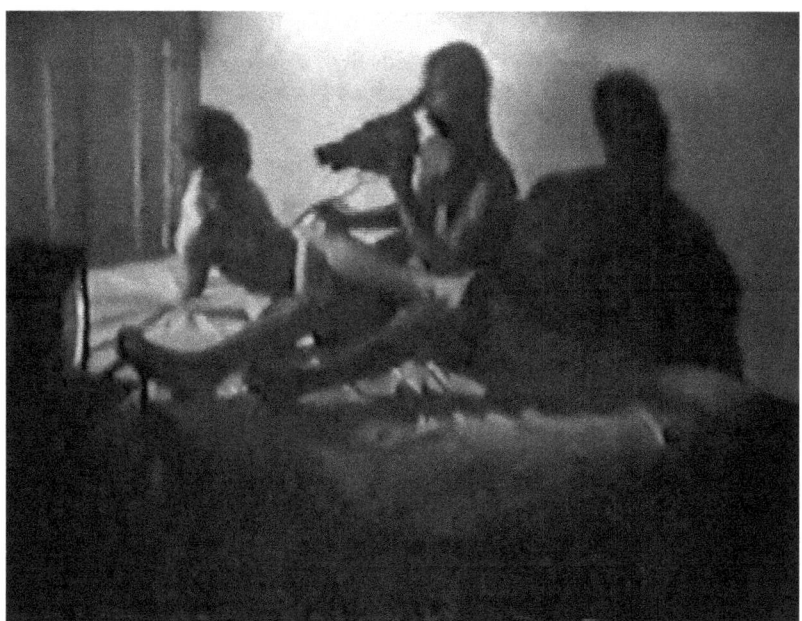

FIGURE 4.6: Filming sex. *Slanted Vision* (1995).

out, a Chinese American man performing sex with a Filipino American man expressedly for this video (that is, there is no romantic justification for the sex here), and, most remarkably, the intrusion of disease into a scene that is supposed to signify a new and improved, sexy and pleasurable vision of intra-Asian homoeroticism. Lustre's poetic allusion to a pilgrimage to Lourdes to find an AIDS cure and the unnamed narrator's mention of HIV-infected semen constitute two crucial moments in the scene that announce the unavoidable framework of HIV/AIDS as the broader context for any project of reeducating desire in the 1990s.[21] Instead of seeing sticky rice desire as a natural manifestation of an essential gay Asian sexuality that has somehow been perverted and co-opted by a white gay racial economy of desire, *Slanted Vision* acknowledges sticky rice as a politically inflected and culturally specific intervention in Western gay male sexual discourses and the politics of sexual representation.

Though *Slanted Vision* historicizes sticky rice desire much more effectively than the other three documentaries (especially in its examination of pornographic representation), I maintain that all four works participate in a similar political project. Taken together, they critique the placement of Asian men on the bottom of the gay sexual hierarchy; sexual performance in the documentaries seeks to make up for the paucity of sexy images of Asian men and to engage the spectator "politically . . . [and] also physiologically" (Waugh 2000, 267). These videos aspire to move the spectator by producing Asian men as desiring subjects and desired objects. A sticky rice eroticism based on familiarity, symmetry, and sameness but also strangeness, imbalance, and novelty triumphs over a rice queenliness based on domination, objectification, and rough sex. That is, an active remasculinized, narcissistic sexual subject, one who touches another Asian man and ends up touching himself, displaces the passive, feminized Asian boy toy whose sexual desirability is predicated on the desire of an absolute Other, the rice queen.

Sticky, Stuck

Unfortunately, for some gay Asian men, this lesson is hard to swallow. I cite here a few major stumbling blocks impeding the way to sticky heaven. The road from object status, Oriental boy toy, to subject status, liberated sticky rice man, is riddled with potholes: the persistent desires and identifications of Asian bottomhood return with a vengeance. For example, in her analysis of *Slanted Vision*, Marks points out that Ma makes room for the pleasures of the bottom position, which she characterizes as "masochistic," "passive," and "feminine" (Marks 2002, 85). She cites two examples: Quentin Lee, reflecting on his star turn in the porn video *Shanghai Meat Company*, claims that being objectified in an Orientalist manner actually made him feel more desirable; another interview subject, Nikki Calma, reports intense pleasure from being tied up and humiliated by a sexual partner, mainly due to the excessive attention he showered on Calma. Similarly, in the "Rice Queen" segment in *China Dolls*, a group of Filipino drag performers bemoan the judgment by the "guardians of morality" in the gay Asian Australian community of the drag performers' desire for white men.

Even the use of rice as the preferred metaphor faces complications. In the introduction to *Rice: Explorations into Gay Asian Culture and Politics*, Song Cho points out that rice constitutes a "life-sustaining staple of Asian cultures" but also represents a dominant "metaphor for gay Asians *and* how we are consumed by white gay culture as exotic 'tricks'" (1998, 1). In the same vein, in *7 Steps to Sticky Heaven*, Asian gay boys identify the same traits that rice queens often mention to account for why they find other Asians attractive: slanted eyes, smooth skin, hairless body, little brown nipples, and cute dick. As Yau Ching observes in an analysis of *7 Steps*, "This is how the tongue-in-cheek structural motif of the sticky rice backfires on itself; how we all

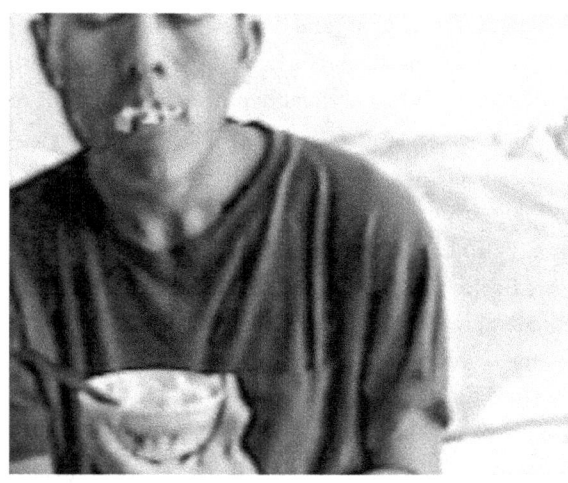

FIGURE 4.7: Eating rice. *7 Steps to Sticky Heaven* (1995).

suddenly become and remain sticky rice; how we all eat it, hate it, love it and . . . eat it—so historically fixed in a position that we actually proclaim it as desire, as home" (1999, 160). A sense of ambivalence about rice as sexual metaphor gets registered in the video itself, specifically in the transitional segments that show the video maker eating from a bowl of rice (figure 4.7). One particular moment late in the video displays a dramatic cut from a high-angle medium close-up of the maker sucking another Asian man's cock to another shot from a similar perspective of him ravenously shoveling rice into his mouth. While the graphic match of sucking rice dick to shoveling rice bowl makes literal the link between cultural sustenance and sexual empowerment, the voraciousness of the sucking and shoveling also bespeaks a certain ambivalence. Do these actions signify insatiable hunger or a force-feeding? Earlier in the same video, Sean Nhan, one of the interviewees, tells an anecdote that highlights the role of insult and the making of sticky rice identity. Nhan and an Asian friend were approached by a white man who attempted to pick them up. After meeting with rejection, the white guy angrily exclaimed, "Ugh, sticky!" and walked off. In response to the unsolicited labeling of "sticky" intended here as an insult, a racial slur of a sort, Nhan walked up to a white guy and kissed him, just to prove that he was not sticky. As he explains, his defensive gesture was based on the assumption that "if you date your own kind, then you're not as good." Nevertheless, Nhan concedes that a "PC-ness" existed within the gay Asian American community (in San Francisco at that time) that pressured Asian men to date other Asians.[22]

Sticky rice politics seeks to reconfigure the connotative links between stickiness (of bodies, objects, surfaces, signs) and disgust. Displacing the formulation of stickiness as slime, a substance that is neither solid nor liquid, that threatens to cling to us, the gay Asian documentaries' deployment of sticky rice reformulates stickiness as desirable contact between racially abject bodies. In an interesting discussion of the experience of stickiness, Sara Ahmed points to the double movement of stickiness: "Stickiness involves a form of relationality, or a 'withness,' in which the elements that are 'with' get bound together. One can stick by a friend. One can get stuck in traffic. Some forms of stickiness are about holding things together. Some are about blockages or stopping things moving. When a sign or object becomes sticky it can function to 'block' the movement (of other things or signs) and it can function to bind (other things or signs) together. Stickiness helps us to associate 'blockages' with 'binding'" (2004, 91). The two senses of stickiness articulated by Ahmed capture well the new form of eroticized racial bonding along with the disciplinary operations found in gay Asian sticky rice politics. For even as sticky rice politics works to refunction "incestuous" Asian-Asian homosexual coupling into a new respectable, egalitarian model of intra-Asian relationality, it inevitably obstructs other forms of social-sexual binding. On the one hand, I want to be clear that I consider sticky rice politics to be an important and powerful intervention in queer cultural politics, not only in North America but across the Asian diaspora. On the other hand, it is necessary to interrogate the legislation of desire that underlies this politicized reeducation of desire. What I am interested in teasing out here is a more complex account of queer Asian sexual subjectivity, one that is informed by shame, disgust, and abjection, as well as pride, attraction, and pleasure.

Bottomhood Is Powerful(?)

In the remainder of the chapter, I look at queer Asian video productions that challenge the shaming and disciplining of desire one finds in the sticky rice documentaries. It should be noted that the historical contexts of production, exhibition, and distribution of these experimental videos overlap with the sticky rice documentaries. This is important to stress because it illustrates that the discussions around Asian bottomhood were varied and contested. In their broader accounts of bottomhood, these videotapes engage not only interracial desire but also other kinds of social issues, including drag, trans masculinity, international sex work, cultural imperialism, HIV/AIDS, and public sex. In doing so, they challenge the privileging of race/ethnicity in sticky rice politics, suggesting that racialized sexuality is invariably underscored by a host of other social and political factors.

Wayne Yung made *Peter Fucking Wayne Fucking Peter* (1994) partly as an effort to address "the 'disconnect' that happens when one's public activist agenda doesn't necessarily match one's private sex life" (Yung and Nguyen 2007, 258). Faithful to its title, the action in the four-minute, thirty-second video is composed of Peter, the video maker's older white boyfriend, fucking Wayne, the Chinese Canadian video maker, and then, Wayne fucking Peter in turn. The innovation of the piece lies in its formal simplicity: one camera, handheld by the person lying on the bottom; one light source, a weak flashlight; and a minimal soundtrack with Yung's poetic voice-over narration accompanied by a jazzy accordion instrumental. Although the title implies that there is a flip-flopping versatility to the sexual acts performed by both men, the narration offers only Yung's perspective. The video is divided into three sections, each dedicated to a part of the action described in the video's title: "This is me as you fuck me"; "This is you fucking me"; and "This is you as I fuck you." Further, it is important to note that though the camera sometimes shows the facial expressions of the fuckee, the voice-over never speaks of how it feels for him to get fucked, only what getting fucked (and fucking) mean. Put differently, bottomhood in *Peter Fucking* is posed in ideological terms. Getting fucked is not experienced and explored for its own sake but is depicted in order to make a political claim.

The bottom position in Yung's video is portrayed as socially, sexually, and politically empowering. Throughout the video, the image track shows low-angle glimpses of a mouth, a nose, closed eyes, a face, nipples, a tummy, a cock, all shot from the point of view of the person lying down, which is not necessarily the perspective of the bottom. For example, over the video's beginning images of Yung from the waist up in semidarkness moving rhythmically up and down, Yung's voice-over announces, "This is me as you fuck me." Gradually, the viewer becomes aware that Yung as the bottom is actually on top, sitting on his lover's cock. The shooting of Wayne getting fucked by Peter in a bottom-riding-on-top position reinforces the narration in the rest of the sequence: "Once I was ashamed to be fucked by a white guy / as if a white cock inside me / could make a houseboy of me / Now I'm proud to be fucked / like I'm proud to be gay / I'm strong / and I like being fucked by a white guy / I'm strong / and I love being fucked by you." In this sequence, Yung invokes assumptions about Asian bottomhood as powerless and degrading in order to directly refute them. What was once shameful is turned into pride, weakness turned into strength, servitude into agency. By riding the white lover's cock, the Chinese sexual performer overcomes abjection and asserts sexual agency. However, as with all strategies of reversal, the positive terms (pride, strength) gain legibility and value only in relation to the negative (shame, weakness). Not surprisingly, the reversal of values reverts back to the original formation. In the third section of the video ("This is you as I fuck you"), Yung proclaims, "Once I was a boy / Too young to fuck a man like you / But now my manhood surges forth / as I thrust my cock deep inside you." In the beginning of the video, the shame of Asian bottomhood is converted into pride due to the boyfriend's individuality ("I'm strong / and I love being fucked *by you*" [emphasis added]). When Wayne gets to fuck Peter, "Wayne" and "Peter" lose all specificity, becoming reduced to "boy" and "man," respectively. The ability to fuck "a man like you" makes a man out of Yung.[23] In this formulation, bottomhood aligns one with youth, while topness accords one masculine power.

The analogy between bottom pride and gay pride in the first section of the video ("Now I'm proud to be fucked / like I'm proud to be gay") is a faulty analogy. Bottomhood is here racialized: it is Peter's *white* cock fucking Wayne's *Chinese* asshole that effectively transforms bottomhood from passivity into power.[24] (To be sure, my reading of Peter's white cock transforming Wayne into a powerful bottom locates another reversal effected by Yung's voice-over monologue: it is the same white cock that potentially renders Yung racially abject by turning him into a houseboy.) Yet the Asian man who proudly takes white cock inside his ass continues risking being mistaken as a houseboy going about his duties. In the second section of the video ("This is you fucking me"), we witness a strong challenge to the binary of bottomhood as either objectification or empowerment. Significantly, it is the only time in the video when bottomhood is explicitly linked with risk and danger. Instead of the visible markers of race and age that underline the other two sections, the distinction between the two lovers here is invisible: "You're HIV positive/I'm HIV negative." In the only shot from the top's POV in the video, we see Peter's cock, wrapped in a condom, moving in and out of Wayne's asshole as Yung discusses the fear he feels in getting fucked, in spite of the protection of the condom. The vulnerability of getting fucked by an HIV-positive partner is emphasized by the fact that Wayne is physically on the bottom as Peter tops him. Unfortunately, Yung does not take up the opportunity to further explore the vulnerability of the bottom partner in anal sex, in allowing oneself to be physically penetrated, to be sure. But also, what does it mean for gay male sexual intimacy to be "protected" by a latex barrier? Instead, he resorts to a simplistic reference to how their love provides him the necessary courage to overcome the fear of contracting HIV and the possibility of losing his lover to it.

According to Yung, *Peter Fucking* was made as a reaction against the bad rap about white-Asian relationships in the gay Asian community in Vancouver at the time, in which "turning sticky" was considered to be a strategy for combating the racism of the white gay community. Seen in this light, Yung's statement that getting fucked by a white guy is an affirmative act should be seen as a protest against a sexual orthodoxy that we witnessed in the sticky rice documentaries. Interestingly, in proclaiming bottomhood as powerful and giving each partner "equal time" in bottoming (and topping), Yung's strategy subscribes to the egalitarian ethos championed in sticky rice relationships and modern racially unmarked gay male relationships. But by refraining from an examination of bottomhood and its ability to affirm vulnerability, receptivity, and risk, rather than as another component of sexual versatility, Yung contains the critical force of bottomhood to undo the distinctions between shame and pride, weakness and strength, abjection and agency. The differences of race, age, and HIV status invoked in the video finally do not make any difference, because love conquers all. As Yung's closing narration announces, "Thank you, Peter. Thank you for trusting me. Thank you for loving me."

A work that offers a more open-ended and productively troubling view of bottomhood is *The Adventures of Iron Pussy III: To Be or Not to Be* (2000), directed by Thai artist Michael Shaowanasai. Moving from the sticky rice politics of gay Hongcouver to the gay sex trade of Bangkok, Thailand, allows us to see how bottomhood also inflects white-Asian interracial relationships in a Southeast Asian context. Although the politics of racialized sexuality is manifested differently in the Thai context, many fruitful resonances can be traced.[25] Because it may seem odd to discuss Shaowanasai's work in a book about Asian American sexual representation, I want to highlight the generative connections that the transnational location of his work provides. In addition to his status as a gay Asian diasporic subject moving between East and Southeast Asia, North America, and Europe, the subject matter explored in his films and videos (the fact that they often deal with sex work), the language used (Thai-accented English), and the subsequent circulation of the work (international festivals, including LGBT and Asian American venues) constitute factors that contribute to a tremendously expansive perspective that challenges the identitarian framework of North American oppositional politics. Shaowanasai's project is not concerned with establishing a visible, out-and-proud masculine gay Asian identity pinned on asserting topness or recuperating bottomhood. Rather, his work displaces the frames of visibility elsewhere by launching a trenchant critique of foreign imperialism — Western and East Asian — through the performance of gender, race/ethnicity, and sex. In doing so, he puts the labor of the queer Thai body on display, most notably in its intense, abject bottomhood. The bottom position is not a sign of powerlessness, but it is not used as a badge of gay Asian pride, either.

The Adventures of Iron Pussy III tells two parallel stories: the first concerns a drag superheroine, Iron Pussy, who does battle with a Chinese female pimp and her two henchmen to protect the livelihood of the go-go boys of Patpong, the heterosexual red-light district of Bangkok as well as the gay neighborhood that caters largely to expatriates and foreign tourists; the second narrative deals with a white "king pimp" who is a serial killer of go-go boys. In both narratives, Thailand, represented by its boy sex trade, is portrayed as a bottom figure, exploited by Chinese capital and Western sex tourists. As such, it is a repository for foreign media, commodities, currency, and cum. The video is, in fact, bookended by two naked male bodies assuming the bottom position: the first depicts it as sexually exploitative and lethal, while the second poses Asian bottomhood as a position of pleasure and danger.

The video opens with an image of a naked young Thai man lying immobile, face down on a bed, legs spread, smooth ass prominently displayed, streams of cum dripping down one butt cheek, a rope wrapped around one wrist (figure 4.8). A white man walks around the body to retrieve a small tape recorder hidden under one of the pillows. He plays the tapes at different points, as if to make sure the recording works; we hear snippets of a male voice speaking English with a strong Thai accent: "OK, I told you no hurt, na? . . . I like your blond hair. I like to make you happy. . . . What can I do for you? . . . I am Thai boy from Isan." The anonymous white man, whose face we never see, quickly exits the room. The camera follows him as he walks along the streets, bumps into a female sex worker, and stops to light her cigarette. Here, the tape cuts abruptly to the other major storyline of *Iron Pussy III*, the superheroine Iron Pussy facing the Chinese villainess Xian Xiaw Hua and her two henchmen, who threaten to take over the boy sex trade of Bangkok. I will return to the white serial killer storyline, but, following the structure of the video, let me first unpack the wicked irony of the superheroine's name.

FIGURE 4.8: To be, or not to be . . . *The Adventures of Iron Pussy III* (2000).

"Iron Pussy" constitutes a fine example of what Peter Jackson (2001, 2) calls "hybridity, complexity, and syncretism" in his examination of the global and local forces shaping the formations of lesbian and gay identities in Asia. With "iron" and "pussy," we have the simultaneous appearance of male/female, masculine/feminine, hard/soft, as well as the pairing of the technological next to the organic, inert matter alongside penetrable space, modernity and tradition. As a moniker for a superheroine campily played by a man in drag, iron pussy also conjures references to the male anus, a "man pussy" necessary for the repertoire of sex acts a sex worker might perform, but one that is impermeable to HIV and other sexually transmitted infections: this rectum is not a grave. In the context of international sex tourism, Iron Pussy represents the indestructible vagina/anus, one that is able to withstand multiple entries, exits, and reentries, a precious resource indeed for a premier sex tourist destination. The iron pussy also has a threatening, sinister side: it is an organ that cannot be worn out or used up, a formidable *vagina/anus dentata* that consumes whatever dares to enter its territory. As in the notorious pussy shows in which women shoot darts with their vaginas or the boy sex shows in which male couples fuck while suspended in midair on metal

FIGURE 4.9: Protecting go-go boys. *The Adventures of Iron Pussy III* (2000).

chains, female and male pussies—that is, bodily cavities that get fucked, used, and abused—must be maintained, exercised, and strengthened in order to guarantee a secure livelihood.

Whereas the didacticism of *Peter Fucking Wayne* asserts that getting fucked in no way compromises one's political commitments, that it is, in fact, as powerful as getting to fuck, *Iron Pussy III* suggests that getting fucked is business as usual. Bottoming—not just receptive anal sex, but any sex acts performed for the customer—enables the efficient functioning of the sex trade and benefits the Thai nation-state by safeguarding the flow of foreign currency into Thailand. As a former go-go boy, and possibly a current male hustler, Iron Pussy battles to defend Thailand from foreign imperialists (female Chinese pimp in *Iron Pussy III*, female Japanese *yakuzas* in *Iron Pussy II*) seeking to exploit Thai sex workers for their greedy benefit (figure 4.9).

Iron Pussy's superpowers are repeatedly shown to be the products of feminized, queer, Thai labor.[26] Not only must Iron Pussy work diligently at her multiple day jobs, but, more importantly, she requires a team of hair, makeup, and costume people in order to create her glamorous image.[27] While Diana Prince magically transforms into Wonder Woman by spinning in circles, Iron Pussy must go to the beauty salon to have her face done. In preparation for a duel with the Chinese female pimp, our Thai heroine must pump iron at the gym. Just as signifiers of femininity like pink tights and eyeliner can be put on, masculine strength in the form of muscles can also be cultivated and developed. In combining these gender markers, Iron Pussy stylishly impersonates the Western gay stereotype: the muscle queen. Feminine qualities from the *kathoey* (Thai male-to-female transgender) are here juxtaposed with masculine traits from a Western-style gay identity. However, there is no happy marriage between the two gender/sex systems in Iron Pussy, but rather a contentious and unstable relationship. Sex parts and gender trappings double as dangerous weapons in *Iron Pussy III*. A detachable "power testicle" tossed into the Chinese villainess's mouth packs a mean punch. As a masculine attribute ordinarily connoting male potency, a beard thrown onto the face of Iron Pussy humiliates and unmans her. The Chinese henchman's ripping off of her female wig simulates decapitation, exposing Iron Pussy's failed masquerade of femininity. However, this symbolic castration actually contains the seed for a repossession of power: Iron Pussy's baby-bouffant wig turns out to be a bomb that blows the bad guys to pieces. Through such subterfuge and guerilla tactics, our nationalist superheroine successfully exterminates the Chinese invaders.[28] It is crucial to point out that the superlabor of Iron Pussy is to wrestle back control of the boy sex industry, not to eliminate the sex trade entirely. As she stands proudly on the deserted Patpong street, her orange glitter cape waving gently, Iron Pussy's voice-over exclaims: "Now, go-go boys of Patpong are safe. They are free to sell themselves and take in foreign currency to boost up our economy. Bangkok is again at peace, to keep up with the title 'Pleasure Paradise of the World.'" Iron Pussy's victory reveals resistance and triumph as partial and contingent. To be sure, the Thai gay pleasure paradise remains a paradise for the foreign sex tourists, and not for the locals who must use their unironic pussies and anuses to maintain it.[29]

Our story doesn't end there. After defeating the Chinese bad guys, another storyline depicts Iron Pussy in her other night job as a male prostitute. Thus, this plot twist indicates that the battle against foreign imperialists continues, with the target shifting from East Asia to the West. We see Iron Pussy enter a hotel, only to reemerge seconds later in his everyday guise as a man, decked out in gay male dress: tight black jeans and tight red muscle shirt. The camera follows him through the streets, stopping to socialize with friends, chatting on his cell phone, and finally meeting up with a male friend, who turns out to be none other than the white john from the beginning of the video. Iron Pussy and the man greet one another with romantic kisses, oblivious to the stares around them; they walk holding hands down Silom Road, the main street of the red-light and gay districts. Suddenly, the camera cuts to the two passionately making out in the white man's room, the same one we saw at the beginning of the video. Clearly the more aggressive partner, Iron Pussy takes off his shirt, unbuttons the white man's shirt, goes down on his knees, peppers kisses on the man's tummy, eagerly sucks on his partner's fingers, and unbuckles his belt. Abruptly, Iron Pussy excuses himself to go to the bathroom. In his absence, we see the white man place his tape recorder under a pillow, thus unequivocally linking him to the figure we saw at the beginning of the tape. Returning from the bathroom, the two men make out fiercely while the camera circles them in close-ups. Finally, Iron Pussy lubes up his asshole, falls on the bed, and adopts the doggy position. He looks back over his shoulders at his white partner (and by implication, us viewers), wriggling his raised ass seductively, expectantly, eagerly. As the camera/the white man moves toward him, the screen cuts to black. A title appears: "To be or not to be?"

The suspense of *Iron Pussy III*'s cliffhanger rests on whether our superheroine will survive. Will a fate similar to that of the murdered male prostitute befall our heroine? What sexual secrets and superpowers might she have up her cape to save herself or to seduce the white serial murderer to keep him from fucking her to death? *Iron Pussy III* contextualizes Hamlet's existential query weighing the tribulations of life and the unknown of death to address questions of economic survival, sex work, HIV/AIDS, transnational sexual identities, pleasure, and danger. Iron Pussy's dilemma echoes Yung's disconnect between private sexual practice and public political identity: a superheroine who combats Chinese imperialists on the streets takes it up the ass from a white Western man in the sheets. But where Yung claims this sex act to be an empowering one due to his white lover's love and trust, that is, his affirmation of Yung as a sexual subject, Iron Pussy's bottom position offered up for his white partner does not lend itself to an ecstatic embrace of bottomhood. For one thing, the boundaries between public and private are much more unstable in *Iron Pussy III* than the ones laid out in *Peter Fucking*. Instead of the intimate fucking by flashlight recorded by handheld camcorder, the performance of sexuality, gender, race, and nationality by Iron Pussy in both her guises as superheroine and gay male prostitute takes place on busy streets, shot and performed as street theater. In an area known as Bangkok's most famous red-light district (catering to both heterosexual and gay clientele) and commercial gay neighborhood, the couple is easily read by passersby as a Thai money boy and a white john. (My point is that such a reading already publicly brands him as a bottom before we see him stripped on all fours.) Even if we characterize their relationship as romantic, as "boyfriends," such an appellation does not necessarily rule out an economic dimension. There is no unified identity politics (e.g., racial-sexual, potato queen–rice queen) to anchor our reading of their relationship. Hence, unlike the showdown between Iron Pussy and the Chinese female pimp, the drawing up of sides—good versus evil, agent versus victim—in the bedroom battle with the *farang* is complicated by the politics of queer desire.

The sight of Iron Pussy naked on his hands and knees, ass poised and beckoning provocatively, suggests more than an instance of victimhood. Unlike the cultural naïveté and obsequious passivity of the white john's last Thai victim ("I like your blond hair. I like to make you happy. . . . I am Thai boy from Isan"), we witness Iron Pussy as the active initiator of the sexual activity: controlling the pace and rhythm, stripping off his clothes, undressing his partner, voraciously licking, kissing, caressing, and falling on his knees. By couching Iron Pussy's bottomhood, and hence his very survival, as a cliffhanger, the video leaves the question of bottomhood as sexual agency or objectification open ended. Is the irresistible desire to get fucked up the ass Iron Pussy's Achilles heel? Is his bottomhood a natural propensity, a cultural adaptation, a sexual preference, and/or an economic necessity? If we follow the logic of Iron Pussy's previous narration, the victory over the Chinese villainess ensures the smooth functioning of the sex trade, and by extension, Thailand's economy. Iron Pussy's tongue-in-cheek injunction for go-go boys to sell themselves for the benefit of the nation represents a strong critique of the Thai nation-state that, while profiting from the sexual labor of its most stigmatized subjects (women, *kathoeys*, gay men), refuses to accord them social recognition. Assuming the bottom position is Iron Pussy doing his part as a good worker and citizen in order to uphold Bangkok's status as Pleasure Paradise of the World. Yet his taking up the position too enthusiastically reveals a modicum of power and pleasure that cannot be reduced to national duty. The deployment of bottomhood-as-cliffhanger reveals that though he might get fucked, Iron Pussy is not fucked over. Finally, narrative conventions of the action-adventure genre lead us to expect Iron Pussy to survive for the next series installment. Iron Pussy's bottomhood flirts with danger and gambles with the white devil, but, we suspect, she will ultimately come out on top.

Just as our analysis of *Iron Pussy III* provides a more multifaceted view of bottomhood that exceeds the regulatory framework of gay Asian sticky rice politics, an examination of the work of Korean American lesbian artist Erica Cho demonstrates that adopting a view from below generates surprising identifications and alliances across genders, races/ethnicities, generations, and sexualities. Along with the practices of her cohorts Lynne Chan, Lala/Felix Endara, and Yvette Choy, Cho's work reflects an exciting, smart, and sexy tendency in Asian American lesbian artistic productions that irreverently resignifies Asian masculinity, a project that is decidedly not invested in the (straight and gay) Asian American male recuperation of masculinity. Refreshingly, Cho consistently poses her resignified masculinity alongside femininity. While she also exhibits an interest in creating playful and sexualized images of queer Asians, her image repertoires and aesthetic strategies are much more promiscuous and wide ranging than the gay Asian documentaries' narrower reference to gay male sexual subcultures. In turning my attention to Asian American lesbian cultural production, I seek to expand the archive of critical bottomhood beyond the purview of Asian American men. Furthermore, in making such a move, I follow the lead of feminist and lesbian scholars, activists, and cultural workers who have imaginatively and courageously theorized, performed, and embodied masculinities beyond the confines of normativity, in both hetero and homosexual guises.

Following in this feminist and lesbian tradition, Cho's reformulation of masculinity is not necessarily linked to what is (already) real, but it also points to possibilities and permutations available through artistic imagination and erotic fantasy. The powerful work of fantasy is exemplified in her passionate re-presentation of the vulnerable ethnic male body in the videotape *We Got Moves You Ain't Even Heard Of (Part One)* (1999).[30] In it, Cho reenacts specific scenes from *The Karate Kid* (dir. John G. Avildsen, 1984) in which Daniel LaRusso (Ralph Macchio), the Italian American transplant from New Jersey, gets beaten up and humiliated by his buffed, blond-haired California high school classmates. Instead of zooming in on the climax when Daniel the underdog triumphs over his opponent at the film's conclusion, Cho finds the moments when Daniel suffers most spectacularly at the hands of the macho bullies most generative for Asian dyke erotic appropriation.

Interestingly, bottomhood crucially determines how we read this dyke of color appropriation.

The video opens with shaky, handheld footage of downtown Los Angeles at night: empty streets, deserted construction sites, and dirty vacant lots. This location of urban decay, dereliction, and danger becomes the setting for queer public sex. Backed by Bananarama's 1983 hit "Cruel Summer," snippets of dialogue from Karate Kid ("Hey, what was that, karate? . . . Bet you can kick some ass. I'd like to learn some. Maybe you could teach me"), and ambient street noises, we see Cho, dressed like a teenage boy in jeans and hoodie sweater, crouched down in a kneeling position, licking the crack of a bare ass. What is more remarkable, this sight of queer sex is intercut with eyeline shots of Macchio as Daniel intently looking on. The shot–reverse shot structure interpellates Daniel as a rapt spectator of a scene of analingus between Cho and an anonymous partner.[31]

This early scene of Cho "kissing ass" establishes the tone for the rest of the video. What might commonly be regarded as a degrading, perverted act is performed as a tender, erotic gesture, its intimacy reinforced by the low lighting and extreme graininess of the image. In the same way, by revisiting key moments in Karate Kid when Daniel is attacked by bullies, Cho lingers fondly and compassionately over scenes of violation through formal techniques of video looping and slow motion. For example, in a sequence of Daniel and his mother at breakfast, through reediting, Cho inserts herself in the place of Daniel. At the command of Daniel's mom ("Are you on something? . . . Then take off the glasses. Now!"), Cho/Daniel slowly removes her dark sunglasses to reveal a big black eye underneath. We gasp along with Daniel's mother as we watch Cho/Daniel reluctantly exposing her bruised eye. The emotional intensity of the scene lies in the transmission of Daniel's plight to Cho; though different in many ways, his racial, class, and gender injuries reverberate with hers. A scene in which Daniel gets attacked and made to eat sand is reenacted by Cho (in character as Daniel wearing a red hooded sweater) repeatedly taking stunt dives into the sand at a deserted beach (figure 4.10). In another reenactment, a particularly humiliating scene in which Daniel gets a plate of spaghetti dumped in the crotch of his white pants in a public restaurant with his female love interest watching nearby is transformed by the video maker into one in which, wearing red-stained white pants like Daniel did in the movie, she uses the spaghetti as "lube" for a dyke masturbation session. Rejecting facile notions of ethnic

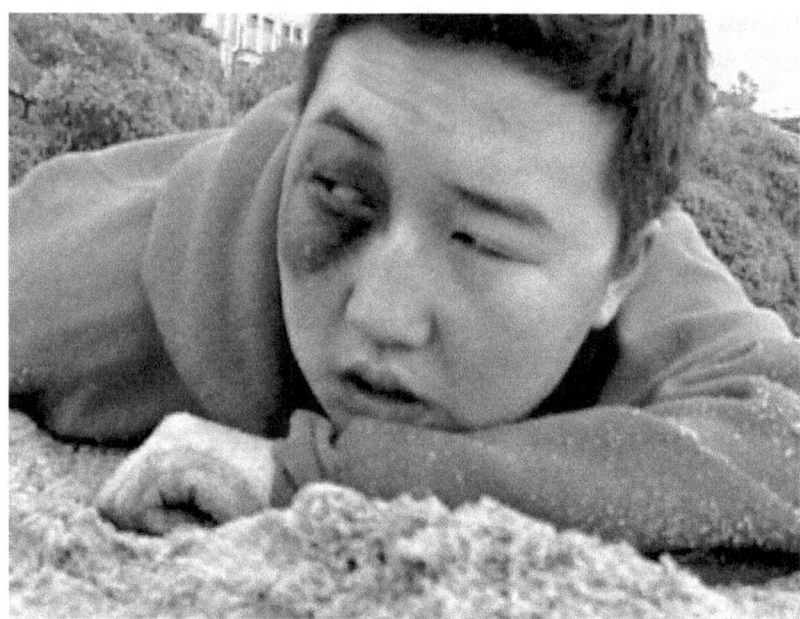

FIGURE 4.10: Eating sand. *We Got Moves You Ain't Even Heard Of (Part One)* (1999).

male empowerment through knee-jerk reclamations of subordinated masculinities, in these reenactments, Cho harnesses affects such as shame and humiliation for their productive potential — mined in these reenactments by the transfiguring of shame and humiliation into sexual pleasure.

It is significant as well that Cho's perverse rearticulation of queer ethnic masculinities is accomplished not by displacing but by recentering femininity. Her boy-dyke masculinity embraces a femme-fag aesthetic and draws on the androgynous style associated with 1970s and 1980s male teen idols (e.g., Macchio, Leif Garrett, Shaun Cassidy, Robby Benson, Matt Dillon, and River Phoenix), who cultivated their sexy prettiness by wearing tight clothes and sporting long feathered hair. This slim, soft, youthful masculinity, while packaged for young adolescent girls, has been adopted by boy-dykes and transfags in recent years in reaction to deglamorized, flannel butch lesbian styles and the hypermasculine, buffed gay clone look. Identifying the narrative logic of the film that inspires her video, Cho states, "In the original narrative of *The Karate Kid*, [Daniel] finds his identity and overcomes his enemies, not by taking up a gun in typical 80s Rambo/Chuck Norris style, but by disguising his training, becoming more invisible and turning into a beautiful crane over water, therefore connecting to femininity and feminine wisdom."[32] Although Macchio's perennially youthful face already connotes a nonthreatening eroticism, Cho's appropriation of his image in *We Got Moves* effectively transforms him into a dyke icon: Daniel comes to resemble a hot baby butch.

While Cho's abject boy-dyke effects a cross-racial, cross-gender movement in modeling himself after Ralph Macchio, the other significant cross-identification in this text is that between Daniel and his older Asian karate master. It is under the tutelage of Mr. Miyagi (Noriyuki "Pat" Morita) that Daniel develops a novel masculine-feminine technique of the self that enables his ultimate triumph over his opponents. Cho's queer idolization brings out the homoerotic potential in the student-teacher relationship between Mr. Miyagi and Daniel that is barely hinted at in the film. Instead of a model of homosexuality based on gender equality, such as Marks and the sticky rice documentaries espouse, Cho revitalizes a prominent form of same-sex relations buried in queer cultural history: the older/younger, mentor/mentee, professor/student, intergenerational relationship that has become tabooed in the contemporary assimilationist gay scene. The deviant sexuality of Mr. Miyagi, an elderly Japanese American handyman without a wife or children, becomes queerly legible through his mentorship of Daniel. Rooted in Daniel's unquestioned submission to Mr. Miyagi's superior Oriental wisdom, their relationship is decidedly not based on the ideal of egalitarianism, reciprocity, or heterosexual reproduction. While the muted interracial homoerotic bond between the two men provides the entry point for Cho's cross-identification with Daniel in his most shameful, abject states, it is necessary to qualify this queer fluidity and to specify its strategy. For unlike Daniel, who goes on to defeat his opponent at the karate tournament (and not surprisingly, win the girl) at the end of the film, Cho remains stuck on the earlier moments of the film, finding an emotional payoff in replaying those humiliating scenes over and over like an obsessed fan with her favorite movie. Instead of moving forward in the narrative to see the underdog overcome his limitations and triumph, Cho's moment of truth involves a repetitive looping back, a constant looking behind to re-touch the past in order to feel and receive it differently.

Here is where Cho's trajectory departs radically from Daniel's in *Karate Kid*. Even as her mimicry of Daniel (lip-syncing his lines; copying his hair, makeup, and costume; imitating his movements) evokes a camp humor with its dyke of color parody of a wounded straight white male, a large part of its queer affect lies in the wide gap between Cho's racialized, queerly gendered body and Daniel/Macchio's white ethnic, adolescent male body. While the traditional Hollywood narrative is easily adjusted to accommodate Daniel/Macchio's conversion from pathetic wimp to underdog hero, it can hardly imagine Cho's faggotized dyke in such a scenario. The force of Cho's fantasy in *We Got Moves* derives from her disruption of the normative trajectory of *Karate Kid*, and, by extension, the American national ethos of success: the little guy who, through sheer hard work and perseverance, rises to the top. Instead, Cho embraces the bullied loser who persists in her pain and suffering, without the reward of redemption in the last reel.[33]

The itinerary from abjection to empowerment has structured the texts we have examined in this chapter. The gay Asian documentaries postulate the conversion from potato queen to sticky rice as analogous to a progression from sex object to sexual subject. Yung's *Peter Fucking Wayne* inverts the logic of the documentaries with its reclamation of the bottom position by articulating a movement from weakness and shame to strength and pride. *Iron Pussy III* interrogates this shift by having its superheroine turn back into a male sex worker; though it leaves the meaning of Iron Pussy's bottom sex act undecidable, the video's narrative riddle ("To be or not to be") links bottomhood with life and death. What is most striking about *We Got Moves* is its explicit rejection of the trajectory from objectification to agency that frames the other works. This is the same progress narrative that underlines different minoritarian political projects (LGBT, Asian American) whose narrative flow tracks a change from shame to pride, from femininity to masculinity, from bottomhood to topness. By dwelling in abject bottomhood, Cho finds eroticism and a degree of power in racial-sexual subjection, and, in so doing, she challenges the equivalence between topness, masculinity, and subjecthood.

In the compulsive return to past injuries, Cho lays bare the intimate, productive relationship between queerness and temporality. As Eve Sedgwick points out, "If queer is a politically potent term, which it is, that's because, far from being capable of being detached from the childhood scene of shame, it cleaves to that scene as a near-inexhaustible source of transformational energy" (1995, 210). By harvesting the "transformational energy" from her bullied adolescence as mediated through the *Karate Kid*, Cho does not idealize the baby dyke as an authentic victim of homophobic violence.[34] It is significant that the restaging of childhood sexual trauma is performed by Cho as mature lesbian artist, one who excavates the terror of the past as material for erotic fantasies in the present. At the same time, her willful clinging to the "childhood scene of shame" challenges the progressive, future-directed bent of minoritarian movement politics that would dismiss such attachments as outdated and pathological. In refusing to get over past grievances (in pop psychology lingo, to learn from the experience, to move on with one's life, and to use it to make one a better person), the narrative of *We Got Moves* follows a different, and queer, time line, one that refuses to go forward, but rather insists on looping back around.[35] In light of the view of queers as "temporally backward . . . as having no past: no childhood, no origin or precedent in nature, no family traditions or legends" (Freeman 2007, 162), Cho relives a childhood, an origin, a popular legend. The power of these revisionist narratives is not undermined even if they are made up, embellished, or digitally enhanced.

The rearward trajectory of *We Got Moves* crystallizes the spatial and temporal coordinates of bottomhood that I have delineated throughout the book. Attending to the spatial-temporal logics of the behind (in the sense of being stuck in time and fixed in a devalued, lowly point of view), my study offers a different model of politics that champions the forging of alliances and affinities with others, as we witnessed in the preceding chapters: Brandon Lee and his FOB costars and viewers, Anacleto and Alison, the Chinese lover and the young French girl, gay Asian men who identify as sticky rice, and Cho and the Karate Kid. To offer some closing thoughts on queer racialized sexual receptivity and its potential for fostering new relations, I turn to a quotidian example of sexual interaction that mobilizes the threatening force of abjection to assert and affirm gay Asian subjecthood.

CONCLUSION

The recentering of femininity in Erica Cho's Asian baby butch take on bottomhood in *We Got Moves You Ain't Even Heard Of (Part One)* provides me the opportunity to highlight the personal and scholarly influence of lesbian writings on butch-femme desire on my thinking around gay Asian American bottomhood. Butch-femme sexuality constitutes a lesbian sex-gender formation that creatively refunctions heterosexual codes into a vital form of queer sociality. In a phrasing that perfectly captures Cho's artistic appropriation in *We Got Moves*, Juana María Rodríguez describes butch-femme as a manner of "disentangl[ing] bodies and acts from preassigned meanings, creating meaning and pleasure anew from the recycled scraps of dominant cultures" (2007, 286). To be sure, significant differences exist between lesbian butch-femme sexuality and gay male top-bottom sexual positions. For one, butch-femme is a sexual aesthetic that encompasses sexual practice and gender expression, whereas top-bottom commonly refers to sexual roles and positions not necessarily linked to gender presentation. Indeed, contemporary gay male discourses of bottomhood stubbornly disavow the imaginative queering of gender and sexual norms found in lesbian butch-femme sexuality. Against gay male repudiations of bottomhood as feminizing, throughout the book, I have insisted on bottomhood as a position—sexual, social, affective, political, aesthetic—and a mode of relationality that is nurtured by alignments with femininity and the feminine. As such, my formulation of gay Asian American bottomhood intervenes in the "hypermasculinization of bottoming" through a strategic rejoining of gender presentation and sexual practice. Instead of resorting to a renaturalization of gender witnessed in such an appellation as "butch bottom," I emphasize gay male bottomhood's social and historical adjacency with various techniques of gender dissidence, including femininity, femmeness, effeminacy, faggotry, sissiness, camp, androgyny, and drag.[1] In addition, factoring in race alongside these various genres of feminized genders enables a refutation of the equation of masculinity with social recognition and legitimacy.

Scholars writing on lesbian femme have described femme femininity as "a femininity that is transgressive, disruptive, and chosen" (Harris and Crocker 1997, 3); the lesbian femme "occupies normality abnormally" (Duggan and McHugh 1996, 155). Thus, against the dismissal of lesbian femme as an inauthentic replica of heterosexual femininity, critics have argued for lesbian femme as a dissident, perverse, sexualized, and desired sex-gender category. Drawing on arguments for lesbian femme as "an empowered category of queer gender" (Textor 1997, 198), I challenge the scorn directed against "femme" in gay male communities by considering gay male femme as similarly perverse, sexualized, and wanted, thus interrogating the conflation of maleness with masculinity, and masculinity with sexual desirability. A more expansive, and queer, horizon of gender embodiment suggests that "for some gay men, femininity may be a desiring position, and conversely, in others it may be what is desirable" (Garlinger 1999, 70). To resuture femininity with bottomhood is to recognize the complex gender differences among men, specifically those that surpass conventional investments in normative masculinity, investments that frequently reek of extreme misogyny and effeminophobia. Instead of the unexamined acceptance of homonormative celebrations of masculine norms, a more productive analysis of male femme attends to important gay male feminine embodiments in the past.[2] By remarking on the association between lesbian femme and gay Asian American bottomhood, I attend to Tania Modleski's important distinction between a "male alignment with femininity" and a "male alignment with *feminism*" (1991, 150, emphasis in original). In doing so, I acknowledge the major influence of feminist and lesbian theories of sexuality and gender on my conceptualization of racialized bottomhood; this recognition also constitutes a politically inflected alliance between feminist-lesbian and queer Asian American male critiques, thus instantiating the reverberation of the term bottomhood with sisterhood.[3] A queer and feminist coalition is privileged over and against gay male aspiration to normalization. Inspired by the capacious redrawing of sociability in butch-femme theory, I seek to expand the boundaries of top-bottom to envelop multiple subject positions. Rodríguez maintains that butch-femme constitutes not identities but a mode of relationality; its "sexual moments and movements belong to no one and can be accessed by anyone" (2007, 284). Echoing Rodriguez, Jewelle Gomez clarifies, "We could just as easily call femme/butch relationships yin/yang, or north/south, or better yet: magnetic" (1998, 150).[4] The complicated negotiation, exchange, and interplay of power and pleasure in butch-femme literature exemplify a sustained attention to social differences and antagonisms as well as the eroticized politicization of the sexual. These dynamics, though specific to lesbian intimacies, are available for different rearticulations by other kinds of femmes and butches, bottoms and tops. Bringing both gender and race (back) to bottomhood reveals it as a magnetic positioning from which to look at, feel out, and relate to the world.

My articulation of gay Asian American bottomhood is not concerned with empirical evidence or with erecting a new sexual essentialism. It is not advocating for another politics of visibility, a call for bottoms to find themselves and proudly come out. Rather, it advances bottomhood as a sexual, social, and political program that one tactically assumes and consciously cultivates. Bottomhood describes a particular way of inhabiting an abject social-sexual-racial positioning situated in relation to other social-sexual-racial positions in a field of power and difference. Bottomhood constitutes a process of subjectification, one involving subjugation while enabling recognition. Not all subjects who are relegated to bottom positions necessarily inhabit bottomhood. Those who dwell in bottomhood capitalize on their own marginalization from heteronormativity. A tactic of the bottom, to paraphrase Michel de Certeau, recognizes its own limitations at the same time that it makes use of the "clever tricks of the 'weak' within the order established by the 'strong'" (de Certeau 1984, 40).[5]

To bring a more recent example to bear on the bottom historiography I have traced throughout the book, in these concluding pages I examine an everyday sexual performance of bottomhood that departs from the cinematic, videographic, and artistic terrains that constitute my objects of analysis in the preceding chapters. My concluding case study is drawn from online media, specifically, gay male sex cruising websites.[6] The analysis of gay Asian male navigation of online gay environments affirms gay Asian male cruisers' creative negotiation of a racialized sexual marketplace where their feminized Asianness places them at a distinct disadvantage. Employing a tactic of the bottom, gay Asian men enact a racial-sexual masquerade that mobilizes exposure and concealment, identity and positioning, to challenge virtual whiteness and interrogate GAM legibility in sexualized online environments. In doing so, they "[create] meaning and pleasure anew from the recycled scraps of dominant cultures."

"look_im_azn"

In spite of the identification of digital divides and "racial ravines" preventing marginalized groups from gaining entry into cyberspace,[7] Asian Americans and queers constitute two minority groups that have been able to assert a marked presence online. It is not surprising then that the Internet is the one arena where one finds a saturation of eroticized images of Asian men: on social networking websites, chat forums, blogs, personal ads, gay porn sites, and sex cruising sites. Gay Asian men (GAMs) combat invisibility through the posting of sexually explicit "self-pics" advertising body parts (chest, stomach, torso, ass, cock); they contest desexualization through the recitation of sexual scripts conveying preferred sexual practices and positions. Like the sticky rice documentaries analyzed in chapter 4, these sexual want ads allow gay Asian men to chip away at mainstream gay porn's monopoly in rendering GAMs as objects of desire. Taking full advantage of the gay "pornification of everyday life" through new media,[8] GAMs become sexual subjects who take control of the expressions of their sexual wants and needs. As part of their negotiations of the new freedoms afforded by online presence and the homonormative constraints that exclude them from the sexual playing field, some GAMs redeploy visual and tactile bodily traits deemed negative and stereotypical in order to compete in the online sexual marketplace: smooth skin, small lean build, toned torso, and a tight hairless ass. However, such empowering articulations of erotic and sexual subjectivity by GAMs have met with virulent rejection by other members of the gay virtual community. The common response posted by non-Asian men—"Sorry, not into Asians. No offense. Just a preference"—implies that preferences are socially and politically innocent, not intended to "offend." Gay Asian male bodies, seen and seen through, are simultaneously acknowledged and made to disappear.

On sex cruising sites, unless one announces otherwise, everyone assumes that one is a white gay man. Gay Asian men who do not declare their Asianness through photos or textual descriptions (in their profiles, screen names, e-mails, or chat conversations) are considered to be hiding or passing.[9] Such a view, however, recenters whiteness as the default category and puts the burden on nonwhite users to confess their difference and deviation from the unspoken norm. Except for face pics and other ancillary clues (such as a check in the Ethnicity box), one economical way for cruisers of color to publicize their race and ethnicity is through the screen name. Yet the decision for a person of color to come out about his race online is not an innocent gesture, but takes on a different kind of political valence in comparison to a white user declaring his whiteness. In a context in which one's racialized body is deemed alien and undesirable, the gesture of embracing GAM abjected identity constitutes a politically meaningful assertion. In the following, I look at two specific tactics employed by GAMs in their navigation of online sex cruising websites: the first is the posting of headless torso pictures, and the second is the use of screen names. The first method makes the GAM body unreadable; the second defiantly declares GAM online presence by rendering it excessively intelligible. In doing so, GAMs pass as something they already are: GAMs, thus confirming Wendy Chun's (2006, 59) point that far from "protect[ing] viewers from becoming spectacles, from being in public," passing turns cruisers into spectacles.

Digital photos take precedence over the written text in online gay cruising, serving as the bait for the instigation of the online cruise. For example, one often comes across the proviso "No Pic = No Chat" (or its more direct version, "No Pic/No Play"); those without photos are commonly ignored and blocked by other users. One finds a variety of photos posted on sites such as Manhunt.net, Adam4Adam.com, and Gay.com, but self-pics generally fall into the categories of face, torso, cock, ass pics, and photos depicting sexual acts such as oral and anal sex.[10] While the sexual exhibitionism inherent to the posting of one's face and cock in the semipublic space of the Internet suggests the risk of (over)exposure and loss of privacy, online cruising actually affords more control over one's image than say, meeting someone in the physical context of a bar. Nevertheless, users of gay dating and sex cruising sites frequently complain about the rampant misrepresentation that occurs on these sites.[11] While they usually protest against the deliberate deception in the use of old and/or fake photos, one can also point to other deceptive strategies employed by online cruisers to put their best face, torso, and cock forward while at the same time maintaining a sense of control and privacy over their virtual image and identity. I refer here to the posting of pictures that are blurry; taken from unique, complimentary angles; tight close-ups; extreme long shots; exceedingly small in size and/or resolution; slick professional studio shots; carefully cropped; and digitally altered. As one Manhunt.net cruiser helpfully points out, "people that look TOO good in pictures generally make it happen that way"—by which he means that they don't actually look that good in real life.

It's safe to say that for many men, the face photo is the deciding factor, the deal maker or deal breaker. Hence, for those who don't have face photos clearly posted, the online cruise (involving e-mails, instant messaging, digital "smiles," the unlocking of photos) commonly concludes with a sharing of face pictures. Not surprisingly, most people will not agree to meet offline for sex without seeing at least one face picture. With this all-important requirement of the face photo in mind, the first tactic I want to discuss concerns the ubiquitous headless torso pics uploaded by Asian men on their profiles. These include shirtless pictures showing whole bodies or featuring the torso from shoulders to tummy; whatever the camera distance, the head is cropped off or digitally obscured (figures C.1 and C.2). Although headless torso photos are used by many users to remain anonymous, I contend that one must factor in the issue of race in the analysis of these headless GAM profiles. For these users, anonymity is not only about protecting one's privacy but also has to do with the conflation of anonymity with virtual whiteness. The headless body shots allow GAMs to emphasize their most attractive body part while remaining discreet. More to the point, this maintenance of anonymity enables GAMs to temporally and performatively "drag out" their racial and ethnic difference. The Asian headless torso exemplifies a self-effacement and a radical decapitation that refuse to make GAM-ness knowable, and thus easily seen, ignored, blocked, and deleted.[12] Here, we find a critique and a tribute to the ideal digital homo body with the cropping off of the Asian face. The sexy Asian torso works online because it resembles and conforms to the ideal body of a young white man, in a context in which such a body functions as the desirable norm. In tilting the focus from head to body, GAM self-defacement shifts the all-knowing, all-assessing stare from the excessively legible Oriental face to the unreadable, deracinated torso.[13]

Exploiting the stereotype of the Asian face as an inscrutable mask, I sug-

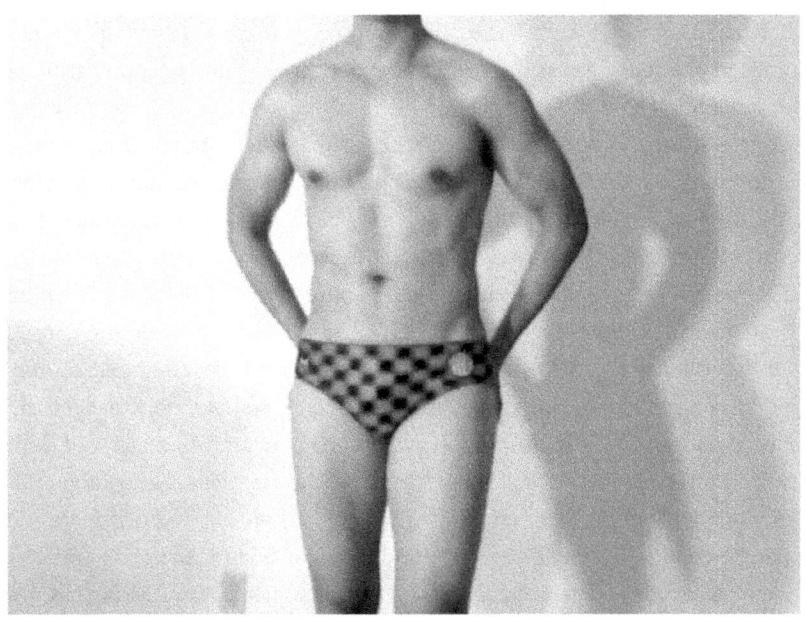
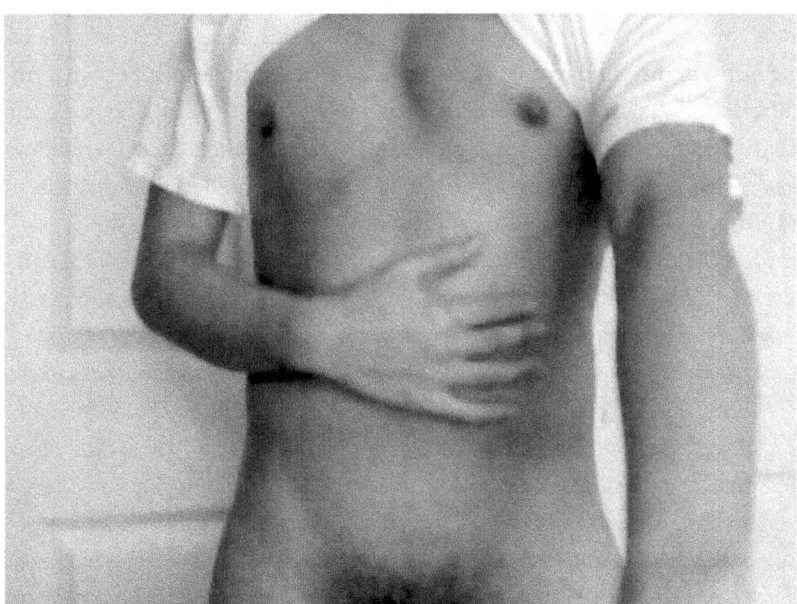

FIGURES C.1 AND C.2: Headless torsos. *look_im_azn* (2011).

gest that GAMs who refuse to make their Asianness transparent in their digital pics are strategically utilizing online control and anonymity to enact a tactical masking. In contrast to the example of "textual masking" (Danet 1998) in previous discussions of virtual cross-dressing and its implication of masquerading as an identity that one is really not, my use of masking draws on Fran Martin's (2003) work on "tactical masking." Martin analyzes the controversial practice of Taiwanese *tongzhi* (queer) activists donning colorful Chinese opera masks in their public appearances, such as parades and press conferences. Read as an ironic "collective coming out," these masks also operate as a critique of homosexual oppression and the ways in which society forces *tongzhi* to wear masks in everyday life (Martin 2003, 191). On the other hand, critics of *tongzhi* masking object that the tactic merely reinforces the social order by reaffirming society's stipulation that *tongzhi* should continue to hide behind masks. Martin writes, "As a tactic of defiant self-effacement or even self-defacement, the *tongzhi* masking tactic implicitly questions the very conditions of visibility within authorized public space — conditions which make it impossible for homosexuals to appear as complete or properly 'faced' (*you lian*) social subjects" (195). Martin's description of the ambivalent deployment of masking provides insight into the double nature of GAM headless torsos: they constitute a tactic that simultaneously contests and reaffirms the dominance of whiteness and the marginalization of Asianness in gay male communities. Even as the sexy, smooth, toned, decapitated GAM torso passes for a racially unmarked ideal homo body, its eventual reattachment to the Asian face undermines gay Asian cruisers' claim to sexual desirability, confirming their abject status once more.[14] At the same time, in arguing for this double movement, Martin's concept of tactical masking troubles conventional assumptions about visibility and empowerment, exposure and camouflage, identity and politics.

The obverse of rendering GAM-ness opaque in the torso-as-mask example is the strategy of embracing GAM identity and abjection by the adoption of racially marked and overdetermined screen names. In the place of the headless torso pictures' aesthetic of defacement and delay, the adoption of GAM screen names exploits the method of in-your-face confrontation. On the gay sex cruising sites under consideration, users employ a resourceful array of screen names. Created not only to be titillating and memorable, but also to communicate crucial information about the bearer of the handle, screen names can designate a geographical location (navytopdc), preferred sexual practices (yngcumdrainer), physical descriptions (hardthicktoo129), play on first names (mmmmMichael), occupation (airforceboy23), affective or poetic reference (heatseeker), object of desire (bklyndad4bklynlad), lifestyle or brand identity (af_guy23), and finally, race and ethnicity. In this category, one finds such names as latinobttmlkn, azntennislegs, ebonykev, but only seldom does one encounter hotwhtcowboi. That is, announcing one's whiteness in cyberqueer space comes across as somehow redundant.[15]

I identify two key tactics employed by GAMs to contest their virtual invisibility: one is the utilization of "GAM" or "AZN" and the other is the miming of Oriental abjection in handles derived from racial slurs. The first tactic exploits the substitutability of Asian as a racial category. The dizzying repetitions and permutations of GAM and AZN bespeak a certain genericness that empties out what GAM-ness as a sexualized racial category might encompass. The repeated modification of GAM and AZN eviscerates their originary stereotypes. Consider this method of self-naming as a critical, campy spin on the common claim that "all Orientals look the same." I cite a list that illustrates a variety of combinations: submissive_gam, sweetie-gam, gam-bttm, gamtop4u, leather_n_gam, smgam4fun, benicegam, inner_beauty-gam, dieselgam77, gam_buddy_69, hot-gam, bbbtmgam, GAM4GBM, gam4glm, gam4gam, GAM4Mature, GAMforService, gamlokng4love, gam-looking4fun, GAMinLA, GAMinSF, gamprofessional, gamweek; Azn4Fun, azn4grabs, azn94107, AznArtFag, aznassfuker, AznAthlete, aznbuttboy, aznchi, AznCock415, azncub4daddies, azndelight, azndirkdiggler, azndreamboi, aznfratdude, azngymbunny, aznjdawg18, AznJOBuddy, aznloverboy1234, aznmassge, AznParkRanger, AZNQTLKN41UV, Aznswimmer389, azntwinkboi24; and my personal favorites, look_im_azn and onemoreazn (figure C.3).

Interestingly, the use of GAM and AZN as parts of gay Asian men's screen names, while allegedly foregrounding gay Asian men's racial difference and their aspiration to be up front about their race, tells us very little about what difference such GAM-ness makes. In its reiteration and interchangeability, GAM becomes a placeholder, a generic type, that must be amended and modified by other traits to make sense: GAMs and AZNs only come into legibility in relation to qualifiers such as geographical location, preferred sex acts, age, occupation, hobbies, economic status, and so on. These GAM screen names foreground identity as a performance that makes visible one's invisibility and illustrates the ways in which the process of visibility conceals as much as it reveals. In addition to commenting on online anonymity and identity tourism, cruisers' strategies of virtual sexual seduction often entail blatant lies about their physical characteristics (age, height, weight, cock

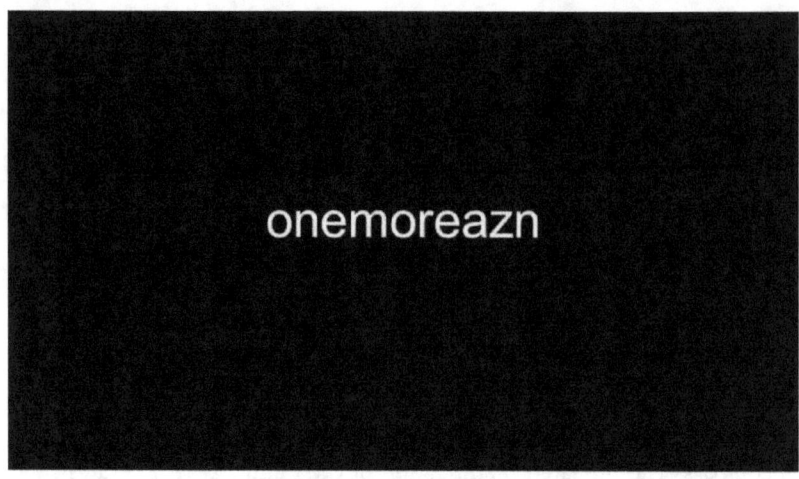

FIGURE C.3: AZN screen name. *look_im_azn* (2011).

FIGURE C.4: Racial slur as screen name. *look_im_azn* (2011).

size, location, occupation), thus making literal post-structuralist theories about the performativity of identities.

In contrast to the generic interchangeability of the GAM handles, another strategy utilized by GAMs is the use of racially abject screen names, one that exploits what Karen Shimakawa (2002, 21) terms Asian American "critical mimesis." These include such screen names as chinkorama, BBChink, chinkytwink, sxy_chink_boi, chinkyme, chinkysmile, chinky_eyez, spunkychink, fucked_up_chink, tj-communist-chink, alex_ugly_chink, chink_daddy, gookbuddy, gook, cracker_gook, KoreanWhoreHouse, japsjaps, jap24, suitntiejapboy, kenjap, shyjap, forricequeenonly, gam_slut_bubble_ ass, asianalslut, notcuteasian, asian_slave, asiangeishaboy, full_azn_service, aznbtmhole, aznpussyboy, and so on (figure C.4).

The enunciation of GAM abjection contests the tyranny of positive representation that seeks to arrest the mobility, multiplicity, and duplicity of GAM subjectivities. Abject GAM screen naming effectively "questions the very conditions of visibility [afforded GAMs] within authorized public space" (Martin 2003, 195)—that is, online gay cruising grounds. To be sure, this "deathly embrace" of GAM abjection powerfully alludes to nonnormative sexual practices, identifications, and desires.[16] Following Shimakawa, I contend that the authors of these "chinky" aliases "critically reterritorialize the position of the 'abject' through mimicry, not necessarily to render Asianness nonabject but to redeploy the threatening force of abjection" (2002, 21). (I would add, this threat of abjection comes with an eroticizing element.) This formulation of abjection highlights Shimakawa's theorization of abjection as a social-historical process, not merely a psychic one. She argues that American national subject formation is constituted by the relegation of Asian Americanness to the status of the national abject, a process marked by an unstable sliding between the domesticated and the foreign, Asian Americanness and Asianness (Shimakawa 2002, 17). She writes, "Abjection, in other words, functions to make Asian Americanness into Asianness. If Asian American identity functions as a site of racial/sexual/national abjection, then it can only be represented (objectified) once it has been radically excluded; as 'ordinary' Americans, Asian Americans are often simply incomprehensible or invisible" (17). Building on Shimakawa's important analysis, my reading of GAM surfing on gay sex cruising sites foregrounds the ways the borders of white gay online space are constituted through the acknowledgment and disavowal of gay Asian male bodies, which, along with other racially marked bodies, are relegated to the edges of the gay cybersexual playing field.

In outlining GAM digital cruising as a technique that necessarily engages accommodation and struggle, I seek to refute the definition of abjection as a psychic failing that plagues all racialized queer subjects. As I have outlined throughout the book, GAM abjection has its origin in specific social, cultural, and historical forces. Theorizing the relationship between gay male subjectivity and abjection as one inflected by power dynamics, David Halperin maintains that "abjection is not a normative notion, not an index of psychological health, but a way of imagining and figuring social relations and their subjective vicissitudes" (2007, 70). Thus, we can say that gay Asian men's negotiated abjection can be seen as a potent response to their marginalization from heteronormative society and gay male subculture. Through the critical mimesis of gay Asian male sexual abjection, GAM online cruisers seek to reimagine and refigure social relations in order to account for their assignment as abject bottom subjects. My reading of GAM online cruising practices shows that Asian bottomhood constitutes the "secret grace" that renders gay Asian men legible as sexual subjects, even if they do not register as such in a society that conflates sexual subjecthood with white masculine aggressivity, control, and power.[17]

In my formulation, gay abjection and Asian abjection collude to render the gay Asian American male a bottom subject. This GAM abjection is accomplished through feminization, that is, the "negative" processes of gendering and sexualization. In the oft-repeated phrase, "No fats, femmes, or Asians," bodily corpulence ("fats"), feminine gender presentation ("femmes"), and race ("Asians") metonymically infect one another. Even as we disaggregate the components of bottomhood, we must not lose sight of the full range of connotations that underlie the bottom position, ones that take into account processes of complicity, conflict, and contradiction. The Asian American male subject draws on the force of abjection and shame in his assumption of bottomhood; but he also productively harnesses the power of shaming mechanisms by performing to the hilt the "improper joy" of Asian American male subjection.[18] That is, Asian American bottomhood constitutes an instance of partial, and at times thwarted, agency. Writing about the myth of the superagent, the all-powerful Internet user, propounded by new media corporate speak, Wendy Chun contends that "vulnerability and a certain loss of control drives communication, drives our using" (2006, 76); Chun thus reminds us that even as we assert ourselves as agential users, inevitably we subject ourselves to regulation and spectacularization. To claim bottomhood as anxious and ecstatic, pleasurable and vulnerable, is to witness the complicated workings of subjectification, one that refuses the choice of either rejecting or celebrating the "fact" of Asian male feminization.

In her work on the archiving of partial gestures and fleeting utterances of queer butch-femme sex, Juana María Rodríguez reminds us that the images, narratives, bodies, and acts that exert a powerful hold on our sexual imaginations and fantasies are inevitably socially and historically located: "That these narratives are often steeped in discourses of heterosexual gender and heteronormative sexuality, barely tinted or boldly coated through figures of racialization, should not surprise us; these are the discourses, images, and performative acts that have hailed us as desiring subjects. That we reproduce these gestures and utterances—a repetition that always occasions a difference—with social bodies that exist outside the logic of gendered and racial normativity produces a gap, a performative abyss, that queer sex steps into and (re)marks" (2007, 286). Insisting on the openness of acts, bodies, and meanings to be reinterpreted and reassigned, Rodríguez points out that it is through queer sex that marginalized subjects can access social recognition and intelligibility. It is my hope that in the preceding pages, my exploration of gay Asian bottomhood has allowed us to attend to the thrill, risk, pain, ecstasy, pleasure, danger, recognition, and joy in recirculating the meanings of sex acts, raced bodies, and gendered positions toward the cultivation of new social scripts and sexual scenarios.

NOTES

Introduction

1. Grindr started its operations on March 25, 2009, and has garnered over six million users in 192 countries across the globe. Ten thousand new users sign up every day. At any moment, 190,000 users are online. In the United States, by March 6, 2013, more than one million users were sending more than seven million messages and two million photos daily; www.grindr.com, accessed April 19, 2013. A straight version of the app, called Blendr, appeared on September 8, 2011.

2. See Rowlson (2011). See Wasley (2011), Weber (2012), and the blog Stop Gay Racism and Internalised Homophobia.

3. In gay sex ads jargon, "masc" is an abbreviation of masculine, "str8-acting" for straight-acting, "DL" for down-low, and "bi" for bisexual. Of these, only DL is racially marked, specifically as a term used for heterosexually or bisexually identified or straight-passing African American (and sometimes Latino) men who present themselves as "thugs," maintain sexual relationships with women, or otherwise feel they are unable to be associated with gayness.

4. Though the subject of my book is Asian American masculinity, there are times in the book when I use "Asian American" and "Asian" interchangeably. I follow the logic

sketched out by JeeYeun Lee when she writes: "On the one hand, since the 1960s, Asian American groups have insisted on being recognized as 'American,' in order to defy dominant views of Asians as perpetual foreigners as well as to provide an alternative to the loaded term 'Oriental.' On the other hand, many first-generation Asian Americans do not identify as Americans. Also, many people of all generations who originate from nations that have endured colonial subjugation in the past and/or neo-colonial relationships in the present, such as the Philippines, reject Americanness: to a certain extent, these people have already been forcibly made 'American' in their own homelands. In addition, racial stereotypes do not distinguish between Asian and Asian American, as they are based on phenotype and imagined cultural traits" (1996, 116). In light of Lee's commentary, it's clear that in the U.S. context, bottomhood marks both Asian and Asian American men, in spite of the differences in cultural and national contexts.

5. The term "remasculinization" originates from Susan Jeffords in her 1989 book *The Remasculinization of America: Gender and the Vietnam War.* Drawing on Jeffords's work, Viet Thanh Nguyen distinguishes his use of the term in the context of Asian American literature as one that draws on American culture's redeployment of masculinist tendencies in the post–Vietnam War period, while at the same time challenging the Orientalist bent of dominant culture's remasculinization: "Jeffords argues that a process of remasculinization occurred in American culture at this time, largely through the discourse of the Vietnam War. In this discourse, the remasculinization of the (white) American male body in literature and film served to counter various cultural, political, and economic changes exceeding the scope of the war that were thought to be eroding the social and material status of the American white male. The turmoil of the war and the economic threat of Asia, with its contribution to the real or imaginary erosion of white male privilege, exacerbated an already present orientalist tendency in American culture to conflate Asians and Asian Americans. While Asian American remasculinization is inevitably influenced by this dominant discourse of remasculinization, it is also antagonistic to its orientalism. Thus, I situate the project of Asian American remasculinization both within and against the dominant American remasculinization, for it partakes in American patriarchy's attempts to continue the masculinization of political and economic public life, but it opposes the racialization and subordination of races that in the past characterized this masculinization of nation-state and civil society" (Nguyen 2000, 133).

6. Lee proudly portrays himself as a groundbreaking sexual performer who treads where no other Asian American man has dared. As he proclaims at his website, "the goal is not really to profit but rather to make a point, a contribution that I like to make to the whole AM [Asian man] sex theme. Also, I know I am doing something that people are going to talk about 100 years from now since this is the first website to emphasize AM sex in America." Nonetheless, such a heroic feat is somewhat undermined by the fact that Lee does not show his face in any of the photographs or videos on the site. In *Masters of the Pillow,* his face is digitally blurred out. So much for straight Asian American male pride porn! See Lee (2012).

7. According to historian David Halperin, these contemporary assignments of value to top-bottom roles find their roots in the practice of "active" sodomy, which can be

traced as far back as the ancient civilizations of Minoan Crete in the Bronze Age to fifteenth-century Renaissance Italy. The partners in these sexual relations are differentiated from one another according to hierarchies of age, class, gender presentation, and sexual role, with the socially superordinate partner penetrating the socially subordinate partner (Halperin 2000, 96). While Halperin argues that the concept of "sex as hierarchy" has since been superseded in modern Western homosexuality grounded on egalitarianism between both partners, it is the case that the concept of the active/masculine/fucker and passive/feminine/fucked in gay male anal sex still obtains in diverse cultures around the world (not to mention within the United States itself). For example, on *activo/passivo* homosexual roles in Brazil, see Parker (1988); in Mexico, see Prieur (1998); see Jackson (1997) on the differentiation between "gay queens" and "gay kings" in Thailand; and see Valentine (2007) for a discussion of how gender and sexuality are perceived among sexual minorities of color in the United States.

8. Bersani elaborates, "*jouissance* refers to an 'erotogenicity' that . . . Freud ascribes not only to the body's entire surface and all the internal organs, but also to any activities and mental states or affective processes (he mentions intellectual strain, wrestling, railway travel) that produce a certain degree of intensity in the organism and in so doing momentarily disturb psychic organization. Following Jean Laplanche, who speaks of the sexual as an effect of *ébranlement*, I call jouissance 'self-shattering' in that it disrupts the ego's coherence and dissolves its boundaries" (1995, 101). See also D. A. Miller's essays, "Anal *Rope*" (1991) and "Visual Pleasure in 1959" (1999), and Lee Edelman's *Homographesis: Essays in Gay Literary and Cultural Theory* (1994) and "*Rear Window*'s Glasshole" (1999).

9. Rather than arguing that queers are just as respectable and responsible as heterosexual citizens, Bersani contends that a more radical response to the demonization of homosexuals during the AIDS epidemic would be to embrace the abjection and threat attributed to gay men due to their hedonist pursuit of disease-spreading promiscuous sex, captured by the one sex act at the heart of the homophobe's fantasy: passive anal sex.

10. *The Joy of Gay Sex* was first published in 1977. Notably, the seduction of "huge donkey dongs" is described as taking place on the visual register, for the authors of the sex manual point out that it is not the penis's impressive length—the "stat" that gay men often mention—but its girth that does damage to the sphincter muscles.

11. In addition to the 1992 and 2003 editions of *The Joy of Gay Sex*, see Morin (1986), Brent (2002), and Underwood (2003).

12. For example, critics such as D. A. Miller and David Halperin have maintained that for gay men to take up the position of "to-be-looked-at-ness" traditionally occupied by women both violates and undermines heterosexual male prerogatives. Halperin states that "what distinguishes the gay male gym body, then, in addition to its spectacular beauty, is the way it advertises itself as an object of desire. Gay muscles do not signify power" (1997, 117). In response to the claims that gay eroticization of dominant masculinity functions as a parodic deconstruction, Leo Bersani asserts that gay male performance of masculinity might be more productively read as a continuing investment in it. He writes, "The logic of homosexual desire includes a potential for a loving identifica-

tion with the gay man's enemies" (Bersani 1987, 208). Far from being deflated and cast out by gay male parody, dominant masculinity structurally informs homosexual desire. On the one hand, gay male desire is constituted by an identification with the masculinist ideal, an internalization of something that is actually oppressive for gay men (heterosexual masculinity); on the other, gay male sexual expression partakes in the male privilege accorded to men within a heterosexist sex/gender system.

13. See Dyer's ([1985] 2002) "Coming to Terms: Gay Pornography," in *Only Entertainment*.

14. The convention of the money shot (i.e., visible ejaculation) in heterosexual moving-image pornography serves two functions: (1) the porn text directs its address to a male viewer, a viewer that can identify with the male performer's pleasure in ejaculating; (2) the cum shot serves as evidence of female pleasure. The perverse porn convention of using an ejaculating penis to signify female pleasure is brilliantly unpacked by Linda Williams (1989) in her influential book *Hard Core: Power, Pleasure, and the "Frenzy of the Visible."* Carried over into gay porn, cum shots reinforce the assumption of the (ideal) male viewer while simultaneously functioning as evidence of the bottom performer's anal pleasure. In other words, the invisible interiority of anal pleasure must be made visible through the bottom performer's penile ejaculation. Admittedly, this description is only one possible explanation for the "perverse" convention in gay porn in showing the bottom's cum shot. I say perverse because it's often the case—especially in contemporary video pornography—for the bottom to jack himself off to ejaculation after the top has pulled out and come. That is, the bottom's coming is not directly the result of getting fucked by the top. In their essay on the operations of the voice in gay porn, Rich Cante and Angelo Restivo (2001) argue that it is the voice that serves to signify anal pleasure.

15. This temporal trajectory is most obvious in pornography shot and exhibited on film. With VHS video in the 1980s and 1990s and the Internet in the 1990s and 2000s, the possibilities for how the work is viewed, in what order, and with what focus in mind have drastically multiplied.

16. The high regard for bottoms is borne out by a star system for bottom performers, including Kevin Williams from the 1980s, Joey Stefano in the 1990s, Jeremy Jordan in the 2000s, and Brent Corrigan in the 2010s. Though these four famous bottom performers (save for Stefano) fit into the category of the "twink" (that is, a young, smooth, slim white man), more recent bottoms who have garnered attention tend to be extremely muscular and butch presenting, as can be seen by recipients of the Hottest Bottom award from the annual gay porn industry Grabby Awards: Matt Cole (2007), Jesse Santana (2008), Brent Corrigan (2009), Vince Ferelli (2010), Angelo Marconi (2011), and Cavin Knight (2012); www.grabbys.com, accessed April 19, 2013.

17. In gay male sex lingo, "Greek active" and "Greek passive" designate inserter in anal sex and insertee in anal sex, respectively; "French active" and "French passive" refer to sucker and suckee in oral sex, respectively. This vocabulary is no longer commonly used, having been replaced by "top" and "bottom." Nowadays, a top that likes to suck cock is referred to as an "oral top." This change in terminology suggests that anal sex has come to be privileged over oral sex.

18. It's noteworthy that the terms "top" and "bottom" are not used in Wittman's dismissals. As he writes (Wittman 1992, originally published in *San Franciso Free Press* in 1970):
These sexual perversions are basically anti-gay:
"I like to make it with straight guys"
"I'm not gay, but I like to be 'done'"
"I like to fuck, but don't want to be fucked"
"I don't like to be touched above the neck" (306)

19. Interestingly, Escoffier observes that "since the late seventies, anal sex had become the narrative focal point of gay porn. While it is difficult to document, the shift away from oral sex as the normative activity to anal sex was one of the major changes that accompanied the sexual revolution of the sixties and seventies" (2009, 185). He notes that porn actors in the 1970s such as Al Parker and Casey Donovan fluidly performed the roles of top and bottom. He calls attention to the "virilization" of gay male culture in the late 1970s in the work of Joe Gage, as part of the trend in the hypermasculine "clone" look (Escoffier 2009). In Gage's classic trucker porn titles *Kansas City Trucking Co.* (1976), *El Paso Wrecking Corp.* (1978), and *L.A. Tool and Die* (1979), white butch clones fuck and get fucked in equal measure without having their masculinity compromised in any way. Escoffier identifies the AIDS epidemic as partly responsible for the shift in gay porn from the reversibility of fucker-fuckee positions to the more rigid top-bottom scenarios. Due to the fact that the bottom is more vulnerable to HIV transmission, the exchangeability of roles championed in 1970s porn transformed into an idolization of the top in 1980s and early 1990s gay porn. The privileging of the top resurrects the gay male fantasy of having sex with a sexual object commonly deemed as out of reach, the ultimate impossible object of desire: the straight man.

In one of Stryker's most popular titles, *Powertool* (dir. John Travis, 1986), one finds: "The bottoms are rarely erect while getting fucked, there is no reciprocity, and most of the sexual roles are exclusively top or bottom" (Escoffier 2009, 210). Escoffier (2009, 295) goes on to note that it was during the 1990s, with the increased professionalization of the gay porn industry, along with the normalization of condoms, that yet another kind of porn star emerged. The professionalized porn actor of 1990s video porn was a consummate performer who did everything, including making out, topping and bottoming, sucking cock and getting sucked, rimming and getting rimmed, and so on. The return to sexual versatility prevalent in the 1970s also came with a concomitant masculine gender presentation. What is new in gay porn from the mid-1990s to the present is an excessive masculinizing of the bottom performer that reads as a defensive response to the feminization of the bottom position.

20. Thanks to Lucas Hilderbrand for this important reference.

21. Versatile, or "vers," is placed between top and bottom in online gay cruising sites' coding of sexual role hierarchies. Vers is often indicated in modified forms such as "vers top" or "vers bottom" that generally indicate an individual's "real" preference as opposed to the sexual position he seeks. Thanks to Dredge Byung'chu Käng for this insight.

22. To be sure, there are cultural sanctions against anal penetration that do not apply to vaginal penetration. However, Merck's criticism is directed at Bersani's appropriative

use of femininity to buttress his argument for the heroization of gay male bottoming. For another source that takes Bersani to task for his problematic treatment of femininity, see Patrick Paul Garlinger's (1999) review essay of *Homos*, "'Homo-Ness' and the Fear of Femininity."

23. Gay barebacking refers to gay male anal sex without the use of condoms, which, as an act, does not necessarily have to be coded as transgressive, as it typically is among those who identify with the gay barebacking subculture. The reasons for the recent popularity of the practice are complex, including safe-sex burnout, the view of AIDS as a manageable disease, the eroticization of risk, sero-sorting (HIV-positive men seeking out other positive men), lack of information, substance abuse, and a backlash against government regulation of gay male sexuality. Visitors to the website Bareback.com encounter the explanation that they should be ready to "fuck and suck without barriers, lectures or bullshit"; they are advised to click "Cum in" to enter the site, or "Pull out" if they are "a wimp, wuss or pussy"; www.bareback.com, accessed January 5, 2013. Bareback.com's "Cum in" puns on the phrase "come in" while suggesting that a visitor should be interested in ejaculating inside his partner's rectum, whereas "Pull out" indicates withdrawing his cock from his partner's asshole before ejaculating.

24. In addition to Dean (2009), see also Halperin (2007) and Bersani and Phillips (2008). In these recent studies, gay barebacking is theorized as gay men's complex negotiations of sexual risk and the cultivation of new modes of relationality after three decades of the AIDS epidemic. Dean performs extended analyses of "bug chasers" (those seeking to get infected) and the visual depictions of these fantasies in bareback porn. Because the top's "gift" of infected ejaculate inside the bottom's rectum cannot be visually recorded, it gets displaced onto what Dean (2009, 135) calls the "reverse money shot," whereby the semen is shown dripping out of the bottom's asshole and collected in measuring cups. Such "breeding" fantasy scenarios put the experience of the bottom center stage. Dean acknowledges the masculinist spectacle of bottomhood when he writes, "Bareback subculture's hypermasculinization of bottoming, its picturing erotic submission as a proof of manhood, could be seen as a compensatory response to modern society's feminization of male homosexuality. . . . Through its commitment to no-excuses submission and no-limits endurance, however, bareback subculture conversely embraces masochism as proof positive of masculinity. That is to say, by remasculinizing masochism, barebackers have made self-loss into a confirmation rather than an effacement of manhood" (2009, 56). Clearly, we have come a long way from the Bersanian renunciation of masculine power and self-shattering *jouissance* of bottoming circa 1987. What is sorely missing from the account above is a feminist and race analysis of barebacking's "compensatory response."

25. Mandy Merck (2000, 165) points out that Bersani's theory "precludes the acknowledgment of the gay male top, as well as women's active eroticism, whether hetero- or homosexually directed." Similarly, Lynda Hart (1998, 90) argues that Bersani's, as well as Kaja Silverman's (1992), theoretical claims for the "emancipatory" force of male masochism rest on the elision of lesbian desire. My discussion of the mutual pleasure and recognition between tops and bottoms constitutes a preliminary corrective to the sidelining of the top in previous gay male scholarship.

26. It is important to refrain from collapsing what is referred to as "passive femininity" in these gay male writings with women's sexual experience. Just as gay male bottomhood complicates and challenges the mere reproduction of passive femininity (as these gay male writers claim), the act of a woman who bottoms for her male or female partner cannot be reduced to any simple enactment of "essential" feminine passivity.

27. In spite of the fetishization of "huge donkey dongs" and the focus on top performers in gay pornography, the relative anonymity of the Internet has enabled the public, albeit virtual, coming out of bottoms on sex cruising sites, a move that effectively unseats gay porn's monopoly in visually registering "legitimate" gay male sexual practices. For instance, in addition to the postings of pictures of large, erect penises, one also finds many pictures of male assholes posed in various bottom positions on these gay sex cruising sites.

28. "Active passivity" and "strength in submission" are two terms deployed by gay male informants of Kippax and Smith (2001) to describe their experiences as bottoms. Challenging the conventional opposition between active political engagement and passive political apathy, Lee Edelman's formulation of "passive agency" "requir[es] the recognition that powerfully 'political' effects can be generated even by those who would seem, from an 'activist' perspective, to be a- or anti-political" (1994, 112–113).

29. Even in cases where a wholehearted embrace of passivity is proclaimed, accessing pleasure through submission paradoxically betrays a certain degree of power. Writing about heterosexual S/M pornography, Linda Williams specifies, "Without a modicum of power, without some leeway for play within assigned sexual roles, and without the possibility of some intersubjective give-and-take, there can be no pleasure for either the victim or the totally identified viewer. There can be no pleasure, in other words, without some power" (1989, 227).

30. In *Intercourse*, Andrea Dworkin makes a similar argument about heterosexual intercourse: "In it [heterosexual intercourse], female is bottom, stigmatized. Intercourse remains a means or the means of physiologically making a woman inferior: communicating to her cell by cell her own inferior status, impressing it on her, burning it into her by shoving it into her, over and over, pushing and thrusting until she gives up and gives in—which is called *surrender* in the male lexicon. In the experience of intercourse, she loses the capacity for integrity because her body—the basis of privacy and freedom in the material world for all human beings—is entered and occupied; the boundaries of her physical body are—neutrally speaking—violated" (1987, 137). Though I find her assessment of the male penis entering the female vagina as an eroticization of "powerlessness and self-annihilation" persuasive to a certain extent, I must point to important differences between heterosexual vaginal penetration and homosexual anal penetration, a distinction that she also makes ("A man has an anus that can be entered, but his anus is not synonymous with entry"; 1987, 122–123). Consequently, where I depart from Dworkin is the assignment of political value to anal penetration and its linkages to powerlessness and self-annihilation.

In an analysis of the "labor of receptivity" in butch-femme sexuality, Ann Cvetkovich (2003, 58) points out that for lesbian femmes whose desires are deemed perverse and deviant, getting fucked by a butch is not necessarily traumatic, but rather constitutes an affirmation and an achievement. The femme expresses the "power and labor of receptivity" by responding to her butch lover through speech, moans, breathing, and body movement. Allowing herself to be penetrated by a lover's hand is not a passive gesture, but an intimate, mutual action: the lover takes her as she in turn takes her lover inside her body. Cvetkovich notes, "One can be penetrated both in order to receive pleasure and in order to give pleasure, and different terms might be used to indicate which is primary. 'Receptivity' can be used to signify both an openness to one's own pleasure and a willingness to give someone else pleasure" (1995, 134). She extends the formulation of penetration to cover not just the penis entering an anus or vagina, but also tongues, fingers, fists, and dildos penetrating mouths, vaginas, and anuses, that is, a proliferation of zones and parts for pleasure giving and taking, with "different kinds of penetration *mean*[ing] different things" (2003, 60, emphasis in original). Indeed, male anal penetration signifies a host of connotations that do not apply to other kinds of bodily penetration. Nevertheless, I find Cvetkovich's argument for lesbian receptivity very compelling, even if it cannot be transcribed to gay male bottomhood without significant qualifications.

31. As Scott reminds us, "the de rigueur application of the concept of double-consciousness to objects of knowledge assigned to the category of 'black,' 'male,' and 'African American' generally finds the 'black male' to be a self-contradicting and self-reinforcing position at once hypermasculine and feminine, exemplifying an erection/castration paradox" (2010, 19). Clearly, this erection/castration paradox does not obtain in the category of "gay," "male," and "Asian American"; instead, the latter subject position, as Eng (2001) helpfully argues, is invariably consigned to the side of castration.

32. In the same vein, Stockton rejects any assertions about the subversiveness of black debasement; instead she devotes her attention to the connections between black debasement and its "attractions," "aesthetic delight," and "creative historical knowing" (2006, 24).

33. Though I am committed to a model of dominance-critique in my rejection of re-masculinization, I don't fully subscribe to a model of dominance-resistance. I am indebted to Damon Young for pushing me to rethink the questions of pleasure, power, and agency in relation to gay Asian American bottomhood.

34. While two chapters offer close readings of major films that have been neglected due to their appraisals as either financial or critical flops, the other two chapters explore marginalized genres, such as gay pornography and experimental video.

35. In spite of the persistent complaints against the egregious sexual and gender stereotyping of Asians by the dominant U.S. media, there have not been many serious inquiries into existing treatments (albeit a small corpus) of explicit sexual representation. For example, Hamamoto's (2000) promisingly titled essay, "The Joy Fuck Club: Prolegomenon to an Asian American Porno Practice" devotes many pages to analyzing an independent narrative film based on a 1961 Asian American novel but doesn't offer extended close readings of any Asian/American pornographic film/video. (The film is *Eat a Bowl of Tea* [dir. Wayne Wang, 1989], based on the novel by Louis Chu [1961].) More alarmingly, Hamamoto neglects the significant contributions of queer Asian American film and videomakers such as Shu Lea Cheang and Ming-Yuen S. Ma, who

have been actively engaged in a "Yellow porno practice" for at least a decade before the time his essay was written.

36. See Hamamoto (2000), Fung (1995), Oishi (2000, 2006), King (2010), Shimakawa (2002), and Mimura (2009).

37. See Sobchack (1992, 2004), Williams (1991, 2008), Clover (1992), and Marks (2000, 2002). Linda Williams (1991) develops the theory of "body genres" in her classic essay "Film Bodies: Gender, Genre, and Excess." I discuss embodied viewership more fully in chapter 3.

38. I thank one of the anonymous readers for helping me understand this crucial connection between my argument for gay Asian bottomhood and Keeling's work on "the black femme function."

Chapter 1: The Rise, and Fall, of a Gay Asian American Porn Star

1. Brandon Lee may not be the first gay Asian American porn star. Hapa (half-Asian, half-white) stars like Jordan Young have been quite successful and even more prolific. However, these stars have never been explicitly coded as Asian but instead have appeared only in mainstream gay videotapes.

2. Gay slang for a generic, cute, boyish, slim, smooth young man, implicitly coded as white.

3. Conducting close readings of three videos in his essay, Fung restricts his analysis to only American-made videos with Asian themes, because the Japanese and Thai productions, he says, "come from cultural contexts about which I am incapable of commenting. In addition, the fact that porn from those countries is sometimes unmarked racially does not mean that it speaks to my experience or desires, my own culture of sexuality" (1991, 164). I adopt an approach similar to Fung's in my analysis of Brandon Lee's videos.

4. The scene in question has Robbie, a white karate student, telling a fellow classmate his sex dream about their karate teacher, Greg. In the dream, shown as a cutaway, Robbie is rescued by Greg from "an evil samurai." As part of his expression of gratitude, Robbie lets Greg fuck him. While Robbie appears as himself (that is, white) in the video up to this point, during the fucking scene, Robbie "turns Japanese": Sum Yung Mahn plays Asian Robbie in the bottoming sequence.

5. The lone named straight male Asian porn actor currently working in the United States is Keni Styles, a British of Thai descent. Styles broke into the business in 2006 in the United Kingdom and only relocated to Los Angeles in 2010. For a wide-ranging analysis of the depictions of heterosexual Asian American men in Hollywood cinema and Asian American independent film and video in the period between 1959 and 2009, see Shimizu (2012).

6. By "Asian-niche," I refer to videos marketed for consumers who seek out porn featuring Asian performers. These videos can be found in the section labeled "Asian" in gay video stores (that is, before video stores were put out of business by digital media platforms such as on-demand and streaming video available on the Internet); other niches include "Black," "Latino," "Amateur," and so on. While the actual demographic of this

Asian niche audience is difficult to ascertain, I argue below that the ideal viewer addressed by these videos, especially in its advertising and packaging, is a gay white man. To be sure, Asian men (and other men of color) also constitute the audience for these productions. I discuss the tension and problems of gay Asian reception of these works briefly at the conclusion of the chapter.

7. Although two of the directors of Brandon Lee's videos remain the same (Chi Chi LaRue and Josh Eliot) and there is an overlap in the time of production (1997–1998), the crossover that I am suggesting is not so much about Lee jettisoning one market or audience for another over a period of time. Instead, I am arguing that there exists a shift in the casting and coding of his image from the Asian-themed videos to the mainstream productions. The relatively small size of the gay porn industry and its rapid production schedule allow for the simultaneity of Brandon Lee's appearance in both the Asian-themed and mainstream tapes or, rather, their contemporaneous release on the market. I argue below that it is precisely the illegibility of this porn actor's racial coding that makes possible his cross-appeal to both mainstream and Asian-niche audiences. His racially mixed face and body make him desirable to both white and Asian men.

8. His titles, after his comeback in 2004, include *Bolt* (dir. Chi Chi LaRue, 2004), *[2] for the Taking* (dir. Chi Chi LaRue, 2004), *Lookin' for Trouble* (dir. Doug Jeffries, 2004), *Wicked* (dir. Chi Chi LaRue, 2005), *Deceived* (dir. Chi Chi LaRue, 2005), *Lights & Darks: An Interracial Spin* (dir. Doug Jeffries, 2005), and *Brandon Lee's Hot Shots* (dir. Chi Chi LaRue, 2005). His output since 2005 has petered out, with only one high-profile leading role, in *Affirmative Blacktion: An Interracial Takeover* (dir. Doug Jeffries, 2010). In that same year, he started a personal food-catering business in San Francisco called Catering by Brandon Lee.

9. The concept of "border cases" comes from Valerie Smith, who uses it to describe "issues that problematize easy assumptions about racial and/or sexual difference, particularly insofar as they demonstrate the interactions between race and gender" (1990, 272).

10. This was Lee's second film; it was also released as *The Chinese Connection*.

11. The notable exception is *Fist of Fury*, where Lee's character, Chen, has a female love interest, Yuan (Nora Miao), whom he wants to marry. In one romantic scene lit by firelight, they confess their enduring love for one another, and he takes her in his arms and kisses her tenderly.

12. However, the issue of Bruce Lee's "asexuality" is complicated by the fact that Chinese codes of masculinity (*wu*, or martial masculinity) stipulate that for a martial arts hero to become involved with a woman is a sign of weakness, of "losing control." Thus, "manliness" in Chinese contexts becomes translated as "asexual" in Asian American critical analyses of Bruce Lee. I am indebted to Chris Berry for bringing the Chinese archetype of *wu* masculinity to my attention. The complex cultural and historical codings of Asian and Asian American masculinities suggest the necessity of situating discussions of Asian American masculinity and sexuality in a transnational context, something that I am unable to undertake here due to space constraints (see Louie 2002).

13. It is important to note that Lee's films do contain extreme violence. One infamous scene of Lee sawing a man's head open and another showing him sticking his fingers

into the villain's torso had to be edited out of the U.S. version of *The Big Boss* (dir. Wei Lo, 1971) in order to escape an X rating.

14. I maintain that most viewers of gay porn concentrate on the spectacle of gay sex rather than on the role of the sexual numbers in working through narrative conflicts. For example, in a porn video review in the San Francisco gay weekly *Bay Area Reporter*, critic John F. Karr faults a video for its "overwrought plotting," which, he claims, "stifle[s] the spontaneity of the sex act, distancing the performers from the naturalness they need to bring to sex." To get a sense of what he means by "overwrought," in the next paragraph, Karr complains of a video that *"drowns in plot scenes of five-minute duration"* (2001, 35, emphasis added). However, below I complicate this knee-jerk dismissal of narrative setups by highlighting the important functions of space and mise-en-scène in Asian-niche gay video porn.

15. The association between martial arts or, more specifically, Bruce Lee, and pornography (albeit heterosexual) is casually made in Paul Thomas Anderson's *Boogie Nights* (1997). In a footnote to his article, Darrell Y. Hamamoto cites this link as "a breakthrough of sorts, [whereby] the exclusion of eroticized Asian American men in the dominant media is subverted" (2000, 82). In the film, Mark Wahlberg's porn actor character, Dirk Diggler, idolizes Bruce Lee and performs "karate chops" in front of the dressing room mirror before his porn shoots.

16. In my use of "West Hollywood" throughout this chapter, I wish to mobilize the full range of connotations associated with this term in the popular imagination; that is, "West Hollywood," like "the Castro" in San Francisco, has come to stand in for a specific brand identity or gay lifestyle constituted by a set of features such as race (whiteness), economic class (upper middle class), gender (male), body-and-fitness consciousness (gym bunny), attitude or worldview (Southern California superficiality)—features that not only construct this sexual minority as an extremely profitable consumer demographic for corporations, but also as a shorthand expression used within the gay community to reference a certain type of gay male identification. In this manner, "West Hollywood" exceeds the physically demarcated zone of this Southern California city and instead signifies what Thomas Waugh has noted as an "intra-sexual identity/class/subculture." Thanks to Thomas Waugh for bringing this critical point to my attention.

17. My focus on space and mise-en-scène of these videos is partly justified due to the fact that most viewers consumed these productions in VHS or DVD formats. Though viewers certainly had the option to watch selectively through fast-forwarding (in the case of VHS) and chapter selections (in the case of DVD), I contend that the racially marked fantasy scenarios are central to the production and marketing of these Asian-niche videos. Porn viewing habits have changed dramatically with the advent of the Internet, where the viewing of clips out of sequence has replaced the consumption of linear narratives. For insightful discussions of how new media have drastically transformed porn consumption, see Patterson (2004); Williams (2008), in particular the concluding chapter; and Hanich (2011).

18. We assume the character is supposed to be Japanese from the earlier credit sequence, which informed us that his name is Tenji Mito.

19. Unlike Brad Davis Mikado and Broc Hiyashi, the other two Asian actors, Hiro Sukowa and Tishiro Ho, speak with pronounced accents.

20. Interestingly, by replacing a terrorizing white "female" boss with a kinder Asian male one, the narrative appears to champion a more "positive" intraracial erotics, coded as nonexploitative. In contrast to Time's lackluster performance bottoming for Paul Morgan in an earlier scene, his scene with Lee is much more passionate. They kiss often. Lee fucks Time very enthusiastically and energetically; Time responds much more verbally than in his scene with Morgan. Like the gay Asian documentaries I discuss in chapter 4, racial sameness trumps class difference. Although Lee still has power over Time as his boss at the brothel, their relationship is deemed less exploitative than the one between Morgan (white john) and Time (Asian prostitute). The affirmative presentation of "sticky rice" coupling appears to acknowledge the desire of a gay Asian viewer, one who might fantasize himself in Time's position bottoming for Lee.

21. To be sure, a common fantasy in gay porn depicts straight men engaging in gay sex due to economic necessity, as can be seen in the wild popularity of Dirk Yates's video series on military guys and online porn sites such as CorbinFisher.com. The difference between these white gay-for-pay and the Asian American productions I'm analyzing lies in the extremely limited roles and fantasy scenarios offered to Asian performers.

22. This description is culled from Bijou Video's review of *Shanghai Meat Company* (dir. Tony Chan, 1991). http://www.alanevideo.com/oldsite/alane/itema02066.html, accessed March 22, 2012.

23. Tsang (1999, 474–475) observes how the culturally unmarked, unspecified "hotel rooms in unnamed cities or countries" in which the videos are filmed suggest the use of underpaid actors from third world countries.

24. I am building on Christopher Ortiz's perceptive reading of gay Chicano/Latino porn videos and adapting it to the Asian American videos. Discussing *Soul and Salsa* (dir. Frank Jeffries, 1988), Ortiz writes, "The text, then, is structured so that the fantasy is not only that of watching men perform specific sexual acts with each other, but that the spectator watches racially coded men—Afro-American and Chicano/Latino men—engage in sexual acts with one another. The text provides an idea of what sex between hot men of color might possibly look like" (1994, 84–85).

25. Based on his appearance in the video, it is difficult to ascertain Brad Davis Mikado's actual race/ethnicity, and I am not concerned with identifying it here. My point is that in *Asian Persuasion*, he is coded as Asian or part Asian with the addition of "Mikado" to his name.

26. Of course the term also activates the word "Asian" embedded in "persuasion." This assonance had been creatively deployed by at least one gay Asian club in Los Angeles (now defunct), which called itself "Persuasian." The simple change in spelling constructs the club as a queer Asian space where Asian men are the objects of pursuit—by white men as well as by other Asian men.

27. The beginning sequence of *Asian Persuasion 2* illustrates most blatantly the intended audience of the video as white men. White blond actor Joey James points the camera at his Asian boyfriend, Tommy Lin, and persuades Lin to perform sex for

James's camera. From shots of James holding the camera and looking into the eyepiece, the visual track switches to James's perspective through the camera's viewfinder, complete with black frame, rectangular lines, red dot, time code, and "REC" lettering. From James's POV, we hear him directing Lin: "play with your balls, show me your ass . . . spread your cheeks out for me," as we see a zoom into Lin's ass crack. Acting as the viewer's privileged stand-in, James, with one hand on the camera, reaches in with the other hand to caress and play with Lin's ass cheeks, inserting his finger easily inside the asshole.

28. Another, even more famous example of a relatively short porn actor with a weight-height-proportional body nicely setting off his humongous genitals is Jeff Stryker. However, we never hear remarks that Stryker's dick (ranging from 7.5 to 10 inches) is out of proportion with his body (5'9") or that it is as big as he is.

29. An interesting difference between the star image of Lee, an Asian American porn star, and other mainstream white gay porn stars can be seen in a product tie-in that follows the video *Chew Manchu* (dir. Mark Jensen, 2000). Though Lee does not appear in the video, he is shown on the box of the Samurai Penis Pump, a prop that was used in the video. (The tag line is "As Seen in 'Chew Manchu.'") The Orientalist marking of Asian male sexuality is neatly condensed in this sexual aid. Whereas white gay porn stars like Jeff Stryker and Ryan Idol endorse "life-sized" dildoes cast from their own penises, Brandon Lee—though allegedly possessing a cock too big for his own body—is used to sell a hollow device for the purpose of inflating the user's/viewer's penis. It wasn't until after his porn comeback that a Brandon Lee SensaFirm Dildo, "modeled after Brandon Lee's own eight inch package," appeared on the market in March 2006.

30. As I argue in the next chapter, an "anal vision" also informs looking relations that threaten illusionist cinematic space in *Reflections in a Golden Eye* (dir. John Huston, 1967).

31. Although one could argue that the phrase "youthful-looking and cute" does not play off any Asian markers, a closer, and more anal, reading uncovers the connection between age and size that conventionally animates a specific popular American conception of Asian men. For instance, many critics have highlighted the way in which Bruce Lee's small stature operates as a disguise that intensifies the moment of his transformation from a harmless, naive bumpkin to a spectacular martial arts hero. Part and parcel of this revelation of agility coupled with sensuality is the pairing of Lee with huge opponents, such as Robert Baker in *Fist of Fury*, Chuck Norris in *The Way of the Dragon*, and Kareem Abdul-Jabbar in *Game of Death* (dir. Robert Clouse and Bruce Lee, 1978). This contrast in size produces in the audience the pleasure of seeing Lee's small lithe body performing high kicks and knocking down his big opponents. For his audiences from marginalized populations, visual pleasure comes from watching the victory of the small downtrodden hero over the giant, menacing other. A similar dynamic is at work in the awe and surprise registered by directors and viewers in reaction to Brandon Lee's big cock on a small body.

32. In this West Hollywood context and in hip LA parlance in general, the San Fernando Valley represents the social death of the dreaded suburbs.

33. In the videos he made after this comeback, Lee's roles are not racially marked;

they include tattoo artist (*Bolt*), party host (*[2] for the Taking*), biker dude (*Lookin' for Trouble*), twink (*Deceived*), and porn video emcee (*Brandon Lee's Hot Shots*). The exceptions are his roles as "porn star Brandon Lee" (*Wicked*), laundromat owner (*Lights & Darks: An Interracial Spin*), and Chinese bar owner (*Affirmative Blacktion: An Interracial Takeover*).

34. Due to space and time constraints, I am unable to explore the reasons for the lack of Asian actors in gay pornography. In addition to Josh Eliot, Chi Chi LaRue bemoans the difficulty of finding Asian actors: "Now it's very hard to find Asian models. . . . They're very private. I think maybe they're worried, maybe their culture doesn't condone this kind of thing, maybe Asian guilt, like Catholic guilt. That's why they'll come and do one or two films and they'll disappear" (quoted in Ko 1999, 85). Similarly, Oggi, an Asian American producer-director of Exotic Videos, suggests, "It would take me forever to find models here; that's one reason why I don't make them in the U.S. . . . The ones I interview, sometimes they will chicken out. When it gets right down to production, they get scared. Asians aren't very brave, not like (non-Asian) American people who don't care. What if my friends or parents see it?" (quoted in Ko 1999, 85). Whether the paucity of Asian actors in gay porn can be attributed to cultural difference or the lack of demand (and adequate rewards) for them, I would reject the individualist and psychological explanations of guilt and timidity. Though he does not provide any hard evidence or theoretical elaboration, Hamamoto attributes the lack of Asian men—or what he refers to as the "exclusion of the Yellow man from video porn"—working in front of the camera to the "pervasive White-supremacist race/sex/power ideology": "The absence of Asian American men in video porn has nothing to do with having the 'right equipment' and the 'desire' to be in the business. The reason is found in the obdurate anti-Asian racism of the dominant society, which is reproduced intact by the thematic conventions of U.S. video porn" (2000, 75). Although I agree with Hamamoto's diagnosis, I still wonder about the dismal showing of Asian men in American porn, an industry riddled with niche and specialty markets always ready to exploit "sexual novelties."

35. Sean Martinez may also be read as Filipino, though I do not think most American porn viewers are savvy enough to be cognizant of the tremendous influence of Spain on Filipino culture. In spite of the fact that on their website, Oh Man! Studios's synopsis of *Glory Holes of L.A.* identifies Sean Martinez as an "Asian newcomer," I would contend that a viewer watching the video without this extratextual information might not automatically make the assumption that Sean Martinez should be read as (only) Asian, let alone specifically Filipino.

36. Looking at American social scientific discourse of the 1930s, David Palumbo-Liu explores how assimilation into American society was thought to enact both somatic and psychic changes in the immigrant's body. He cites the work of anthropologist Franz Boas and the federally sponsored Immigration Commission in order to show how this discourse asserted that presence on "American soil" brought about changes in the European immigrant's head form. For instance, the European Jew's round head elongated, while the southern Italian's long head transformed to a shorter length. Whereas the faces and bodies of Eastern European and Mediterranean immigrants were amenable

to appreciable changes once in the United States, "'orientals' . . . were not susceptible to such transformation, no matter how intense or lengthy their exposure" (Palumbo-Liu 1999, 86). Thus the commission believed Asians should be excluded from the nation since they were seen as unalterably foreign and unassimilable. Palumbo-Liu discusses the work of sociologist Robert E. Park, who suggested that Asians could erase the physical signs of racial difference, and thus assimilate into the nation, through intermarriage with white Americans. Twenty years later, in the 1950s, the long process of intermarriage advocated by Park to biologically efface racial difference was rejected in favor of the more immediate technology of plastic reconstructive surgery to speed up what before would have taken generations. The physical reconstruction ensures an attendant psychic transformation, thus making one's interior conform to the new Americanized face. Significantly, plastic surgery cannot turn Asian subjects into white Americans; they are transformed, rather, into white ethnics. They resemble Mexicans or Italians; their facial mimicry remains "not quite, not white."

37. John Wirfs, personal email, April 26, 2001.

38. In the precondom era of gay 1970s porn when the roles of top and bottom were not as rigid, the ingestion of cum was a common act taking place at the end of a sex scene, performed by either partner regardless of the role of top or bottom. Safer sex guidelines during the 1980s and 1990s AIDS era discouraged the exchange of bodily fluids, and the eating of cum fell out of favor in porn; it has since made a comeback, in the widely popular genre of barebacking porn and, increasingly, in mainstream porn.

39. Even if we allow that Lee's bottom performance was medically and cinematically faked (the use of Viagra to maintain an erect penis while getting fucked; the editing together of two cum shots from separate days into one scene), it remains the case that within the diegesis, these two components constitute a good bottom performance.

40. It should be noted that this range is extremely limited in mainstream gay video porn, where the repertoire of sex acts is restricted to jacking off, kissing, minimal nipple play, rimming, fellatio, topping, and bottoming. Echoing straight pornographic conventions, a scene in gay porn typically progresses from foreplay (kissing, mutual masturbation, rimming) to anal intercourse.

41. "Brandon Lee (pornographic actor)," Wikipedia, http://en.wikipedia.org/wiki/Brandon_Lee_%28pornographic_actor%29, accessed January 20, 2013.

42. Throughout this essay, I have argued that the ideal viewer constructed by the Brandon Lee videos (and Asian-themed gay video pornography in general) is a gay white man. However, the insertion of my own experience and reactions to these tapes in these pages—in addition to my citations of Richard Fung and my friend John Wirfs, a self-professed Brandon Lee fan—do offer some evidence that there exists an active gay Asian audience intellectually engaged with, and getting off to, this pornography. My personal interest in explicit sexual representation (of which gay moving-image pornography occupies a central position) arises from my own experimental video practice concerning issues around queer Asian American sexuality and identity as they intersect with and are articulated through popular cultural forms.

The most sustained interventions in homoerotic Asian American visual representation have taken place in the realm of queer experimental film and video. In place of amateur or commercial porn production, the realm of low/no-budget queer Asian experimental film and video is the one key area where the problematic depiction of the Asian male body in gay video porn comes under interrogation. It is also where more alternative and complex—not to mention smart, campy, and sexy—accented voices and "slanted visions" (to invoke the title of one of Ming-Yuen S. Ma's videos) are articulated. In addition, venues such as lesbian and gay film festivals around the world, Asian American (and Asian Canadian) film festivals, and the few remaining nonprofit alternative art exhibition spaces continue to lend support and offer exposure to this critical work. Some of the most exciting film and video makers engaged in these issues include Richard Fung (*Orientations*, 1984; *Chinese Characters*, 1986; *Steam Clean*, 1990; *Dirty Laundry*, 1996; *Sea in the Blood*, 2000), Wayne Yung (*The Queen's Cantonese*, 1998; *Search Engine*, 1999; *Field Guide to Western Wildflowers*, 2000; *My German Boyfriend*, 2004; *Asian Boyfriend*, 2006), Stuart Gaffney (*My Lover's Aunt Porn*, 2000; *Transgressions*, 2002), Ho Tam (*Season of the Boys*, 1997; *99 Men*, 1998; *Matinee Idol*, 1999; *Discopedia*, 2007), Michael Shaowanasai (*Exotic 101*, 1998; *The Adventures of Iron Pussy III: To Be or Not to Be*, 2000), and Ming-Yuen S. Ma (*Toc Storee*, 1992; *Slanted Vision*, 1995; *Sniff*, 1997). I discuss the work of Yung, Ma, and Shaowanasai in depth in chapter 4.

On queer Asian American experimental film and video, see Oishi (2000, 2003). For a brief overview of queer Asian American cinema and the politics of curating such work in Asian American film festivals, see Han (1998).

43. It must be noted that everyone has an accent. The accents that we don't hear as accents are considered the standard accent, such as those adopted by television news anchors. Some accents are marked as proper, upper class, and educated, such as a British accent. In the United States, what is heard as an Asian accent is decidedly not a desirable accent to have.

44. More frequently, one finds a failure to measure up to such an ideal, as when a high-pitched, queeny, Valley Girl accent belies the handsome face, muscular body, and big dick, thus effectively branding such an actor as a "muscle Mary."

45. Cante and Restivo, citing Daniel Harris, have this to say about gay porn actors' voices and their "ownership" of the social spaces that they occupy: "Harris describes the frequent disjunction between the spaces inhabited by the characters and the characters themselves, in terms of the tangible (in the case of the spaces) as well as more intangible (in the case of the models) class signifiers that circulate both within and beyond the actual tapes. The characters in the 'diegesis' simply don't seem to have the literal or figurative capital to command the spaces in which they perform. Usually, this is most evident as soon as the character/actor delivers his lines" (Cante and Restivo 2004b, 121).

46. In making this point, I'm drawing on Cante and Restivo's insight that the voice in gay porn, among other functions, is charged with providing authentic evidence of the actor's enjoyment of sex acts, especially anal pleasure. As they write, "If the come shot can't signify anal pleasure, and the erection (or even flaccidity, to be contrarian) can't do this either, . . . it would indeed seem to be anal pleasure that the voice is standing in for" (2001, 223). At the start of the scene, Rusty communicates his pain in get-

ting fucked in Mandarin. But as the scene progresses, he notes Tommy's handsomeness and sexiness, in English and Mandarin. As Tommy continues to energetically fuck him, Rusty registers his increasing pleasure, asking for "more, more," and affirms in Mandarin that he feels "very good." I am indebted to Lucetta Kam, Dave Zhou, and Julian Liu for the translation of this critical scene.

47. For an excellent discussion of the conceptual and political distinctions and overlaps between immigration and diaspora, see Mimura's (2009) chapter "Diaspora, or Modernity's Other: Theorizing Asian American Identity and Representation" in *Ghostlife of Third Cinema*.

48. José B. Capino makes the same argument for Asian pornography when he suggests that Asian actors disrupt Orientalist characterizations and narratives through self-distanciating, camp performance: "Self-reflexive distanciation is also achieved in Asian porn through strategies of camp performance, and is especially heightened when Asian actors are camping along. . . . Asian drag degenerates into Asianness-as-drag, making Asianness function like the complex of sex roles, assumed/performed identities, subcultural expressions, and gender reconfigurations that comprise such porn cinema personas as dominatrices, daddies, leatherfolk, nymphomaniacs, slaves and masters, and the like" (2006, 215).

In both *Lights & Darks* and *Affirmative Blacktion*, the social and economic power Lee wields as a ruthless Asian businessman, one who subjects his customers and employees to physical and psychological abuse, is ultimately regulated and contained in the concluding sequences of both videos when he is forced to sexually service customers and employees. Bottoming is marked as punishment in both narratives. However, as in all gay porn, sexual coercion and punishment in the storyline are invariably contradicted by the sexual performances themselves. That is, what is supposed to be narratively coded as punishment is always performed and experienced as something pleasurable and wanted onscreen. Once the sex begins, everyone seems to immediately forget that the characters are being forced, coerced, punished. Nevertheless, it is noteworthy that in both of these videos, "interracial" is familiarly coded as black and white. Lee is the only Asian character in both videos and, interestingly, the one targeted by the other characters for his racism. *Lights & Darks* ends with him getting fucked by Kennedy and orally servicing Razor, without any narrative explanation of the nature of Lee's relationship to the two men besides a sexual one. In *Affirmative Blacktion*, he is murdered by his employees Matthew Rush and Rod Daily after bottoming for both of them.

49. In gay American slang, blatino refers to men of black and Latino heritage.

50. A prime example of Asianness as drag can be found in *With Sex You Get Egg Roll* in the character of restaurant owner–boy brothel madam Miss Ling (Lilienne Li), played by a cisgendered Filipino American woman who looks like a drag queen in her super-tight dress, plunging neckline, spaghetti straps, and excessive shiny jewelry. Most strikingly, her campy lines are spoken in an accented, broken English (including the occasional replacement of Rs with Ls): "Listen Mister, I tell you one more time. You come twice, you pay twice. No more special order for you. You don't come here no more. [She hangs up the phone and starts to count her large wad of cash] . . . [On another call] Yes,

Mr. Smith. You want pork fried lice [sic]? Noodle? Sweet and sour chicken. OK, I send you right away. Excuse me? You want egg roll? Ahhh, that's special. With sex you get egg roll!"

51. My claim here is echoed by Capino's call to read Asian porn "alternatively": that is, "to read symptomatically the converse of white desire, which we might tentatively (and awkwardly as well as problematically) refer to as 'Asian desire.' We might look at how the Asian characters' sexual desires are articulated within the diegesis of the videos. . . . Alternatively, the impromptu statements and involuntary kinesthetic responses of Asian actors while in the thrall of coitus evince less legible but nonetheless perceptible ways by which both the desires and pleasures of Asian figures are encoded" (Capino 2006, 216).

Chapter 2: Reflections on an Asian Bottom

1. These themes are drawn from a review in the *Christian Science Monitor* (1967).

2. The novel is set sometime before World War II. Huston explained the updating of the story's setting to the postwar period to "ease searching for [prewar] props" (Russo and Merlin 2005, 139).

3. "Zorro David's portrayal as Anacleto, the houseboy, is bad and sad enough to send the gay movement back thirty years. It's reviling, degrading and, like a horrible traffic accident, impossible to ignore. No wonder Brando's character is desperate to keep his little secret. Look at his role model! This was David's first and only film role. You see? There is justice" (Brumburgh 2001). In an otherwise astute analysis of the figure of the houseboy and "alternative structures of feeling, belonging, and kinship" (See 2009, 108) in queer Filipino American performance art, Sarita See unfortunately dismisses any productive potentialities in the character of Anacleto, and David's performance, when she comments: "David produces a horrifyingly homophobic and racist caricature. . . . Anacleto is a mere appendage to the ailing, white military wife. . . . In a number of ways Huston's movie exemplifies how Hollywood's depiction of queer, obsessive, and/or perverse desires—the longing for something and someone wonderful—inevitably ends in their prohibition, frustration, and thwarting" (121–122). Although I don't dispute See's observation regarding the curtailing of perverse desires in the conclusion of *Reflections*, I do think it profitable to examine the generative moments that precede the shutting down of those queer desires.

4. On June 27, 1969, at the Stonewall Inn, a gay bar located in New York City's Greenwich Village frequented by transvestites and drag queens, patrons responded to a common police raid by fighting back and inciting a violent three-day riot. Activists and historians have cited this event as a momentous shift in gay politics. Whereas the homophile organizations prior to 1969 sought to gain homosexual recognition through quietist and assimilationist tactics, Stonewall sparked a militant turn in lesbian and gay movement politics. My reading of *Reflections* contests this neat periodization and teleological narrative of gay liberation by looking back at a historical moment considered to be socially and politically retrograde.

5. A number of commentators writing on McCullers's work have pointed out that her

coded depictions of homosexual characters reflect the repressive sexual mores of the sociohistorical context in which she was writing. Indeed, McCullers herself personally subscribed to the discourse of sexual inversion and named herself an invert.

The delineation of homosexuality in both the book and the film locates the truth of homosexuality as gender deviance. As the blurb on the back cover of my 1966 Bantam Book paperback copy asserts, "The Captain. Half man and half woman, he was irresistibly drawn to his wife's lover." Nevertheless, I concur with Russo's point that Huston's presentation of homosexuality goes over the top in its deployment of sexual inversion, especially in the characterization of the publicly butch Penderton, who is shown as an inveterate queen in private: studying a black-and-white postcard of the Apollo Belvedere, caressing a stolen silver spoon, and applying cold cream on his face. The not-so-subtle depictions of Anacleto's and Penderton's homosexuality through the means of effeminacy are nothing new. In the first chapter of *The Celluloid Closet*, devoted to the long tradition of sissies in the movies, Russo writes, "Homosexuality in the movies, whether overtly sexual or not, has always been in terms of what is or is not masculine" ([1981] 1995, 4).

6. As Richard Dyer explains in an essay on the importance of typification and gay representation, "A major fact about being gay is that it doesn't show. . . . There are signs of gayness, a repertoire of gestures, expressions, stances, clothing, and even environments that bespeak gayness, but these are cultural forms designed to show what the person's person alone does not show: that he or she is gay" (quoted in White 1999, 145). Similarly, Dana Takagi observes the distinctions between gayness and Asianness: "The first [distinction] . . . is the relative invisibility of sexual identity compared with racial identity. While both can be said to be socially constructed, the former are performed, acted out, and produced, often in individual routines, whereas the latter tends to be more obviously 'written' on the body and negotiated by political groups. Put another way, there is a quality of voluntarism in being gay/lesbian that is usually not possible as an Asian American" (1995, 24–25). While I understand the distinctions made by Dyer and Takagi on the cultural repertoires and performative routines of gayness in contradistinction to the racial markers on the "person's person," I would interrogate both critics' assumptions of choice and voluntarism when it comes to making one's homosexuality visible. Ask a proto-gay sissy teenager, of any race/ethnicity, how much choice he has in controlling the information circulated about his sexual identity.

7. Although much lip service has been given to the heroism of gender dissidents (queens, transgender folks, butch lesbians) who paved the way for lesbian and gay liberation in the post-Stonewall era, it is evident that nelly queens, butch women, and other gender queers have been marginalized in contemporary lesbian and gay public culture. In the gay male context, a quick perusal of any online gay personals forum would alert the reader to the hysterical fear and loathing of any potential respondent who might be feminine or femme in any remote way. It is important to note that my intervention is firmly situated within the current homonormative moment of LGBT politics. Gay liberation movement discourses of the late 1960s and 1970s were much more radical and critical of heteronormative structures, as can be glimpsed by such tracts as "Cocksucker" (Anonymous 2003, originally published in *Fag Rag* in 1971) and

"Indiscriminate Promiscuity as an Act of Revolution" (Shively 2003, originally published in a joint issue of *Gay Sunshine/Fag Rag* in 1974). Although he does not locate his work within the gay liberation movement—in fact, he was very critical of gay movement politics for its assimilationist bent—the film criticism of Parker Tyler (1973), most notably in his book *Screening the Sexes: Homosexuality in the Movies*, reveals a cheeky, witty, and very irreverent take on the representation of queers in the cinema. Most productively for our current discussion, Tyler was not interested in sanitized versions of homosexuals in the movies. His queer approach is exemplified by an ironic, campy style of writing as well as his obvious pleasure in proliferating terms to describe homosexual types in movies. To cite a chapter "Homeros in Uniform," we find a listing of "Soldiers, supersoldiers, subsoldiers, high and low schoolboys, fascist finaglers, draft-board daisies, boyish bonnes, lessoning lesbians, kingly kampfs, and a pansy poet of prison cells" (x–xi).

8. My reading is indebted to Martin Manalansan's distinction between "wearing" and "declaring" gay identity: "Filipino gay men argue that identities are not just proclaimed verbally, but are also felt (*pakiramdaman*) or intuited. The swardspeak term *ladlad ng kappa* suggests how identity is something 'worn' and not always 'declared.' It is this act of 'wearing' identity that makes public arenas for gay identity articulation superfluous" (2003, 34).

9. The various connotations of effeminacy include: "womanish, unmanly, enervated, feeble; self-indulgent, voluptuous; unbecomingly delicate or over-refined" (OED, quoted in Sinfield 1994, 26).

10. To be sure, the attribution of sexual and social immaturity to nonwhite subjects constitutes a common trope in colonial anthropology and other Western social scientific discourses. These same pseudo-scientific discourses also deem homosexual subjects to be immature and arrested in development. Writing on the interface between sexology and comparative anatomy in the sexual construction of African American women and lesbians, Siobhan B. Somerville observes, "Sexologists writing in the late nineteenth and early twentieth centuries inherited [the] tendency to racialize perceived sexual ambiguity" (2000, 27). For instance, the "findings" of African American women's allegedly abnormal buttocks and genitalia and white lesbians' large clitorises were employed to prove their primitive hermaphroditism and justified as evidence of their "bodies as anomalous 'throwbacks' within a scheme of cultural and anatomical progress" (29).

11. Remarking on McCullers's list of characters, Robert K. Martin (1992) points out that, unlike those who come before him on the list ("two officers, a soldier, two women"), Anacleto as "a Filipino" is ungendered. Curiously, in this ranking, Anacleto's racial difference trumps his maleness. One doesn't have to read many pages to see the reasons why Anacleto doesn't quite count as a man.

12. On this point, see Butt (2005), especially his chapter "Idol Gossip: Myths of Genius and the Making of Queer Worlds" (51–73).

13. In the same passage, Alison does allow that "as a painter Anacleto had great talent—of that she was sure" (74).

14. Thanks to Greg Youmans for this reference. To be fair, in the introduction to his

book *How to Do the History of Homosexuality* in which the essay is reprinted, Halperin (2002) explicitly acknowledges some of the drawbacks of his postulation of the modern homosexual and its problematic spatial-temporal partition of the past-present, the West and the rest. At least one other critic has made a comparable argument in relation to male same-sex eroticisms in Asia. In his essay "Global Gaze/Global Gays," Dennis Altman (1997) offers an account of "the emergence of a western-style politicized homosexuality in Asia." Though he warns Western scholars and activists about the dangers of postulating a universalized gay identity, he goes on to narrate an origin story in which globalization is responsible for importing "modern," "Western-style" models of homosexuality to Asian countries. The traits of this "modern homosexuality" include masculine-presenting men replacing "would-be women"; gay male couplings supplanting married men who engage in surreptitious "homosex"; and closeted gays publicly coming out and embracing gay identity, politics, and community (Altman 1997, 422–423). However, as Lisa Rofel has forcefully pointed out, "Altman's Western origin story of gay liberation places Asian gays forever in the place of deferred arrival" (2007, 91). Still, I must admit that the ideal of egalitarian homo-relations Halperin and Altman, among other critics, describe exerts a powerful hold on Euro-American lesbians and gays in the contemporary LGBT assimilationist moment. In chapter 4, I take up these very issues again in my discussion of gay Asian American sticky rice politics.

15. I suggest that such an expansion of dissident gender styles and presentations also allows room for the effeminate straight man and masculine straight woman.

16. The main reason Halperin gives for separating out effeminacy and modern homosexuality is that historically, effeminacy designated excessive heterosexual desire in men. Essentially womanizers, effeminates rejected masculine endeavors such as business, politics, and war; instead they devoted their energies to the sexual pursuit of women. In contrast to normatively masculine men who seek to replace their sensual appetites with austere control and regulation of the body, effeminate men undercut their virility by directing disproportionate erotic attention to women, some by employing "makeup and perfumes, elaborate grooming, and prominent jewelry" (Halperin 2000, 93). Although I appreciate Halperin's careful historicization of effeminacy as a mode that was traditionally adopted by straight men, it still remains unclear how such a distinction serves to help us better understand the construction of homosexuality today. For in spite of the fact that effeminacy has historically signified male heterosexual excess, effeminacy is linked overwhelmingly to homosexuality in this day and age, however problematic that linkage may be. In his latest book, *How to Be Gay*, Halperin (2012) examines carefully and thoughtfully many of the issues around gay femininity that I discuss in this chapter. His primary project is to provide a nonbiological, nonpsychological, which is to say social, account for the ways in which gay male culture is coded as feminine and how much of it lies outside of the sexual realm. He points out, rightly, that masculinity constitutes "a key erotic value for gay men" that confers "sexual dignity . . . [and] erotic prestige and desirability," while gay male effeminacy signifies "a throwback, a symbol of age-old homophobic prejudice" (Halperin 2012, 306). The most interesting and insightful part of his analysis is the argument that gay femininity has little to do with women, but exists as a "form of gender atypicality" specific to gay men:

"As a proxy identity, 'femininity' is a clear expression of gay male gender dissidence, a rejection of standard, canonical, established forms of heterosexual masculinity. But that doesn't mean that gay 'femininity' necessarily signifies an actual identification with *women*. However much it may *refer* to women, which it obviously does, it is not always or essentially *about* women" (318). In my discussion of the queer domestic bond between Alison and Anacleto below, I am less committed to demarcating a clear boundary between gay male femininity and "female" femininity. In my estimation, it is more productive to highlight the overlaps, blurrings, and connections between the two embodiments of femininity, in order to work toward a queer feminist analysis of nonnormative gender expressions.

17. The notable exception is Joon Oluchi Lee's wonderful essay, "The Joy of the Castrated Boy." Responding to Eng, Lee's "embracing [of] racial castration" perfectly describes Anacleto's blissful identification with femininity (2005, 44).

18. For example, two key agendas of the LGBT movement today consist of gay marriage and gay adoption. Similarly, Asian American academic scholarship and popular journalistic discourses continue to focus on questions relating to the maintenance and disintegration of families, from the generation gap of earlier decades to the parachute kids and astronaut parents in today's transnational era.

19. In the same vein, Robert K. Martin (1992) has identified Anacleto's status as a eunuch.

20. Here the narration reveals Alison's pitying and patronizing, yet maternal attitude toward the houseboy: "He was seventeen years old, but his sickly, clever, frightened face had the innocent expression of a child of ten. When they were making preparations to return to the States, he had begged her to take him with her, and she had done so. The two of them, she and Anacleto, could perhaps find a way to get along in the world together but what would he do when she was gone?" (McCullers [1941] 1966, 49). Another clue to read the bond between mistress and houseboy as a mother-child relation is the link between the name Anacleto and the word "anaclitic." In Freudian psychoanalytic theory, an infant's anaclitic object choice is a sexual object choice that is "propped" upon self-preservative functions, functions often provided by the mother. I thank one of the anonymous reviewers for this insightful observation.

21. Anacleto adds, "And while we are about it, we might order an extra yard or so. Then I can have a jacket." We might say that both he and Alison are "cut from the same cloth."

22. In his study of public health in nineteenth-century San Francisco's Chinatown, Shah (2001) coins the term to encompass such phenomena as female-headed households among female prostitutes and their children, male workers living together in bunkhouses, and cross-class and multiracial opium dens.

23. The characterizations of Alison as "desexed" (Baker 1967, B23) and Anacleto as an "artistic half-male" (Champlin 1967, D14) are culled from popular reviews, in the *Chicago Tribune* and the *Los Angeles Times*, respectively.

24. Interestingly, Patricia White discusses the pairing of black maids and white mistresses in Hollywood cinema as one significant way in which lesbian connotations are produced. Similarly, one might suggest that Anacleto's identification with Alison's fail-

ure at white heterosexual femininity enables a different set of queer connotations. In the book, McCullers writes about Morris Langdon's observations of Alison's and Anacleto's verbal mirroring in the following way: "It always made the Major [in the film he is a colonel] feel rather eerie to listen to them talking together in the quiet room. Their voices and enunciation were so precisely alike that they seemed to be softly echoing each other. The only difference was that Anacleto spoke in a chattering, breathless manner, while Alison's voice was measured and composed" ([1941] 1966, 35). The opposition between Alison's measured tone of voice and Anacleto's breathless chatter, though undoubtedly conjuring up the stereotype of the breathy gay lisp, nevertheless highlights Alison's role as the well-spoken mentor to Anacleto's enthusiastic mentee.

25. In a perverse way, we can read Anacleto's performance of sympathetic childbirth not only as the ultimate feminizing act but also as a sexualizing one. Thanks to Linda Williams for this point.

26. Their unequal relationship bears out Heather Love's warning against the idealization of queer friendship in queer studies. While affirming the potential of queer friendship to undermine heteronormative sociality, Love points out that we must also attend to the "impossible or interrupted intimacy" of such relations, marked as they are by "betrayal, disappointment, [and] loss" (2007, 74–75). See Love (2007), especially her chapter "The End of Friendship: Willa Cather's Sad Kindred" (72–99).

27. The importance of Anacleto's queer alliance with Alison's infirm femininity can be productively posed against the representation of Penderton's homosexuality, which is markedly masculinist. McCullers's portrayal of Penderton's sexual inversion exploits what Sarah Gleeson-White calls the "toxic codes" of homosexual desire, including the "rejection of women, sexual impotence, narcissism, and decadence" (2003, 38).

28. In *Impossible Desires*, Gayatri Gopinath offers a brilliant analysis of the queering of "home" by those who cannot afford the mobility of leaving home for the freedom promised elsewhere. As she astutely comments, "'Home' is a space that is ruptured and imaginatively transformed by queer diasporic subjects even as they remain within its confines. This queer transformation of the diasporic 'home' constitutes a remarkably powerful challenge to dominant ideologies of community and nation in ways that may very well escape intelligibility within a logic of visibility and 'coming out.' . . . Thus the construction of 'queers' being 'like Asian American' in their alienation from 'home' needs to be rearticulated in light of the ways in which queer diasporic subjects—and queer female diasporic subjects in particular—inhabit and transform home space rather than simply existing in exilic relation to it" (2005, 79). Gopinath's insight is especially resonant when we consider that while Alison and Anacleto's queer domestic bond fervently contests "dominant ideologies of community and nation," it is running away from home that results in the killing off of the two characters (literally in the case of Alison and metaphorically for Anacleto).

29. Anacleto's influence is tremendous, especially given the fact that his total screen time is approximately thirteen minutes in a film whose total running time is one hour and forty-eight minutes. His sudden disappearance bears out See's point regarding the exploitation of domestic work, its "simultaneous, contradictory disposability and indispensability" (2009, 121).

30. Along with Alison and the dead infant Catherine, these are the types of people that Anacleto cherishes, as revealed in McCullers's novel. Similarly, Alison considers other people "loathsome" in comparison to herself and Anacleto: "Everyone she had known in the past five years was somehow wrong—that is, everyone except [her friend Captain] Weincheck and of course Anacleto and little Catherine" (McCullers [1941] 1966, 68). These two characters' self-assessments bear out Jonathan Dollimore's (1991, 263) observation that the intimate relation between femininity and male homosexuality should not be an affront to either one. In McCullers's oeuvre, freaks occupy a pride of place as figures of identification and desire. Witness the following oft-cited passage from *The Member of the Wedding* regarding twelve-year-old Frankie: "She was afraid of all the Freaks, for it seemed to her that they had looked at her in a secret way and tried to connect their eyes with hers, as though to say: we know you. She was afraid of their long Freak eyes. And all the years she had remembered them, until this day" (McCullers [1946] 2004, 20).

31. A number of critics have argued that historically, certain talented actors assigned to play stereotypical characters were able to transcend the stereotypes due to the ways they played those roles. Donald Bogle ([1973] 2004) ascribes a critical function to the performances of black female stars such as Hattie McDaniel, Ethel Waters, and Dorothy Dandridge. Vito Russo ([1981] 1995, 36) lauds the "charming and winning" contributions of character actors Franklin Pangborn, Eric Blore, and Grady Sutton, who specialized in sissy roles in the 1930s. White (1999, 146) focuses on the lesbian-coded supporting types such as "nurses, secretaries, career women, nuns, companions, and housekeepers" in the career of Agnes Moorehead; she also looks at lesbian-coded supporting characters played by Ethel Waters and Mercedes McCambridge. The key element of these critics' arguments for the metacritical function of these queer and black actors' supporting performances is the fact these actors played similar roles across a body of films. Hence, their effects are partly based on an intertextual repetition that produces a sense of pleasurable recognition and defamiliarization for the viewer. Therein lies the difficulty with making a similar case for Zorro David's performance as Anacleto. Because this was his only screen role, the question of the audience's resistant spectatorship is more difficult to establish. Yet a few contemporary critics did note David's standout performance. For the *Washington Post*, he performed his part with "vivid élan" ("Brando and Miss Taylor" 1967, H2). The *New York Times* notes that he played the part "amusingly and waspishly" (Crowther 1967, 59) and *Sight and Sound* contends that the film is "nearly stolen" by David and Julie Harris (Taylor 1968, 99). In reviews panning David's excessive performance, the negative evaluations at times come across as protests against the mere thought that such a character might exist.

32. For example, before Brando signed on, other actors considered for the role of Penderton included Montgomery Clift, Robert Mitchum, Lee Marvin, Rod Steiger, Jason Robards, and William Holden. The choice of Brando echoes the casting of the two major female leads in that it capitalized on these actors' sexualized star personas. Elizabeth Taylor won her first Oscar for playing a sexually promiscuous young woman, Gloria Wandrous, in *Butterfield 8* (dir. Daniel Mann, 1960) and her second Oscar for the role of the boozy Martha in *Who's Afraid of Virginia Woolf?* (dir. Mike Nichols, 1966).

Her other notable roles preceding *Reflections* include highly sexualized women in such films as *Cat on a Hot Tin Roof* (dir. Richard Brooks, 1958), *Suddenly, Last Summer* (dir. Joseph L. Mankiewicz, 1959), and *Cleopatra* (dir. Joseph L. Mankiewicz, 1963). Though her box office clout ebbed at the end of the 1960s, she started out the decade as the highest-paid actress in Hollywood. The casting of Julie Harris benefits from the actress's queer star text. Her association with Carson McCullers began with her starring role as the tomboy protagonist Frankie in *The Member of the Wedding* in both the Broadway play (1950) and the film adaptation (dir. Fred Zinnemann, 1952), for which she received an Academy Award nomination for Best Actress. She played another queer-coded character (the spinster aunt Eleanor Lance) in the lesbionic ghost movie *The Haunting* (dir. Robert Wise, 1963). Brando came to *Reflections* with an Oscar under his belt (Best Actor for *On the Waterfront* [dir. Elia Kazan, 1954]), along with Best Actor nominations for five other films. I discuss Brando's star text below in note 34. I cite these accomplishments of three of *Reflections*'s leads to clarify that, indeed, they were solidly established stars honored for their acting talents. For the role of Anacleto, producers considered casting a young Puerto Rican actor named Jamie Sanchez who had appeared with Rod Steiger in *The Pawnbroker* (dir. Sidney Lumet, 1964). They saved money by going with David by paying him Screen Actors minimum, that is, a tenth of the salary Sanchez would have commanded (Russo and Merlin 2005, 84).

33. A pointed example related in *Troubles* shows how David's cutting humor takes gay culture as the norm. Referring to Huston's country of residence, David is quoted as saying, "I thought [*Reflections* producer] Mr. Ray Stark said Fire Island, but it turned out to be Ireland" (Russo and Merlin 2005, 84). A similar campy attitude infuses his playing of Anacleto.

34. In addition to the Method techniques, his choice of roles also bespeaks a certain consistency, roles that James Naremore describes as "homosexual fantasy figures": an ethnic stud (*A Streetcar Named Desire* [dir. Elia Kazan, 1951] and *The Fugitive Kind* [dir. Sidney Lumet, 1959]), a biker (*The Wild One* [dir. Laslo Benedek, 1954]), and a cowboy (*One-Eyed Jacks* [dir. Marlon Brando, 1961]). Naremore mentions the threatening sexual persona that Brando brings to all of his roles, especially a "'bisexual' effect" that contrasts sharply with other leading men of the 1940s (John Wayne, Clark Gable, and Gregory Peck), but that reverberates with his 1950s contemporaries (James Dean, Montgomery Clift, and Elvis Presley) (Naremore 1988, 194–195).

35. I am borrowing Stephen Cooper's (1993, 107) marvelous description.

36. In addition to these sightings of bottoms, we might add another key image of bottomhood: Alison's breasts. By cutting off her nipples (body tissue that becomes erect and secretes milk), she renders them round, smooth, and bottom-like. Twice in the film, Leonora mentions Alison's act of self-mutilation to Langdon as evidence of Alison's unstable mental state. To Langdon's suggestion that Alison is getting better because she hasn't tried to do anything like that again, Leonora rejoins, "What she did is something a lady can only do once, now, isn't it?" The implication here is that Alison's cutting off of her nipples desexualizes her, disqualifying her as a suitable sexual partner for Langdon. I suggest, however, that the site of Alison's feminine erogenous zone has traveled from boobs to buttocks, from front to behind. Unseen but repeatedly invoked, Alison's breast-

bottom, that is, a mother's bottom pleasure, is the most unimaginable and threatening of all. This reading is indebted to D. A. Miller's fascinating account of Elizabeth Taylor's voluptuous breasts (her "front") as a visual displacement of the gay male "behind" in an essay on another queer film, *Suddenly, Last Summer* (dir. Joseph L. Mankiewicz, 1959); see Miller (1999).

37. In the book, this perilous ride produces an epiphany in Penderton: "And having given up life, the Captain suddenly began to live. A great mad joy surged through him. . . . He was conscious of the pure keen air and he felt the marvel of his own tense body, his laboring heart, and the miracle of blood, muscle, nerves, and bone. The Captain knew no terror now; he had soared to that rare level of consciousness where the mystic feels that the earth is he and that he is the earth" (McCullers [1941] 1966, 59–60).

38. In a speech given to Langdon and Leonora, Penderton waxes hypnotic about the attractions of life among enlisted men: "And they're seldom out of one another's sight. They eat and they train and they shower and they play jokes and go to the brothel together. They sleep side by side . . . and the friendships — my Lord. There are friendships formed that are stronger than the fear of death. And they're never lonely; they're never lonely. And sometimes I envy them."

39. My reading of Private Williams's view from below builds upon Stephen Cooper's incisive analysis of these sequences in relation to the spectator-screen relationship: "The spectator-voyeur must deal with a voyeurism problematized precisely by the construction of that narrative gap in which Private Williams is seen seeing nothing more than an upstairs lighted window: This is no peep show, but a showing forth of the politics of cinematic looking, an implicit indictment of films that would suture their spectators into unquestioning passivity" (1993, 105–106). Interestingly, if we follow Cooper's line of argument, it is Williams's onscreen passive looking that shakes the film spectator out of her passive viewing.

40. To be sure, besides Anacleto's flamboyant effeminacy, the sequences showing Penderton actively cruising Williams constitute the most powerful evidence of homosexuality in the film: the look of one man at another articulated in the classic shot–reverse shot structure.

41. Katz (1996) cites the quotation from an unpublished interview of Arnheim by John Jones, conducted on October 16, 1965.

42. A major reason for the critical and popular success of European art cinema (and its freer, more sophisticated representation of sexual themes) was the fact that these films did not have to get approval from the Production Code. At the time of the release of *Reflections*, a transition was under way from the Production Code to the new Motion Picture Association of America rating system still in operation today. During this period, Hollywood was no longer deterred by a negative evaluation by the Production Code. Indeed, *Reflections* was widely released even with a C rating (for "condemned") by the National Catholic Office for Motion Pictures. By this time, such a rating was even thought to help films do better at the box office (see Monaco 2003).

43. And it was the Technicolor version that was circulated in subsequent repertory and retrospective exhibitions and on VHS. It was not until its November 2006 DVD release that the desaturated version was restored.

44. This point is partly supported by the fact that most critics fixated on Huston's color experiments in their reviews of the film.

45. Huston's war documentaries include *Report from the Aleutians* (1943), *The Battle of San Pietro* (1945), and *Let There Be Light* (1946). See also Edgerton (1993). Most relevant for our discussion at hand is both critics' observations that these documentaries evince a shift in sentiment, from patriotic conviction in American military projects to a critical disenchantment toward the atrocities of war. *Let There Be Light*, a film about shell-shocked soldiers returning to civilian life after World War II, was suppressed by the Pentagon for more than three decades. It finally had a national theatrical run in 1981.

46. Benshoff's texts include *The Strange One* (dir. Jack Garfein, 1957), *Billy Budd* (dir. Peter Ustinov, 1962), *Reflections in a Golden Eye* (1967), *The Sergeant* (dir. John Flynn, 1968), and *The Gay Deceivers* (dir. Bruce Kessler, 1969).

47. I would like to thank Douglas Crimp for the email correspondence about *Reflections* and for making the text of his lecture on the film available to me.

Chapter 3: *The Lover's* "Gorgeous Ass"

1. The explicit (hard-core) depiction of "an Asian male in a full nude scene in a major film" had already occurred in Nagisa Oshima's *Ai no corrida* (*In the Realm of the Senses*, 1976).

2. It should be noted that the charge of pornography (i.e., of being a low genre) must be tempered by the film's various high-art credentials. The film is based on Marguerite Duras's novel *L'Amant* (1984), an international best seller and recipient of the Prix Goncourt; directed by Annaud, known for pseudo-arty productions such as *Quest for Fire* (1981) and *The Name of the Rose* (1986); produced by noted producer-director Claude Berri; cowritten by Gérard Brach, a longtime collaborator of Roman Polanski; and narrated by famous French actress Jeanne Moreau. In addition to the decision to translate the French literary text into an English-soundtrack film, Annaud's casting of English model Jane March and well-known Hong Kong actor Tony Leung Ka Fai further contributes to the film's international credentials and cachet.

3. I am tracing one possible itinerary marking the film's location shoots and the actor's image circulation, and registering San Francisco as the place where I first caught sight of Leung's gorgeous ass on the movie screen.

4. Duras's novel and Annaud's film have received scant attention in the Asian American scholarly context; however, they have inspired erotic poetry and prose by Asian American writers dealing with interracial (Asian man–white woman) desire. For example, one finds two short stories in the 1995 anthology *On a Bed of Rice: An Asian American Erotic Feast*: "Afterimages of Leung Kar Fai," by Wagner Wai Jim Au (1995), and "The Lover," by David Mura (1995b). In both of these stories, the film *The Lover* functions as the erotic, sexual, and emotional inspiration for the narratives, hard-core sexual activity in "Afterimages" and an emotional reminiscence of a past love affair in "The Lover." In his poetry collection *The Colors of Desire*, Mura (1995a) employs Duras's work (*The Lover* and *Hiroshima Mon Amour*) as an intertext for several of his poems. In one poem, he rewrites Duras's interracial scenarios by inserting a Japanese American

soldier doing a tour of duty who has an affair with a French woman ("The Blueness of the Day," 23–40).

In a fascinating essay about interracial (black female–Asian male) desire, "The Black Asianphile," African American female writer Latasha Natasha Diggs professes her desire for "Asian dick" by giving a biographical tour from her girlhood crushes on local Chinese restaurant workers to her appreciation of Bruce Lee's glistening "latissimus dorsi" in his kung fu fight scenes and Tony Leung's sexual performances in *The Lover*. It is noteworthy that her "Asian male fetish" finds its catalyst in Hong Kong martial arts movies, anime, and Asian literatures, although one finds Hong Kong movies and American films with Asian male characters dominating her chapter. Even as she notes the racist bent of Hollywood's representation of Asian men, Diggs reveals her immense pleasure in consuming them: "When Hollywood began to feature more Asian men in the eighties, the roles let me down while still holding me controlled supernaturally. The heroes were always white boys. The Asian dudes always had mushrooms for a haircut and they always looked like little boys. The only sexy ones were the evil-doers or the idiots" (2003, 195). Diggs's essay constitutes an unexplored and undertheorized area of studies about racialized sexuality, in particular, what happens when the frame of reference is based on black female subjectivity and the desire for nonnormative masculinities of color.

5. The section heading is culled from Jeanne Moreau's voice-over description of the Chinese lover: "This is what he does in life. He makes love, nothing else."

6. In the wider scheme of things, neither of the protagonists is actually punished for their sexual transgressions. The Chinese lover gets to sow his wild oats and marry his arranged bride; the girl gets to return to France, a dream come true for most whites in the colonies. Thanks to Ji Sung Kim for this point.

7. Focusing on three big-budget French films from 1992 (*Indochine*, dir. Régis Wargnier; *Dien Bien Phu*, dir. Pierre Schoendoerffer; and *The Lover*), Norindr (1996) describes these productions as "filmic memorials," examples of "colonial blues" undergirding an imperialist nostalgia.

8. A distinctive cue to reread Duras's text as a revision of women's romance novels comes from Duras herself. In the screenplay-novel *L'Amant de la Chine du Nord* (1991) (translated as *The North China Lover* [1992])—her rewriting of *L'Amant* as a corrective to Annaud's film project—she offers in a footnote: "*Some pointers for a movie.* . . . Shoot the lovers, The Book as Pulp Novel" (Duras 1992, 72).

9. It is important to distinguish Asian-white interracial relationships by the race and gender of the partners. In her book about Asian-white miscegenation in the American context, Koshy argues, "The white man-Asian woman dyad has historically been more serviceable to signifying the assimilability of Asian Americans than the Asian man-white woman dyad, which typically emplotted the cultural impossibility and sexual danger of incorporating Asians into the nation" (2004, 22). Though the issue of national assimilability does not apply in Annaud's film, the coding of the Chinese lover as sexually dangerous certainly underscores the racial-sexual taboo of their relationship. To be sure, the young girl's sexual affair with the Chinese man, because it is consensual, reinforces her humiliation and degradation in the French colonial community. Another

interesting example in which the white woman's decision to go with an Asian man signifies her masochistic desire for sexual degradation can be found in Luis Buñuel's *Belle de Jour* (1967). The scene in question has Catherine Deneuve's Severine Serizy enthusiastically agreeing to go to bed with a fat Asian client (Iska Khan) with a mysterious box (that is, a perverse sexual fetish too bizarre for the camera to show) after the other prostitutes turned him down.

10. As the Chinese man tells her on their first meeting on the ferry, "It's so surprising, a young white girl on a native bus. . . . And you're pretty. You can do anything you like." The comment suggests that her eccentric appearance and nonconventional movement (riding a local bus) are possible due to her race privilege.

11. Sean Metzger also finds a similar regulation of Asian masculinity in Annaud's film. He argues that the film ultimately controls and contains Asian masculinity and sexuality in the context of French colonialism and imperialism in Indochina, in spite of an "oscillation of power defin[ing] the Chinese man's masculinity throughout the text" (Metzger 2002, 118). Though more nuanced than Hagedorn's blanket dismissal, on closer examination, one finds that the basis of Metzger's assessment of Asian masculinity in *The Lover* turns on very limited and conventional criteria of what constitutes desirable, and normative, masculinity: Asian masculine agency is determined by the power to initiate sexual activity, to sexually penetrate the female protagonist, to turn her into a properly desiring heterosexual subject—that is, Asian masculine agency is figured as the desire to be on top.

12. In a formulation that reverberates with Eve Sedgwick's (2003, 36) claim for shame as "deconstituting and foundational" of identity, Judith Butler observes that the work of subjection involves an interpellative process "by which subjects are formed in subjugation" (1997a, 27). She points out that, at times, "we find ourselves preferring the occasion of being derogated to the one of not being addressed at all" (27). Glossing the complicated itineraries through which subjects are formed, Butler reminds us that we must take care to distinguish "agency" from "mastery" (26). I contend that such a slippage occurs in the simplistic reversal of subject/object, masculine/feminine in the readings offered by critics who diagnose racial objectification in the French girl's treatment of the Chinese lover. That is, the girl's accession of sexual subjectivity is conflated with sexual dominance.

13. We find such couplings to be indelibly marked by social taboo, transgression, and danger in the history of Hollywood cinema. For example, one can name early productions like *The Cheat* (dir. Cecil B. DeMille, 1915), *Broken Blossoms* (dir. D. W. Griffith, 1919), and *The Bitter Tea of General Yen* (dir. Frank Capra, 1933) and recent ones such as *Anna and the King* (dir. Andy Tennant, 1999) and *Kiss of the Dragon* (dir. Chris Nahon, 2001). For a study of white-Asian interracial relationships in Hollywood film, see Marchetti (1993). Eugene Franklin Wong (1978) has identified the racist casting practice of "role segregation" in Hollywood representation of interracial sex. Whereas the cinematic representation of miscegenation favored the depiction of white male and Asian female pairings (whether as actors or characters), the depiction of interracial sex between an Asian male actor and a white female actress was strictly forbidden during the studio era; however, such couplings were allowed if the Asian male character was

played by a white actor in yellowface. Laura Kang points out that the meticulous, phobic management of racialized bodies onscreen propagated by racist casting practices reveals that "'yellowfacing' . . . was neither an effort at a mimetic representation of sociological realities or the lack of available Asian actors and actresses to perform a range of other configurations of desire and sexuality" (2002, 106). In the following, I go on to consider the scandalous difference that is put into play when "the 'simulated effect' of interracial sex" (in Kang's terms, 2002, 107) is produced by a "real" Asian male body and an "actual" white female one.

14. See, for example, Liz Constable's (2004) essay on the affect of shame in Simone de Beauvoir and Catherine Breillat, "Unbecoming Sexual Desires for Women Becoming Sexual Subjects: Simone de Beauvoir (1949) and Catherine Breillat (1999)"; Sally R. Munt's (2008) *Queer Attachments: The Cultural Politics of Shame*; Elspeth Probyn's (2005) *Blush: Faces of Shame*; Roderick Ferguson's (2003) *Aberrations in Black: Toward a Queer of Color Critique*; David M. Halperin and Valerie Traub's (2010) *Gay Shame* anthology; Frances Negrón-Muntaner's (2004) discussion of shame as constituting and generative of Puerto Rican national identity in *Boricua Pop: Puerto Ricans and the Latinization of American Culture*; and Hiram Perez's (2005) "You Can Have My Brown Body and Eat It, Too!" The latter two critics have advanced powerful critiques of gay shame theory's sidelining of race. Responding to Halberstam's point about the feminizing operation of shame, Negrón-Muntaner calls attention to the ways shame is also "racially engendered" (Gonzalez 2010, 90). Referencing "[Douglas] Crimp and other (white) theorists" writing on shame, she cautions, "being socially constituted by shame is not desirable for most people who are so hailed. Yes, shame is culturally 'productive.' But I find the narcissism that shame brings forth politically problematic, especially if one becomes enamored of it. . . . I do not desire shame on anyone for my personal or political enjoyment. For if one's greatest political priority is to 'resist' normalization rather than contest the 'evil eyes' of shame, it probably means that one is pretty 'normal' already and should take a better look at that new location" (Gonzalez 2010, 95–96). In my reading of the Chinese lover's and the French girl's relationship, I attend to the simultaneity of race, gender, class, and sexuality in the ways their shame gets played out.

15. As the phrase from Stockton's book title, "beautiful bottom," and its reverberation in my chapter title, "gorgeous ass," indicate, aesthetics and bottomhood, that is to say, adopting a view from below, expands our psychic and corporeal purview and allows us to be open and receptive to a different "angle of attraction" (Stockton 2006, 25).

16. In his reading of the girl's costume as articulated in the book, Norindr identifies a different strategy, not mimicry or assimilation, but one that exploits visibility and exhibitionism beyond the purview of the eroticized male gaze, redirecting such attention to her goal of monetary gain (1996, 120–121).

17. This characterization positions the lover as an outsider as well, another colonial presence in Indochina. See Metzger (2002), Lessard (2007), and Ha (2009) for the historical background concerning these two competing colonial powers in Indochina. One important consequence of Duras's depiction of the young girl and Chinese lover as members of the colonizing groups is that the sexual policing of native men and Euro-

pean women described by Stoler doesn't obtain in quite the same way in *The Lover*. Although the Chinese lover risks arrest and punishment for having sex with a white adolescent girl, as a member of the wealthy Chinese minority he would be able to use his money to buy his way out of any potential prosecution.

18. It is instructive to compare this portrayal of the Chinese lover to the portrayal of the Japanese architect in *Hiroshima Mon Amour*. As Duras writes in her screenplay notes regarding the portrait of the Japanese man: "He's a man of about forty. Tall. With a fairly 'Western' face. . . . In short, he is an 'international' type. What makes him attractive should be immediately apparent to everyone as being that quality found in men who have reached maturity without succumbing prematurely to fatigue, without having resorted to subterfuge" (2003, 26–27). The revealing modifiers in this characterization are certainly the phrases "a fairly 'Western' face" and "an 'international' type" as racially marked descriptors that qualify, and bolster, the virile masculinity of the Japanese lover.

19. See Lessard (2007).

20. The depiction of the Chinese man's conspicuous consumption also distinguishes him from the majority of Chinese in Vietnam. Marie-Paule Ha points out that "the absence of any conspicuous display of socio-economic rank markers among the Chinese never ceased to puzzle the French administrators. In their reports, they frequently talked about the difficulties they had in differentiating the owners of Chinese businesses from their employees or even the coolies when visiting their premises" (2009, 196). She gives the following reasons for the Chinese's lack of conspicuous consumption: these men came from poor places in China and were also uneducated and unskilled; they planned to return to China and were saving their earnings to send back to their families in China; and they wanted to blend in in order to avoid stirring up resentment from both the native and French populations. Seen in this light, the Chinese lover's excessive display suggests his family's immense affluence, his desire to broadcast this fact through the use of French luxury goods, and his lack of concern for the opinions of the indigenous or colonial communities.

21. Winston compares *L'Amant* unfavorably to *Un Barrage* and attributes the popularity of *L'Amant* to its empty, vacuous style: "it tells of a *colon* girl's first sex with an older Chinese man in a fragmented and postmodern style that pays no mind to the historical, social, and cultural contexts that the 1950 novel rendered explicit" (2001, 71).

22. In spite of these kinds of assessments, it is clear that Duras confidently asserted her high literary and cultural cachet during this last phase of her career. These critics' dismissals of *L'Amant* should be tempered with the fact that the novel garnered tremendous praise from other critics and the enthusiasm of her readers. As Winston points out, "This work of its author's winter was so successful that it won the literary prize designed to recognize the first work of a young unknown: the prix Goncourt. . . . [The Goncourt jury] may have recognized the unavoidability of recognizing a writer who had produced so much, earned an international reputation, been around so long, sold well at home and abroad" (2001, 70–71). Winston goes on to observe that Duras strategically used her literary capital for financial gain as well as to maintain control over the reception of her work: she sold the rights to the book to provide her son a generous

inheritance; and she wrote *L'Amant de la Chine du Nord* as a response to Annaud's film, publishing it before the film's release in theaters as a way of authorizing her side of the story (Winston 2001, 76).

23. To be sure, such criticism is borne out by Annaud's non-self-reflexive Orientalist descriptions of the "delayed spell" Vietnam exerted on him: "the 'Flemish' beauty of the endless plains, the bustling of life on the canals and on the river, the continuous presence of water. Captured also: the smiling seriousness of this ascetic population, so integrated, blended into the background, eternal. Its extraordinary dignity in the face of misery. And then, the unique relics of French presence, with its caricature Napoleonic order of avenues and monuments, the quaint charm of the Parisian 'Belle Epoque' architecture, that feeling of resort towns, or an end-of-the-century 'Riviera,' moved to the equator. Jewels in the midst of ruins. The 'good' side of poverty" (Annaud quoted in Norindr 1997, 141). In addition to his blatant Orientalism, critics also cite his depiction of the native population as faceless, nameless hordes relegated to the background in order to assure an authentic atmosphere.

24. Molly Haskell calls this scene the most erotic and exciting moment in the film. Interestingly, she misattributes the "active" partner in this scene: "The most erotic moment is that in which Jane Marsh [sic] reaches over in the limousine and touches the slender, slightly darker male hand, confirms the awakening of desire—or maybe just desire for desire—and initiates the love affair" (Haskell 1992, 33). This scene does not appear in Duras's original novel, but was added in *The North China Lover* (1992). In the latter book, it is the girl—here renamed the child—who first reaches over to touch the Chinese man's hand. However, unlike the explicit sexualization of this scene in the film, as a discreet sexual foreplay number of sort, the treatment of the girl's fondling of his hand in *North China Lover* is much more playful and childlike, albeit with clear sexual undertones; see Duras (1992, 32–33).

25. This formulation supplements conventional readings of Duras's text as one of prostitution, but from the girl's vantage point. For example, Haskell (1992) has pointed out that it is the girl who takes and profits from the Chinese lover, not merely for financial gain and amusement; but ultimately, the "author" has transformed this "emotional trauma" into the material for her life's work, recycling this "primal story" over and over again in screenplays, novels, and films.

26. The following passage from Duras's 1984 novel confirms the intimate linkage between identity-producing habitual shame and its transformation into "shame creativity," expressed as the defining component of the lovers' sexual engagement: "I say we lived out of doors, poverty had knocked down the walls of the family and we were all left outside, each one fending for himself. Shameless, that's what we were. That's how I came to be here with you. He is on me, engulfed again. We stay like that, riveted, moaning amid the din of the still external city" (1984, 45). Interestingly, Levinas's theorization of shame turns on the example of the nude body to articulate the self's inability to flee from itself: "What appears in shame is therefore precisely the fact of being chained to oneself, the radical impossibility of fleeing oneself to hide oneself from oneself, the intolerable presence of the self to itself. Nudity is shameful when it is the obviousness of our Being, of its final intimacy. And the nudity of our body is not the nudity of a ma-

terial thing that is antithetical to the spirit but the nudity of our entire Being, in all its plenitude and solidity, in its most brutal expression, of which one cannot not be aware" (quoted in Agamben 2002, 105). At least one movie critic forges a connection between the actors' performance of sex (in all their naked splendor) and their culpability for shame, that is, their shamefulness/-lessness. As Brian D. Johnson writes in his review in *Maclean's*, "March's immaturity as an actress delivering dialogue with her clothes on is more embarrassing than anything she does with her clothes off. In fact, it is only during the lovemaking scenes that *The Lover* makes sense—as a celebration of skin-deep sensuality" (1992, 108).

27. See as well Jeanne Vaccaro's interesting discussion of "felt" as an "anti-fabric" that encompasses "a tactile sensation and emotion, as in that which is felt" (2010, 253). Echoing Sedgwick's comments about the nondualism of touch, Vaccaro brings felt's nonhierarchical makeup to an analysis of transgender embodiment whereby "aesthetic and identificatory practices . . . are not defined by binaries of depth/surface or before/after" (2010, 254).

28. Bersani continues, "It was perhaps in early play with that much-shamed organ that we learned about the *rhythms* of power, and we were or should have been initiated into the biological connection between male sexuality and surrender or passivity" (1995, 101). Writing about masturbation and homosexuality, Sarah Gleeson-White comments that "both are 'unnatural' because they defy reproductive sexuality. Furthermore, masturbation involves the eroticisation of one's own body and thus might be construed as a homosexual act. . . . It is the trope of the hands that is tied up with forbidden desire, masturbatory and homosexual" (2003, 53). These two critics' arguments confirm my earlier claim about the lesbionic and queer uses of the hand in the lovers' affective, social, and sexual bonds. I use "lesbionic" (rather than lesbian or homoerotic) to gesture toward the lesbian-coded erotic labor of the hand described by Merck above.

29. The link between the two men is explicitly made with a graphic match of the sleeping Japanese lover's hand with that of the dead German lover shown in a flashback.

30. Indeed, as an iconic image of the film, it appears on the DVD cover of the film from the Criterion Collection.

31. To be sure, one can detect in these dismissals the conservative Anglo-American tendency to view with suspicion any attempt to marry art and explicit sexual representation. As Linda Williams points out in an essay on cinema and the sex act, "In the U.S., we have grown so used to the separation of pornography from art that we tend to assume—sometimes rather hypocritically—that any arousal response is antithetical to art and any emotionally complex art antithetical to arousal" (2001, 22).

32. In his erotic short story, "Afterimages of Leung Kar Fai," Wagner Wai Jim Au writes about a white woman who begins to notice Asian men after watching Annaud's film. Between passages about one Asian male lover blowing opium smoke up her vagina and another erupting in Cantonese as he comes, one finds a detailed description of one of the sex scenes in *The Lover*. Most remarkable for our discussion here is Au's stress on both of the characters' asses; it bears mention that though narrated in the third person, the story is told from the woman's perspective: "Then he is fucking her on the dusty

floor, without preamble. . . . She has a firm, spacious butt, a Gallic horse's ass; it makes her back arc off the ground as he thrusts into her. . . . His own ass is beautiful. It's a slender ass, the ass of an earnest choirboy. And as she watches them fuck from straight on, she can see it just over his straining shoulders; she can see it, hovering and kneading above the girl's cunt" (Au 1995, 219). This marvelous gloss of the scene, with its enthusiastic focus on the partners' buttocks, supports my point about the film's sexual heat, and realism, as residing in Leung's scrumptious ass.

33. One of Williams's central arguments is that this phallocentric drive toward "maximum visibility" is totally inadequate in its goal to represent female pleasure and desire.

34. In addition to the question of sexual realism, the issue of period verisimilitude, the realistic re-presentation of French colonial Saigon in the late 1920s also dominates the commentary around the film. While most critics derided the sex scenes as stilted and unconvincing, they lauded the "heart-breaking nostalgic beauty" (Denby 1992, 68) of the cinematography and the authentic reconstruction of the colonial setting. (Indeed, the film was nominated for an Academy Award for cinematography.) In spite of the numerous obstacles and the absurd expenses of shooting in Vietnam (*The Lover* being the first Western production shot in the country), Annaud insisted on shooting the film on location due to the poverty-stricken country being "so much closer to eternal Asia" than its neighbors, such as Malaysia, Thailand, and the Philippines, which have stood in for Vietnam in previous Hollywood films (Galbraith 1992, 1). For an excellent discussion and critique of Annaud's "phantasmatic love affair with Indochina," his desire to transform Duras's "imaginative geography" into naked reality, see Norindr's (1996) chapter, "Filmic Memorials and Colonial Blues: Indochina in Contemporary French Cinema" in *Phantasmatic Indochina*, especially 139–145.

35. Providing more proof of his honest eroticism, Annaud is quick to point out that he did not use body doubles in the love scenes, because "there is a way to move a finger or move an arm to get a special thrill. If you don't have that, you have something mechanical" (Krupp 1992, 195).

36. For instance, even in rare instances when Asian men do act as romantic leads opposite white women in mainstream productions (Sessue Hayakawa in *The Cheat*, Chow Yun-fat in *Anna and the King*, Jet Li in *Kiss of the Dragon*), these interracial pairings are invariably depicted as deviant, either as sexual threat or as innocent flirtation. For an extended examination of Asian men in Hollywood cinema, as well as Asian American independent film and video, martial arts movies, and pornography, see Celine Parreñas Shimizu's (2012) *Straitjacket Sexualities: Unbinding Asian American Manhoods in the Movies*, especially chapter 5 on the careers of romantic leading men James Shigeta and Jason Scott Lee. In addition to Shigeta and Lee, who constitute exceptions to deviant Asian man–white woman interracial pairings in Hollywood film, other recent examples include John Cho and Kal Penn (in pairings with a Latina and a white woman, respectively) in *Harold and Kumar Escape from Guantanamo Bay* (dir. Jon Hurwitz and Hayden Schlossberg, 2008) and Korean actor Jang Dong-Gun (coupled with Kate Bosworth) in *The Warrior's Way* (dir. Sngmoo Lee, 2010).

37. The practice of "mooning" engaged in by young men can be seen as a management of this straight male sexual anxiety. By humorously and/or aggressively exposing

their asses to unsuspecting viewers, the mooners intend to offend and insult the persons subjected to the sight of a naked, penetrable ass, thus feminizing and emasculating the viewers in the process. Yet, like other acts performed in all-male environments (locker room communal shower, stag party porn viewing, circle jerks), the homoeroticism of flashing one's male buttocks must be continually invoked and disavowed. Discussing the homoerotics of the men's restroom, Lee Edelman notes the anxiety that infuses the restroom stall and its particular dynamics of anal release: "For the satisfaction that such [intestinal] relief affords abuts dangerously on homophobically abjectified desires, and because that satisfaction marks an opening onto difference that would challenge the phallic supremacy and coherence of the signifier on the men's room door, it must be isolated and kept in view at once lest its erotic potential come out" (1994, 161).

38. Glossing Vivian Sobchack's phenomenological description of the film experience, Laura Marks writes: "If one understands cinema viewing as an exchange between two bodies—that of the viewer and that of the film—then the characterization of the film viewer as passive, vicarious, or projective must be replaced with a model of a viewer who participates in the production of the cinematic experience. Rather than witnessing cinema as through a frame, window, or mirror, Sobchack argues, the viewer shares and performs cinematic space dialogically" (Marks 2002, 13). I argue that the sight of Leung's moving bare buttocks moves the viewer to share and co-construct cinematic space, by putting into motion an "intersubjective eroticism" (Marks 2002, 13) animated by sight, sound, and touch.

39. Sobchack argues that all of our senses, not merely our sight but also hearing, touch, smell, and taste, are activated in our movie-watching experience. The term she invents to describe this viewer, the "cinesthetic subject," conjoins the term "cinema" with synesthesia and coenesthesia and is used to articulate the "intercommunication of the senses" in our experience of cinema and the subject who "both touches and is touched by the screen—able to commute seeing to touching and back again *without a thought*" (Sobchack 2004, 71, emphasis in original). Also pertinent for our discussion is Marks's point that tactile visuality enables an ethical relation between viewer and object, an encounter in which the viewer relinquishes her mastery and the object remains unknowable: "By engaging with an object in a haptic way, I come to the surface of myself . . . , losing myself in the intensified relation with an other that cannot be known" (2002, 19). This statement resonates well with Crimp's (2002) argument for an ethico-political potential of "collectivities of the shamed."

40. In a close reading of *Sweet Sweetback Baadasssss Song*'s five sex scenes, Linda Williams notes that although Van Peebles's ass is spectacularly featured in the scenes and "functions metonymically for his front" (2008, 96), it is shown barely moving; the sex act itself is performed with no apparent pleasure. A quick glimpse of Sweetback's front in one scene reveals a flaccid penis. Williams argues that even in a movie Huey Newton named as the "first truly revolutionary Black film" (quoted in Williams 2008, 99), one that celebrates black male sexual prowess and potency, Van Peebles's sexual performances were framed by the popular stereotypes of Uncle Tom and the hypersexual black buck. The threat of black male sexuality is thus managed and contained. Curiously, in contrast to Van Peebles's limited pelvic movement, Leung's sexual perfor-

mance is marked by his rigorous pelvic thrusts. It is noteworthy that it is only in the sex scenes that Leung's Chinese lover really comes alive.

41. Williams writes, "From behind Mede's back, we see a powerfully built black man, naked buttocks prominently displayed, with a white woman kneeling at his feet. This scene clearly puts Mede's body, not Blanche's, on display.... Taking 'control,' he lifts her briefly up and then onto the bed where he lies on her. Once again, it is his body, especially his buttocks, that is on display as the camera glides along its length to reveal her feet caressing his thighs" (2004, 295). In addition, the simultaneous eroticization and containment of black male prowess can be seen in an earlier scene in the film in which a black male slave is hung upside down naked and beaten on his exposed buttocks inside a barn. The white plantation patriarch's son, Hammond (Perry King), is instructing another slave in the proper way to beat his fellow slave so as not to injure him. As the beating progresses, Hammond breaks out into a sweat and leaves the barn. Though the narrative suggests that Hammond's departure is due to his uneasiness around physical violence, one might also attribute a (homo)erotic dimension to his uneasiness. This reading is bolstered by the fact that in the scene immediately preceding this one, we see Hammond naked in his bedroom as he limps from the background of the shot to the foreground to the bedside of one of his female slaves. Hammond's flaccid cock is clearly, and casually, depicted. Along with Hammond's lame leg and the portrayal of the character as nonnormatively masculine, the exposure of his white dick constitutes a nonthreatening, domesticated sexuality. Coming right after Hammond's floppy full frontal, the paddling of black male buttocks in the following scene activates connotative links between the punishment of black men for their sexual prowess and white male sexual lack.

42. The similarity of the two actors' bodies—barring the color of their skin and their sex—in terms of their slim, lithe build, smoothness, and toned musculature are especially pronounced and exploited in the third sex scene, in which an explicit confusion of bodies is mobilized in a rapid montage of abstract close-ups of sweaty body parts in order to evoke the sexual merging between the two. The emphasis on the "golden silky" body of Tony Leung in the film serves to underscore a different type of masculinity I discuss above, as well as suggesting a possible lesbionic (nonphallic) reading of the sexual scenes in the film, with their focus on manual eroticism and on the male body being "caught from behind."

43. As a result, even gay-themed narrative films invariably shy away from frontal male nudity, lest they become associated with pornography, thus bestowing their commercial kiss of death. For all of Annaud's purported desire to portray sex and sexuality honestly, the director readily conformed to Hollywood industry standards in proffering just the right amount of naked exposure of Tony Leung's body in order to ensure the wide exhibition and distribution of his film, in spite of the fact that he was also selling *The Lover* as a European art film. The MPAA initially gave Annaud's film an NC-17 rating; however, after cutting three minutes of footage and resubmitting the film on appeal, the film was granted an R rating. For an excellent analysis of a recent cycle of international films that bring explicit depictions of sex to "serious" (nonpornographic) art cinema, see Linda Williams's (2008) chapter, "Philosophy in the Bedroom: Hard-

Core Art since the 1990s" in *Screening Sex*. The corpus she examines includes *The Idiots* (dir. Lars von Trier, 1998), *Nine Songs* (dir. Michael Winterbottom, 2004), *Shortbus* (dir. John Cameron Mitchell, 2006), *Intimacy* (dir. Patrice Chéreau, 2001), *Romance* (dir. Catherine Breillat, 1999), *Fat Girl* (dir. Catherine Breillat, 2001), and *Anatomy of Hell* (dir. Catherine Breillat, 2004). It is worth noting that all of these films prominently feature shots of hard erect penises. It should also be pointed out that not all of these films achieve the demystification of the phallus of which Lehman (1993) speaks, nor was that their aim.

44. A parallel reticence around explicit visual representation of the male body is also found in Hong Kong cinema. As Travis Kong writes, "In contrast with Western aesthetics of masculinity the Chinese ideal has always been the desexualized male body. In mainstream popular culture in Hong Kong the naked male body is seldom exposed. When a stripped man appears it is usually in a comedy" (2005, 65). However, he goes on to note an increase in the exhibition of male bodies since the 1980s, as a result of influences from Western popular culture and the capitalist commodification of gay male identity through the spectacularization of the male body.

45. See Hocquenghem ([1972] 1993) for a fascinating discussion of "the phallic signifier and the sublimation of the anus." As Brett Farmer succinctly explicates, Hocquenghem "contends that the gay subject's reclamation of the anus as a pleasurable site of erotic passivity subverts the primacy of the penis on which dominant constructions of masculinity depend, thereby opening up those constructions to the destabilizing effects of a plurality of erotic sites" (Farmer 2000, 207). See Edelman (1994) and Miller (1991).

46. Along the same vein, in a powerful rebuttal to Edelman's revision of the primal scene as a "spectacle of gay male sex," Susan Fraiman proposes female anal eroticism or, more precisely, the mother's anus, as "the most unthinkable pleasure of all," one possessing the conceptual leverage to radically subvert the "imperatives of heterosexuality" linking the mother to reproduction (Fraiman 2003, 134–137).

47. The dialogue between the two men is not in either of Duras's books.

48. To be fair, she does challenge such a victimization with the following question, posed after he has finished and buttoned up his fly: "How much is what we did worth? In a brothel, how much does it cost to do what you just did to me?"

Chapter 4: The Politics of Starch

1. In effect, Marks is drawing on a significant body of work in feminist film theory that has productively challenged and expanded upon the Mulveyian paradigm of the male gaze, specifically in the writings of such critics as Teresa de Lauretis, Tania Modleski, Judith Mayne, Linda Williams, and Carol Clover, among others. In addition, Marks's s/m model of looking, especially when applied to pornography, also parallels the arguments made by gay male critics in distinguishing the separate project of gay pornography from its heterosexual counterpart, especially in response to antipornography feminists who collapsed the two as manifestations of patriarchal oppression and degradation of women (see Waugh 1985).

2. Indeed, Marks does acknowledge, albeit only in passing, the obstacles of other dif-

ferences in the S/M exchange: "Power differentials that obtain outside the S/M relationship, such as class and ethnicity, test the participants' ability to play with their mutual boundaries" (2002, 84). I would respond by saying, when do factors such as "class and ethnicity" (in addition to gender and race) not obtain inside S/M or any other relationships?

3. I want to note that in including Wayne Yung's video in this grouping, I am employing a broad understanding of what constitutes documentary practice, since one can make the case that *The Queen's Cantonese* might be better characterized as an experimental videotape. However, I feel justified in my expanded categorization of Yung's work due to the blurring of these formal distinctions in the realm of queer film and video. As Chris Holmlund and Cynthia Fuchs acknowledge in the introduction to their anthology on gay, lesbian, and queer documentary, "firm distinctions among documentary, fiction, and avant-garde films and videos are increasingly untenable" (1997, 2). Admitting that "no 'straight' lines can be drawn around documentary," they go on to argue that "the force of these films, television shows, and videos stems from the fact that they remain *narratives grounded in some version of actuality and experience, involving social actors, as opposed to characters*" (11, emphasis added).

4. White-Asian pairings of similar age and economic status are becoming the norm à la *The Wedding Banquet*. Until recent years, it was very uncommon to find visible Asian-Asian gay couples in the Western gay scene. In this context, white men are "potato"; hence an Asian who exclusively dates white men is a "potato queen."

5. I remember a running joke from the 1990s that goes: What do you call an Asian man who dates another Asian man? Sticky rice. What do you call a white man who dates another white man? Normal.

6. The rejection of bottomhood is especially troubling because the sticky rice coupling between two gay Asian men—subjects coded as feminized, as "sisters," lesbians, and bottoms—can be potentially resignified as a sexual and social alliance based on feminine, lesbionic, bottom values, instead of a way of superseding them through remasculinization.

7. However, as I pointed out in chapter 2 in my discussion of Anacleto's effeminacy, oftentimes nonnormative gender presentations are read as signs of homosexuality. Relatedly, for some people, their sex or racial identity evades direct legibility.

8. I must also acknowledge another significant enabling context for the production of these works: a new queer Asian visibility in the 1990s as a result of political organizing around gay, Asian identity issues as well as HIV/AIDS activism, education, and prevention targeted to Asian American communities.

Throughout the 1980s and 1990s, community-based organizations dedicated to the education and prevention of AIDS adopted frank discussions of gay sex practices and the various risks for HIV and other sexually transmitted infections in safer-sex pamphlets, along with multimedia campaigns such as flyers, posters, stickers, buttons, T-shirts, and advertising at bus shelters, in subways, and on billboards. Most significant for my study at hand, safe-sex videos were produced by nonprofit AIDS organizations as part of the effort to provide life-saving information in light of the U.S. government's media blackout. As Cindy Patton, Richard Fung, Douglas Crimp, Greg Bordowitz, and others have documented, these safe-sex videos utilized the codes and conventions of explicit, hard-core gay male pornography to eroticize safe sex in the service of the reeducation of desire. In the same period, the gay porn industry instituted the use of condoms in all of its productions. The bottom partner, whether the sucker in oral sex or the fuckee in anal sex, was thought to be more vulnerable to infection if semen were deposited in his mouth or rectum, respectively. Due to the higher risk of contracting HIV for the bottom partner, bottomhood was instrumental in discussions of AIDS discourse throughout the 1980s and 1990s. In recent years, the development of protease inhibitors has resulted in the characterization of AIDS as a "manageable disease." Nevertheless, bottomhood continues to hold pride of place in the "post-AIDS" era when we take into account the emergence of barebacking sex in the past two decades, as can be seen in the creation of new "BB" subcultures and the immense popularity of barebacking in gay pornography. The key issues attached to bottomhood—sexual risk, intimacy, danger, desire, and psychological and physical vulnerability—stubbornly endure from the early days of the AIDS epidemic to the present-day normalization of the disease. Far from a leftover relic from the toxic, homophobic past, this continuity confirms the continuing relevance of bottomhood in the present.

9. These videos bear out Martin Manalansan's argument that for queer immigrants of color, "mobility is not only about the actual physical traversing of national boundaries but also about the traffic of status and hierarchies *within* and across such boundaries" (2003, 9). For an interesting discussion of a parallel body of queer Asian videos in the context of queer diaspora, see Mimura's (2009) chapter, "Diaspora Sexualities: Asian American Queer Video in the World System," in his book *Ghostlife of Third Cinema: Asian American Film and Video*.

10. In the jargon of personal ads on- and offline in the 1990s and 2000s, GAM stands for gay Asian male. The term was used in casual conversation among gay Asian men as a tongue-in-cheek shorthand reference. In recent years, "gaysian" has become the term of choice among younger gay Asian men in the United States.

11. The joke of nominating Vancouver as Pearl of the Orient comes out of the most recent wave of immigrants from Taiwan, China, and Hong Kong beginning in the late 1980s. Most significantly, the early 1990s witnessed a large influx of Chinese from Hong Kong, escaping the imminent turnover of the city to China. Hence, Vancouver was dubbed Hongcouver due to the arrival of the wealthy Hong Kong people who entered Canada as part of the "entrepreneurial class," who proceeded to set up new Chinatowns in the suburbs. Thanks to Wayne Yung for filling me in on the Hongcouver phenomenon (personal e-mail, November 18, 2005).

12. In contrast to the clash of the ethnoscape of the Asian male donning a coolie hat video keyed in front of the homoscape of a white pornographic scene in Fung's earlier video *Chinese Characters* (1986), Waugh reads the train corridors and compartments in Fung's video *Dirty Laundry* (1996) as a confident and more successful convergence of the two disjunctive scapes (Waugh 2002, 71). While the Asian male in *Chinese Characters* can access the white gay porn scenario only through the magic of video editing (e.g., the blue screen, video keying), the gay Chinese Canadian protagonist in *Dirty Laundry* has a sexual encounter with another Chinese Canadian man (a train attendant) aboard

the train. Thus, as I understand his argument, Waugh is suggesting that while in the earlier video, the Asian man is clearly demarcated from gay (white) culture, in the latter video, the ethnoscape converges more seamlessly with the homoscape by the consummation of sticky rice desire, especially within the historically resonant setting of Chinese Canadian history (the train).

13. Appadurai defines "ethnoscape" as "the landscape of persons who constitute the shifting world in which we live: tourists, immigrants, refugees, exiles, guest workers, and other moving groups and individuals constitute an essential feature of the world and appear to affect the politics of (and between) nations to a hitherto unprecedented degree" (1996, 41).

14. To be sure, gay pornography has changed greatly since Dyer made this claim in 1985. Although it remains the case that a prodigious cock size continues to be a highly prized feature of gay porn actors and the money shot is still de riguer, the ability to perform as a bottom is a skill that is frequently noted by porn reviewers and fans. Because anal intercourse constitutes the central sex act in mainstream gay video porn, the performances of both the top and the bottom are eroticized by the viewer. Arguably, bottoming is considered to require more skill than topping—for example, the impressive talent of accommodating unusually large cocks up one's asshole. In addition, viewers' appreciation of the bottom can also be attributed to the excitement of seeing a normatively masculine-appearing man (well-built, well-hung, butch in mannerism) getting fucked, the thrilling dissonance that Dyer refers to in the quotation. The high estimation of bottoming can be seen in at least two other phenomena: the idolization of porn stars known for their expertise as bottoms (such as Joey Stefano and Kevin Williams); and the tendency of top porn actors to add bottoming to their sexual repertoire as a way of diversifying their porn persona, as discussed in chapter 1. In regards to the latter practice, to be a versatile performer has once more become the norm (as was the case in the 1970s; see Escoffier 2009).

15. It should be noted that in spite of the egalitarian ethos advanced by pundits and scholars of contemporary Western gay male culture, an abiding investment in power and hierarchy persists. For example, besides racial difference, top and bottom roles in gay male pornography are marked by many other differences, including body type, musculature, penis size, age, class, gender presentation, nationality, presence or absence of body hair, hair color, and so on. To be sure, many of these characteristics are often articulated through commonsense assumptions about racial difference.

16. Manalansan's queer Filipino informants describe a similar sense of ambivalence about the rice bars located in New York City. While they view them as spaces offering camaraderie, they also see rice bars as "sites of alienation and exclusion." Manalansan writes: "Rice bars are among the most overtly Asian and Orientalized gay spaces in New York. . . . Rice bars, according to gay lore, were popularly or stereotypically seen to be unsophisticated institutions with outdated music that catered to a clientele made up of older homely (mostly white) men and naïve immigrant Asian men" (2003, 82). The issue of a safe gay Asian space has been a vexed one for gay Asian American political and community organizing since its beginnings in the early 1980s. Bracketing the different trajectories of gay male and lesbian organizing, gay male organizations invari-

ably must come to terms with the decision of whether to open the group for the participation of white men, or to keep it as an Asian-only space. For a very nuanced and local analysis of this problem, see Wat's (2002) discussion of the formation of Asian/Pacific Lesbians and Gays in Los Angeles.

17. In contrast to Dyer's recuperative gesture, John Champagne argues for the antiproductivity of gay porn. Following Bataille, Champagne posits that the use value of gay porn lies in its status as "nonproductive expenditure," one example of "cultural forms that on a phantasmatic level counter modern disciplinary society's 'economical' deployment of the body in the service of subject formation" (1995, 30).

18. The reader might notice that I have alternated between first- and third-person pronouns in discussing my video *7 Steps*. This move was done purposefully to establish some distance between my position as a critic and maker of the video. In doing so, I want to remark on the distinctions between the sexual performer in the video, the person who shot and edited the footage, and the scholar who submitted the work to analysis two decades later. Here, I offer Glen Mimura's sharp, generous reading of my double role in the documentary:

Most provocative is Nguyen's participation—self-conscious and self-reflexive—on both sides of the camera. He is the only sexual actor who does not, like his interviewees, tell his own story; instead, he enacts particular relations within and around representation. The video artist represents himself as an object of desire, a bottom fucked by his white "x-boyfriend"; yet he remains the maker in control of his own (and others') portrayals. In this respect, the [sexual] vignette teases the stereotypical coding of Asian men as inherently submissive in mainstream, commercial gay porn. Nguyen chooses his role here as bottom, contrary to the *sticky rice* ethos introduced in the first part [of the video], just as he also chooses to be the top in his sexual encounter with his Asian American partner. His participation demonstrates that erotic desire is more complicated than such namings as *sticky rice* allow. Several of the interviewees acknowledge as much, but it is Nguyen's participation (as onscreen sexual subject and object, and as maker who composes the images) that most powerfully, and playfully, broadens the meaning of sexuality across media representation and lived experience. (2009, 144)

19. I borrow this wonderfully evocative phrase from Thomas Waugh (1996).

20. The poem details his mother's request to go to Lourdes with Lustre to pray to the Virgin for an AIDS cure for him.

21. Indeed, one of the central concerns of *Slanted Vision* is the impact of HIV/AIDS on the sexual practices of Asian Pacific Islander gay men. The third and final chapter of the video is called "Culinary: The Cooking Show," which is a spoof of *Yan Can Cook*. In the place of Yan, we have Martina, a Filipino drag queen, and her trusty Asian nerd assistant demonstrating a recipe for Chicken Fuk Yew, that is, safe sex practices utilizing dildoes, zucchinis, dental dams, and a willing chicken, among other latex and organic ingredients.

22. For an interesting example of reeducating desire in a lesbian context, see Chris Straayer's (1996) fascinating discussion of the lesbian porn film *Erotic in Nature* (1985). The controversy around this early example of "real" lesbian porn (as opposed to fake

lesbian porn targeted to heterosexual men) arises from its being subjected to the judgment of the lesbian community for its representation of authentic lesbian sex. Glossing the slippage between the reeducation of desire and the policing of desire, Straayer writes: "Claiming the lesbian 'community' as its rightful audience, the lesbian porn industry broke through the private-public split only to be met head-on by identity politics. Viewers looked for a visual representation of themselves, often prioritizing reality-checking over fantasy experience. . . . Certain characters, especially exaggerated femmes, were criticized (perhaps by ki kis) for not looking like 'lesbians.' Various sexual acts (for example, penetration and 'air-fucking') were admonished as inherently or symbolically heterosexual" (1996, 213). There are clear parallels between the policing of lesbian sex in this lesbian porn film and the sticky rice projects I have been discussing.

23. Interestingly, Yung's use of "man" and "boy" to designate top and bottom positionings, respectively, echoes the dialogue between Jacob Scott and Brandon Lee in *Fortune Nookie* when Scott asks Lee whether he wants to fuck Scott like a man or like a boy. In both Yung's video and *Fortune*, youth, immaturity, and femininity ("boy") are aligned with Asian bottomhood, while age, experience, and masculinity ("man") are linked with white topness.

24. Racial markers are announced from the beginning of the video: "This is me as you fuck me / You're white / I'm Chinese."

25. As I have argued elsewhere, "gay Asian" as a category is peculiar to the identity politics in Western countries where Asians constitute a minority population (Yung and Nguyen 2007). It has minimal purchase in an Asian country like Thailand, where sexual identity is understood along other registers, such as gender, class, nation, and morality. However, a publicly visible gay culture exists where one finds couplings of older white man–younger Asian man resembling the rice queen–potato queen paradigm in the West. Relatedly, middle-class gay Thai men are seeking out East Asian partners in order to distinguish themselves from low-class sex workers seen on the arms of older *farangs* (white foreigners); this phenomenon sometimes is labeled "sticky rice" by East Asians cognizant of its use in the gay Asian communities in San Francisco, Vancouver, and Sydney. For more in-depth analyses of gay male and transgender politics, interracial relationships, and the media in Thailand, see Käng (2011, 2012).

In addition, my reframing of *Iron Pussy* in the present discussion of works produced in the Asian diaspora finds support in the personal biography of Shaowanasai. His father went to medical school at the University of Pennsylvania in the early 1960s, and Shaowanasai was born in Philadelphia. His family moved back to Thailand, and he grew up there. He came back to the United States to attend art school at the San Francisco Art Institute and went on to receive his MFA at the School of the Art Institute of Chicago. Thus, although Shaowanasai still holds an American passport, he considers himself a Thai artist and lives and works in Bangkok. As someone who has lived and participated extensively in both American and Thai gay communities in his frequent shuttling back and forth across the Pacific, Shaowanasai's life story challenges any absolute division between Asian and American gay identities, what Dennis Altman describes as the conflict between Asianness on the one hand and the desire of gay Asian men to align themselves with a universal (read Western) gay identity on the other.

26. Iron Pussy's feminized Thai labor is markedly different from that of the Chinese female pimp's and her two henchmen's more masculinized arsenal. The former has recourse to a low-tech beauty and exercise regimen (the beauty parlor and the gym); the Chinese pimp, Xian Xaiw Hua, and her toughs, Ping Ping and Hua Xiaw Hua, however, possess fancy technological gadgets, such as "killer chopsticks," "rice bowl from hell," and "hairy killer thing [testicle]."

27. One of Shaowanasai's inspirations for Iron Pussy's look is Thai actress Petchara Chaowarat, who was wildly popular in 1960s and 1970s Thai cinema. Iron Pussy's alter ego is constantly shifting. In the previous installment, *The Adventures of Iron Pussy II: Bunzai . . . Chaiyo!* (1999), she disguises herself as Monkol, a Clark Kent–like office worker; in *Iron Pussy III*, she masquerades as an unnamed male prostitute who hooks up with a white john; in the feature film *The Adventures of Iron Pussy* (co-directed with Apichatpong Weerasethakul, 2003), Iron Pussy punches the clock as a 7-Eleven store clerk. In the most recent installment, "Iron Pussy: A Kimchi Affair" (dir. Visit Sasanatieng, 2010), she poses as a line cook in a restaurant.

28. It is highly significant that these Chinese invaders who threaten to take over the boy sex trade of Bangkok are depicted as martial arts movie villains, whose kung fu fighting is set against Iron Pussy's Thai kickboxing. Thus, economic domination is consolidated through cultural imperialism, exemplified by the inundation of Chinese-language popular cinemas across Southeast Asia. In recent years, there has been a shift from Chinese to Korean cultural influence in Southeast Asia, a phenomenon commonly referred to as Hallyu, or Korean wave. This shift is thematized in "Iron Pussy: A Kimchi Affair," where the superheroine travels as a spy for hire to Busan, Korea. Indeed, the short is part of *Camellia* (dir. Visit Sasanatieng, Isao Yukisada, and Jang Joon-hwan, 2010), a South Korean–funded omnibus production also known as the Busan Project. All three films were shot in Busan, with their romantic narratives taking place in the South Korean city as well.

29. To be fair, I should note that *Iron Pussy III* advances a much more complicated view of sex workers' self-determination than my sentence here suggests. On the one hand, the video highlights the agency of sex workers in improving their individual lots. On the other hand, they remain subservient to the Thai state, in the sense that their sexual labor is used by the nation to promote economic development.

30. Cho made the tape under the pseudonym Clover Paek.

31. In *Karate Kid*, Daniel is looking at Ali (Elisabeth Shue), his female love interest. Cho substitutes the wholesome heterosexual object of desire with her own image of "dirty" queer butt sex.

32. Erica Cho, personal e-mail, December 1, 2005.

33. For an interesting analysis of queer feminist theories and practices of failure, see Halberstam (2011).

34. In response to the call for reclaiming the childhood scene of shame, Judith Halberstam suggests that queer critics end up "idealizing youth itself, the territory of gay shame after all" (2005b, 221–222).

35. As Halberstam notes, "Queer time . . . [is] the embrace of late childhood in place of early adulthood or immaturity in place of responsibility. It is a theory of queerness as

a way of being in the world and a critique of the careful social scripts that usher even the most queer among us through major markers of individual development and into normativity" (Dinshaw et al. 2007, 182).

Conclusion

1. I am drawing here on Eve Sedgwick's important observation that one of the most significant accomplishments by the modern lesbian and gay movement has been the delinking of gender from sexuality. She notes, "the conceptual need of the gay movement to interrupt a long tradition of viewing gender and sexuality as continuous and collapsible categories—a tradition of assuming that anyone, male or female, who desires a man must by definition be feminine; and that anyone, male or female, who desires a woman must by the same token be masculine. That one woman, *as a woman*, might desire another; that one man, *as a man*, might desire another . . . [represent] powerful, subversive assertions" (1993, 157, emphasis in original). However, Sedgwick is quick to point out that "one serious problem with this way of distinguishing between gender and sexuality is that, while denaturalizing sexual object-choice, it radically *re*naturalizes gender" (1993, 159, emphasis in original).

2. See for example the narration of male homosexual embodiments of various femininities in Chauncey (1994).

3. In the creative and critical writings of Joan Nestle, Amber Hollibaugh, Madeleine Davis, Jewelle Gomez, Minnie Bruce Pratt, Kara Keeling, and Juana María Rodríguez, among others, one finds complex theorizations of the negotiation and exchange of power in lesbian butch-femme sexuality. In the wake of second-wave feminism in the 1970s and the sex wars of the 1980s, butch-femme was demonized as a product of a patriarchal hangover and characterized as an embarrassing playacting-out of heterosexual roles. As a result, various writers, scholars, artists, and activists have courageously spoken out against the scapegoating and dismissal of butch-femme sexuality in the name of feminism. Specifically, they insist on its difference from heterosexual models. Writing about her experience as a femme in the 1950s, Nestle testifies, "Butch-femme relationships, as I experienced them, were complex erotic statements, not phony heterosexual replicas. They were filled with a deeply Lesbian language of stance, dress, gesture, loving, courage, and autonomy" (1987, 100). Laura Harris and Liz Crocker argue for femme as "a sustained gender identity" and "a reshaped femininity" (1997, 1–3). The queering of gender codes and performances are accorded positive values by Jewelle Gomez: "For me the erotic tension of being a lesbian lives in that place where unexpected elements come together: the stone-butch woman who knows how to turn a hem, or looks like a little girl when she laughs. Or the high femme with her skirt hiked up as she changes a tire. The tension of where the unexpected comes together is what makes being a lesbian, and being a femme, interesting. It is also what makes being a lesbian a political act" (1998, 106). Gomez's eloquent statement exemplifies a common tactic in 1990s lesbian and gay scholarship and activism with the promotion of "gender fuck," the fluid blurring of feminine and masculine gender codes. More recently, other commentators have emphasized the fixity of butch-femme, a tenacious

attachment to "heterosexual roles" that delivers and intensifies erotic tension and release, as can be seen in the following sexual scenario described by Juana María Rodríguez: *"he pushes the tip inside her, she bleeds; he ejaculates, she conceives"* (2007, 285, emphasis in original).

4. The embrace of sex positivity against the forces of misogyny, sexism, homophobia, racism, and classism in these texts offers a rich, generative model of my own thinking about the feminization and racialization of bottomhood missing in gay male accounts. The most forceful statement made for the de-essentialization of butch-femme and top-bottom positionings comes from Esther Newton and Shirley Walton: "Biological males are not necessarily tops, nor are those who use male gender symbols. This applies to butch lesbians and gay men and, thousands of years of cultural mythology notwithstanding, to straight men" (1984, 246).

5. I am rearticulating de Certeau's (1984) formulation of "tactic of the weak."

6. My analysis is culled from three of the most popular sites based in the United States as of October 2008: Manhunt.net, Adam4Adam.com, and Gay.com. The research for this conclusion was conducted between 2005 and 2008, and is drawn from web-based cruising. My broad claims about the discrimination against Asian men also apply to more recent digital cruising on smartphone apps such as Grindr and Scruff, though the specifics (for instance, screen names) are different.

7. I borrow the phrase "racial ravines" from Logan Hill (2001).

8. See Sharif Mowlabocus's (2007) chapter, "Gaydar: Gay Men and the Pornification of Everyday Life."

9. That is, the tactic of making one's Asian race less legible (e.g., using a chest photo without showing a face) in the hope that one can hook another cruiser before race is disclosed is considered disingenuous.

10. Furthermore, on sites such as Manhunt.net, pics are divided into two groups, public and private. Public pics—usually face and torso—are visible to everyone, while private pics must be unlocked by the user. Unlocking one's private pic is akin to virtually flashing oneself, a digital self-exhibition that communicates one's interest in the recipient of one's unlocked pic. An innovation in the era of online cruising, the practice of virtual sexual exhibitionism serves to garner profits for these gay websites: the more one pays, the more flesh one gets to see. What's interesting in this case is the provider of the flesh content is not a porn model but other real people like the user himself.

11. It is not uncommon for users to state in their ads, "Please look like your pics. I do." Some users include a date stamp from their digital cameras or webcams as proof that their photos are recent.

12. I am not arguing that there are more pictures of headless Asian torsos online than, say, headless Latino torsos; rather, what is remarkable is the fact that in no other arena in North American visual culture does one find such a concentration of eroticized images of Asian male flesh. What's more, these are self-representations created by GAMS in order to exploit their resemblance to an ideal gay male body part: namely, a smooth, hairless, toned, buffed torso. The common practice of GAMS posting torso shots can be gleaned from the following line in one user's Grindr profile: "BiLad26" claims that he is an "expert on picking Asian torso pics from afar" (found on Douchebags of

Grindr). Thus, he suggests that he is not "fooled" by Asian men's torsos, and implies that he is not interested in Asians. My casual observations of black users' torso pics on these same sex cruising sites suggest a similar logic as the headless GAM torso pics; that is, oftentimes black users' torsos also are illegible as "black" due to cropping, lighting, and digital filters.

13. Writing about gay personal ads from the 1960s to the 1990s, Daniel Harris identifies the headless torso photos as originating in "escort ads," where they were accorded "their own disreputable section of the newspaper, a journalistic skid row of sleazy photographs of decapitated men squeezing the bulges of their wet jockey shorts above headlines that read 'Throat Plug,' 'Eat at Pete's,' and 'Super Hung Fresh Grade "A" Stud'" (1997, 53). The use of the headless torso in online personal ads confirms Harris's observation that gay assimilation has resulted in an increase in the marketization of gay relationships and the commodification of gay male bodies, which he dismissively equates with pornography: "These novelized vignettes [in 1980s print gay personals] represent an advanced stage in the commercialization of the subculture in that gay men now perceive and represent sex through the lens of pornography, a highly commercial genre that has become the screen or filter that blurs and distorts our erotic experiences" (1997, 58). Though I find the obsessive quantification of male body parts (known as "stats") that litters gay personal ads troubling, I disagree with Harris's blanket characterization of pornography as "distortions" of authentic gay male sex. I suggest that pornography serves an important function in shaping and constituting gay male subjecthood in the post-Stonewall era, for better and for worse.

14. This concept of body as mask displaces the unhelpful gay rhetoric around shame and pride connected to the face—giving, losing, or saving face—to a more profitable (and sexy) one around voyeurism and exhibitionism tied to the body part, normally associated with issues of fetishization and objectification so generative in gay male sexual culture—for example, the realm of pornography.

15. In a cursory search on Gay.com, I found that "white" or "GWM" only comes up as a screen name or headline of an ad when the poster of the profile is a white man looking for men of color or a man of color seeking white men; thus, whiteness becomes visible when set against the nonwhite.

16. I am animating Sheng-Mei Ma's (2000) evocative phrase describing the complicated intertwining of Orientalism and Asian American identity formation.

17. According to Halperin, the gay male subject's agential rejoinder to abjection cannot be reduced to a voluntaristic, conscious gesture or a completely fortuitous act. Describing Jean Genet's embrace of his abjected state in *The Thief's Journal*, Halperin (2007, 83) characterizes abjection as "a secret grace" that redeems Genet from total contempt.

18. I borrow this phrase from Anne Cheng (2001, 35).

BIBLIOGRAPHY

Adam Gay Video Directory 2001. 2000. Los Angeles: Knights Publishing.
Agamben, Giorgio. 2002. *Remnants of Auschwitz: The Witness and the Archive.* Trans. Daniel Heller-Roazen. Cambridge, MA: MIT Press.
Ahmed, Sara. 2004. *The Cultural Politics of Emotion.* Edinburgh: Edinburgh University Press.
Altman, Dennis. 1996. "On Global Queering." *Australian Humanities Review* (July). Accessed January 12, 2013. http://www.australianhumanitiesreview.org/archive/Issue-July-1996/altman.html.
Altman, Dennis. 1997. "Global Gays/Global Gaze." GLQ 3 (4): 417–36.
Altman, Dennis. 2001. *Global Sex.* Chicago: University of Chicago Press.
Angelo, Gregory T. 2005. "The Accidental Birth of an Anarchist." *Next* 13 (1): 12–14.
Anonymous. (1971) 2003. "Cocksucker." In *Sexual Revolution,* ed. Jeffrey Escoffier, 513–15. New York: Thunder's Mouth Press.
Appadurai, Arjun. 1996. "Disjuncture and Difference in the Global Cultural Economy." In *Modernity at Large: Cultural Dimensions of Globalization,* 40–52. Minneapolis: University of Minnesota Press.

Arnheim, Rudolf. (1931) 2004. "In Praise of Character Actors." In *Movie Acting: The Film Reader*, ed. Pamela Robertson Wojcik, 205–6. New York: Routledge.

Au, Wagner Wai Jim. 1995. "Afterimages of Leung Kar Fai." In *On a Bed of Rice: An Asian American Erotic Feast*, ed. Geraldine Kudaka, 217–25. New York: Anchor Books.

Ayres, Tony. 1999. "China Doll: The Experience of Being a Gay Chinese Australian." *Journal of Homosexuality* 36 (3/4): 87–97.

Baker, Robb. 1967. "'Eye' Focuses on Lonely World of Its People (Movie Review)." *Chicago Tribune*, October 13, B23.

Benshoff, Harry. 2007. "Representing (Repressed) Homosexuality in the Pre-Stonewall Hollywood Homo-military Film." In *Sleaze Artists: Cinema at the Margins of Taste, Style, and Politics*, ed. Jeffrey Sconce, 71–95. Durham, NC: Duke University Press.

Berlant, Lauren. 2007. "Slow Death (Sovereignty, Obesity, Lateral Agency)." *Critical Inquiry* 33: 754–80.

Berlant, Lauren, and Michael Warner. 1998. "Sex in Public." *Critical Inquiry* 24 (2): 311–31.

Bernard, Jami. 1992. "Movie Review (The Lover)." *New York Post*, October 30, 29.

Bersani, Leo. (1987) 1988. "Is the Rectum a Grave?" In *AIDS: Cultural Analysis, Cultural Activism*, ed. Douglas Crimp, 197–222. Cambridge, MA: MIT Press.

Bersani, Leo. 1995. *Homos*. Cambridge, MA: Harvard University Press.

Bersani, Leo, and Adam Phillips. 2008. *Intimacies*. Chicago: University of Chicago Press.

Billson, Anne. 1992. "A Frameful of Rogering." *New Statesman and Society* (June 19): 20–21.

Blum-Reid, Sylvie. 2003. *East-West Encounters: Franco-Asian Cinema and Literature*. London: Wallflower.

Bogle, Donald. (1973) 2004. "The 1950s: Black Stars." In *Movie Acting: The Film Reader*, ed. Pamela Robertson Wojcik, 191–204. New York: Routledge.

Bordowitz, Gregg. 1993. "The AIDS Crisis Is Ridiculous." In *Queer Looks: Perspectives on Lesbian and Gay Film and Video*, ed. Martha Gever, John Greyson, and Pratibha Parmar, 209–24. New York: Routledge.

"Brando and Miss Taylor in Huston Film (Movie Review)." 1967. *Washington Post* (R.I.C.), October 12, H2.

Brent, Bill. 2002. *The Ultimate Guide to Anal Sex for Men*. San Francisco: Cleis Press.

Brown, Georgia. 1992. "Bonjour Tristesse." *Village Voice*, November 3, 58.

Brumburgh, Gary. 2001. "John Huston's depressing, oddly compelling adaption of Carson McCullers' best-selling social elegy is, still and all, a misfire." Internet Movie Database. Online posting, October 18. Accessed November 29, 2013. http://www.imdb.com/title/tt0062185/reviews-12.

Burger, John R. 1995. *One-Handed Histories: The Eroto-Politics of Gay Male Video Pornography*. Binghamton, NY: The Haworth Press.

Butler, Judith. 1993. *Bodies That Matter: On the Discursive Limits of Sex*. New York: Routledge.

Butler, Judith. 1997a. *Excitable Speech: A Politics of the Performative*. New York: Routledge.

Butler, Judith. 1997b. *The Psychic Life of Power: Theories in Subjection*. Stanford, CA: Stanford University Press.

Butler, Judith. 2004. *Undoing Gender*. New York: Routledge.
Butt, Gavin. 2005. *Between You and Me: Queer Disclosures in the New York Art World, 1948–1963*. Durham, NC: Duke University Press.
Canby, Vincent. 1992. "A French Girl, a Chinese Lover and Colonial Days in Old Vietnam." *New York Times*, October 30, C5.
Cante, Rich, and Angelo Restivo. 2001. "The Voice of Pornography: Tracking the Subject through the Sonic Spaces of Gay Male Moving-Image Pornography." In *Keyframes: Popular Cinema and Cultural Studies*, ed. Matthew Tinkcom and Amy Villarejo, 207–27. New York: Routledge.
Cante, Rich, and Angelo Restivo. 2004a. "The Cultural-Aesthetic Specificities of All-Male Moving-Image Pornography." In *Porn Studies*, ed. Linda Williams, 142–66. Durham, NC: Duke University Press.
Cante, Rich, and Angelo Restivo. 2004b. "The 'World' of All-Male Pornography: On the Public Place of Moving-Image Sex in the Era of Pornographic Transnationalism." In *More Dirty Looks: Gender, Pornography and Power*, 2nd ed., ed. Pamela Church Gibson, 110–26. London: British Film Institute.
Capino, José B. 2006. "Asian College Girls and Oriental Men with Bamboo Poles: Reading Asian Pornography." In *Pornography: Film and Culture*, ed. Peter Lehman, 206–19. New Brunswick, NJ: Rutgers University Press.
Capino, José B. 2010. *Dream Factories of a Former Colony: American Fantasies, Philippine Cinema*. Minneapolis: University of Minnesota Press.
Champagne, John. 1995. "Gay Pornography and Nonproductive Expenditure." In *The Ethics of Marginality: A New Approach to Gay Studies*, 28–56. Minneapolis: University of Minnesota Press.
Champlin, Charles. 1967. "'Reflections' Tours the Southern Gothic Style." *Los Angeles Times*, October 8, D14.
Chan, Jachinson. 2001. *Chinese American Masculinities: From Fu Manchu to Bruce Lee*. New York: Routledge.
Chan, Jeffery Paul, Frank Chin, Lawson Fusao Inada, and Shawn Wong, ed. 1991. *The Big Aiiieeee! An Anthology of Chinese American and Japanese American Literature*. New York: Meridian.
Chauncey, George. 1994. *Gay New York: Gender, Urban Culture, and the Making of the Gay Male World, 1890–1940*. New York: HarperCollins.
Chen, Tina. 2005. *Double Agency: Acts of Impersonation in Asian American Literature and Culture*. Stanford, CA: Stanford University Press.
Cheng, Anne Anlin. 2001. *The Melancholy of Race: Psychoanalysis, Assimilation, and Hidden Grief*. New York: Oxford University Press.
Chiao, Hsiung-Ping. 1981. "Bruce Lee: His Influence on the Evolution of the Kung Fu Genre." *Journal of Popular Film and Television* 9 (1): 30–42.
Chin, Frank, and Jeffery Paul Chan. 1972. "Racist Love." In *Seeing through Shuck*, ed. Richard Kostelanetz, 65–79. New York: Ballantine.
Ching, Yau. 1999. "Can I Have MSG, an Egg Roll to Suck on and Asian American Media on the Side?," 147–61. In *Foodculture: Tasting Identities and Geographies in Art*. Toronto: YYZ Books.

Cho, Song, ed. 1998. *Rice: Explorations into Gay Asian Culture and Politics*. Toronto: Queer Press.

Christian Science Monitor (I.S.). 1967. "Reflections in a Golden Eye (Movie Review)." October 20, 6.

Chun, Wendy Hui Kyong. 2006. *Control and Freedom: Power and Paranoia in the Age of Fiber Optics*. Cambridge, MA: MIT Press.

Clarke, Eric O. 2000. *Virtuous Vice: Homoeroticism and the Public Sphere*. Durham, NC: Duke University Press.

Clover, Carol J. 1992. *Men, Women, and Chain Saws: Gender in the Modern Horror Film*. Princeton, NJ: Princeton University Press.

Combahee River Collective. 1983. "The Combahee River Collective Statement." In *Home Girls: A Black Feminist Anthology*, ed. Barbara Smith, 172–82. New York: Kitchen Table, Women of Color Press.

Constable, Liz. 2004. "Unbecoming Sexual Desires for Women Becoming Sexual Subjects: Simone de Beauvoir (1949) and Catherine Breillat (1999)." *MLN* 119: 672–95.

Cooper, Stephen. 1993. "The Undeclared War: Political *Reflections in a Golden Eye*." In *Reflections in a Male Eye: John Huston and the American Experience*, ed. Gaylyn Studlar and David Desser, 97–116. Washington, DC: Smithsonian Institution Press.

Corday, J. Keller. 2005. "Wild and Wicked—and Now Versatile!" *Unzipped*, November, 18–21.

Corliss, Richard. 1992. "Saigon Mon Amour." *Time*, November 2, 70.

Crimp, Douglas, ed. (1987) 1988a. *AIDS: Cultural Analysis/Cultural Activism*. Cambridge, MA: MIT Press.

Crimp, Douglas. (1987) 1988b. "How to Have Promiscuity in an Epidemic." In *AIDS: Cultural Analysis/Cultural Activism*, ed. Douglas Crimp, 237–71. Cambridge, MA: MIT Press.

Crimp, Douglas. 2002a. "Mario Montez, for Shame." In *Regarding Sedgwick: Essays on Queer Culture and Critical Theory*, ed. Stephen M. Barber and David L. Clark, 57–70. New York: Routledge.

Crimp, Douglas. 2002b. *Melancholia and Moralism: Essays on AIDS and Queer Politics*. Cambridge, MA: MIT Press.

Crimp, Douglas. 2004. "Scraping About the Round Hole." Presentation at LGBT Studies: Local, National, and Global Perspectives Conference, Syracuse University, New York, October 23.

Crimp, Douglas, and Adam Rolston. 1990. *AIDS Demo Graphics*. Seattle, WA: Bay Press.

Crowther, Bosley. 1967. "The Screen: 'Reflections in a Golden Eye' Opens (Movie Review)." *New York Times*, October 12, 59.

Cvetkovich, Ann. 1995. "Recasting Receptivity: Femme Sexualities." In *Lesbian Erotics*, ed. Karla Jay, 125–46. New York: New York University Press.

Cvetkovich, Ann. 2003. *An Archive of Feelings: Trauma, Sexuality, and Lesbian Public Culture*. Durham, NC: Duke University Press.

Danet, Brenda. 1998. "Text as Mask: Gender, Play, and Performance on the Internet." In *Cybersociety 2.0: Revisiting Computer-Mediated Communication and Community*, ed. Steven G. Jones, 129–58. Thousand Oaks, CA: Sage Publications, Inc.

Daney, Serge. 1992. "Falling Out of Love." *Sight and Sound* (July): 14–16.

Dean, Tim. 2009. *Unlimited Intimacy: Reflections on the Subculture of Barebacking*. Chicago: University of Chicago Press.

de Certeau, Michel. 1984. *The Practice of Everyday Life*. Trans. Steven F. Rendall. Berkeley: University of California Press.

Denby, David. 1992. "Last Tango in Saigon." *New York*, November 9, 68–69.

Dent, Gina. 1992. "Black Pleasure, Black Joy: An Introduction." In *Black Popular Culture*, ed. Gina Dent. Seattle, WA: Bay Press.

Desser, David. 2000. "The Kung Fu Craze: Hong Kong Cinema's First American Reception." In *The Cinema of Hong Kong: History, Arts, Identity*, ed. Poshek Fu and David Desser, 19–43. Cambridge: Cambridge University Press.

Diggs, Latasha Natasha. 2003. "The Black Asianphile." In *Everything but the Burden: What White People Are Taking from Black Culture*, ed. Greg Tate, 191–202. New York: Broadway Books.

Dinshaw, Carolyn, Lee Edelman, Roderick A. Ferguson, Carla Freccero, Elizabeth Freeman, Judith Halberstam, Annamarie Jagose, Christopher Nealon, and Nguyen Tan Hoang. 2007. "Theorizing Queer Temporalities: A Roundtable Discussion." GLQ 13 (2–3): 177–95.

Dollimore, Jonathan. 1991. *Sexual Dissidence: Augustine to Wilde, Freud to Foucault*. New York: Oxford University Press.

Doyle, Jennifer. 2007. "Between Friends." In *A Companion to Lesbian, Gay, Bisexual, Transgender, and Queer Studies*, ed. Molly McGarry and George E. Haggerty, 325–39. Oxford: Blackwell.

Duggan, Lisa, and Kathleen McHugh. 1996. "A Fem(me)inist Manifesto." *Women and Performance* 8 (2): 150–60.

Duras, Marguerite. 1985. *The Lover*. Trans. Barbara Bray. New York: HarperCollins.

Duras, Marguerite. 1992. *The North China Lover*. Trans. Leigh Hafrey. New York: New Press.

Duras, Marguerite. 2003. "Notes." *Hiroshima Mon Amour*. Dir. Alain Resnais. Criterion Collection DVD.

Dworkin, Andrea. 1987. *Intercourse*. New York: Free Press.

Dyer, Richard. 1990. *Now You See It: Studies in Lesbian and Gay Film*. New York: Routledge.

Dyer, Richard. (1985) 1992. "Coming to Terms: Gay Pornography." In *Only Entertainment*, 121–34. New York: Routledge.

Dyer, Richard. 1997. "The White Man's Muscles." In *Race and the Subject of Masculinities*, ed. Harry Stecopoulos and Michael Uebel, 287–314. Durham, NC: Duke University Press.

Dyer, Richard. (1994) 2002. "Idol Thoughts: Orgasm and Self-Reflexivity in Gay Pornography." In *The Culture of Queers*, 187–203. New York: Routledge.

Edelman, Lee. 1994. *Homographesis: Essays in Gay Literary and Cultural Theory*. New York: Routledge.

Edelman, Lee. 1999. "*Rear Window*'s Glasshole." In *Out Takes: Essays on Queer Theory and Film*, ed. Ellis Hanson, 72–96. Durham, NC: Duke University Press.

Edelman, Lee. 2004. *No Future: Queer Theory and the Death Drive.* Durham, NC: Duke University Press.

Edgerton, Gary. 1993. "Revisiting the Recordings of Wars Past: Remembering the Documentary Trilogy of John Huston." In *Reflections in a Male Eye: John Huston and the American Experience*, ed. Gaylyn Studlar and David Desser, 33–61. Washington, DC: Smithsonian Institution Press.

Eng, David L. 2001. *Racial Castration: Managing Masculinity in Asian America.* Durham, NC: Duke University Press.

Eng, David L. 2010. *The Feeling of Kinship: Queer Liberalism and the Racialization of Intimacy.* Durham, NC: Duke University Press.

Eng, David L., and Alice Y. Hom. 1998. "Introduction: Q & A: Notes on a Queer Asian America." In *Q & A: Queer in Asian America*, ed. David L. Eng and Alice Y. Hom, 1–21. Philadelphia: Temple University Press.

Escoffier, Jeffrey. 2003. "Gay-for-Pay: Straight Men and the Making of Gay Pornography." *Qualitative Sociology* 26 (4): 531–55.

Escoffier, Jeffrey. 2009. *Bigger Than Life: The History of Gay Porn Cinema from Beefcake to Hardcore.* Philadelphia: Running Press.

Espiritu, Yen Le. 1997. *Asian American Women and Men: Labor, Laws, and Love.* Thousand Oaks, CA: Sage.

Espiritu, Yen Le. 2003. *Home Bound: Filipino American Lives across Cultures, Communities, and Countries.* Berkeley: University of California Press.

Espiritu, Yen Le. 2008. *Asian American Women and Men: Labor, Laws, and Love*, 2nd ed. Lanham, MD: Rowman & Littlefield Publishers.

Farmer, Brett. 2000. *Spectacular Passions: Cinema, Fantasy, Gay Male Spectatorships.* Durham, NC: Duke University Press.

Feld, Rose. 1996. "[Review of] *Reflections in a Golden Eye.*" In *Critical Essays on Carson McCullers*, ed. Beverly Lyon Clark and Melvin J. Friedman, 28–29. New York: G. K. Hall.

Feng, Peter X. 2002a. *Identities in Motion: Asian American Film and Video.* Durham, NC: Duke University Press.

Feng, Peter X., ed. 2002b. *Screening Asian Americans.* New Brunswick, NJ: Rutgers University Press.

Ferguson, Roderick. 2003. *Aberrations in Black: Toward a Queer of Color Critique.* Minneapolis: University of Minnesota Press.

Fore, Steve. 2001. "Life Imitates Entertainment: Home and Dislocation in the Films of Jackie Chan." In *At Full Speed: Hong Kong Cinema in a Borderless World*, ed. Esther C. M. Yau, 115–41. Minneapolis: University of Minnesota Press.

Foucault, Michel. 1996. *Foucault Live: Collected Interviews, 1961–1984*, ed. Sylvère Lotringer. Trans. Lysa Hochroth and John Johnston. New York: Semiotext[e].

Fraiman, Susan. 2003. *Cool Men and the Second Sex.* New York: Columbia University Press.

Freccero, Carla. 2005. *Queer/Early/Modern.* Durham, NC: Duke University Press.

Freeman, Elizabeth. 2005. "Time Binds, or, Erotohistoriography." *Social Text* 84–85: 57–68.

Freeman, Elizabeth. 2007. "Introduction (Special Issue on Queer Temporality)." GLQ 13 (2–3): 159–76.
Fuller, Graham. 1992. "Jane March" (Interview). *Interview*. September, 90–93.
Fung, Richard. 1991. "Looking for My Penis: The Eroticized Asian in Gay Video Porn." In *How Do I Look?*, ed. Bad Object-Choices. Seattle, WA: Bay Press. 145–68.
Fung, Richard. 1993. "Shortcomings: Questions about Pornography as Pedagogy." In *Queer Looks: Perspectives on Lesbian and Gay Film and Video*, ed. Martha Gever, John Greyson, and Pratibha Parmar, 355–67. New York: Routledge.
Fung, Richard. 1995. "The Trouble with 'Asians.'" In *Negotiating Lesbian and Gay Subjects*, ed. Monica Dorenkamp and Richard Henke, 123–30. New York: Routledge.
Galbraith, Jane. 1992. "Steam from Saigon: Forget the Sex, Director Says—How About Those Hot Locations?" *Los Angeles Times*, October 30, 1.
Garlinger, Patrick Paul. 1999. "'Homo-Ness' and the Fear of Femininity." *Diacritics* 29 (1): 57–71.
Gleeson-White, Sarah. 2003. *Strange Bodies: Gender and Identity in the Novels of Carson McCullers*. Tuscaloosa: University of Alabama Press.
Glück, Robert. 2004. "The Glass Mountain." In *Bottoms Up: Writing about Sex*, ed. Diana Cage, 1–5. New York: Soft Skull Press.
Gomez, Jewelle. 1998. "Femme Erotic Independence." In *Butch/Femme: Inside Lesbian Gender*, ed. Sally R. Munt, 101–8. London: Cassell.
Gonzalez, Rita. 2010. "*Boricua* Gazing: An Interview with Frances Negrón-Muntaner." In *Gay Shame*, ed. David M. Halperin and Valerie Traub, 88–100. Chicago: University of Chicago Press.
Gopinath, Gayatri. 1996. "Funny Boys and Girls: Notes on a Queer South Asian Planet." In *Asian American Sexualities: Dimensions of the Gay and Lesbian Experience*, ed. Russell Leong, 119–27. New York: Routledge.
Gopinath, Gayatri. 2005. *Impossible Desires: Queer Diasporas and South Asian Public Cultures*. Durham, NC: Duke University Press.
Ha, Marie-Paule. 2009. "The Chinese and the White Man's Burden in Indochina." In *China Abroad: Travels, Subjects, Spaces*, ed. Elaine Yee Lin Ho and Julia Kuehn, 191–207. Hong Kong: Hong Kong University Press.
Hagedorn, Jessica, ed. 1993. *Charlie Chan Is Dead: An Anthology of Contemporary Asian American Fiction*. New York: Penguin.
Halberstam, Judith. 1998. *Female Masculinity*. Durham, NC: Duke University Press.
Halberstam, Judith. 2005a. *In a Queer Time and Place: Transgender Bodies, Subcultural Lives*. New York: New York University Press.
Halberstam, Judith. 2005b. "Shame and White Gay Masculinity." *Social Text* 84–85: 219–33.
Halberstam, Judith. 2011. *The Queer Art of Failure*. Durham, NC: Duke University Press.
Halperin, David M. 1996. "More or Less Gay-Specific." *London Review of Books* 23 (5): 24–27.
Halperin, David M. 1997. *Saint Foucault: Towards a Gay Hagiography*. New York: Oxford University Press.

Halperin, David M. 2000. "How to Do the History of Male Homosexuality." *GLQ* 6 (1): 87–123.

Halperin, David M. 2002. *How to Do the History of Homosexuality*. Chicago: University of Chicago Press.

Halperin, David M. 2007. *What Do Gay Men Want? An Essay on Sex, Risk, and Subjectivity*. Chicago: University of Chicago Press.

Halperin, David M. 2012. *How to Be Gay*. Cambridge, MA: Belknap.

Halperin, David M., and Valerie Traub, eds. 2010. *Gay Shame*. Chicago: University of Chicago Press.

Hamamoto, Darrell Y. 2000. "The Joy Fuck Club: Prolegomenon to an Asian American Porno Practice." In *Countervisions: Asian American Film Criticism*, ed. Darrell Y. Hamamoto and Sandra Liu, 59–89. Philadelphia, PA: Temple University Press.

Hamamoto, Darrell Y., and Sandra Liu, eds. *Countervisions: Asian American Film Criticism*. Philadelphia: Temple University Press.

Han, Ju Hui Judy. 1998. "Creating, Curating, and Consuming Queer Asian American Cinema: An Interview with Marie K. Morohoshi." In *Q & A: Queer in Asian America*, ed. David L. Eng and Alice Y. Hom, 81–94. Philadelphia: Temple University Press.

Hanich, Julian. 2011. "Clips, Clicks and Climax: Notes on the Relocation and Remediation of Pornography." *Jump Cut: A Review of Contemporary Media* 53. Online journal. Accessed November 26, 2013. http://www.ejumpcut.org/archive/jc53.2011/Hanich2/1.html.

Harris, Daniel R. 1991. "Effeminacy." *Michigan Quarterly Review* 30 (1): 72–81.

Harris, Daniel R. 1997. *The Rise and Fall of Gay Culture*. New York: Hyperion.

Harris, Laura, and Elizabeth Crocker. 1997. *Fem(me): Feminists, Lesbians, and Bad Girls*. New York: Routledge.

Hart, Lynda. 1998. *Between the Body and the Flesh: Performing Sadomasochism*. New York: Columbia University Press.

Haskell, Molly. 1992. "You Saw Nothing in Indochina." *Film Comment* 29 (January/February): 31–33.

Hill, Logan. 2001. "Beyond Access: Race, Technology, Community." In *Technicolor: Race, Technology, and Everyday Life*, ed. Alondra Nelson and Thuy Linh N. Tu, with Alicia Headlam Hines, 13–33. New York: New York University Press.

Hocquenghem, Guy. (1972) 1993. *Homosexual Desire*. Trans. Daniella Dangoor. Durham, NC: Duke University Press.

Holmlund, Chris, and Cynthia Fuchs. 1997. *Between the Sheets, in the Streets: Queer, Lesbian, Gay Documentary*. Minneapolis: University of Minnesota Press.

Hoppe, Trevor. 2011. "Circuits of Power, Circuits of Pleasure: Sexual Scripting in Gay Men's Bottom Narratives." *Sexualities* 14 (2): 193–217.

Huston, John. 1980. *An Open Book*. New York: Knopf.

Jackson, Earl, Jr. 1994. "Desire at Cross(-Cultural) Purposes: *Hiroshima, mon amour* and *Merry Christmas, Mr. Lawrence*." *positions: east asia cultures critique* 2 (1): 133–174.

Jackson, Earl, Jr. 1995. *Strategies of Deviance: Studies in Gay Male Representation*. Bloomington: Indiana University Press.

Jackson, Peter A. 1997. "Kathoey > < Gay > < Man: The Historical Emergence of Gay

Male Identities in Thailand." In *Sites of Desire, Economies of Pleasure*, ed. Lenore Manderson and Margaret Jolly, 166–190. Chicago: University of Chicago Press.

Jackson, Peter A. 2001. "Pre-Gay, Post-Queer: Thai Perspectives on Proliferating Gender/Sex Diversity in Asia." In *Gay and Lesbian Asia: Culture, Identity, Community*, ed. Gerard Sullivan and Peter A. Jackson, 1–26. New York: Harrington Park Press.

Jeffords, Susan. 1989. *The Remasculinization of America: Gender and the Vietnam War*. Bloomington: Indiana University Press.

Johnson, Brian D. 1992. "Sexual Wildlife: Three Movies Explore the Jungle of Passion." *Maclean's*, November 9, 108.

Kaminsky, Stuart M. 1976. "Italian Westerns and Kung Fu Films: Genres of Violence." In *Graphic Violence on the Screen*, ed. Thomas R. Atkins, 46–67. New York: Monarch Press.

Käng, Dredge Byung'chu. 2011. "Queer Media Loci in Bangkok: Paradise Lost and Found in Translation." *GLQ: A Journal of Lesbian and Gay Studies* 17 (1): 169–91.

Käng, Dredge Byung'chu. 2012. "Kathoey 'In Trend': Emergent Genderscapes, National Anxieties and the Re-Signification of Male-Bodied Effeminacy in Thailand." Special issue, "Queer Asian Subjects," *Asian Studies Review* 36 (4): 475–94.

Kang, Laura Hyun Yi. 2002. *Compositional Subjects: Enfiguring Asian/American Women*. Durham, NC: Duke University Press.

Karr, John F. 2001. "Flip-Flopping Fun." *Bay Area Reporter*, March 29, 35.

Katz, Jonathan. 1996. "Passive Resistance: On the Success of Queer Artists in Cold War American Art." *L'image* 3. QueerCulturalCenter.org Accessed July 13, 2008. http://www.queerculturalcenter.org/Pages/KatzPages/KatzLimage.html.

Kauffmann, Stanley. 1992. "Making Love." *New Republic*, December 28, 24–25.

Keeling, Kara. 2007. *The Witch's Flight: The Cinematic, the Black Femme, and the Image of Common Sense*. Durham, NC: Duke University Press.

Kim, Daniel Y. 2005. *Writing Manhood in Black and Yellow: Ralph Ellison, Frank Chin, and the Literary Politics of Identity*. Stanford, CA: Stanford University Press.

Kim, Elaine H. 2003. "Interstitial Subjects: Asian American Visual Art as a Site for New Cultural Conversations." In *Fresh Talk, Daring Gazes: Conversations with Asian American Art*, ed. Elaine H. Kim, Margo Machida, and Sharon Mizota, 1–50. Berkeley: University of California Press.

King, Homay. 2010. *Lost in Translation: Orientalism, Cinema, and the Enigmatic Signifier*. Durham, NC: Duke University Press.

Kippax, Susan, and Gary Smith. 2001. "Anal Intercourse and Power in Sex." *Sexualities* 4 (1): 413–34.

Ko, Claudine. 1999. "My Search for Brandon Lee." *Giant Robot* 14: 83–85.

Kong, Travis S. K. 2005. "Queering Masculinity in Hong Kong Movies." In *Masculinities and Hong Kong Cinema*, ed. Pang Lai-kwan and Day Wong, 57–80. Hong Kong: Hong Kong University Press.

Koshy, Susan. 2004. *Sexual Naturalization: Asian Americans and Miscegenation*. Stanford, CA: Stanford University Press.

Kracauer, Siegfried. (1960) 2004. "Remarks on the Actor." In *Movie Acting: The Film Reader*, ed. Pamela Robertson Wojcik, 19–27. New York: Routledge.

Krupp, Charla. 1992. "Did They or Didn't They?" *Glamour*, October, 195.

Laplance, Jean, and Jean-Bertrand Pontalis. 1986. "Fantasy and the Origins of Sexuality." In *Formations of Fantasy*, ed. Victor Burgin, James Donald, and Cora Kaplan, 5–34. London and New York: Methuen.

Lawrence, Doug. 1998. "Asian Persuasion." *Adam Video XXX Showcase*, May, 45.

Lawrence, Doug, ed. 2001. *The Films of Josh Eliot*. Los Angeles: Knights Publishing.

Lee, Helen, and Kerri Sakamoto, ed. 2002. *Like Mangoes in July: The Work of Richard Fung*. Toronto: Insomniac Press.

Lee, JeeYeun. 1996. "Why Suzie Wong Is Not a Lesbian: Asian and American Lesbian and Bisexual Women and Femme/Butch/Gender Identities." In *Queer Studies: A Lesbian, Gay, Bisexual, and Transgender Anthology*, ed. Brett Beemyn and Mickey Eliason, 115–32. New York: New York University Press.

Lee, Joon Oluchi. 2005. "The Joy of the Castrated Boy." *Social Text* 84–85: 35–56.

Lee, Quentin. 1993. "Between the Oriental and the Transvestite." *Found Object* 2: 45–66.

Lee, Rick. 2012. "Biography." In *Asian Man: The Sex Adventures of Asian Man*. Accessed December 20, 2012. http://asian-man.com/asianmannew/biography.htm.

Lee, Robert G. 1999. *Orientals: Asian Americans in Popular Culture*. Philadelphia: Temple University Press.

Lehman, Peter. 1993. *Running Scared: Masculinity and the Representation of the Male Body*. Philadelphia: Temple University Press.

Lehman, Peter, ed. 2006. *Pornography: Film and Culture*. New Brunswick, NJ: Rutgers University Press.

Lessard, Micheline R. 2007. "Organisons-nous! Racial Antagonism and Vietnamese Economic Nationalism in the Early Twentieth Century." *French Colonial History* 8: 171–201.

"Le top 10 des icons gay asiatiques." 2006. *Baby Boy*, April, 28–29.

Ling, Jinqi. 1997. "Identity Crisis and Gender Politics: Reappropriating Asian American Masculinity." In *An Interethnic Companion to Asian American Literature*, ed. King-Kok Cheung, 312–37. New York: Cambridge University Press.

Lo, Kwai-Cheung. 1996. "Muscles and Subjectivity: A Short History of the Masculine Body in Hong Kong Popular Culture." *Camera Obscura* 39: 105–25.

Louie, Kam. 2002. *Theorising Chinese Masculinity: Society and Gender in China*. Cambridge: Cambridge University Press.

Love, Heather. 2007. *Feeling Backward: Loss and the Politics of Queer History*. Cambridge, MA: Harvard University Press.

Lowe, Lisa. 1996. *Immigrant Acts: On Asian American Cultural Politics*. Durham, NC: Duke University Press.

Lurie, Rod. 1992. "Movie Review (The Lover)." *Los Angeles Magazine*, November, 153–56.

Ma, Ming-Yuen S. 2002. "Untitled." In *Like Mangoes in July: The Work of Richard Fung*, ed. Helen Lee and Kerri Sakamoto, 60–61. Toronto: Insomniac.

Ma, Sheng-Mei. 2000. *The Deathly Embrace: Orientalism and Asian American Identity*. Minneapolis: University of Minnesota Press.

Manalansan, Martin F., IV. 2003. *Global Divas: Filipino Gay Men in the Diaspora*. Durham, NC: Duke University Press.

Manalansan, Martin F., IV. 2010. "Servicing the World: Flexible Filipinos and the Unsecured Life." In *Political Emotions*, ed. Janet Staiger, Ann Cvetkovich, and Ann Reynolds, 215–28. New York: Routledge.

Marchetti, Gina. 1993. *Romance and the "Yellow Peril": Race, Sex, and Discursive Strategies in Hollywood Fiction*. Berkeley: University of California Press.

Marks, Laura U. 2000. *The Skin of the Film: Intercultural Cinema, Embodiment, and the Senses*. Durham, NC: Duke University Press.

Marks, Laura U. 2002. *Touch: Sensuous Theory and Multisensory Media*. Minneapolis: University of Minnesota Press.

Martin, Fran. 2003. *Situating Sexualities: Queer Representation in Taiwanese Fiction, Film and Public Culture*. Hong Kong: Hong Kong University Press.

Martin, Robert K. 1992. "Gender, Race, and the Colonial Body: Carson McCullers's Filipino Boy, and David Henry Hwang's Chinese Woman." *Canadian Review of American Studies* 23 (1): 95–106.

McCullers, Carson. (1941) 1966. *Reflections in a Golden Eye*. New York: Bantam.

McCullers, Carson. (1946) 2004. *The Member of the Wedding*. New York: Houghton Mifflin.

McPherson, Hugo. 1996. "Carson McCullers, Lonely Huntress: [*Reflections in a Golden Eye*]." In *Critical Essays on Carson McCullers*, ed. Beverly Lyon Clark and Melvin J. Friedman, 143–46. New York: G. K. Hall.

Merck, Mandy. 2000. *In Your Face: 9 Sexual Studies*. New York: New York University Press.

Metzger, Sean. 2002. "Filmic Revisions of Vietnam and the MIAs (Male Indochinese Asexuals)." *Quarterly Review of Film & Video* 19: 107–21.

Miller, D. A. 1991. "Anal *Rope*." In *Inside/Out: Lesbian Theories, Gay Theories*, ed. Diana Fuss, 119–41. New York: Routledge.

Miller, D. A. 1999. "Visual Pleasure in 1959." In *Out Takes: Essays on Queer Theory and Film*, ed. Ellis Hanson, 97–125. Durham, NC: Duke University Press.

Mimura, Glen M. 2009. *Ghostlife of Third Cinema: Asian American Film and Video*. Minneapolis: University of Minnesota Press.

Modleski, Tania. 1982. *Loving with a Vengeance: Mass-Produced Fantasies for Women*. New York: Routledge.

Modleski, Tania. 1991. *Feminism without Women: Culture and Criticism in a "Postfeminist" Age*. New York: Routledge.

Monaco, Paul. 2003. *The Sixties, 1960–1969*. Berkeley: University of California Press.

Morin, Jack. 1986. *Anal Pleasure and Health: A Guide for Men and Women*. Burlingame, CA: Yes Press.

Morland, Iain. 2009. "What Can Queer Theory Do for Intersex?" GLQ 51 (2): 285–312.

Motion Picture Herald. 1967. "*Reflections in a Golden Eye* (Movie Review)." October 25, Volume 237, Number 43: 733.

Mowlabocus, Sharif. 2007. "Gaydar: Gay Men and the Pornification of Everyday Life." In *Pornification: Sex and Sexuality in Media Culture*, ed. Kaarina Nikunen, Susanna Paasonen, and Laura Saarenmaa, 61–72. New York: Berg.

Muñoz, José Esteban. 1996. "Ghosts of Public Sex: Utopian Longings, Queer Memories." In *Policing Public Sex: Queer Politics and the Future of AIDS Activism*, ed. Dangerous Bedfellows, 355–72. Boston, MA: South End Press.

Muñoz, José Esteban. 1999. *Disidentifications: Queers of Color and the Performance of Politics*. Minneapolis: University of Minnesota Press.

Munt, Sally R. 1997. "Orifices in Space: Making the Real Possible." In *Butch/Femme: Inside Lesbian Gender*, ed. Sally R. Munt, 200–209. London: Cassell.

Munt, Sally R. 2008. *Queer Attachments: The Cultural Politics of Shame*. Burlington, VT: Ashgate.

Mura, David. 1995a. *The Colors of Desire: Poems*. New York: Anchor Books.

Mura, David. 1995b. "The Lover." In *On a Bed of Rice: An Asian American Erotic Feast*, ed. Geraldine Kudaka, 370–83. New York: Anchor Books.

Murray, Stephen O. 2000. *Homosexualities*. Chicago: University of Chicago Press.

Naficy, Hamid. 2001. *An Accented Cinema: Exilic and Diasporic Filmmaking*. Princeton, NJ: Princeton University Press.

Naremore, James. 1988. *Acting in the Cinema*. Berkeley: University of California Press.

Negrón-Muntaner, Frances. 2004. *Boricua Pop: Puerto Ricans and the Latinization of American Culture*. New York: New York University Press.

Nestle, Joan. 1987. *A Restricted Country*. Ithaca, NY: Firebrand Books.

Nestle, Joan, ed. 1992. *The Persistent Desire: A Femme-Butch Reader*. Boston: Alyson Publications, Inc.

Newton, Esther, and Shirley Walton. 1984. "The Misunderstanding: Toward a More Precise Sexual Vocabulary." In *Pleasure and Danger: Exploring Female Sexuality*. Boston: Routledge & Kegan Paul.

Nguyen, Mimi. 2007. "Bruce Lee I Love You: Discourses of Race and Masculinity in the Queer Superstardom of JJ Chinois." In *Alien Encounters: Popular Culture in Asian America*, ed. Mimi Nguyen and Thuy Linh Nguyen-Tu, 271–304. Durham, NC: Duke University Press.

Nguyen, Viet Thanh. 2000. "The Remasculinization of Chinese America: Race, Violence, and the Novel." *American Literary History* 12 (1–2): 130–157.

Norindr, Panivong. 1996. *Phantasmatic Indochina: French Colonial Ideology in Architecture, Film, and Literature*. Durham, NC: Duke University Press.

Oishi, Eve. 2000. "Bad Asians: New Film and Video by Queer Asian American Artists." In *Countervisions: Asian American Film Criticism*, ed. Darrell Hamamoto and Sandra Liu, 221–24. Philadelphia: Temple University Press.

Oishi, Eve. 2003. "Bad Asians, the Sequel: Continuing Trends in Queer API Film and Video." *Millennium Film Journal* 41: 33–41.

Oishi, Eve. 2006. "Visual Perversions: Race, Sex, and Cinematic Pleasure." *Signs: Journal of Women in Culture and Society* 31 (3): 641–674.

Okada, Jun. 2005. "The PBS and NAATA Connection: Comparing the Public Spheres of Asian American Film and Video." *Velvet Light Trap* 55: 39–51.

Ongiri, Amy Abugo. 2002. "'He Wanted to Be Just Like Bruce Lee': African Americans, Kung Fu Theater and Cultural Exchange at the Margins." *Journal of Asian American Studies* 5 (1): 31–40.

Ortiz, Christopher. 1994. "Hot and Spicy: Representation of Chicano/Latino Men in Gay Pornography." *Jump Cut* 39: 83–90.

Palumbo-Liu, David. 1999. "Written on the Face: Race, Nation, Migrancy, and Sex." In *Asian/American: Historical Crossings of a Racial Frontier*, 81–115. Stanford, CA: Stanford University Press.

Parker, Richard. 1988. *Beneath the Equator: Cultures of Desire, Male Homosexuality, and Emerging Gay Communities in Brazil*. New York: Routledge.

Parreñas, Rhacel Salazar. 1998. "'White Trash' Meets the 'Little Brown Monkeys': The Taxi Dance Hall as a Site of Interracial and Gender Alliances between White Working Class Women and Filipino Immigrant Men in the 1920s and 30s." *Amerasia Journal* 24 (2): 115–34.

Patterson, Zabet. 2004. "Going On-line: Consuming Pornography in the Digital Era." In *Porn Studies*, ed. Linda Williams, 104–123. Durham, NC: Duke University Press.

Patton, Cindy. 1991. "Safe Sex and the Pornographic Vernacular." In *How Do I Look? Queer Film and Video*, ed. Bad Object-Choices, 31–63. Seattle, WA: Bay Press.

Patton, Cindy. 1996. "Visualizing Safe Sex." In *Fatal Advice: How Safe-Sex Education Went Wrong*, 118–38. Durham, NC: Duke University Press.

Patton, Cindy. 1999. "How to Do Things with Sound." *Cultural Studies* 13 (3): 466–487.

Perez, Hiram. 2005. "You Can Have My Brown Body and Eat It, Too!" *Social Text* 84–85: 171–91.

Phillips, Gene D. 2001. "Talking with John Huston." In *John Huston: Interviews*, ed. Robert Emmet Long, 36–43. Jackson: University Press of Mississippi.

Prieur, Annick. 1998. *Mema's House, Mexico City: On Transvestites, Queens, and Machos*. Chicago: University of Chicago Press.

Probyn, Elspeth. 2005. *Blush: Faces of Shame*. Minneapolis: University of Minnesota Press.

Proschan, Frank. 2002. "Eunuch Mandarins, Soldats Mamzelles, Effeminate Boys, and Graceless Women: French Colonial Constructions of Vietnamese Genders." *GLQ* 8 (4): 435–467.

Puar, Jasbir K. 1998. "Transnational Sexualities: South Asian (Trans)nation(alism)s and Queer Diaspora." In *Q & A: Queer in Asian America*, ed. David L. Eng and Alice Y. Hom, 405–422. Philadelphia: Temple University Press.

Rigg, Jonathan. 2003. "Exclusion and Embeddedness: The Chinese in Thailand and Vietnam." In *The Chinese Diaspora: Space, Place, Mobility, and Identity*, ed. Laurence J. C. Ma and Carolyn Cartier, 97–115. Lanham, MD: Rowman and Littlefield.

Rodriguez, Juana María. 2003. *Queer Latinidad: Identity Practices, Discursive Spaces*. New York: New York University Press.

Rodriguez, Juana María. 2007. "Gesture and Utterance: Fragments from a Butch-Femme Archive." In *A Companion to Lesbian, Gay, Bisexual, Transgender, and Queer Studies*, ed. George E. Haggerty and Molly McGarry, 282–91. Malden, MA: Blackwell.

Rofel, Lisa. 2007. *Desiring China: Experiments in Neoliberalism, Sexuality, and Public Culture*. Durham, NC: Duke University Press.

Romney, Jonathan. 1992. "L'amant (The 'Lover')." *Sight and Sound*, July, 38–39.

Rowlson, Alex. 2011. "Not Just a Preference: Alex Rowlson Goes Head-to-Head with the Troubling Terminology of Our Desires." FAB, December 10. Accessed October 26, 2012. http://www.fabmagazine.com/story/not-just-a-preference.

Ruddy, Karen. 2006. "The Ambivalence of Colonial Desire in Marguerite Duras's *The Lover*." *Feminist Review* 82 (1): 76–95.

Russo, Vito. (1981) 1995. *The Celluloid Closet*, rev. ed. New York: HarperCollins.

Russo, William, and Jan Merlin. 2005. *Troubles in a Golden Eye*. Philadelphia: Xlibris.

Scott, Darieck. 2010. *Extravagant Abjection: Blackness, Power, and Sexuality in the African American Literary Imagination*. New York: New York University Press.

Sedgwick, Eve Kosofsky. 1993. "How to Bring Kids Up Gay: The War on Effeminate Boys." In *Tendencies*, 154–64. Durham, NC: Duke University Press.

Sedgwick, Eve Kosofsky. 1995. "Shame and Performativity: Henry James's New York Edition Prefaces." In *Henry James's New York Edition: The Construction of Authorship*, ed. David Bruce McWhirter, 206–39. Stanford, CA: Stanford University Press.

Sedgwick, Eve Kosofsky. 1996. "Queer Performativity: Warhol's Shyness/Warhol's Whiteness." In *Pop Out: Queer Warhol*, ed. Jennifer Doyle, Jonathan Flatley, and José Esteban Muñoz, 134–43. Durham, NC: Duke University Press.

Sedgwick, Eve Kosofsky. 2003. *Touching Feeling: Affect, Pedagogy, Performativity*. Durham, NC: Duke University Press.

See, Sarita Echavez. 2009. *The Decolonized Eye: Filipino American Art and Performance*. Minneapolis: University of Minnesota Press.

Shah, Nayan. 2001. *Contagious Divides: Epidemics of Race in San Francisco's Chinatown*. Berkeley: University of California Press.

Shaviro, Steven. 1993. *The Cinematic Body*. Minneapolis: University of Minnesota Press.

Shimakawa, Karen. 2002. *National Abjection: The Asian American Body Onstage*. Durham, NC: Duke University Press.

Shimizu, Celine Parreñas. 2004. "Master-Slave Sex Acts: *Mandingo* and the Race/Sex Paradox." *Wide Angle* 21 (4): 42–61.

Shimizu, Celine Parreñas. 2005. "The Bind of Representation: Performing and Consuming Hypersexuality in Miss Saigon." *Theatre Journal* 57: 247–65.

Shimizu, Celine Parreñas. 2007. *The Hypersexuality of Race: Performing Asian/American Women on Screen and Scene*. Durham, NC: Duke University Press.

Shimizu, Celine Parreñas. 2012. *Straitjacket Sexualities: Unbinding Asian American Manhoods in the Movies*. Stanford, CA: Stanford University Press.

Shimizu, Celine Parreñas, and Helen Lee. 2004. "Sex Acts: Two Meditations on Race and Sexuality." *Signs: Journal of Women in Culture and Society* 30 (1): 1385–402.

Shively, Charles. (1974) 2003. "Indiscriminate Promiscuity as an Act of Revolution." In *Sexual Revolution*, ed. Jeffrey Escoffier, 516–26. New York: Thunder's Mouth Press.

Silverman, Kaja. 1992. *Male Subjectivity at the Margins*. New York: Routledge.

Silverstein, Charles, and Edmund White. 1977. *The Joy of Gay Sex*. New York: Simon and Schuster.

Silverstein, Charles, and Felice Picano. 1992. *The New Joy of Gay Sex*. New York: HarperCollins.

Silverstein, Charles, and Felice Picano. 2003. *The Joy of Gay Sex*, rev. and expanded 3rd ed. New York: HarperCollins.

Sinfield, Alan. 1994. *The Wilde Century: Effeminacy, Oscar Wilde and the Queer Moment*. New York: Columbia University Press.

Sinfield, Alan. 2004. *On Sexuality and Power*. New York: Columbia University Press.

Smith, Jack. (1962) 1997. "The Perfect Filmic Appositeness of Maria Montez." In *Wait for Me at the Bottom of the Pool: The Writings of Jack Smith*, ed. J. Hoberman and Edward Leffingwell, 25–35. London: Serpent's Tail/High Risk.

Smith, Valerie. 1990. "Split Affinities: The Case of Interracial Rape." In *Conflicts in Feminism*, ed. Marianne Hirsch and Evelyn Fox Keller, 271–87. New York: Routledge.

Sobchack, Vivian. 1992. *The Address of the Eye: A Phenomenology of Film Experience*. Princeton, NJ: Princeton University Press.

Sobchack, Vivian. 2004. *Carnal Thoughts: Embodiment and Moving Image Culture*. Berkeley: University of California Press.

Somerville, Siobhan B. 2000. *Queering the Color Line: Race and the Invention of Homosexuality in American Culture*. Durham, NC: Duke University Press.

Sragow, Michael. 1992. "Guns & Lovers." *New Yorker*, November 16, 132–33.

Staley, Jeffrey S., and Laurie Edson. 2001. "Objectifying the Subjective: The Autobiographical Act of Duras's *The Lover*." *Critique: Studies in Contemporary Fiction* 42 (3): 287–98.

Stockton, Kathryn Bond. 2006. *Beautiful Bottom, Beautiful Shame: Where "Black" Meets "Queer."* Durham, NC: Duke University Press.

Stoler, Ann Laura. 2002. *Carnal Knowledge and Imperial Power: Race and the Intimate in Colonial Rule*. Berkeley: University of California Press.

Stop Gay Racism and Internalised Homophobia. 2013. Accessed November 25. http://stopracismandhomophobiaongrindr.wordpress.com.

Straayer, Chris. 1996. *Deviant Eyes, Deviant Bodies: Sexual Re-orientations in Film and Video*. New York: Columbia University Press.

Stringer, Julian. 1997. "'Your Tender Smiles Give Me Strength': Paradigms of Masculinity in John Woo's *A Better Tomorrow* and *The Killer*." *Screen* 38 (1): 25–41.

Tajima, Renee. 1989. "Lotus Blossoms Don't Bleed: Images of Asian Women." In *Making Waves*, ed. Asian Women United of California, 305–9. Boston, MA: Beacon Press.

Takagi, Dana Y. 1995. "Maiden Voyage: Excursion into Sexuality and Identity Politics in Asian America." In *Asian American Sexualities: Dimensions of the Gay and Lesbian Experience*, ed. Russell Leong, 21–36. New York: Routledge.

Tasker, Yvonne. 1997. "Fists of Fury: Discourses of Race and Masculinity in the Martial Arts Cinema." In *Race and the Subject of Masculinities*, ed. Harry Stecopoulos and Michael Uebel, 315–36. Durham, NC: Duke University Press.

Taylor, John Russell. 1968. "*Reflections in a Golden Eye* (Movie Review)." *Sight and Sound*, spring, 99.

Teo, Stephen. 1997. *Hong Kong Cinema: The Extra Dimensions*. London: British Film Institute.

Textor, Alex Robertson. 1997. "Marilyn, Mayhem, and the Mantrap: Some Particularities of Male Femme." In *Fem(me): Feminists, Lesbians, and Bad Girls*. New York: Routledge. 198–209.

Thomson, David. (1989) 2004. "The Lives of Supporting Players." In *Movie Acting: The Film Reader*, ed. Pamela Robertson Wojcik, 207–10. New York: Routledge.

Ting, Jennifer P. 1995. "Bachelor Society: Deviant Heterosexuality and Asian American Historiography." In *Privileging Positions: The Sites of Asian American Studies*, ed. Gary Y. Okihiro, Marilyn Alquizola, Dorothy Fujita Rony, and Wong K. Scott, 271–80. Pullman: Washington State University Press.

Ting, Jennifer P. 1998. "The Power of Sexuality." *Journal of Asian American Studies* 1 (1): 65–82.

Tsang, Daniel. 1999. "Beyond 'Looking for My Penis': Reflections on Asian Gay Male Video Porn." In *Porn 101: Eroticism, Pornography, and the First Amendment*, ed. James Elias, Veronica Diehl Elias, Vern L. Bullough, Gwen Brewer, Jeffrey J. Douglas, and Will Jarvis, 473–47. Amherst, NY: Prometheus.

Turan, Kenneth. 1992. "Steam from Saigon: Hard-Breathing; 'The Lover' Too Much in Love with Itself." Calendar. *Los Angeles Times*, October 30, 1.

Tyler, Parker. 1973. *Screening the Sexes: Homosexuality in the Movies*. New York: Anchor Press.

Underwood, Steven G. 2003. *Gay Men and Anal Eroticism: Tops, Bottoms, and Versatiles*. Binghamton, NY: Harrington Park Press.

Vaccaro, Jeanne. 2010. "Felt Matters." *Women & Performance: A Journal of Feminist Theory* 20 (3): 253–266.

Valentine, David. 2007. *Imagining Transgender: An Ethnography of a Category*. Durham, NC: Duke University Press.

Wang, Yiman. 2005. "The Art of Screen Passing: Anna May Wong's Yellow Yellowface Performance in the Art Deco Era." *Camera Obscura* 20: 159–191.

Wasley, Andy. 2011. "Profile Prejudice." So So Gay, February 25. Accessed December 19, 2012. http://sosogay.org/2011/profile-prejudice/.

Wat, Eric C. 2002. *The Making of a Gay Asian Community: An Oral History of Pre-AIDS Los Angeles*. Lanham, MD: Rowman & Littlefield Publishers.

Waugh, Thomas. 1985. "Men's Pornography: Gay vs. Straight." *Jump Cut* 30: 30–35.

Waugh, Thomas. 1996. *Hard to Imagine: Gay Male Eroticism in Photography and Film from Their Beginnings to Stonewall*. New York: Columbia University Press.

Waugh, Thomas. 2000. "Walking on Tippy Toes: Lesbian and Gay Liberation Documentary of the Post-Stonewall Period 1969–1984." In *The Fruit Machine: Twenty Years of Writing on Queer Cinema*, 246–71. Durham, NC: Duke University Press.

Waugh, Thomas. 2002. "Fung: Home and Homoscape." In *Like Mangoes in July: The Work of Richard Fung*, ed. Helen Lee and Kerri Sakamoto, 66–77. Toronto: Insomniac.

Wayne, Bruce, ed. 2000. *Gay Adult Video Star Directory*. Laguna Hills, CA: Companion Press.

Weber, Marten. 2012. "Egg, Banana, and Coconut: Are Gays More Racist?" February 25. *The Huffington Post*. Accessed November 29, 2013. http://www.huffingtonpost.com/marten-weber/gay-racism_b_1295368.html.

Wexman, Virginia Wright. 1993. *Creating the Couple: Love, Marriage, and Hollywood Performance*. Princeton, NJ: Princeton University Press.

White, Patricia. 1999. *Uninvited: Classical Hollywood Cinema and Lesbian Representability*. Bloomington: Indiana University Press.

Williams, Linda. 1989. *Hard Core: Power, Pleasure and the "Frenzy of the Visible."* Berkeley: University of California Press.

Williams, Linda. 1991. "Film Bodies: Gender, Genre, and Excess." *Film Quarterly* 44 (4): 2–13.

Williams, Linda. 2001. "Cinema and the Sex Act." *Cineaste* 27 (1): 22–25.

Williams, Linda. 2004. "Skin Flicks on the Racial Border: Pornography, Exploitation, and Interracial Lust." In *Porn Studies*, ed. Linda Williams, 271–308. Durham, NC: Duke University Press.

Williams, Linda. 2006. "Of Kisses and Ellipses: The Long Adolescence of American Movies." *Critical Inquiry* 32: 288–340.

Williams, Linda. 2008. *Screening Sex*. Durham, NC: Duke University Press.

Willis, Sharon. 1987. *Marguerite Duras: Writing on the Body*. Urbana: University of Illinois Press.

Winston, Jane Bradley. 2001. *Postcolonial Duras: Cultural Memory in Postwar France*. New York: Palgrave Macmillan.

Wittman, Carl. (1970) 1992. "Refugees in Amerika: A Gay Manifesto." In *Homosexuality and Government, Politics and Prisons*, ed. Wayne R. Dynes and Stephen Donaldson, 297–311. New York: Routledge.

Wojcik, Pamela Robertson, ed. 2004. *Movie Acting: The Film Reader*. New York: Routledge.

Wong, Eugene Franklin. 1978. *On Visual Media Racism: Asians in the American Motion Pictures*. New York: Arno Press.

Wong, Sau-ling Cynthia. 1993. "Subversive Desire: Reading the Body in the 1991 Asian Pacific Islander Men's Calendar." *Critical Mass: A Journal of Asian American Cultural Criticism* 1 (1): 63–74.

Wong, Sau-ling Cynthia, and Jeffrey J. Santa Ana. 1999. "Gender and Sexuality in Asian American Literature (Review Essay)." *Signs: Journal of Women in Culture and Society* 25 (1): 171–226.

Yeager, Jack Andrew. 2001. "Colonialism and Power in Marguerite Duras's *The Lover*." In *Of Vietnam: Identities in Dialogue*, ed. Jane Bradley Winston and Leakthina Chau-Pech Ollier, 224–35. New York: Palgrave.

Yung, Wayne, and Nguyen Tan Hoang. 2007. "Queer Hongcouver and Other Fictions." In *Reel Asian: Asian Canada on Screen*, ed. Elaine Chang, 250–63. Toronto: Coach House.

VIDEOGRAPHY

The Adventures of Iron Pussy. 2003. Dir. Apichatpong Weerasethakul and Michael Shaowanasai. Kick the Machine.
The Adventures of Iron Pussy II: Bunzai . . . Chaiyo! 1999. Dir. Michael Shaowanasai. Joanna Stien, cumeat@yahoo.com.
The Adventures of Iron Pussy III: To Be or Not to Be. 2000. Dir. Michael Shaowanasai. Joanna Stien, cumeat@yahoo.com.
Affirmative Blacktion: An Interracial Takeover. 2010. Dir. Doug Jeffries. All Worlds Video.
Anatomy of Hell. 2004. Dir. Catherine Breillat. CB Films.
Anna and the King. 1999. Dir. Andy Tennant. Fox 2000 Pictures and Lawrence Bender Productions.
Asian Boyfriend. 2006. Dir. Wayne Yung. Video Out.
Asian Force. 1991. Dir. Tony Chan. HIS Video.
Asian Knights. 1985. Dir. Ed Sung. William Richhe Productions.
Asian Persuasion. 1997. Dir. Josh Eliot. Catalina.
Asian Persuasion 2. 1998. Dir. Brad Austin. Catalina.
Belle de Jour. 1967. Dir. Luis Buñuel. Allied Artists Pictures.

Below the Belt. 1985. Dir. Philip St. John. California Dream Machine Productions.
The Best of Brandon Lee. 1999. Dir. Chi Chi LaRue and Josh Eliot. Catalina.
A Better Tomorrow 3. 1989. Dir. Tsui Hark. Golden Princess Film Production Ltd. and Film Workshop.
The Big Boss. 1971. Dir. Wei Lo. Golden Harvest Company.
Big Guns 2. 1999. Dir. Josh Eliot. Catalina.
Billy Budd. 1962. Dir. Peter Ustinov. Allied Artists Pictures.
The Bitter Tea of General Yen. 1933. Dir. Frank Capra. Columbia Pictures Corporation.
Bolt. 2004. Dir. Chi Chi LaRue. Rascal Video.
Bound. 1996. Dir. Andy and Larry Wachowski. Dino De Laurentiis Company.
Boy's? 1996. Dir. Hau Wing-choi. Shui Goh.
Brandon Lee's Hot Shots. 2005. Dir. Chi Chi LaRue. Rascal Video.
Broken Blossoms. 1919. Dir. D. W. Griffith. D. W. Griffiths Productions.
Butterfield 8. 1960. Dir. Daniel Mann. Afton-Linebrook and Metro-Goldwyn-Mayer.
Camellia. 2010. Dir. Wisit Sasanatieng, Isao Yukisada, and Jang Joon-hwan. Busan Metropolitan City.
Cat on a Hot Tin Roof. 1958. Dir. Richard Brooks. Metro-Goldwyn-Mayer and Avon Productions.
The Cheat. 1915. Dir. Cecil B. DeMille. Jesse L. Lasky Feature Play Company.
Chew Manchu. 2000. Dir. Mark Jensen. Catalina.
China Dolls. 1997. Dir. Tony Ayres. Film Australia Ltd.
Chinese Characters. 1986. Dir. Richard Fung. Vtape.
Cleopatra. 1963. Dir. Joseph L. Mankiewicz. Twentieth Century Fox Film Corporation.
Crème of Sum Yung Gai. 2004. Dir. uncredited. Catalina.
The Crimson Kimono. 1959. Dir. Samuel Fuller. Globe Enterprises.
The Crow. 1994. Dir. Alex Proyas. Miramax Films.
Daughter of Shanghai. 1937. Dir. Robert Florey. Paramount Pictures.
Deceived. 2005. Dir. Chi Chi LaRue. Rascal Video.
Dial "S" for Sex. 1998. Dir. Chi Chi LaRue. Catalina.
Dien Bien Phu. 1992. Dir. Pierre Schoendoerffer. Flach Film and Mod Films.
Dirty Laundry. 1996. Dir. Richard Fung. Vtape.
Discopedia. 2007. Dir. Ho Tam. Vtape.
Dragon: The Bruce Lee Story. 1993. Dir. Rob Cohen. Universal Pictures.
Eat a Bowl of Tea. 1989. Dir. Wayne Wang. American Playhouse.
El Paso Wrecking Corp. 1978. Dir. Joe Gage. Joe Gage Films.
Emmanuelle. 1974. Dir. Just Jaeckin. Trinacra Films.
Enter the Dragon. 1973. Dir. Robert Clouse. Concord Productions Inc., Golden Harvest Company, Sequoia Productions, and Warner Bros.
Erotic in Nature. 1985. Dir. Cristen Lee Rothermund. Tigress Productions.
Exotic 101. 1998. Dir. Michael Shaowanasai. Joanna Stien, cumeat@yahoo.com.
Fat Girl (À ma seour!). 2001. Dir. Catherine Breillat. CB Films.
Field Guide to Western Wildflowers. 2000. Dir. Wayne Yung. Video Out.
Fist of Fury. 1972. Dir. Wei Lo. Golden Harvest Company.

Flower Drum Song. 1961. Dir. Henry Koster. Universal International Pictures and Fields Productions.
Forever Bottom! 1999. Dir. Nguyen Tan Hoang. Video Out.
Fortune Nookie. 1998. Dir. Chi Chi LaRue. Catalina.
The Fugitive Kind. 1959. Dir. Sidney Lumet. Pennebaker Productions.
Game of Death. 1978. Dir. Robert Clouse and Bruce Lee. Concord Productions Inc. and Golden Harvest Company.
The Gay Deceivers. 1969. Dir. Bruce Kessler. Fanfare Films.
Glory Holes of L.A. 1997. Dir. Bianco Piagi. Oh Man! Studios.
Harley's Crew. 1998. Dir. Chi Chi LaRue. Catalina.
Harold and Kumar Escape from Guantanamo Bay. 2008. Dir. Jon Hurwitz and Hayden Schlossberg. New Line Cinema.
The Haunting. 1963. Dir. Robert Wise. Argyle Enterprises.
Heathers. 1989. Dir. Michael Lehmann. New World Pictures.
He's a Woman, She's a Man. 1994. Dir. Peter Chan. United Filmmakers Organisation.
Hiroshima Mon Amour. 1959. Dir. Alain Resnais. Argos Films.
The Idiots. 1998. Dir. Lars von Trier. Zentropa Entertainments.
Indochine. 1992. Dir. Régis Wargnier. Sony Pictures Classics.
Intimacy. 2001. Dir. Patrice Chéreau. Téléma.
Kansas City Trucking Co. 1976. Joe Gage. Joe Gage Films.
The Karate Kid. 1984. Dir. John G. Avildsen. Columbia Pictures.
Kiss of the Dragon. 2001. Dir. Chris Nahon. Twentieth Century Fox Film Corporation.
L.A. Tool and Die. 1979. Dir. Joe Gage. HIS Video.
Lights & Darks: An Interracial Spin. 2005. Dir. Doug Jeffries. Channel 1 Releasing.
look_im_azn. 2011. Dir. Nguyen Tan Hoang. Video Out.
Lookin' for Trouble. 2004. Dir. Doug Jeffries. Channel 1 Releasing.
The Lover. 1992. Dir. Jean-Jacques Annaud.
The Lovers. 1994. Dir. Tsui Hark. Film Workshop and Paragon Films Ltd.
Mandingo. 1975. Dir. Richard Fleischer. Dino De Laurentiis Company and Paramount Pictures.
Masters of the Pillow. 2004. Dir. James Hou. Avenue Films.
Matinee Idol. 1999. Dir. Ho Tam. Vtape.
The Member of the Wedding. 1952. Dir. Fred Zinnemann. Stanley Kramer Productions.
My German Boyfriend. 2004. Dir. Wayne Yung. Video Out.
My Lover's Aunt Porn. 2000. Dir. Stuart Gaffney. Self-distributed, stuart@aya.yale.edu.
The Name of the Rose. 1986. Dir. Jean-Jacques Annaud. Neue Constantin Film, Cristaldi-film, and Les Films Ariane.
Nine Songs. 2004. Dir. Michael Winterbottom. Revolution Films.
99 Men. 1998. Dir. Ho Tam. Vtape.
Oh! My Three Guys. 1994. Dir. Derek Chiu. Regal Films Co. Ltd.
One-Eyed Jacks. 1961. Dir. Marlon Brando. Pennebaker Productions.
On the Waterfront. 1954. Dir. Elia Kazan. Horizon Pictures and Columbia Pictures Corporation.

Orientations. 1984. Dir. Richard Fung. Third World Newsreel.
Pacific Fever. 1991. Dir. Frank Ross. P.M. Productions.
Pacific Rim. 1997. Dir. Mitchell Dunne. Catalina.
The Pawnbroker. 1964. Dir. Sidney Lumet. Landau Company.
Peking Opera Blues. 1986. Dir. Tsui Hark. Cinema City and Film Workshop.
Peter Fucking Wayne Fucking Peter. 1994. Dir. Wayne Yung. Video Out.
Peters. 1999. Dir. Dane Preston. Great Dane Productions.
Powertool. 1986. Dir. John Travis. Catalina.
Prison on Fire. 1987. Dir. Ringo Lam. Cinema City.
The Queen's Cantonese. 1998. Dir. Wayne Yung. Video Out.
Quest for Fire. 1981. Dir. Jean-Jacques Annaud. International Cinema Corporation.
Reflections in a Golden Eye. 1967. Dir. John Huston. Warner Bros./Seven Arts Productions.
Romance. 1999. Dir. Catherine Breillat. Flach Film.
Sea in the Blood. 2000. Dir. Richard Fung. Vtape.
Search Engine. 1999. Dir. Wayne Yung. Video Out.
Season of the Boys. 1997. Dir. Ho Tam. Vtape.
The Sergeant. 1968. Dir. John Flynn. Warner Bros./Seven Arts.
7 Steps to Sticky Heaven. 1995. Dir. Nguyen Tan Hoang. Video Out.
Shanghai Meat Company. 1991. Dir. Tony Chan. HIS Video.
Shortbus. 2006. Dir. John Cameron Mitchell. THINKFilm.
Skin on Skin. 2004. Dir. Darrell Y. Hamamoto. No distributor.
Slanted Vision. 1995. Dir. Ming-Yuen S. Ma. Third World Newsreel.
Sniff. 1997. Dir. Ming-Yuen S. Ma. V Tape.
Soul and Salsa. 1988. Dir. Frank Jeffries. Adam & Company.
Stag Party. 1998. Dir. Chi Chi LaRue. All Worlds Video.
Steam Clean. 1990. Dir. Richard Fung. Vtape.
The Strange One. 1957. Dir. Jack Garfein. Horizon Pictures and Columbia Pictures Corporation.
A Streetcar Named Desire. 1951. Dir. Elia Kazan. Charles K. Feldman Group and Warner Bros.
Suddenly, Last Summer. 1959. Dir. Joseph L. Mankiewicz. Horizon Pictures and Columbia Pictures Corporation.
Sweet Sweetback Baadasssss Song. 1971. Dir. Melvin Van Peebles. Cinemation Industries.
Swordsman II. 1992. Dir. Ching Siu-Tung. Film Workshop.
Throat Spankers. 1998. Dir. Josh Eliot. Catalina.
Toc Storee. 1992. Dir. Ming-Yuen S. Ma. Third World Newsreel.
Transgressions. 2002. Dir. Stuart Gaffney. Self-distributed, stuart@aya.yale.edu.
[2] for the Taking. 2004. Dir. Chi Chi LaRue. Unzipped Video.
The Warrior's Way. 2010. Dir. Sngmoo Lee. Rogue and Relativity Media.
The Way of the Dragon. 1972. Dir. Bruce Lee. Concord Productions Inc. and Golden Harvest Company.
We Got Moves You Ain't Even Heard Of (Part One). 1999. Dir. Clover Paek. Erica Cho, ericarcho@gmail.com.
Who's Afraid of Virginia Woolf? 1966. Dir. Mike Nichols. Warner Bros.

Wicked. 2005. Dir. Chi Chi LaRue. Rascal Video.
The Wild One. 1954. Dir. Laslo Benedek. Stanley Kramer Productions.
With Sex You Get Egg Roll. 1999. Dir. Peter Romero. Catalina.
Word is Out. 1978. Dir. Mariposa Film Group: Nancy Adair, Peter Adair, Andrew Brown, Rob Epstein, Lucy Massie Phenix, and Veronica Selver. Milestone Films.
Yellowcaust: A Patriot Act. 2004. Dir. Darrell Y. Hamamoto. No distributor.

INDEX

abjection: national, 93, 96, 180, 203; racial, 14, 19, 20–21, 45, 60–63, 69–70, 112, 166, 176, 178, 189, 190, 195, 197, 200–204; sexual, 15, 121, 179, 209n9, 252n17

Adam4Adam.com, 197, 251n6

Adventures of Iron Pussy III, The: To Be or Not to Be (dir. Michael Shaowanasai), 179–86, 190, 222n42, 248–49nn25–29

Affirmative Blacktion: An Interracial Takeover (dir. Doug Jeffries), 62, 67–68, 216n8, 220n33, 223n48

agency, 12, 20, 60–61, 73, 92, 119, 190; lateral, 21, 89; mastery and, 235n12; partial, 88, 204; passivity and, 17, 132–33, 140, 156, 213n28; pleasure and, 19; sexual, 70, 117, 143, 178, 185, 235n11, 249n29; social, 114, 145. See also Berlant, Lauren; Sedgwick, Eve; Cheng, Anne

Ahmed, Sara, 176

Altman, Dennis, 227n14, 248n25

Anacleto (character in *Reflections in a Golden Eye*): bodily comportment of, 75, 76, 86, 94, 106–7; bottomhood of, 74, 89, 97–98, 100; as contrast to the military, 77, 94; dismissal of character by gay critics, 73, 96; disapearance of, 73, 90, 108, 229n29; effeminacy of, 72–76, 78–79, 83, 86, 225n5; and the English language, 78; masculinity and, 85; performance of Zorro David as, 92–97, 224n3, 230–31nn31-33; racial difference of, 76, 84, 89, 226n11; in relation to Major Weldon Penderton, 97–98, 103–4, 106–7; relationship with Alison Langdon, 72–73, 83–90, 94, 226n13, 228n16, 228nn20–21, 228–29n24, 229nn27–28, 230n30; significance of the name of, 228n20; title of *Reflections in a Golden Eye* and, 103

anal sex, 6, 74, 212n23; ecstasy and, 8, 13; eroticism and, 3, 7–9, 74, 105, 243n46; fear of,

anal sex (continued)
  31; in gay pornography, 10, 12, 31, 37–38, 46, 47, 55–60, 65–66, 211n19, 215n4, 218n20, 221nn39–40, 222–23n46, 246n14; HIV/AIDS and, 209n9, 244–45n8; orgasm and, 16; pleasure of, 15–16, 46, 66, 222–23n46; power and, 8, 13, 16, 19, 31, 177–78, 213–14n30; as punishment, 31, 215n4, 223n48; as social taboo, 13, 15, 17, 211–12n22; top-bottom dynamics in, 6, 11, 16, 17–18, 178–79, 208–9n7, 210n17, 211n18. *See also* barebacking; bottom position; top position
"anal vision," 102–6, 107, 149, 219n30
Annaud, Jean-Jacques, 111, 114, 117, 119, 121–22, 127–28, 139, 140–41, 145, 233n2, 233n4, 235n11, 238n23, 240nn34–35, 242n43. *See also Lover, The*
anus, 15–17, 105, 144, 164, 213n27; and Asian men, 24, 72, 166, 181; bottomhood and, 6, 7, 17, 107, 139, 243n45; in gay pornography, 10, 46, 47, 56, 57–58, 218–17n27. *See also* anal sex
Appadurai, Arjun, 163, 246n13
Arnheim, Rudolf, 91–92, 105, 232n41
asexuality, 23–24, 34–35, 72, 91, 97, 119, 216n12
Asian/American men: accent of, 38, 40, 61–69, 168, 218n19; assimilation into the US of, 6, 45, 49, 203, 207–8nn4–5, 220–21n36; as audience of gay Asian-niche pornography, 216n6–7, 221–22n42; bottomhood and, 48, 70, 74, 81, 112–13, 151–52, 154, 156, 174, 176, 177–180, 193–95, 204–5; as bottom in gay sex, 3, 20–21, 31, 36, 60, 61, 247n18; buttocks of, 112, 114, 137–40, 143–45, 180, 184–85, 239–40n32; definition of the term, 207–8n4; desirability and, 2, 44, 60, 155, 164–65, 171, 174, 176; in gay pornography, 5–6, 30–33, 37–70, 166, 172, 208n6, 215–216n6, 218n20, 220n34, 221n42, 223n48; as immigrants, 38, 39, 40–42, 64–67, 69–70, 246n16; in mainstream Western films, 31, 91–92, 112–13, 119, 189, 234n4, 235–36n13, 240n36; as poorly endowed, 2, 38, 143, 144, 147 (*see also* penis); racialized gendering of, 80–81, 83, 91, 119, 126–27; in sex cruising websites, 1–2, 196–204, 251–2n12; in sexual relation with other Asian/American men (*see* "sticky rice" relationships); as sexual threat, 4, 52, 53, 82, 83; smoothness of, 139,

169–170; in heterosexual pornography, 5–6, 208n6, 215n5; as well-endowed, 35, 45–48 (*see also* penis); white men and, 164–65, 177–79, 180, 184–86; white women and, 111–12, 116, 139–40, 233–234n4, 234–35n13, 239–40n32; as youthful, 38, 49, 178, 219n31, 248n23. *See also* effeminacy; fantasy; feminization; Hollywood; Lee, Brandon; masculinity; Orientalism; remasculinization; stereotypes
Asian American studies, 2, 5, 20, 21–22, 66, 80, 82, 159
Asian Knights (dir. Ed Sung), 31
Asian Man: The Sex Adventures of Asian Man (website), 5, 208n6
Asian Persuasion (dir. Josh Eliot), 32, 37–38, 39–41, 43–46, 47, 51, 58, 218n25
Asian Persuasion 2 (dir. Brad Austin), 32, 55–56, 58, 65–66, 70, 218–19n27
asshole. *See* anus
autoeroticism, 56. *See also* masturbation
Ayres, Tony, 155, 164, 168–71. *See also China Dolls*
AZN (Asian), 201–2. *See also* Asian/American men: in sex cruising websites

"bachelor societies," 4, 19
bakla, 79
barebacking, 13–14, 212n23–24, 245n8
Below the Belt (dir. Philip St. John), 31
Benshoff, Harry, 109, 233n46
Berlant, Lauren, 21, 24, 89
Bersani, Leo: on abjection, 209n9; on bottomhood, 7–8, 12–13, 211–12n22, 212n24–25; on gay masculinity, 209–10n12; on jouissance, 209n8; on passivity, 133, 239n28; and the re-education of desire, 166–67. *See also* "Is the Rectum a Grave?"
Best of Brandon Lee, The (dir. Chi Chi LaRue and Josh Eliot), 32, 43
Big Guns 2 (dir. Josh Eliot), 32, 49
"black femme," 28, 215n38
black men, 155, 207n3, 214nn31–32; bottomhood and, 20, 121; buttocks of, 142, 144, 241–42nn40–41; in gay pornography, 49, 62, 68–69, 223n48; masculinity of, 142–43; penis of, 49; racial stereotyping of, 4; in sex cruising websites, 252n12

bottomhood: abjection and, 30, 60, 69, 195; aesthetics of, 108, 236n15; bottom position and, 2, 180, 190, 195, 251n4; as critique of heteronormativity, x, 14; disidentification with, 19; as ecstasy, 8, 12–13, 184, 204; effeminacy and, 74, 80, 194; femininity and, 9, 12, 19, 156–57, 194, 213n26, 231–32n36; feminization and, 6–7, 14, 113, 244n6; in gay pornography, 31, 48, 54, 56, 60, 68; HIV/AIDS and, 244n8; as humiliation, 8, 20, 121; hypermasculinization of, 13, 194, 212n24; pleasure of, 14–19, 20, 59–60, 70, 180; power and, 21, 69, 176–79; race and, 19, 20, 81, 89, 96–97, 121, 152, 178 (*see also* Asian/American men; black men); as sexual agency, 185–86; as social alliance, 14, 83, 89, 244n6; as social positioning, 152, 195; as submission, 17, 18, 156; as subversion, 20; vulnerability and, 17, 113, 179, 245n8. *See also* anus; Asian/American men; black men; houseboy; lesbianism; masculinity; passivity; receptivity; shame; visibility politics

bottom position, *viii*, ix–x, 154; agency and, 73, 247n18; definition of, 6–7; as emasculation, 14; emergence of the concept, 11–13, 210–11nn17–18; as empowerment, 177–79; in gay pornography, 10, 31, 46, 47, 48, 54–60, 210n16, 211n19, 246n14 (*see also* Brandon Lee: as bottom); hierarchy and, 208n7; HIV/AIDS and, 245n8; masochism and, 8; passivity and, 213n26, 213n28; pleasure of, 8, 14–17, 20, 66, 121, 174, 210n14; physiological dimension of, 9; race and, 20–21, 61–62, 76; in sex cruising websites, 196, 213n27; in sex trade, 41, 180, 184; as socially unintelligible, 28. *See also* Asian/American men; bottomhood; feminization

Brando, Marlon, 71, 72, 92, 93, 95–96, 108, 109, 110, 224n3, 230–31n32, 231n34. *See also* Penderton, Major Weldon; *Reflections in a Golden Eye* (film)

Bulosan, Carlos, 82, 90

butch-femme sexuality, 193–95, 204, 213–14n30, 250–51nn3–4

Butler, Judith, 18, 113, 235n12

buttocks: bottom position and, 6, 8, 10, 13, 55–58, 178, 180, *181*, 184–85, 219n27; as displacement of penis, 113, 142–44, 147; and proximity with the penis, 16; as representing sexual potency, 112, 137–40, 142–45, 149, 239–40n32, 241–42nn40–41; of women, 98, 226n10, 231–32n36, 239–40n32. *See also* Asian/American men; black men

Cante, Rich, 10, 39, 63–64, 161, 210n14, 222n46

Capino, José B., 56, 223n48, 224n51

Catalina Video, 29, 44, 45, 49, 56, 65; Far East Features series of, 32, 39, 42, 52

Celluloid Closet, The (book, Vito Russo), 73, 225n5

Chan, Jachinson, 5

Chan, Jackie, 31, 34

Chen, Jean Russo, 51

Cheng, Anne, 21

Chew Manchu (dir. Mark Jensen), 42, 52, 219n21

Chiao, Hsiung-Ping, 34–35

Chicano/Latino men, 41–42, 49, 52, 218n24, 223n49

Chin, Frank, 4

China Dolls (dir. Tony Ayres), 155, 168–71, 174

Chinese Characters (dir. Richard Fung), 171, 222n42, 245n12

Ching, Yau, 174–75

Cho, Erica, 186–91, 193, 249nn30–31

Cho, Song, 174

Chow Yun-fat, 31, 34, 141, 240n36

Chun, Wendy, 197, 204

Clover, Carol, 105, 243n1

cock. *See* penis

colonialism: in Indochina (Vietnam), 114, 116, 118–20, 122–24, 126–28, 147–48, 234n7, 234–35n9, 236–37n17, 237n20, 240n34; in the Phillipines, 53, 76–77, 82–84; sexual, 226n10

coming out, 75, 157–59, 164, 167, 200, 227n14

Constable, Liz, 124, 236n14

Cooper, Stephen, 102–3, 106, 108–9, 231n35, 232n39

counterpornography, 23, 155, 163

Crème of Sum Yung Gai (director uncredited), 52

Crimp, Douglas, 109–10, 236n14, 241n39, 244n8

Crockett, Sam, 38, 45

cum shot, 10, 66, 138, 210n14, 212n23–24, 221n39

cumming. *See* ejaculation
Cvetkovich, Ann, 213–14n30

David, Zorro, 71, 231n33; casting of (in *Reflections in a Golden Eye*), 93, 231n32; discovery of, 92; identification with the character of Anacleto of, 92, 96–97; review of performance of, 73, 94–95, 224n3, 230n31
de Beauvoir, Simone, 124, 236n14
de Certeau, Michel, 195, 251n5
Dean, Tim, 13–14, 212n24
desexualization, 4, 34, 42, 82, 83, 97, 141, 155, 163, 196, 231n36, 243n44
Dial "S" for Sex (dir. Chi Chi LaRue), 32, 45, 49–50
diaspora: Asian, 163, 168, 170–71, 176, 223n47, 248n25; queer, 66–67, 79, 159, 160–63, 168, 172, 179, 229n28, 245n9
dick. *See* penis
digital media, 25, 215n6. *See also* sex cruising websites
Dirty Laundry (dir. Richard Fung), 222n42, 245–46n12
"disaffection," 89
documentary: 22, 160; gay affirmative, 157; performance-based, 157–58; queer, 244n3; "sticky rice" relationships in, 152, 155, 156–63, 166–67, 170–76. *See also 7 Steps to Sticky Heaven*; *China Dolls*; *Queen's Cantonese, The*; *reeducation of desire*; *Slanted Vision*
Duras, Marguerite, 145, 147, 233n2, 237n18, 237–38n22, 238n24; ahistoricism in, 115–16, 127–28; as inspiration, 233–34n4; racialization of romance in, 117–20, 148, 236–37n17; shame in, 120, 121, 124, 238n26; tactility of skin and, 139. *See also Hiroshima Mon Amour*; *L'Amant*; *L'Amant de la Chine du Nord*
Dworkin, Andrea, 213n30
Dyer, Richard, 10, 133, 157–58, 164, 166–67, 170, 225n6, 246n14, 247n17

Edelman, Lee, 7, 144, 209n8, 213n28, 241n37, 243n46
effeminacy: of Asian/American men, 23–24, 42, 72, 76, 82, 127, 155; connotations of, 226n9; as enabling, 72–73, 76, 96; gender dissidence and, 79–80, 194, 227n15; marginalization of, 14, 75; redefinition of, 11; signi-

fying homosexuality, 74–75, 78–81, 83, 91, 225n5, 227n16, 244n7; theatricality of, 86, 93, 95; voice of actors and, 63, 75. *See also* Anacleto; femininity
egalitarianism: in gay male relationships, 154, 189, 227n14; LGBT politics and, 12; as modern, 209n7, 246n15; in "sticky rice" relationships, 176, 179
ejaculation: 66, 251n3; in bareback sex, 212nn23–24; facial, 56–57, 59; pleasure and, 10, 15, 16, 210n14. *See also* cum shot
Eliot, Josh, 32, 45, 51, 216n7, 220n34. *See also Asian Persuasion*; *Best of Brandon Lee, The*; *Big Guns 2*; *Throat Spankers*
Emmanuelle (dir. Just Jaeckin), 111, 117
Eng, David L., 6, 18–19, 81, 159, 168, 170, 228n17
Enter the Dragon (dir. Robert Clouse), 34
Escoffier, Jeffrey, 12, 58, 211n19
Espiritu, Yen Le, 4, 80, 83
ethnoscape, 163, 168, 170, 245–46nn12–13

fantasy: Asian/American men as objects of, 41, 56; Asian/American men as subjects of, 66–67, 164; from the bottom point of view, 10, 16, 186, 190, 211n19, 212n24; colonialism and, 88, 127–28, 240n34; gay figures of, 2, 212n24; generic scenarios of, 38–39, 42, 49, 218n21; homophobia and, 209n9; as "nonproductive expenditure," 247n17; racialization of, 42, 52–53, 64, 218n24; setting and, 37, 38, 42–43, 172; voice and, 63–65
femininity: as abject, 70, 121; anal sex and, 7, 12, 13–14, 16, 209n7, 212n22; and association with the arts, 77; colonialism and, 118, 119; as desirable, 72, 194; failed, 86, 228–29n24; gay male culture and, 227–28n16, 230n30, 250nn1–2; lesbian femme and, 194, 250n3; marginalization of, 14, 76; queerness and, 84, 90; racialization of, 19–20, 142, 214n31, 228n17, 244n6; recentering of, 188, 193; sexual roles and, 152, 174, 181; shame and, 120–21, 124, 126. *See also* Anacleto; bottomhood
feminization: of Asian/American men, 4–6, 14, 24–25, 31, 80–82, 118–19, 204; bottom position and, 11, 13, 212n24; shame and, 121, 236n14. *See also* bottomhood
fetishism, 71, 81, 156, 252n14; colonialism and,

280 INDEX

128; penile, 213n27; racial, 18, 135, 234n4, 235n9; verbal, 64

Filipino men: 71, 173, 174, 220n35; gay identity of, 226n8, 246n16; identification with white women, 72; racialized gendering of, 80–81, 226n11; sexuality of, 52–53, 81–82. *See also* Anacleto

Fist of Fury (dir. Wei Lo), 33, 216n11, 219n31

FOB (fresh off the boat), 40, 49, 63–64, 67, 70

Forster, Robert, 72, 102. *See also* Williams, Private L. G.

Fortune Nookie (dir. Chi Chi LaRue), 32, 39–41, 43–44, 46, *48*, 51, *54*, *55*, 58, 67, 70, 248n23

Freccero, Carla, 79

Freeman, Elizabeth, 149

fucking. *See* anal sex; vaginal sex

Fung, Richard: on Asian men in gay pornography, 18–19, 31, 48, 166, 215n3; on Asian spectatorship of gay pornography, 41, 156, 221–22n42; as filmmaker of color, 158, 163, 245n12; and the reeducation of desire, 167, 244–45n8. *See also Chinese Characters*; *Dirty Laundry*; "Looking for My Penis"

Gage, Joe, 211n19

GAM (gay Asian male), 160, 196–204, 251–52n12. *See also* Asian men: in sex cruising websites

Game of Death (dir. Robert Clouse and Bruce Lee), 219n31

"gay-for-pay," 41, 58, 218n21

Gay.com, 197, 251n6, 252n15

gay pornography. *See* pornography, gay

gender: based on racialization, 3, 25, 80–81, 113, 156, 159, 165, 204, 226n11; nonnormative expression of, 2, 7, 9, 63, 73, 74–76, 78–80, 83, 91, 117–18, 140–41, 183, 186–87, 189, 194–95, 225n5, 225n7, 227–28nn15–16, 250–51n3; performance of, 8, 14, 182–3; sex act and, 11–13, 211n19; sexual identity and, 144, 209n7, 250n1, 251n4

getting fucked. *See* anal sex; bottom position

Gleeson-White, Sarah, 104, 229n27, 239n28

Glory Holes of L.A. (dir. Bianco Piagi), 51, 220n35

Gomez, Jewelle, 195, 250n3

Gopinath, Gayatri, 168, 229n28

Grindr, 1–2, 207n1, 251n6, 251–52n12

Hagedorn, Jessica, 119, 235n11

Halberstam, Judith, 7, 121, 124, 249–250nn34–35

Halperin, David: on abjection, 203–4, 252n17; on gay eroticization of donimant masculinity, 209n12; on models of homosexuality, 78–79, 236n14; on sexual roles, 11, 208–9n7, 217n16

Hamamoto, Darrell Y., 5–6, 22–24, 214–15n35, 217n15, 220n34. *See also Skin on Skin*

Harlequin romance, 117

Harris, Daniel, 11, 75, 222n45, 252n13

Harris, Julie, 72, 95–96, 230–31nn31–32. *See also* Langdon, Alison

Haskell, Molly, 139, 238nn24–25

Hayakawa, Sessue, 240n36

Heathers (dir. Michael Lehmann), 50

heteronormativity: anal sex and, 8; as marginalizing minority subjects, 22, 24, 195, 204; nation-state and, 163, 168; opposition to, x, 5, 14, 19, 73, 80, 82, 90; reinforcement of, 91, 143–44

Hiroshima Mon Amour (dir. Alain Resnais), 115, 133–36, 139, 233n4, 237n18

HIV/AIDS, 7, 11, 18, 159, 173, 176, 178–79, 184, 212n24, 221n38, 244–45n8, 247n21

Hocquenghem, Guy, 7–8, 144, 243n45

Hollywood: acting in, 95, 97 (*see also* Method acting); interracial pairings in, 228–29n24, 235–36n13, 240n36; representation of Asian/American men in, 31, 51–52, 93, 96, 234n4, 240n36; sexual representation in, 143, 232n42, 242n43. *See also* pornography, gay

Hom, Alice Y., 6, 159

homonormativity, 66–67, 158, 194, 196, 225n7

homophobia: anal sex and, 14, 209n9; gender inversion and, 73, 224n3, 227n16; remasculinization and, 4, 121

homoscape, 163, 168, 170, 245–46n12

Hongcouver, 163, 179, 245n11

houseboy: asexuality of, 72, 97; as an Asian stereotype in films, 91, 172; bottomhood and, 76, 89, 100, 107–8, 177–78; as challenge to normative family relations, 84–85; effeminacy and, 73, 75, 224n3; power relations and, 87–88; as premodern homosexual, 79; as sexual threat, 83; topness and, 31. *See also* Anacleto; *Reflections in a Golden Eye* (film)

Huston, John, 71, 72, 89; casting in *Reflections in a Golden Eye* and, 92–93, 96; setting of *Reflections in a Golden Eye* and, 224n2; war documentaries by, 108–9, 233n45. *See also Reflections in a Golden Eye* (film)
hypercorporeality, 86. *See also* Anacleto: bodily comportment of
hypermasculinity, 13, 80, 142, 188, 194, 211n19, 212n24, 214n31
hypersexuality, 22, 42, 49, 52, 91, 241n40

In the Realm of the Senses (dir. Nagisa Oshima), 233n1
Indochina, 113, 115–116, 118, 126–28, 235n11, 236n17, 240n34. *See also Lover, The*
Indochine (dir. Régis Wargnier), 234n7
interracial relationships: in blaxploitation films, 142, 242n41; colonialism and, 128, 148; in Hollywood films, 235–36n13, 240n36; in literature, 115–16, 233–34n4 (see also *L'Amant*); national assimilation and, 234n9. *See also* bottomhood: race and; *Lover, The*; *Hiroshima Mon Amour*; reeducation of desire; "sticky rice" relationships
"Is the Rectum a Grave?" (Leo Bersani), 7, 12, 209n8

jacking off. *See* masturbation
Jeffords, Susan, 208n5
Jeffries, Doug, 57, 62, 208n15, 216n18. *See also Affirmative Blacktion: An Interracial Takeover*; *Lights & Darks: An Interracial Spin*
Joy of Gay Sex, The, 8–9, 11–12, 209nn10–11

Käng, Dredge Byung'chu, 211n21
Kang, Laura, 22, 236n13
Karate Kid, The (dir. John G. Avildsen), 186–91, 249n31
kathoey, 183, 185
Keeling, Kara, 28, 90, 215n38, 250n3
Killer, The (dir. John Woo), 141
Kim, Elaine, 4, 22
King, Homay, 22
Ko, Claudine, 29
Kong, Travis, 141, 243n44
Koshy, Susan, 43, 81–82, 86, 90, 115–16, 234n5
kung fu, 35, 52, 234n4, 249n28

L'Amant (Marguerite Duras), 114, 127–28, 233n2, 234n8, 237nn21–22. *See also Lover, The*
L'Amant de la Chine du Nord (Marguerite Duras), 127, 145, 238n22, 238n24
Langdon, Alison (character in *Reflections in a Golden Eye*), 100–101; reconstructed femininity of, 84–86, 88–90, 92, 228n23, 228–29n24, 229n27, 231–32n36; relationship with Anacleto of, 72–73, 77–78, 82, 83, 86–87, 89, 94, 96, 103–4, 107, 116, 228n16, 228nn20–21, 229n28, 230n30
Laplanche, Jean, 42, 209n8
LaRue, Chi Chi, 29, 32–33, 57, 216nn7–8, 220n34. *See also Best of Brandon Lee, The*; *Dial "S" for Sex*; *Fortune Nookie*; *Wicked*
Lee, Brandon (Jon Enriquez): accent of, 38, 54, 67–69; as assimilated Asian American, 33, 49–51, 54, 219–20n33; audience of, 221n42; as bottom, 58–60, 221n39, 223n48; changing of sexual role of, 54–58, 62; in comparison with Bruce Lee, 35–36; cross-over into mainstream gay porn, 32, 50, 51, 54, 216n7; discovery of, 29–30; as ethnic Filipino, 52–53, 220n35; as first gay Asian/American porn star, 215n1; masturbation and, 56; merchandising of, 219n29; Orientalist fantasies and, 42–44; penis of, 35, 37–38, 45–48; racial ambiguity of, 51, 216n7; as Sean Martinez (porn pseudonym), 51–53, 220n35; as top, 30–31, 33, 35–37, 48; video output of, 32, 216n8. *See also Asian Persuasion*; *Asian Persuasion 2*; *Best of Brandon Lee, The*; *Dial "S" for Sex*; *Fortune Nookie*; *Peters*; porn stardom; *Wicked*
Lee, Brandon (son of Bruce Lee), 29, 33, 51
Lee, Bruce, 29, 33–36, 61, 216–17nn11–13, 217n15, 219n31, 234n4. *See also Game of Death*; *Way of the Dragon, The*
Lee, Joon Oluchi, 19–20, 228n17
Lee, Quentin, 172, 174
Lee, Rick, 5–6, 208n6
Lee, Robert G., 83
Lehman, Peter, 143–45, 243n43
lesbianism: bottomhood and,190–91, 212n25, 244n6; pornography and, 247–48n22; sexual roles in, 193–95, 213–14n30, 250–51nn3–4 (*see also* "black femme"; butch-femme relationships); visual representation of, 91,

130, 186, 188, 226n10, 228–29n24, 230n31, 239n28
Leung Ka Fai, Tony, 111–12; buttocks of, 113, 137–40, 142–44, 145, 148–49, 233n3, 241n38; casting of (in *The Lover*), 140, 233n2, 242n42; criticism of performance of (in *The Lover*), 119; and physical distinction from white male bodies, 133, 242n42
Lights & Darks: An Interracial Spin (dir. Doug Jeffries), 62, 67–69, 216n8, 220n33, 223n48
look_im_azn (dir. Nguyen Tan Hoang), 202
"Looking for My Penis" (Richard Fung), 18, 19, 31, 41, 156, 166, 215n3
Love, Heather, 20, 229n26
Lover, The (dir. Jean-Jacques Annaud): dismissed as soft-core pornography, 111–12, 137, 233n2; masculinity in, 112–13, 119, 126, 131, 133, 139–40, 142–43, 144, 145, 148–49, 235n11, 242n42; nudity in, 137–40; press reviews of, 137–38, 239n26; racial and sexual shame in, 120–28, 132, 137, 139, 145; sexual realism in, 138; transgression in, 117–18, 236–37n17. See also *L'Amant*; Leung Ka Fai, Tony
Lowe, Lisa, 67, 80
Lustre, Napoleon, 172–73, 247n20

Ma, Ming-Yuen S., 155, 171–72, 174, 214–15n35, 222n42. See also *Slanted Vision*
Macchio, Ralph, 186–190
Mahn, Sum Yung, 31, 215n4
Manalansan, Martin, 79, 89, 168, 226n8, 245n9, 246n16
Mandingo (dir. Richard Fleischer), 142
Manhunt.net, 197–98, 251n6, 251n10
March, Jane, 111, 133, 137, 139, 142, 233n2, 239n26. See also *Lover, The*
Marchetti, Gina, 52
Marks, Laura: on the bottom position, 174; on haptic visuality, 140, 241nn38–39, 243n1; on gender egalitarianism, 154–55, 189, 243–44n2; on watching gay pornography, 152–53
martial arts films, 33, 35–36, 51–52, 113, 163, 216n12, 217n15, 219n31, 234n4, 240n36, 249n28
Martin, Fran, 200
Martin, Robert K., 84, 226n11, 228n19
masculinity: Asian/American, 3–6, 14, 18, 21, 23–26, 30, 33, 48, 59–61, 63, 70, 80–82, 112–13, 119, 125–27, 131, 139–44, 186, 216n12, 235n11, 237n18, 242n42, 243n44; black, 49, 142–43, 241–42nn40–41; bottomhood and, 13, 14, 16, 73, 97, 212n24; dominant, 9, 113, 119, 209–10n12, 243n45; gay reclamation of, 121 (*see also* remasculinization); martial arts films and, 34–35; normative, 78, 141, 145, 194, 227n16; nation-state and, 34; phallic, 7–8, 12, 19; queer, 188–90; racialized, 142–43, 234n4 (*see also* "racial castration"); in gay sex cruising profiles, 207n3; in sexual roles, 209n7, 211n19; simultaneous expression with femininity of, 181–83, 249n26; topness and, 9, 15, 178; *wen* and *wu*, 141, 216n12; white, 108, 156, 204, 242n41, 248n23. See also hypermasculinity
Masters of the Pillow (dir. James Hou), 5, 208n6
masturbation, 16, 49–50, 55, 57, 66, 133, 172, 187, 210n14, 221n40, 239n28; solo, 56, 58, 70
McCullers, Carson, 71, 84, 92–93, 104, 224–25n5, 226n11, 228n20, 229n24, 229n27, 230n30, 231n32, 232n37. See also *Reflections in a Golden Eye* (book)
Merck, Mandy, 12, 130, 137–38, 211–12n22, 212n25, 239n28
Method acting, 93, 95, 231n34
Metz, Christian, 105
Metzger, Sean, 235n11
Mikado, Brad Davis, 37–39, 43–44, 46, 51, 218n19, 218n25. See also *Asian Persuasion*
Miller, D. A., 7, 144, 209n8, 209n12, 232n36
Mimura, Glen, 22, 223n47, 245n9, 247n18
misogyny, 4, 13–14, 75, 194, 251n4
Modleski, Tania, 13, 117, 194–95, 243n1
money shot. *See* cum shot
Moreau, Jeanne, 125, 130, 131, 136, 233n2, 234n5
Morin, Jack, 16–17
Morita, Noriyuki "Pat," 189
MPAA (Motion Picture Association of America), 143, 242n43
Munt, Sally R., 144, 236n14
Mura, David, 233n4

Naficy, Hamid, 62–63
Naremore, James, 231n34
Négron-Muntaner, Frances, 236n14

Nestle, Joan, 250n3
New Joy of Gay Sex, The, 11–12
New Queer Cinema, 158
Nguyen, Viet Thanh, 208n5
Norindr, Panivong, 115, 118, 127, 234n7, 236n16, 240n34
North China Lover, The (Marguerite Duras). See *L'Amant de la Chine du Nord*
nudity, 133, 137, 138, 147, 238–39n26; female, 98, 103, 106, 131, 137; male, 99–100, 102–4, 112, 132, 139, 143–44, 180, 242n41, 242–43n43–44

Oishi, Eve, 22, 222n42
oral sex, 37–38, 46, 47, 58, 64, 65, 172, 175, 210n17
Orientalism, 43, 49, 51, 238n23; abjection and, 201–03; Asian/American men and, 68, 208n5, 246n16; fantasies based on, 52–53, 62, 64, 66–67; pornographic locales and, 42; sexual representation and, 223n48
Ortiz, Christopher, 41–42, 218n24

Palumbo-Liu, David, 220–21n36
passivity: as agency, 17, 133, 138, 213n28; in anal sex, 7–8, 11, 16, 18, 209n7, 209n9, 210n17; bottomhood and, 9, 17, 174; of film viewers, 104–5, 232n39; in heterosexual sex, 119, 132, 146; lesbian sex and, 214n30; pleasure in, 213n29, 243n45; in premodern homosexual models, 78–79
Patton, Cindy, 63–65, 244–45n8
Penderton, Major Weldon (character in *Reflections in a Golden Eye*): body language of, 75, 98; casting of Marlon Brando as, 95–96, 230n32; closeted homosexuality of, 72, 74, 84, 97–100, 101, 107–9, 225n5, 232nn37–38, 232n40; in comparison with Anacleto, 78, 151, 229n27; receptive gaze of, 103–4; on the subject of Anacleto, 106–7
Perez, Hiram, 159, 236n14
penis: censorship of, 138, 143–44, 147, 242n43; erection of, 60, 143, 213n27, 243n43; eroticism and, 166; flaccidity of, 241n40, 242n41; from a female point of view, 153–54, 234n4; largeness of, 8, 35, 37–38, 44–46, 47, 48, 49, 142, 144, 213n27, 219n28, 219n31, 246n14; male subjecthood and, 82, 144; and proximity with the anus, 16; in sex cruising websites, 196, 197–98; smallness of, 49, 61, 70, 143; as substituted by other body parts, 130, 241n40; topness and, 19, 30; visibility of, 24, 144–45. See also black men; Brandon Lee; ejaculation; phallocentrism
Peter Fucking Wayne Fucking Peter (dir. Wayne Yung), 177–79, 182, 184, 190
Peters (dir. Dane Preston), 32, 50–51
phallocentrism, 8, 130, 144, 240n33
point of view: of the bottom, 10, 28, 46, 101; of FOB Asian/Americans, 70
Pontalis, Jean-Bertrand, 42
pornography, gay: accent in, 62–69, 160; Asian/American bottomhood in, 18, 58–61, 152, 247n18; Asian names in, 43, 51–52; Asian niche, 30, 32, 42, 51–52, 54, 58, 70, 215–16nn6–7; compared to heterosexual pornography, 5–6, 210n14, 213n29, 243n1; fantasy scenarios in, 64, 66–67, 218n21, 218n24; gay male subjecthood and, 252n13; HIV/AIDS and, 56, 221n38, 245n8; martial arts films and, 35–36, 217n15; narrative and, 35, 41, 43, 217n14; performance in, 10, 35, 41, 54, 58, 60, 62, 66, 68, 166, 221n39, 223n48, 224n51; as privileging the bottom, 10, 46, 66, 212n24; as privileging the top, 9–10, 211n19; polarization of sexual roles in, 11–12; as providing knowledge of the body, 164, 166; public space and, 39, 161; racial difference and, 41–43, 66, 166, 246n15; rarity of Asian/Americans in, 220n34; realism in, 137–38; settings of, 38–39, 41–44, 49–51; sex cruising sites and, 213n27; sexual repertoires in, 12, 57–58, 62, 221n40; soundtrack in, 36, 63–65, 222–23n46; spectatorship of, 41–44, 56–57, 66, 69–70, 217n14, 217n17, 221–22n42; watched by straight women, 152–54; West Hollywood and, 30, 37, 44, 49–50, 217n16; as "world-making," 39, 161. See also Asian/American men; porn stardom
porn stardom: Americanness and, 32–33, 36–37, 54; Asianness and, 31, 36–37, 58–59, 60–61, 65; bottom performers as, 210n16, 246n14; penis size and, 45–46, 47, 48, 48; topness and, 12, 30, 56–57, 59; versatility and, 211n19. See also Lee, Brandon (Jon Enriquez)

"potato queen," 155–56, 160–61, 162, 166–67, 168, 185, 190, 244n4, 248n25
power relations, 12, 31, 40, 90, 116, 154
Prison on Fire (dir. Ringo Lam), 141
Proschan, Frank, 127
Puar, Jasbir K., 159, 168

Queen's Cantonese, The (dir. Wayne Yung), 155, 160–64, 167, 168, 222n42, 244n3
queer of color critique, 20, 90, 121, 158–59
queer domesticity, 74, 83–90, 112, 228n16, 229n28. *See also* Anacleto: relationship with Alison Langdon
queer relationality, 83–84, 85, 87, 89, 90, 109, 194, 195
queer studies, 2–3, 9, 20, 21–22, 120, 159, 229n26
queer theory, 8, 18, 23, 168

race: femininity and, 19, 194, 204 (*see also* "racial castration"); in relation to sexuality, 18, 20, 31, 81, 158–59, 169–71, 195, 225n6; in sex cruising websites, 197–98, 201, 251n9. *See aso* Asian/American men; black men; bottomhood; Chicano/Latino men; interracial relationships; race: in gay pornography; white men
"racial castration," 19, 73, 81, 144–45
racism, 4–6, 14, 23, 80, 119, 148, 156; in the gay community, 165, 171, 179; in gay pornography, 49, 62, 69, 166, 220n34, 223n48; in mainstream Western films, 91, 93, 96, 224n3, 235–36n13; in sex cruising websites, 28 (*see also* Asian/American men: in sex cruising websites)
receptivity: in anal sex, 17–18, 139; bottomhood and, 112–13, 149, 179; in butch-femme sexuality, 213–14n30; filmic gaze and, 103, 105, 106 (*see also* "anal vision")
reeducation of desire, 155–56, 163–74, 176, 245n8, 247–48n22
Reflections in a Golden Eye (book, Carson McCullers), 71, 77, 84, 92, 100, 104, 224–25n5, 228n20, 228–29n24, 229n27, 230n30, 232n37
Reflections in a Golden Eye (film, dir. John Huston): acting styles in, 93–97; casting in, 93, 96, 230–31n32; color experiment in, 105–6; effeminacy in, 74–77; inversion of social hierarchy in, 100; low-angle shots in, 100–101, *101*, *102*; "anal vision" in, 102–5; nudity in, 98, *99*, 102–3, 106; plot of, 72–73; press criticism of, 75–76, 92, 108, 230n31; queer domesticity in, 83, 85–90; rating system and, 232n42; sexual inversion in, 73, 77, 79, 108, 225n5
remasculinization: of Asian/American men, 2, 4, 6, 14, 30, 33, 35, 73, 113, 174, 208n5; of the bottom position, 12, 212n24
Restivo, Angelo, 10, 39, 63–64, 161, 210n14, 222nn45–46
"rice bar," 161, 164–65, 246n16
"rice queen," 155, 161, 162, 167, 171, 174, 185, 248n25. *See also* "potato queen"; "sticky rice" relationships
Riggs, Marlon, 155, 158
rimming, 10, 57–58, 211n19, 221n40
Rodríguez, Juana María, 193, 195, 204–5, 250–51n3
Rofel, Lisa, 227n14
Russo, Vito, 73, 74, 93, 95–96, 97–98, 107–8, 225n5, 230n31. *See also Celluloid Closet, The* (book)

sadomasochism (S/M), 7, 74, 152, 154, 156–57, 213n29, 243–44n2
Scott, Darieck, 20–21, 142, 214n31
Scott, Jacob, 40, 54–55, 248n23
Sedgwick, Eve: on agency, 88, 132, 138, 239n27; on delinking of gender and sexuality, 250n1; ideological mode of analysis and, 24; on shame, 114, 120–21, 124, 190, 235n12
See, Sarita, 83–84, 224n3
7 Steps to Sticky Heaven (dir. Nguyen Tan Hoang), 155, 160, 165–69, 174–75, 247n18
sex cruising websites: bottomhood in, 204; headless torso pictures in, 28, 196, 197–201, 251nn9–11, 252n13; racism in, 1, 197–98, 201, 204–5, 251n9; screen names in, 28, 197, 201–203, 251n6, 251–52n12, 252n15
sexual inversion, 73, 78, 79, 108, 225n5, 229n27
sexual representation: explicit, 31, 152, 214n35, 221n42, (*see also* documentary; pornography, gay); as illegitimate and under-researched in scholarship, 3–4, 21–22, 24; in mainstream Western films, 143–44 (see

sexual representation (*continued*)
    also *Lover, The*; *Reflections in a Golden Eye* [film]); positive-negative images and, 5, 23; race and, 155, 156, 158, 164, 171, 173 (*see also* race: in gay pornography). *See also* visibility politics
sexual roles: as fixed, 12, 33, 41, 62, 208–9n7, 211n19, 250–51n3; as fluid, 11–12, 153–54, 189; gender difference and, 12, 79; power dynamics in, 17. *See also* bottom position; top position
sexuality: Asian/American scholarship on, 21–24, 159; as identity, 157, 159, 161, 168, 225n6, 248n25; nationality and, 33, 42, 159, 215n3; Orientalism and, 44, 52–53, 219n29; the penis and, 82; privileged over gender, 78, 79–80; public space and, 161; racialization of, 62, 72, 118, 195; regulation of, 113, 118; retooling of (Asian male), 171; as threat, 53, 81–82, 241–42n40. *See also* bottomhood; butch-femme sexuality
sex work, 40–41, 179–82, 249n29
Shah, Nayan, 85, 228n22
shame: bottomhood and, 17, 177–78, 179; female subjectivity and, 124, 136; formation of identity and, 120, 236n14; in *L'Amant* (book), 238n26; male subjectivity and, 19, 144, 204, 239n28; queer theory of, 120–21; rhetoric of, 252n14; sexual pleasure and, 188; shamelessness and, 122, 126, 128, 133; specularity and, 134; in *The Lover*, 121–28, 130–33, 138–39, 146–47
Shanghai Meat Company (dir. Tony Chan), 52, 172, 174, 218n22
Shaowanasai, Michael, 179–80, 222n42, 248n25, 249n27. *See also Adventures of Iron Pussy III, The: To Be or Not to Be*
Shaviro, Steven, 104–5
Shimakawa, Karen, 22, 202–3
Shimizu, Celine Parreñas, 22–24, 215n5, 240n36
Sinfield, Alan, 75–76
Skin on Skin (dir. Darrell Y. Hamamoto), 5
Slanted Vision (dir. Ming-Yuen S. Ma), 152–55, 160, 171–74, 222n42, 247n21
Smith, Jack, 97
Sobchack, Vivian, 140, 241nn38–39
sodomy. *See* anal sex

Somerville, Siobhan B., 226n10
spectatorship: "body genres" and, 24–25; embodied, 25, 140, 241nn38–39; haptic visuality and, 139–40, 153–54, 241n39; passivity and, 104–5, 232n39; perverse, 23; receptive gaze and, 103, 105–6; resistant, 34–35, 36, 230n31; supporting characters in films and, 91–92, 230n31. *See also* pornography
stereotypes: of Asian/American men, ix–x, 30, 68, 196, 198, 201, 247n18 (*see also* Asian/American men: bottomhood and); Asian/American scholarship and, 21–22; in mainstream Western films, 79, 91, 96, 163, 230n31; in pornography, 30, 40–41, 171–72, 219–20n33; racialized sexual, 42, 49, 241n40. *See also* visibility politics
"sticky rice" relationships, 169; desire for, 165; as empowering, 155–56, 161; egalitarianism and, 168–69,; eroticism of, 167, 170, 174; as heterogenous field, 172–73; insult and, 175; pedagogy and, 163, 167, (*see also* reeducation of desire); politics of, 175–76; queer spaces and, 159, 161–63
Stockton, Kathryn Bond, 20, 121, 214n32, 236n15
Stoler, Ann Laura, 118, 123, 148, 236–37n17
Stonewall, 224n4; LGBT politics after, 11, 73–74, 79–80, 100, 225–26n7, 252n13; LGBT politics before, 109
Stringer, Julian, 141
Stryker, Jeff, 12, 58, 59, 211n19, 219nn28–29
sucking. *See* oral sex
supporting characters, in films, 91–92, 230n31
Sweet Sweetback Baadasssss Song (dir. Melvin Van Peebles), 142, 241–42n40

Tasker, Yvonne, 33–35
Taylor, Elizabeth, 71, 72, 92, 93, 102–3, 106, 109, 230–31n32, 232n36. *See also Reflections in a Golden Eye* (film)
Thailand, 179–80, 182, 185, 248n25. *See also Adventures of Iron Pussy III, The: To Be or Not To Be*
Thomson, David, 91–92
Throat Spankers (dir. Josh Eliot), 32
Ting, Jennifer, 83
Tompkins, Sylvan, 120
tongzhi activism, 200

topness: autoeroticism and, 56, 70; esteemed in gay culture of, 8–9; instability of, 54, 56–59, 70, (see also Lee, Brandon: changing of sexual role of); self-sufficiency and, 70; as constitutive of American masculinity, 33, 38; white men and, 18, 177–78

top position: in bareback sex, 13, 212n24; definition of, 6–7; emergence as a concept, 11–12, 210–11nn17–19; in gay pornography, 10, 30–31, 33, 35–38, 48, 54–61, 69–70, 246nn14–15 (see also Lee, Brandon: as top; white men: in gay pornography); pleasure of, 15–16, 212n25; passivity of, 17, 55; visual representation of buttocks and, 112, 137, 139, 143. See also sexual roles

touch: embodied spectatorship and, 25, 139–40, 241nn38–39; in gay porrnography, 15, 154; the hand and, 113, 128–36, 238n24; nondualism of, 132, 138, 239n27; shame and, 133; as socially binding, 130, 132, 146; in "sticky rice" relationships, 167–69, 174; as terrorizing, 134, 146

Tsang, Daniel, 42, 43–44, 218n23

Tyler, Parker, 103, 226n7

Underwood, Steven G., 15–16

vaginal sex, 12, 107, 130, 138, 211n22, 213–14n30

Van Peebles, Melvin, 142, 241–42n40. See also *Sweet Sweetback Baadasssss Song*

versatility, 12, 42, 58, 60–62, 177, 211n21. See also bottom position; top position

Vietnam: French colonialism and, 127–28; Orientalist view of, 238n23, 240n34; status of the Chinese in colonial era in, 126, 237n20; war in, 108, 208n5

visibility politics: bottomhood and, 24, 74, 108, 113, 195; remasculinization and, 14; in sex cruising websites, 196, 200–201, 203; sexual identity and, 225n6, 229n28, 244n8; "transnational sexualities" and, 159. See also sexual representation

vulnerability: "anal vision" and, 104; of Asian men during colonialism, 119–20 (see also *Lover, The*); bottom position and, 17–18, 113, 178–79, 211n19, 245n8; of buttocks, 139, 142, 147; masculinity and, 23; nudity and, 133; of the penis, 144; shame and, 146; of white women during colonialism, 118 (see also *Lover, The*)

Wat, Eric, 164–65, 247n16

Waugh, Thomas, 157–58, 163, 217n16, 245–46n12, 247n19

Way of the Dragon, The (dir. Bruce Lee), 34, 219n31

We Got Moves You Ain't Even Heard Of (Part One) (dir. Erica Cho), 186–91, 193

white men: Asian/American men's desire for, 155, 167; as audience of gay pornography, 41, 44, 70, 215–16nn6–7, 218–19n27; in gay pornography, 9–10, 40, 45–46, 49–50, 57–8, 68, 210n16, 211n19, 215n2, 215n4, 219n29; in interracial relationships, 179, 235–36n13, 244n4, 248n25; penis of, 144, 242n41; in sex cruising websites, 2, 197, 201, 252n15. See also masculinity

White, Patricia, 91–92, 228n24, 230n31

Wicked (dir. Chi Chi LaRue), 33, 54–55, 57–60, 62, 216n8, 220n33

Williams, Linda: on "body genres," 215n37; on the sex act in films, 239n31, 242–43n43; on female pleasure, 63, 240n33; on heterosexual pornography, 138, 210n14, 213n29; on interracial sex, 142, 148, 241–42nn40–41

Williams, Private L. G. (character in *Reflections in a Golden Eye*): Major Weldon Penderton's obsession with, 98, 100, 107–8, 232n40; nudity of, 72, 98, 99, 100, 138; view from the bottom and, 102, 232n39; voyeurism of, 101–4, 106, 109

Winston, Jane Bradley, 127, 237–38nn21–22

With Sex You Get Egg Roll (dir. Peter Romero), 42, 52, 223n50

Wittman, Carl, 12, 211n18

Wong, Eugene Franklin, 235n13

Woo, John, 140–41. See also *Killer, The*

Word Is Out (dir. Mariposa Film Group), 160

Yates, Dirk, 218n21

"yellowface," 62, 67–68, 236n13

Yung, Wayne, 155, 160, 163, 177–79, 184, 190, 222n42, 244n3, 245n11, 248n23. See also *Peter Fucking Wayne Fucking Peter*; *Queen's Cantonese, The*

www.ingramcontent.com/pod-product-compliance
Lightning Source LLC
Chambersburg PA
CBHW051049230426
43666CB00012B/2625